DOCTRINAL
DIMENSIONS
New Perspectives on Gospel Principles

DOCTRINAL DIMENSIONS

New Perspectives on Gospel Principles

DUANE S. CROWTHER

ISBN: 0-88290-286-5
Library of Congress Catalog No.: 86-081779
Horizon Publishers Catalog & Order No.: 1028
First Printing, 1986

Printed and distributed
in the United States of America by

Horizon
Publishers
& Distributors, Incorporated
50 South 500 West P.O. Box 490
Bountiful, Utah 84010-0490

www.horizonpublishers.biz

Preface

Today, more than ever before, a battle is being waged for the hearts, minds and souls of men. As the climactic events of the last days draw nearer, there are voices clamoring for the attention and allegiance of all who will listen, inviting them to embrace a varied spectrum of social, political, psychological and theological philosophies.

Religious factions find themselves in the center of the arena, and proponents of many doctrines and dogmas are exerting their influence on others more than ever before.

During the past several decades, The Church of Jesus Christ of Latter-day Saints, with more than 30,000 full- and part-time missionaries laboring in the field, has experienced unprecedented growth, rising to a worldwide membership of more than 6,000,000. This growth has come in a period when the populations of many other Christian denominations have diminished or barely held their own. In some cases, the Latter-day Saints have reaped jealousy and envy from others who have experienced less success.

This jealousy has spawned a growing covey of individuals who are writing religious hate-literature, and targeting Mormonism with it. Such literature is not new, but recent releases have enjoyed more-than-deserved prominence because of the increased utilization of modern marketing and advertizing techniques.

In response, Latter-day Saints authors have begun challenging the many errors they are propagating. This book is one such response. It focuses on the strong Biblical basis of the restored gospel and speaks out forcefully in defense of the faith.

Doctrinal Dimensions is a compilation of nine cassette tape discussions written and recorded by the author between 1980 and 1986. The discussions selected all have a missionary orientation, and they all carry a strong message in defense of the gospel of Jesus Christ as it is embodied in The Church of Jesus Christ of Latter-day Saints.

1

It is anticipated that there will be new insights in the book—new thoughts to think—for readers with various backgrounds: non-members who are pondering whether they should join the Church, new members who are seeking to grow in their understanding of gospel principles, and established Latter-day Saints who are striving to reaffirm their committment to gospel fundamentals while gaining additional perspectives and understandings.

Those who are called to preach the gospel to others will find the book particularly valuable. It presents a wide variety of materials and historical "capsules" which can be adapted and incorporated into missionary presentations when needed, providing useful answers to frequently asked questions.

The book is based primarily in the Bible, with the exception of the chapter which presents doctrinal evidences that Mormons are Christians. That chapter, due to its subject matter, draws most of its materials from the Book of Mormon. The chapter on Joseph Smith draws mainly on early LDS Church history for its sources, and the final chapter, "Recognizing Techniques of Deception in Anti-Mormon Literature," is based in the main on observations of approaches used by current critics of the Church.

The informal conversational tone of the tapes has been maintained. Scriptural passages, when quoted, have been presented in paragraph form, with the punctuation and capitalization of the King James Version retained. There has been slight editing to adapt the material from spoken to written form; the text remains essentially the same as in the taped version, however. Footnotes and additional documentation have been added to several chapters to increase reader understanding and utilization.

It is my sincere desire that *Doctrinal Dimensions* will strengthen the faith and testimony of many Latter-day Saints, and that it will cause many others who are not yet members to embrace the gospel of Jesus Christ and come into the Church. May it become a useful instrument which helps bring to pass the Lord's eternal plan is my humble prayer, offered in the name of Jesus Christ, our Savior.

Duane S. Crowther

Contents

BIBLICAL PROOFS
OF THE
RESTORED CHURCH
13

BIBLICAL PROOFS
OF THE
BOOK OF MORMON
48

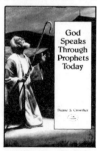

GOD SPEAKS
THROUGH PROPHETS
TODAY
72

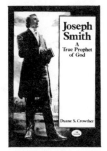

Joseph Smith
A
True Prophet
of God

Duane S. Crowther

JOSEPH SMITH—
A TRUE PROPHET
OF GOD
96

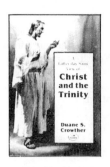

A LATTER-DAY SAINT VIEW OF CHRIST AND THE TRINITY
126

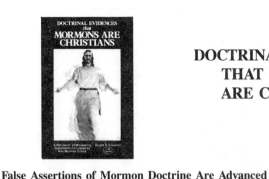

DOCTRINAL EVIDENCES
THAT MORMONS
ARE CHRISTIANS
161

8

God's Eternal
Plan of
Salvation

Duane S. Crowther

GOD'S ETERNAL
PLAN OF
SALVATION
204

ARE *YOU* SAVED?— A MORMON'S VIEW OF FAITH, WORKS, GRACE AND SALVATION
230

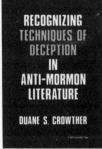

RECOGNIZING TECHNIQUES OF DECEPTION IN ANTI-MORMON LITERATURE
266

Biblical Proofs of the Restored Church

Duane S. Crowther

My Brothers and Sisters and Friends,

I appreciate very much the opportunity to come and be with you today. It's a pleasure to be invited into your midst, and I regard it as an honor to be asked to speak to you. I appreciated the sweet prayer that was offered as the invocation at the beginning of this meeting. I want you to know that I've been praying, and seeking the Spirit of the Lord to be with me today, because I want to speak to you about two of the most important subjects in the entire gospel teachings of Jesus Christ.

An Overview: The Apostasy and Restoration

Let me review with you two basic doctrines which are taught repeatedly in your Bible:

1st., the teaching that there was to be a universal apostasy, in which the authority of Christ's Church was completely removed from the earth, by about the 2nd century A.D., and

2nd., the Biblical doctrine that God would restore His Church and gospel to the earth in the last days.

I'd first like to summarize those doctrines. Then I would like to turn to the scriptures to increase our understanding of those teachings, and invite you to turn to each of the passages with me if you brought your Bible. If you don't have your scriptures, I'll ask you to write down the passages, and then go home and review them and others that are pertinent to those subjects. Please devote some time to renewing your understanding of these key teachings about the Church of Jesus Christ.

Doctrine No. 1—We believe that Christ, in His day, organized His Church here upon the earth, that He called men to labor in His Church, giving them power and authority to act in His name by ordaining them to his Holy Priesthood. This Priesthood was extended to others by a series, or "chain" of ordinations, by those who held that Priesthood and were authorized to ordain others. Christ based His Church on a foundation of apostles and prophets. He gave revelation to those men who guided it. Each of these characteristics that He placed in His Church was a characteristic of the true Church of Jesus Christ.

We believe there came a time, shortly after the death of the Savior, when those who were His chief followers, His 12 apostles and other key disciples, were taken, one by one, and were martyred for the cause. As their lives were taken, **there was a break in the chain of authority which Christ had established, and there occurred a falling away, or an apostasy—a turning away from the doctrines of God to the doctrines of man,** taught by individuals functioning without proper authority to act in the name of Christ. We believe the scriptures clearly tell us that there was to be an apostasy, and that the Bible described it as already starting to take place in the time of Paul and his contemporaries.

The Bible teaches us there was to be a great apostasy in which Satan would make war on the early saints and overcome them, substituting a counterfeit church that lacked authority to act in the name of God in place of The Church established by Jesus Christ. It also teaches that God, in His wisdom, provided that His Church would be restored to the earth in the last days, in preparation for the triumphal return of the Savior.

That there would be a complete apostasy, in which the power and authority to act in the name of Jesus Christ would be completely removed from the face of the earth, is a major teaching of the Bible. We believe that for any church to be the true Church of Christ today, it must accept as a major tenet the doctrine that there was a complete apostasy following the days of Christ, in which the authority to represent Jesus Christ was completely taken from the earth.

Doctrine No. 2—We believe that Jesus, because of His love for His people, saw fit to *restore* His Church and His gospel here upon the earth in these latter days. Just as the Bible tells us there was to be an apostasy, it also proclaims, clearly and unequivocally, that there was to be a restoration of the gospel and of the Church in these last days. We believe that if a church is truly the church of Jesus Christ today, it must be a restored church. It must accept and preach both the Biblical doctrines of the universal apostasy and the restoration of the Church of Jesus Christ. It must proclaim itself to *be* the *restored* church of Jesus Christ, and must be able to explain, step-by-step, each historical event which fulfilled the many Biblical prophecies of the restoration.

I know of only one church which fully accepts both the Biblical doctrines of the apostasy and of the restoration, and asserts that it literally *is* the restored Church of Jesus Christ—the only church with legitimate priesthood power to represent Christ today. That church is The Church of Jesus Christ of Latter-day Saints—the Mormons. The scriptural strength of its doctrines, coupled with the devotion of approximately 30,000 energetic missionaries serving full or part time at their own expense, and aided by the sweet promptings of the Holy Spirit, have made this church one of the fastest growing churches on earth. In this day of spiritual tribulation, when many Christian denominations are declining, the restored Church of Jesus Christ is rapidly expanding on a world-wide basis, preparing the way for the coming of our Lord and Savior.

My purpose today is to bear witness to you that the Bible speaks in abundance of these two doctrines, and to help you understand the many Biblical verses that teach these vital doctrines. I've had to choose only those passages that would be most appropriate because I knew we didn't have too much time. I would like you to turn to them in your scriptures as we talk about them, please, and then write down these passages and prayerfully review them all in your own homes.

Biblical Prophecies of the Apostasy

Paul's Prophecies—They Will Not Endure Sound Doctrine

Let's discuss the doctrine of the universal apostasy first. Please turn to the Book of *Acts, chapter 20, verses 28 to 30.* Here Paul is talking to the congregation at Ephesus where he is visiting, and he gives them a very specific warning. Did you get the reference? Acts 20:28 to 30. He says this: "Take heed therefore unto yourselves, and to all the flock, over which the Holy Ghost hath made you overseers, to feed the church of God, which he hath purchased with his own blood. For I know this, that *after my departing shall grevious wolves enter in among you, not sparing the flock. Also of your own selves shall men arise, speaking perverse things, to draw away disciples after them.*"

So here Paul knew that shortly after his departure from that congregation, the saints at Ephesus would see the apostasy starting to take place. He warned that people from outside the Church would come in, trying to draw away followers after them, and even among their own Church members, people would begin to change the doctrines of Christ and substitutes in their places the doctrines of men.

Turn with me now, to *Second Timothy,* further on in the New Testament, to *chapter 4, verses 3 and 4,* where Paul was writing to one of his converts, a valiant man by the name of Timothy. Paul gave this warning, "The time will come when *they will not endure sound doctrine;* but after their own lusts shall they heap to themselves teachers, having itching ears; And they shall *turn away their ears from the truth, and shall be turned unto fables."* That was his warning to Timothy.

Earlier, in the same letter, in *Second Timothy, chapter three, verses one through five,* he gave another warning about the apostasy to come. He told Timothy, "This know also, that *in the last days perilous times shall come.* For men shall be lovers of their own selves, covetous, boasters, proud, blasphemers, disobedient to parents, unthankful, unholy, Without natural affection, trucebreakers, false accusers, incontinent, fierce, despisers of those that are good, Traitors, heady, highminded, lovers of pleasures more than lovers of God. *Having a form of godliness, but denying the power thereof:* from such turn away."

That was Paul's description of those who would come in a latter day when men would have the form and appearance of godliness, but would lack the power to act in the name of God. He warned that that time was coming, and taught Timothy that even in that day as it began, they must turn away from those men who would lead them astray.

Paul Foretells Identifying Characteristics of the Apostate Church

Would you please turn just one book earlier in the New Testament, to *First Timothy, chapter four, verses one through three,* where we get one of the most specific prophecies anywhere in scripture of that church which was to be formed, but which would change its doctrines to be very different from the doctrines of Jesus Christ. This is what Paul wrote:

"Now the Spirit speaketh expressly, that in the latter times some shall depart from the faith, giving heed to seducing spirits, and doctrines of devils; Speaking lies in hypocrisy; having their conscience seared with a hot iron."

And then here are those characteristics by which he identified that apostate church—as a church that would be *"Forbidding to marry, and commanding to abstain from meats."* Well now, what church was it that appeared there in the first two or three centuries following the death of Christ, and what are two of the doctrines by which that church can today be identified? We know of a denomination who says that they go all the way back and that the very first pope was the Apostle Peter. Latter-day Saints certainly agree that Peter was the leader of the church in the time of Christ, but we don't think Peter was the first pope. Papal leadership didn't begin until many years later.

But the church that came into being following Peter's time has long been identified by doctrines which fulfill this prophecy. Even today, as we read about them, we find a struggle going on in that church because priests within that church aren't happy with the church's doctrine of celibacy. The priests want to marry and have families, and yet they are sworn to be celibate and aren't allowed to take a wife. And we also see in that same church the other characteristic that Paul prophesied. For centuries they had meatless Fridays, didn't they? Even today every time you go to a restaurant throughout the land, what do you see featured on the menu on Friday? Fish dinners, right? Why? Because that church decided that they mustn't eat meat on certain days of the week.

Here's Paul, clearly prophesying way back in New Testament times, giving two characteristics to identify that church which was to take the place of the Church of Jesus Christ—that they would be celibate and that they would forbid their members to partake of meats on certain days. Paul couldn't have been more specific in identifying the apostate church that was to come into being when priesthood authority was lost.

John's Prophecy: Satan to Overcome the Saints

Let me give you another passage which is vital in its message because in it the apostle John prophesied that there was to come a time when the Church of Jesus Christ would be *completely removed* from the face of the earth, and Satan would extend his rule over every family, and language, and nation. That passage is in the Book of Revelation, the thirteenth chapter. Much could be said about this chapter, but let me review what's happening beforehand. If you read the page before, you see that John the Revelator is prophesying that there would come a great beast, and a dragon that gives power to the beast. Bible commentators give various explanations concerning this beast and the time of his coming. But they all agree that it is evil in nature and Satanically inspired because the beast opens his mouth in blasphemy against God, and wars against the saints of God until he overcomes them.

Then, in *Revelation, 13th chapter, verses 7 and 8,* John writes that "It was given unto him *to make war with the saints,* and *to overcome them:* and *power was given him over all kindreds, and tongues, and nations.* And *all* that dwell upon the earth shall worship him." How complete was to be the apostasy, then? It was to extend to all nations, and all kindreds and all tongues, wasn't it? *Every man* who lived upon he earth was then to be denied the power and gospel of Jesus Christ for a time.

Paul's Prophecy: A Falling Away Before the Lord Comes in Glory

Why would that be allowed to happen? Why would God set up a church here upon the earth and then allow it to be taken from the earth? I think that's certainly one of the questions we must consider from the scriptures. I would like you to turn back to *Luke, the 11th chapter, verses 49 and 50,* and find the answer to that question with me, where the Savior gives us the necessary understanding. The passage reads this way:

"Therefore also said the wisdom of God, I will send them prophets and apostles, and some of them they shall slay and persecute"—and then he tells why he would allow it to happen— *"That the blood of all the prophets, which was shed from the foundation of the world, may be required of this generation."*

The Savior has told us that that generation which crucified him and nailed him to the cross was the most wicked generation that had ever lived upon this earth. Here in Luke, the Lord said he would allow his church to be taken from the face of the earth and permit evil men to persecute and to martyr his leaders, that a testimony might be left against that generation.

The Savior's Explanation: Why the Apostles Would Be Martyred

Other Bible passages also tell us about Satan's efforts to substitute his counterfeit church in the place of Christ's true Church. One of the most powerful of these passsages is found in *Second Thessalonians, chapter two, verses three and four.* Paul discovered the early converts in Thessalonika thought the second coming of Christ was so near they had stopped working and taking care of their homes and providing for their daily needs. Paul wrote to them to tell them that Christ wasn't coming yet, and that important events would precede His coming. One of those events was to be a "falling away," when people would be deceived by Satan's representative who would come right into the highest place within the Church.

Referring to Christ's coming in glory with the phrase "that day," Paul wrote: "Let no man deceive you by any means: for *that day shall not come,* except there come a *falling away first,* and that man of sin be revealed, the son of perdition; Who opposeth and exalteth himself above all that is called God, or that is worshipped; so that *he as God sitteth in the temple of God,* shewing himself that he is God."

So here's Biblical doctrine, clearly stated: that there *had* to be a "falling away," or an apostasy—a substituting of Satan's influence in place or the true Church of Christ, before the Savior can come again. We already read John the Revelator's prophecy that the apostasy would be complete—that Satan would make war against the Saints and gain control over every kindred, and every tongue and every nation.

Peter's Prophecy: False Teachers Will Bring in Damnable Heresies

The apostle Peter also warned of the apostasy, when the doctrines of men would be substituted for the true doctrine and authority of Jesus Christ. He wrote about it in *Second Peter, chapter two, verses one and two.* After talking about false prophets in Old Testament times, he told the New Testament church: "There shall be *false teachers among you,* who privily shall *bring in damnable heresies,* even denying the Lord that brought them, and bring upon themselves swift destruction. And *many shall follow* their pernicious ways. . . ."

John's Warning: The Spirit of Antichrist Already Being Manifested

The apostle John knew the apostasy was already beginning in his day and he tried to help the Saints discern between truth and error. Back then, truth was easier to discern before Satan complicated matters by substituting a false Christian church with a host of counterfeit doctrines for the true Church of Jesus Christ. Then people either accepted or rejected Christ. Now, many churches acknowledge that Jesus was the Christ, the son of God, but those same churches teach only a part of Christ's gospel, and mingle it with the teachings of men, and those churches lack the authorization and power to act in God's name in the ordinances that prepare men for salvation.

But John's words at least show us that the apostasy was already beginning in his day, and his counsel has great meaning for all who are seeking the truth today. *First John, chapter four, verses one through three:* "Beloved, believe not every spirit, but *try the spirits* whether they are of God: because many false prophets are gone out into the world. Hereby know ye the Spirit of God: Every spirit that confesseth that Jesus Christ is come in the flesh is of God: And every spirit that confesseth not that Jesus Christ is come in the flesh is not of God: and *this is that spirit of antichrist,* whereof ye have heard that it should come; and *even now already is it in the world.*"

Time after time the scriptures show that an apostasy was already beginning in New Testament times—that Satan was causing men to *change* the doctrines of Christ, to abandon the true Church of Christ and substitute in its place a counterfeit church—one that would *resemble* Christ's true church but would *deceive* the people and thus prevent them from attaining the salvation and glory Christ intended for them.

Paul's Warnings: The Apostasy Already Happening

The apostasy was happening rapidly in New Testament times. We see the apostle Paul's great concern in his Epistles to the Galatian saints. *Galatians, chapter one, verses six and seven:* "I marvel that *ye are so soon removed* from him that called you into the grace of Christ *unto another gospel:* Which is not another; but there be some that trouble you, and would pervert the gospel of Christ." Paul could see the apostasy taking place, with Satan substituting just enough error to rob men of the keys of salvation, while leaving them a counterfeit church that would lull them into a false security.

Look in *Second Corinthians 11, verse 13*, where Paul wrote of men involved in the falling away. He observed that "Such men are *false apostles, deceitful workers,* transforming themselves into the apostles of Christ."

In his epistle to *Titus*, in the *first chapter*, Paul lashed out against those who were leading the saints into apostasy, calling them "vain talkers and deceivers," and in *verse 16* he summarized the false and unauthorized status of those in Satan's counterfeit church: *"They profess that they know God; but in works they deny him,* being abominable, and disobedient, and unto every good work reprobate."

The Apostasy A Basic Doctrine of the Bible

This is the scriptural pattern concerning the doctrine of the apostasy. The Bible teaches clearly and unequivocally that there was to be a falling away from the true gospel of Jesus Christ that the falling away was already beginning in the day of the New Testament Church, that Satan would make war on the saints and would have the appearance of godliness, but would lack and deny the authority and power to truly act in the name of God. The Bible teaches that the apostasy was to be complete—that the authority to act in the name of God would be removed entirely from the earth.

If you believe in the Bible, of necessity you must accept the doctrine of apostasy because that doctrine is taught in a broad pattern of scripture that just can't be ignored. If your church truly believes in the Bible, it must teach and accept the doctrine of the universal apostasy, and must freely acknowledge that the true Church of Jesus Christ was completely removed from the earth shortly after the time of Christ. And then, if your church still claims to have the power and authority to teach the true gospel of Jesus Christ and to exist and function as his authorized representative today, your church must be able to demonstrate from its history that God somehow gave it new power and authority, and restored the true gospel and authorization to represent Jesus Christ, that was completely taken from the earth during the great apostasy.

You need to examine the matter very carefully because your eternal standing before God depends on the answer. Is your church the true church of Jesus Christ, or is it a descendant of the great counterfeit?

You might want to compare the New Testament Church founded by Jesus Christ to a tree. Christ planted it, and it grew rapidly. But when the apostasy occurred, the tree was cut off and completely severed from its life-giving roots. The trunk lay there without any source of new life, with

changes occurring in it as men substituted apostate doctrines for the doctrines of Christ's true gospel, and Catholicism came into being. The trunk
continued to change and decay for many years, until Luther and Calvin
and other reformers tried to generate new life by establishing offshoots that
were protesting against the excesses of the trunk. But if there is no life
in the trunk, could there be life in the branches? If the Catholic trunk lacked
authority to act in the name of God, could the Protestant branches draw
authority from the dead wood from which they sprang? The answer is
obvious.

Basic Protestant Doctrines—An Effort to Overcome Catholic Power

As the reformation took place, Catholicism held power over the people
through two teachings which had been pushed to the extreme, but which
the people accepted. Catholicism taught, first, that man couldn't be saved
unless he received the sacraments of the Catholic church, and second, that
only the pope held the authority to read and interpret scripture. The Protestants attempted to counteract these two powerful holds on the people
by swinging the pendulum to the other extreme. They taught that no religious ordinances or sacraments were necessary—that man can be saved
by faith alone. And they decided that there was no need for authority to
act in God's name—anyone could organize a church and God would
accept it. Just reading the Bible was authority enough. Those substitute
teachings became very popular, and they broke the powerful hold Catholicism had on the people—but they were just as counterfeit as the Catholic
teachings they superceded.

Six Characterisics of Christ's New Testament Church

Let's look, for a few minutes, at the Church Christ established in New
Testament times, and try to list several characteristics by which it was identified. Some people maintain, by the way, that Christ really didn't establish a church—that the church didn't come into being until after his death.
But in the *eighteenth chapter of Matthew, verse 17,* the Lord taught that
if a man had a dispute with someone he couldn't resolve privately, he should
"tell it unto the church." And earlier in the chapter, in *verse 3,* he told
his followers, "Except ye *be converted,* and become as little children, ye
shall not enter into the kingdom of heaven." So there can be no doubt that
the church already had been organized by Christ in his day.

That church had many characteristics by which it could be identified, and if a church today claims to be the true church of Jesus Christ, it's safe to assume that church would have those same characteristics now. But by the same token, we must recognize that if a church does not have those same characteristics, it can't be Christ's true church today. Fair enough?

Then let's draw from the scriptures six characteristics by which Christ's church can be identified.

Priesthood—The Authority to Act in the Name of God

First, the Church of Jesus Christ had priesthood power—the authority to act in God's name. Men were called into the ministry by the Lord, and given priesthood authority by an ordinance called the "laying on of hands" where a man already holding the priesthood would lay his hands on the other man's head and ordain him, transferring the priesthood power to him through that ordinance.

Men couldn't just decide they wanted to serve God and suddenly have authority just by making that decision, or by reading the scriptures, or by going to theological school. Jesus told his disciples in *John 15:16,* for instance, "Ye have not chosen me, but *I have chosen you, and ordained you . . . "*

The Bible is filled with examples of people who tried to use priesthood power when they weren't entitled to it because they hadn't been ordained. *Acts 19:13-16* tells us about the seven sons of Sceva who tried to cast evil spirits out of a man in the name of Jesus without holding the priesthood. The evil spirit answered them, "Jesus I know, and Paul I know, but who are ye?" And then the man filled with the evil spirits attacked the seven brothers and drove them out, leaving them naked and wounded.

Or consider *Acts 19, verses 1 through 6.* When Paul came to Ephesus he found people there who had been baptized by someone who lacked authority. Paul knew that was the case because the people hadn't been taught the basic doctrines of Christ by the individual who baptized them. In this case, they didn't even know that the Holy Ghost existed. So what did Paul do? He baptized them again because he knew it was necessary that they be baptized by someone who held true priesthood authority. (Now you remember that when your conscience and your love for Jesus Christ force you to grapple with the question of whether you have been baptized by someone holding the proper authority to baptize you in the name of Jesus Christ.)

So that's the first characteristic of Christ's New Testament Church. His leaders and church workers held the priesthood—God's authorization to represent Jesus Christ and to preach and perform the necessary ordinances in His name.

A Chain of Ordinations—Priesthood Received from Authorized Priesthood Holders

The second characteristic was closely related to the first one—there had to be a chain of ordinations extending down to every man who held the priesthood. Every person had to receive the priesthood from someone who previously held it, and in a manner repeatedly described in the scriptures. Just having a strong desire to serve God doesn't constitute an authorized call to the priesthood today any more than it did in New Testament times. The apostle Paul was very emphatic about how someone was to receive the priesthood. As he discussed the subject in *Hebrews 5:4*, he wrote, "No man taketh this honor unto himself, but *he that is called of God, as was Aaron.*"

That's the key—a man can't just decide that he wants the priesthood—he must be called of God through the prescribed scriptural procedure, and then be ordained by one who holds priesthood authority. And that chain of priesthood ordinations must continue unbroken all the way back to Jesus Christ. If the chain has even one missing or invalid link, there is no valid priesthood power beyond that lost link.

And what is the scriptural procedure by which men were called to the priesthood? It consisted basically of three parts:

First, inspiration came to one in authority, revealing that the individual was to be called to priesthood office. Second, the name of the individual was presented to the congregation for approval, and third, the person was ordained to priesthood office by one already holding priesthood authorization.

When Moses' brother, Aaron, was called to the priesthood, we see those three steps being followed in *Exodus, chapter 28, verses 1, 3 and 41.*

Moses' successor was called in the same way, using the same three-step procedure. Let me read you of his call in *Numbers 27, verses 18 through 23:* "The Lord said unto Moses, Take thee Joshua the son of Nun, a man in whom is the spirit, and lay thine hand upon him"—there's the first step, revelation to the person in authority—"And set him before Eleazar the priest, and before all the congregation . . ." —there's the second step:

CHAIN OF AUTHORITY

Just as electricity can only light a home if there is an unbroken connection with the source of the power, Latter-day Saints believe that a man must be able to trace his authorization to act in God's name to the Savior if he is to perform the ordinances of Christ's Church. This authority was completely removed from the earth during the great apostasy and all mankind lost the privilege of acting in God's name. It is only through the restoration of Christ's Church and priesthood to Joseph Smith that the authority to act in the name of God is again available to man. Now every ordained priesthood holder in the Church of Jesus Christ of Latter-day Saints can trace his authority back to Jesus Christ through a chain of ordinations. An example of this direct chain of priesthood ordinations is the one shown below which is the author's.

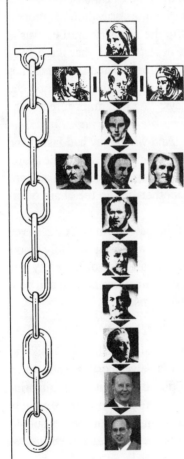

Jesus Christ, the source of priesthood authority, is the "Lamb . . . foreordained before the foundation of the world . . ."[1]

Peter, James, and John were ordained by Jesus Christ. The Savior told his apostles, "Ye have not chosen me, but I have chosen you, and ordained you . . ."[2]

Joseph Smith was given the Melchizedek Priesthood and was ordained to the apostleship in June, 1829, by the apostles Peter, James, and John.[3]

Oliver Cowdery was also ordained to the Melchizedek Priesthood in June, 1829, by Peter, James, and John.[4] David Whitmer was ordained a High Priest by Oliver Cowdery on October 25, 1831. Martin Harris was ordained a High Priest on June 3, 1831 by Lyman Wight, who had been ordained a High Priest on that date by Joseph Smith.

In response to a commandment from the Lord[5] the three witnesses to the Book of Mormon chose and ordained the first quorum of the Twelve Apostles of which Brigham Young was a member, on February 14, 1835.

George Q. Cannon was ordained an apostle by Brigham Young on August 26, 1860.

Heber J. Grant was ordained an apostle by George Q. Cannon on October 16, 1882.

Melvin J. Ballard was ordained an apostle by Heber J. Grant on January 7, 1919.

Don Q. Crowther was ordained a High Priest by Melvin J. Ballard on December 22, 1928.

Duane Swofford Crowther, the author, was ordained an elder by his father, Don Q. Crowther, on September 13, 1953.

1. I Peter 1:19-20   3. D & C 27:7-8, 12-13   4a. HC 1:176   6. HC 2:180-200
2. Jn. 15:16   4. Ibid   5. D & C 18:26-39

presentation to the congregation. And finally in verse 23, "And *he laid his hands upon him, and gave him a charge, as the Lord commanded* by the hand of Moses." So there was the third step. Moses ordained Joshua, through the laying on of hands, extending the chain of ordinations another vital link.

We see the same procedure repeatedly in New Testament times, but one instance is particularly instructive because it shows both how men are given authority and how they are not. Saul of Tarsus, who had been an enemy to the Church, was visited by the Savior on the road to Damascus, yet that didn't constitute a call in the ministry nor give him priesthood authority. He wasn't given the priesthood nor called to the ministry until he was at Antioch, more than a year later. We read in *Acts 13:1-3* that there were priesthood holders at Antioch, men who were prophets and teachers. They were the ones who received the revelation to give Saul the priesthood and to send him on a mission. The scripture says: "As they ministered to the Lord, and fasted, the Holy Ghost said, *Separate me Barnabas and Saul for the work whereunto I have called them.* And when they had fasted and prayed, and *laid their hands on them,* they sent them away." So once again, here were men, already holding priesthood authority, extending that authority to Paul, and as they did so they added another link in the chain of ordination.

Notice, now—having a glorious vision of the Savior himself didn't even give Saul authority. Being healed, or baptized, or receiving the Holy Ghost didn't give Saul priesthood authorization. Saul had to be ordained by one already holding the priesthood so the chain of ordinations is valid and continued, and "no man taketh this honor unto himself. . . ."

Twelve Apostles—The Foundation of the Church

The third characteristic of Christ's New Testament Church I'd like to mention was that it was built on a foundation of twelve apostles. Paul, when he was writing to new church members in Ephesus, taught them this principle. He said in *Ephesians 2:19 and 20* that "Ye are no more strangers and foreigners, but fellow citizens with the saints, and of the household of God; And are *built upon the foundation of the apostles and prophets,* Jesus Christ himself being the chief corner stone."

So the very foundation of the New Testament Church was the apostles and prophets, and I'd like you to list them separately as the third and fourth characteristics of the New Testament Church—twelve apostles being the third characteristic and prophets the fourth one.

One of the most important events in the New Testament was recorded at the beginning of the book of Acts. It is significant because it teaches us the Lord wants 12 apostles, not 11 or 13, to guide his church. You'll remember that Judas betrayed the Savior and then took his own life, so there were only eleven apostles left. By that time, the Church had been in existence for several years and was undoubtedly much larger. Two men were worthy to be named apostles: Barnabas and Matthias. Since the Church was larger, they could easily have called them both to be apostles, but the eleven knew better—they knew that the membership of their quorum was fixed at twelve, so they chose only one, and the *first chapter of Acts, verses 23 through 26,* tells us that it was Matthias that was "numbered with the eleven apostles." So the third characteristic of the New Testament Church was that it was built upon the foundation of 12 apostles.

Prophets—Authorized Spokesmen for God

The apostles were also prophets, and prophets are the fourth characteristic of Christ's true church. A prophet is a man authorized to receive revelation from God to guide the Church. In *Amos, chapter 3, verse 7,* that great prophet observed that "Surely *the Lord God will do nothing, but he revealeth his secret unto his servants the prophets."* In *Hosea, chapter 12, verse 10,* the Lord said, *"I have also spoken by the prophets, and I have multiplied visions, and used similitudes, by the ministry of the prophets."*

How long will prophets be needed on the earth? The apostle Paul gave the answer in the *4th chapter of Ephesians, verses 11 through 13.* Paul was writing about Christ's guidance of the New Testament Church when he said, *"He gave some, apostles; and some, prophets;* and some, evangelists; and some, pastors and teachers; For the *perfecting of the saints,* for the *work of the ministry,* for the *edifying of the body of Christ.* . . ." And then he told us how long prophets and apostles will be needed upon the earth: *"Till we all come in the unity of the faith,* and of the knowledge of the Son of God, unto a perfect man, unto the measure of the stature of the fullness of Christ." Has mankind reached that stage yet? Of course not! Authorized prophets are needed to be God's spokesmen on the earth today, just as they were necessary in New Testament times.

Revelation—God's Word Revealed to Man

A fifth characteristic of Christ's New Testament Church was that its prophets received revelation from God. A prophet isn't God's spokesman unless God speaks through him, and when God gives his word to the prophet, that word is called revelation. When a prophet prophesies, that prophecy is revelation.

Revelation is vital—it's God's communication to man. It's essential in God's church. As it says in *Proverbs 29:18,* "Where there is no vision, the people perish." That's why Paul wrote to the saints at Thessalonika in *First Thessalonians 5:19 and 20:* "Quench not the Spirit. *Despise not prophesyings."*

Revelation to a prophet is the process by which God teaches eternal truths to His people. Paul knew that. In *Galatians 1:11 and 12* he wrote: "But I certify you, brethren, that the gospel which was preached of me is not after man. For I neither received it of man, neither was I taught it, but *by the revelation of Jesus Christ."*

When new revelation is written down, and formally accepted by the Church, it becomes Scripture. Revelations to the early Church were written down and became new scripture—parts of the New Testament. In all ages, the existence of, and acceptance of new scripture is one way you can tell if a church really does receive revelation and have prophets, or not.

Now let's summarize for a minute. We've learned that there were characteristics that identified the true Church of Jesus Christ in New Testament times. I taught you five of them, and it's important that you remember them. Would you please memorize them in order as I review them with you? Make every effort to impress them on your mind because you'll need to know them later on. What are they?

First: *priesthood power*, given by the laying on of hands through one who already holds priesthood authority.

Second: *a chain of ordinations*, all the way back to Jesus Christ, so it can be demonstrated that the person who ordains someone else holds valid authority.

Third: *12 apostles*, because they were the foundation of the New Testament Church.

Fourth: *prophets*, God's spokesmen who conveyed the word of God to the church—and

Fifth: *revelation*, God's messages of guidance to direct the Church from day to day.

Recognition that a Universal Apostasy Would Occur

These characteristics were so essential that I'm going to repeat them again. *Priesthood power, a chain of ordinations, 12 apostles, prophets* and *revelation*. And since we've already learned that the New Testament Church knew there was going to be a falling away from the gospel of Christ, I'm going to add another characteristic to our list: *Christ's Church recognized that there was going to be a universal apostasy*—that's characteristic number six.

Are Catholicism or Protestantism the True Church of Christ?

There are dozens of other characteristics of the true church that can be identified from the scriptures, but rather than take the time to do so, I'm going to summarize a lot of early Christian history in just a few paragraphs, and tell you what happened to these essential characteristics.

After the death of Christ, persecution increased against the Church. Within the next several decades, enemies of the church slew the apostles and other leaders, inflicting horrible deaths upon them. As their lives were taken, the chain of ordinations was broken and continuity of Church leadership was interrupted. Soon there no longer were twelve apostles. Those apostles were also prophets, so revelation to the church through God's authorized prophets also ceased. Without the chain of ordinations, and without the guidance of apostles and prophets, false beliefs and improper practices began to creep in. Soon the priesthood was lost and the church had completed its transformation. No longer was it the Church of God—it had become the church of men, in fulfillment of the New Testament prophecies we've already read. As Paul described it, it was now a church "having a form of Godliness, but denying the power thereof."

It had no prophets, and therefore received no revelation, so those characteristics were lost and ceased to be important. No longer were there twelve apostles, so other forms of church government were adopted, which eventually evolved into the papacy and the college of cardinals. The chain of ordinations had been broken, so the priesthood was lost. Oh yes, people were still ordained to church responsibilities, but priesthood authorization, and power, and the correct priesthood procedures and organizations were long since gone.

Other changes came into the church: a changed concept of the nature of God, the worship of saints and of the virgin Mary, baptism by sprinkling, religious images, celibacy, the rosary, the doctrine of transubstantiation, the doctrine of the immaculate conception, the dogma of papal infallibility, the doctrine of purgatory, the sale of indulgences, the Spanish inquisition, corrupt popes excommunicating each other, and much more.

The tree was cut off from its life-giving roots, and the trunk was dead. Neither the trunk, nor the branches which sprang from it as they protested its decadency, were the true church of Jesus Christ. They were organizations of men, "having a form of Godliness," but lacking the power and authorization to act in the name of God.

A Modern Test: Do the Churches of Today Have the Six Characteristics?

How can you know all these things happened? How can you really be sure? The easiest way is to use the characteristics of Christ's New Testament Church as your guide. Ask yourselves: Does the Catholic Church believe in revelation and new scripture today? No! It doesn't even believe in revelation, so can it possibly have prophets today? No. Is it led by 12 apostles? No. Does it accept the Biblical teaching that there was a universal apostasy that cut the chain of ordinations and left men without authorization to act in God's name as his legally appointed representative? No. Without apostles and prophets and revelation, and with the chain of ordinations broken, can the Catholic priest of today, or the pope, possibly hold valid priesthood power? No. And without valid priesthood power, can the sacraments its members have received be valid and accepted by God? The answer, unfortunately, is no. And without any of the six essential characteristics, can the Catholic Church be the true church of Jesus Christ on the earth today? No.

And what about the Protestants? Do they believe in new revelation and new scripture? No. Do you even know one that claims to have a prophet? No. Do they have 12 apostles? No. Do they have an unbroken chain of ordinations? (How could they, when they all spring from Catholicism? If the trunk is dead, do the branches have life?) No. Then do they have the power of the priesthood, with valid authorization to act in the name of God? No. How could they? Where could they get it from? They reject the Catholics, so they can't get it from them. And they reject revelation, so they can't get it direct from God. There's no other source, so they can't possibly have priesthood authority to act in God's name. And without the six essential characteristics, can the protestant churches be the true church of God on the earth today? No!

You owe it to yourself to ask these questions about your own church. Does it believe in revelation? Does it have prophets? Twelve apostles? A valid chain of priesthood ordinations back to Christ? Priesthood authority? Does it accept the Biblical doctrines of the universal apostasy, with all its implications? And if it does not have the six essential characteristics of Christ's New Testament Church, can it be the true church of Jesus Christ? And the most important question of all must follow—can you come unto Christ, and attain the eternal rewards you seek through it, if it is not Christ's true church?

Beware of Satan's Counterfeits

Let's talk about what Satan wants to do for a minute. I think what he wants you to do is to be lulled into complacency. He wants you to accept a counterfeit and think you have the real thing. He wants you to think you've arrived without even letting you get on the right plane. He wants you to accept his counterfeit and never question nor evaluate nor challenge its validity until your time of mortal probation is passed and you are caught in his grasp after you die.

Let me share with you four passages of scripture that tell what God has said about people who accept Satan's counterfeits instead of rendering obedience to His counsel and commandments given through the true church of God. Please write them down, and then go home and re-read them, and ponder them with care because your eternal future hinges on how you respond to them.

The first is in *Matthew, chapter seven, verses 21 through 23: "Not every one that saith unto me, Lord, Lord, shall enter into the kingdom of heaven; but he that doeth the will of my Father which is in heaven. Many will say to me in that day, Lord, Lord, have we not prophesied in thy name? and in thy name have cast out devils? and in thy name done many wonderful works? And then I will profess unto them, I never knew you: depart from me, ye that work iniquity."* Can you see the danger of thinking that the counterfeit will be accepted for the real thing? God just won't accept the counterfeit.

Please write down the second passage, too: *Matthew 15:7 through 9.* It's a prophecy of Isaiah that was quoted by the Savior. It was applicable in

Isaiah's time, and it applied in Christ's day, and before we're through we'll see that it has special meaning for us in our day, too. Jesus said to people who were living the counterfeit instead of the true gospel: "Ye hypocrites, well did Esaias prophesy of you, saying, This people draweth nigh unto me with their mouth, and honoureth me with their lips; but *their heart is far from me. But in vain they do worship me, teaching for doctrines the commandments of men."* How valid is it to accept the counterfeit and live by men's teachings? Jesus said, "In vain they do worship me!" That's a frightening thought.

The third passage is *Romans 10: verses two and three:* "I bear them record that *they have a zeal for God, but not according to knowledge.* For they being ignorant of God's righteousness, and going about to establish their own righteousness, *have not submitted themselves unto the righteousness of God."* And that's the crux of the matter—No matter how zealous for God you are, if you want God's eternal rewards, you have to submit yourself to God's righteousness, and that can only be done through God's Church, under the direction of men holding valid priesthood authorization. You can't just walk down the street and turn in at any old gate that strikes your fancy—you have to turn in at the narrow gate that will lead you up the path to your real destination.

And that brings us to our fourth scripture: *Matthew 7:13 and 14,* where Jesus talks about the strait, or narrow gate that leads to his kingdom: *"Enter ye in at the strait gate:* for wide is the gate, and broad is the way, that leadeth to destruction, and many there be which go in thereat: Because *strait is the gate, and narrow is the way, which leadeth unto life, and few there be that find it."*

And those are the warnings God has given us about accepting Satan's counterfeits instead of seeking and finding and coming into the fold of the true Church of Jesus Christ.

Now let's summarize. First, we've discussed the Biblical doctrine that there is to be a universal apostasy following the era of the New Testament Church, and we've seen how those prophecies came to pass. Then we've identified six characteristics of the true Church of Jesus Christ, seen how they were lost from the earth, and found that none of those characteristics are found in Catholicism or in the Protestant Churches of modern Christiandom. And third, we've examined God's warnings concerning the danger of believing that even zealous activity in a church not authorized by Jesus Christ will bring us the eternal rewards we desire. The task that remains is for us to examine the broad pattern of Biblical prophecies that tell us God intended to restore His Church to the earth in the latter days, and form the basis for my bold assertion that the true Church of Jesus Christ today can only be a church that has been restored through divine revelation.

Events in the Restoration of the Church of Jesus Christ

Before we turn to our Bibles to examine these prophecies, let me review for you just briefly the events that took place in that restoration which placed the Lord's church once again on the earth.

There came a day in the spring of 1830 when a young man chosen of God went out into the woods near his home, seeking an answer to the question which was preying on his mind, "Which church should I join?" That young man, not yet 15 years of age, had heard a preacher explain, while holding a revival near his home, a Bible passage that made an important promise. Joseph decided he would apply that promise found in the Epistle of *James, the first chapter, the fifth verse,* that says, "If any of you lack wisdom, let him ask of God, that giveth to all men liberally, and upbraideth not," and then the scripture makes the pledge, "and it shall be given him."

Young Joseph Smith went into the woods near his home in upper New York. He knelt there and prayed. In response to his prayer he was visited by two heavenly personages. One pointed to the other and said, "Joseph, this is My Beloved Son. Hear Him!"

And there Joseph talked with God the Father and with His Son, Jesus Christ. And he asked that question, "which church should I join?" To his surprise he was told that none of the churches upon the face of teh earth was the church that he should join, and he learned that God's concern was that men would draw near to Him with their lips but that their hearts were far from Him, that they were teaching for commandments the doctrines of men rather than the doctrines of God. In other words, God affirmed to Joseph at that time that there had been an apostasy—the power and authority to act in the name of God had been lost and that the true doctrines of the Church of Jesus Christ were not on the earth.

Three-and-a-half years went by as Joseph waited patiently for further instructions, until finally, he poured out his heart to his Heavenly Father in his bedroom one night, on September 21st, 1823. In response to his prayer, an angelic personage appeared, told him his name was Moroni, gave him indication that he, Moroni, had lived here upon the American continent some 1400 years before, and that he was the one who had buried some metallic plates in a nearby hill. Moroni said that those plates were the record of God's dealings with the people who lived here in the Americas.

Joseph was shown in a vision where the plates were buried. That same night, as he talked with Joseph, Moroni taught him that the fullness of the everlasting gospel was contained in those plates. Moroni also gave him warning of the great judgments which are to come upon the earth in the last days.

Three times that night, and again the following day, Moroni appeared to Joseph, repeating and adding to his message. Joseph told his father what had happened, and his father sent him to that hill which he had seen in vision. There Joseph found the plates. But as he went to take them from the hill, the angel appeared to him once again and told Joseph that he wasn't to take those plates yet, but that he was to return to the hill each year on that same day and be taught and trained. For four years the Angel Moroni came and met with Joseph to teach him, preparing him to translate those plates and to restore to the earth that inspired record. That book is named after the father of Moroni, the man who preserved and abridged those records. It is known throughout the world today as the Book of Mormon.

Joseph Smith received those plates and was able to begin the translation in the fall of 1827, but the translation was not finally completed until 1829.

While Joseph and his friend and scribe, Oliver Cowdery, were working diligently on the translation, they encountered a passage that dealt with the doctrine of baptism. They knew they hadn't been baptized, so Joseph and Oliver decided, on May 15th, 1829, to seek in prayer an answer to the commandment that was given to them in the scriptures that they should be baptized.

As they sought in prayer for that answer, they were again visited by a heavenly being who identified himself as John the Baptist, that great prophet who baptized our Lord and Savior. John laid his hands upon their heads and conferred upon them the priesthood of Aaron, or the lesser priesthood, as it is referred to today. That priesthood has the power to baptize. With them holding that priesthood, he gave them the commandment that they should baptize each other, and they did just that. So Joseph and Oliver were baptized through the power of the priesthood which John conferred upon them.

A month later, in June 1829, Peter, James and John, the three leaders of the Twelve Apostles in the Lord's Church in the meridian of time, appeared to Joseph and Oliver. They restored to them the higher priesthood—

the "Holy Priesthood after the Order of the Son of God," often called the Melchizedek Priesthood. These three great leaders of Christ's church in ancient times gave them the same great power which they held—the power of the apostleship—and restored to them the keys of the kingdom; giving them the authority to function in the higher ordinances of the gospel; giving them power to perform sealings and to unite people together for all eternity—that same sealing power which they held in the meridian of time.

The gospel unfolding continued. By the authority of the apostleship given to them, and in obedience to a direct commandment from God, Joseph Smith and Oliver Cowdery actually restored Christ's church to the earth—the same Church that had previously been led by Peter, James, John, and the other apostles following Christ's day. The restored Church was officially reorganized on April 6, 1830.

But the restoration process continued all the way down to 1836, when on April 3rd, in Kirtland, Ohio, the Savior appeared and accepted a temple there which had been built to his name, and then Moses appeared and restored the keys for the gathering of the House of Israel. Then Elijah appeared and restored other priesthood keys which were designed to turn the hearts of the children to the fathers and the hearts of the fathers to the children.

We know that in those appearances we have the basis for much of the restoration of the gospel of Jesus Christ. We know that some of that restoration process still lies ahead of us. There are things that still have to come forth. We look forward to those things and to the future revelations that will bring them forth.

Biblical Prophecies of Restoration Events

Nebuchadnezzar's Dream: God's Kingdom to Be Established and Fill the Earth

With that brief historical sketch as a background, let's look now at some of the Biblical prophecies of the restoration of God's true church. Turn with me to the Old Testament, to the Book of Daniel, and let's review one of the most significant revelations ever given to man. It's interesting that this revelation was given to a person who wasn't even in God's church. It was given to a pagan king, Nebuchadnezzar. In his dream he saw an image of a man. You should understand that that image was like a calendar representing events to take place down through time. The statue had a head of gold, a breast and arms of silver, and it had a belly and thighs made of brass. It had legs of strong iron, and it had feet that were part of iron and part of clay. And then Nebuchadnezzar saw that from way up on a mountain a stone came rolling down and hit the image on its feet. The image fell over and was broken. And then Nebuchadnezzar watched as the stone grew and grew until it filled the whole earth, and he saw that it remained upon the earth.

Nebuchadnezzar wanted to know what the vision meant. He asked all of his soothsayers and wise men and astrologers to tell him the meaning. But the problem was that he forgot what he had seen so he couldn't even give them a hint. Because they couldn't interpret the dream, he threatened to put them to death. Then the Lord spoke to one of those wise men, his young prophet, Daniel, showed him the dream, and told him to go and to interpret the dream to Nebuchadnezzar.

Daniel told the king that what he had seen was a vision of the future of the major world kingdoms which were to come down through the ages, and he said, "Now king, you're a king among kings and you and Babylonia represent that head of gold." He said another kingdom was to follow Babylon, and history tells us that was the Medes and the Persians who came a couple of hundred years later. A third kingdom was to follow them, and that was Greece, which the dream represented as the belly of brass. Then there was to come a strong kingdom: Rome, the iron of the legs. It was in the Roman era that the Savior came here upon the earth, wasn't it? He came and established his church in the days of the Romans.

But Nebuchadnezzar saw that there was still another part to the image, the feet, made part of iron and part of clay, that we now know represented the mixture of strong and weak European nations that descended from the Roman empire.

Now the important message of the vision is that it would be in those days that the stone was to hit the image, and swell, and fill the whole earth. Read with me in *Daniel 2:44* how the prophet summarized the message of this important vision to king Nebuchadnezzar. Daniel said, "In the days of these kings," meaning those kings represented by the feet, part of iron and part of clay—the mixed kingdoms that descended out of the Roman empire—*"in the days of these kings shall the God of heaven set up a kingdom, which shall never be destroyed."*

Now what's he saying? Not in the days of Christ, during Roman rule, but in the days of those kingdoms *after* the days of the Roman empire, would

NEBUCHADNEZZAR'S DREAM AND IT'S INTERPRETATION

(Daniel, Chapter 2)

The gold head represented the Babylonian Empire 667-538 B.C.

The silver breast and arms represented the combined empires of the Medes and Persians 538-331 B.C.

The belly and thighs of brass represented the Macedonian (Greek) empire. 331-161 B.C.

The meridian of time— the period of Christ's earthly ministry.

The stone which broke the image was a kingdom to be established by the God of heaven.

The legs of iron represented the Roman Empire. 161 B.C.-431 A.D.

The feet of a mixture of iron and clay represented the variety of strong and weak kingdoms which formed after the collapse of the Roman empire and which still exist today.

The image was a Calendar which showed the future kingdoms of the earth.

The Major Messages of the Prophecy

1. The time when God would set up his kingdom upon the earth was to be in the last days, not during Christ's ministry in the first century A.D.

2. The prophecy makes it clear that no Church has a valid claim to being Christ's kingdom if it maintains that it has continued in an unbroken succession since Christ's earthly ministry, for such a belief violates the many Biblical prophecies of the apostasy.[1] On the contrary, the prophecy shows that Christ's kingdom was to be re-established in a later era — the last days.

Other Messages of the Prophecy

1. Christ's kingdom will be a great kingdom which will fill the whole earth. (Dan. 2:35)

2. Christ's kingdom will break in pieces and consume earthly kingdoms. (Dan. 2:44)

3. Christ's kingdom shall never be destroyed or left to another people; it shall stand forever.

4. The prophecy is not only religious but political in nature. Christ's kingdom will be both religious and political.[2]

1. See chapter XII.

2. For discussion of the dual nature of the kingdom of God and a reporting of substantiating statements of this idea, see Prophecy — Key to the Future. chapters V and XV.

God set up his kingdom which was never to be destroyed. And then Daniel said, "And *the kingdom shall not be left to other people, but it shall break in pieces and consume all these kingdoms and it shall stand forever.* Forasmuch as thou sawest that the stone was cut out of the mountain without hands, and that it brake in pieces the iron, the brass, the clay, the silver, and the gold; the great God hath made known to the king what shall come to pass hereafter: and the *dream is certain, and the interpretation thereof sure."*

Here, then, is a major revelation that tells us that the time when God's kingdom would be set up for the last time, and fill the whole earth, was not during Christ's ministry in the meridian of time, but later—after Rome was gone and when Europe would consist of a conglomerate of strong and weak kingdoms.

The Restoration Period: The Times of Restitution of All Things

Turn with me over to the New Testament again, to Acts, the third chapter, and there read one of those other passages that tells that the Church of Jesus Christ was to be established in the last days. And we read it there in *Acts 3, verses 19 through 21.* You remember what's happening here. Peter and John are preaching, and Peter says these words, "Repent ye therefore, and be converted, that your sins may be blotted out, when the times of refreshing shall come from the presence of the Lord"—and this is the period we're talking about—that time of refreshing in the last days. "And he shall send Jesus Christ, which before was preached unto you." Now Christ had already come and gone by then, right? Peter wasn't talking about that day; he was talking about a time in the last days when Christ would be sent to the earth here again and he said, *"He shall send Jesus Christ,* which before was preached unto you: *Whom the heaven must receive until the times of restitution of all things."* So we know from the book of Acts that there was to be a time in these last days when there was to be a time of restitution—or restoration—of all things.

All Things to Be Gathered in the
Dispensation of the Fulness of Times

If all things were to be restored in preparation for Christ's coming, could his true church have remained on the earth? Would there be a need to restore all things if an authorized church was here and functioning? No, and the need for a complete restoration makes the reality of the universal apostasy more apparent. Turn to the book of *Ephesians, the first chapter, verses 9 and 10,* if you would please, and let's read another of those passages that talk about the latter day era of the restoration. Paul is writing about what God has done to us here as he says, "Having made known unto us the mystery of his will, according to his good pleasure which he hath purposed in himself: That *in the dispensation of the fulness of times he might gather together in one all things in Christ, both which are in heaven, and which are on earth;* even in him." And that's what's happening in these last days, isn't it? God is restoring those things which have been taken away from the earth, gathering here upon the earth all of those things which have to be here in preparation for his coming. It's the era, or dispensation, of the fulness of times.

Paul's Allusion: the Appearance of the Father and the Son

Those three passages are all general references to the restoration in the last days. Let's move now to passages that refer to specific events that transpired in the restoration process. Some of the passages we'll read are very specific. Others are more general and are only passing allusions. But each verse has its place.

Turn to the Book of *Titus,* if you would, please, *chapter two, verse 13.* It's back further here in the New Testament, after Timothy. This is one of those verses that is just an allusion to an event in the restoration. Yet how else can it be explained except that it is a reference to that first vision which came to the Prophet Joseph Smith. Paul told Timothy the Saints were to be looking forward to a significant future event. He said the Saints were to be "looking for that blessed hope, and the glorious *appearance of the great God and our Saviour Jesus Christ."* Now who is the Great God? It's God the Father, isn't it? Paul was talking about a time when the Father and the Son would appear together. And when else did they appear, save at that time when Joseph Smith was visited by the Father and the Son?

Paul, 1800 years before, knew that there was to be an appearance of the great God and His Son, Jesus Christ. He knew it would happen. If someone says Paul wasn't talking about the first vision experienced by Joseph Smith, when Joseph saw both the Father and the Son, he should be able to tell you what other future appearance of the Father and the Son Paul was referring to. And your friend won't be able to do that.

John's Prophecy: An Angel Bringing the Everlasting Gospel

The second event in the restoration process was the coming of the Angel Moroni to Joseph Smith on September 21, 1823. And what did Moroni do? He told Joseph that the fulness of the everlasting gospel was contained in those metal plates of the Book of Mormon, and he warned of the judgments which were to come in the last days. John, the Revelator, foresaw the coming of an angel in the last days with those two identical messages. Remember how we read in Revelation, chapter 13 about the apostasy which was to come? Just a few verses later, in *Revelation 14:6-7*, we find John's prophecy of the angel that was to come, proclaiming those identical messages. John wrote: "I saw another *angel* fly in the midst of heaven, *having the everlasting gospel to preach unto them that dwell on the earth,* and to every nation, and kindred, and tongue, and people, Saying with a loud voice, *Fear God,* and give glory to him; *for the hour of his judgment is come:* and worship him that made heaven, and earth, and the sea, and the fountains of waters."

That's the prophecy. The angel coming to visit the earth was to have the everlasting gospel. Now what did Moroni say was in the plates of the Book of Mormon? The fulness of the everlasting gospel. And what was to be the message of the angel John saw? Fear God because the judgments of the last days were to come. John looked down through time and saw that there would come an angel who would have those two messages together, bringing the fulness of the everlasting gospel and the message that we must fear God, for the hour of his judgment is come, and that's exactly what Moroni did.

Now, would John have prophesied that an angel would bring the fulness of the everlasting gospel if it were already to be found among the churches of the day? Of course not. And if someone says that Moroni didn't fulfill John's prophecy, he should be ready to say when and to whom the angel came. And he can't do it. And if he says that the angel hasn't come yet, you should remind him that the angel was to bring the fulness of the everlasting gospel with him and ask him what implication that has concerning the status of his church. Can it be the true church without the everlasting gospel?

Isaiah's Prophecy: Apostasy, Then the
Vision of All in a Sealed Book

Now would you please turn back to one of the most amazing passages in all scripture, back in the Book of *Isaiah, the 29th chapter.* Surely Isaiah had keen insights into those things that were to happen in these last days. This passage has so many correlations with last days' events, it would take an hour to go over it all, but let me just read a series of verses that start with *verse 9,* and point out what he's talking about. He refers, first of all, to the apostasy, and then he talks about the coming forth of a sealed book.

Maybe I should review for you just a little bit more of the history of what happened as the Book of Mormon was restored. Remember that Joseph received the plates but that two-thirds of them were sealed, and he wasn't allowed to open that portion. But he was allowed to translate the rest of it. He copied some of the characters and sent them with a man named Martin Harris. He told Martin, "I want you to go find the learned men of the day and show these characters to them and get their certificate that these are valid, ancient characters."

Martin Harris went to New York, and he talked to a man by the name of Charles Anthon. Charles Anthon, bless his heart, was a kind of a pompous fellow and he wanted to do some exciting things. He saw the chance to get in on what he thought was a major archaeological find, so he wrote out a certificate saying those were true and valid hieroglyphic characters. He gave it to Martin Harris. As Martin started to leave, Dr. Anthon wanted to prolong the conversation so he asked, "How is it that this man Joseph Smith found out about these characters and these gold plates that you're talking about?" Martin Harris told him that an angel of God appeared and told Joseph the location of them. And Professor Anthon thought, "Oh, Oh! I'm getting into hot water in a hurry here," so he said, "Let me see that certificate." He took it and tore it up and said, "You bring the plates to me and I'll translate them," which was a fallacious thing to say because at that time they didn't yet have the ability to translate Egyptian hieroglyphics in America, but he wanted a chance at it anyway. Martin Harris said, "I can't bring them because part of the plates are sealed," and then Professor Anthon said the significant words that fulfilled Bible prophecy, "I cannot read a sealed book."(See *Joseph Smith—History, 1:63-65.*)

Well, we're going to see how Isaiah foresees that little event, and then we're going to read on a couple of verses further and see how Isaiah prophesies the first vision which the Prophet Joseph received, and Isaiah quotes those very words which the Savior said to Joseph Smith in the spring of 1820. Let's read it, starting with the apostasy at *Isaiah 29, verse 9:* "Stay yourselves, and wonder; cry ye out, and cry: they are drunken, but not with wine; they stagger, but not with strong drink. For the *Lord hath poured out upon you the spirit of deep sleep, and hath closed your eyes: the prophets and your rulers, the seers hath he covered.*"

Isaiah saw that because of the apostasy, a time would come when people on the earth would no longer receive revelation—everyone would be cut off from revelation from God. Then he says, "And the vision of all...," in other words, the way the whole world in these last days is to understand the scriptures, "And the *vision of all is become unto you as the words of a book that is sealed,* which men deliver to one that is learned, saying, Read this, I pray thee: and he saith, *I cannot; for it is sealed:* And the book is delivered to him that is not learned, saying, Read this, I pray thee: and he saith, I am not learned." Well, I've told you the story of how Martin Harris gave the characters of the book to Charles Anthon and it was Anthon that said, "I cannot read a sealed book." And we believe it was Joseph Smith himself who said, "Lord, I'm not learned, I can't translate that." And yet the Lord gave him power. Through the power and spirit of revelation, Joseph translated that sealed book. And what did the Lord say? The vision of all is to be found in that book which was sealed. In other words it has a message of importance to all mankind and would come in a time when all revelation had been cut off.

Let's read on. "Wherefore the Lord said, Forasmuch as this people draw near me with their mouth, and with their lips do honour me, but have removed their heart far from me, and their fear toward me is taught by the precept of men: Therefore, behold, I will proceed to do a marvelous work among this people, even a marvellous work and a wonder; for the wisdom of their wise men shall perish, and the understanding of their prudent men shall be hid."

In other words God was going to overcome the learning of the proud, the scholars, and substitute in its place the vision of all through a man through whom he had revealed his word. That man was the prophet Joseph Smith.

Then Isaiah comes over here in verse 18 and he says, *"In that day shall the deaf hear the words of the book,* and the eyes of the blind shall see out of obscurity, and out of darkness." And so he's talking very clearly about a book which is to come forth in the last days. Notice those words of the prophecy: "This people draw near me with their mouth, and with their lips do honour me, but have removed their heart far from me, and their fear toward me is taught by the precept of men . . . " Those are almost the exact words Jesus spoke to Joseph Smith in Joseph's first vision. (See *Joseph Smith—History 1:19.*)

Now the Latter-day Saints understand the fulfillment of each of these verses in Isaiah 29, but I've never found anyone else who will even attempt to interpret the passage in detail. And there's more that explains about how the Book of Mormon will come forth in the earlier verses of Isaiah 29, but we won't take time to read them.

Malachi's Prophecy: The Coming of John the Baptist

Now consider the next event that happened in the restoration process. We've talked about the first vision, and we've talked about the coming of Moroni and the restoration of the Book of Mormon.

John the Baptist came on May 15, 1829. He restored the power of the priesthood. Did you know his coming was prophesied, in very specific terms, in the book of Malachi, the last book in the Old Testament? The Lord says this, in *Malachi three, verses one to three.* "Behold, *I will send my messenger, and he shall prepare the way before me:* and *the Lord, whom ye seek, shall suddenly come to his temple,* even the messenger of the covenant, whom ye delight in: behold, he shall come, saith the Lord of hosts. But *who may abide the day of his coming?* and who shall stand when he appeareth? for he is *like a refiner's fire,* and like fullers' soap: And he shall sit as a refiner and purifier of silver: and he shall purify the sons of Levi, and purge them as gold and silver, that they may offer unto the Lord an offering in righteousness."

Let's go back and review what's being said. The Lord says that he was going to send a messenger to prepare the way before his coming. But what coming is described here? Is this his coming where he was born as a lowly baby in a manager? No, this is Christ's coming in glory, isn't it—where he comes in power. Malachi says Christ will come like a refining fire— remember the earth is to be burned and cleansed at his Second Coming. And he comes like fullers' soap—that's a strong lye soap, isn't it? So Malachi's prophecy is that the Lord will send a messenger to prepare the way before him when he comes in glory.

Now, cross reference a passage with that. Turn over to Luke the seventh chapter, verses 27 and 28, and see something that the Savior said early in his earthly ministry. At this time John the Baptist had made some strong accusations against the ruler of the day, and that ruler had taken John and placed him in prison. Then John's disciples had come to see the Savior and tell him about it. In that context, the Savior talked to his other followers about John the Baptist, and said, in *Luke 7:27 and 28:* "This is he, of whom it is written, Behold, I send my messenger before thy face, which shall prepare thy way before thee. For I say unto you, Among those that are born of women there is not a greater prophet than John the Baptist." So here the Savior cites that passage in Malachi and says John the Baptist is the man who would fulfill that prophecy, and yet the prophecy was talking about Christ's future coming in glory, when the world will be cleansed by fire. So the Savior clearly identifies John as the one who would come and prepare the way before him. Latter-day Saints know that John the Baptist came on May 15, 1829, in direct fulfillment of the prophecy, but no other church makes any claim concerning it at all.

Sealing Powers Restored by Peter, James and John

Well, turn to one other passage. Who came next in the restoration process? It was Peter, James and John, wasn't it? There isn't a Bible passage that talks about their coming in the last days, specifically, but we have something far more important in words that the Savior said in *Matthew, the 16th chapter, verses 13 through 19.* You remember that in this passage the Savior had turned to his disciples and had asked them who people thought he was, and they'd answered and said, well, some people say that you're John and some say that you're Elias, and some say that you are Jeremiah, one of the prophets. And then Christ said, "But whom say ye that I am?" Simon Peter spoke up and said, "Thou art the Christ, the Son of the living God." Then the Savior said these important words to Peter: "Blessed art thou, Simon Bar-jona: for flesh and blood hath not revealed it unto thee, but my Father which is in heaven. And I say also unto thee, That *thou art Peter, and upon this rock I will build my church;* and the gates of hell shall not prevail against it. And *I will give unto thee the keys of the kingdom of heaven: and whatsoever thou shalt bind on earth shall be bound in heaven:* and whatsoever thou shalt loose on earth shalt be loosed in heaven."

Now, what was the Savior saying? Latter-day Saints recognize that Peter was the leader of the church in those days. It was that same Peter who came back in these last days and established once again the powers of the higher priesthood here upon the earth and restored the authority of the apostleship to Joseph Smith. How do we know that we have the higher priesthood here upon the earth? How do we know that we Mormons have the keys of the kingdom? Well, what was Peter in possession of? The power to seal on earth as in heaven, right? How many churches do you know of this day that even claim to have the power to bind on earth, so that we'll be bound in heaven? The Latter-day Saints are the only church, for instance, that even claim to bind, or seal couples together in eternal marriage, so the partners are together after death. No other church even claims to be able to bind couples throughout eternity—they all teach "to death do ye part." The same Peter whom the Savior talked to and said, "you have the keys of the kingdom," came back in these last days and restored the power of the apostleship, the power of the Melchizedek Priesthood, and the sealing power here upon the earth once again. We know that Peter, with his two helpers, James and John, came and restored those powers and that we have them in the church today.

Malachi's Prophecy: Elijah to Turn the Hearts of Children to their Fathers

Let's look at just one more passage that deals with one of those specific events of the last days when the Church was restored. Remember I talked to you about what happened on April 3, 1836 in the Kirtland Temple where first the Savior, and then Moses, and then Elijah, appeared. Elijah restored the keys which would turn the hearts of the fathers to the children and the hearts of the children to the fathers as he gave us directions concerning temple work and genealogical research. We find his coming prophesied way back in the last two verses of the Old Testament, in the Book of Malachi. Turn there, if you would, to *Malachi 4, verses 5 and 6,* where the Lord makes this promise through his prophet Malachi: "Behold I will send you Elijah the prophet before the coming of the great and dreadful day of the Lord: And he shall turn the heart of the fathers to the children, and the heart of the children to their fathers, lest I come and smite the earth with a curse." How many other churches tell you of the coming of Elijah the Prophet? How many other churches tell you the date and time and the place of the occasion? None. How many other churches speak of any of these passages? How many other churches know that there was to be a complete and universal apostasy?

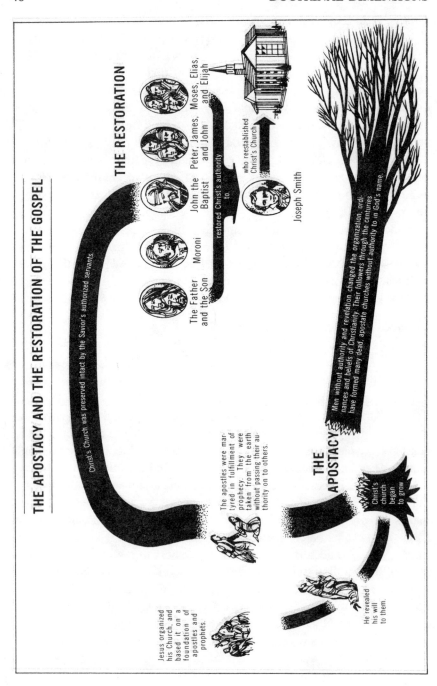

THE APOSTACY AND THE RESTORATION OF THE GOSPEL

THE RESTORATION

Christ's Church was preserved intact by the Savior's authorized servants.

The Father and the Son

Moroni

John the Baptist

Peter, James, Moses, Elias, and Elijah

restored Christ's authority to

who reestablished Christ's Church

Joseph Smith

The apostles were martyred in fulfillment of prophecy. They were taken from the earth without passing their authority on to others.

Jesus organized his Church, and based it on a foundation of apostles and prophets.

THE APOSTACY

Christ's church began to grow

He revealed his will to them.

Men without authority and revelation changed the organization, ordinances and beliefs of Christianity. Their followers through the centuries have formed many dead, apostate churches without authority to in God's name.

In contrast, how many churches somehow try to trace their claims back to the original church but have no valid claim to priesthood authority? The Catholics say, oh yes, Peter was the first pope, and we go back and, yes, there were some bad popes, and yes, we had our problems, but the church still continues and we go back to Peter. They say that. We say that was like the trunk of a tree, and the Lord took his ax and he cut off that tree at the base, didn't he? He chopped down the tree because of the apostasy. Then he came and planted a new tree and restored the gospel in these last days. The Protestants say, Oh, the Catholics were bad and corrupt and they had their indulgences, and their evil ways, and they talk about Martin Luther with his theses that he nailed on the door of the chapel. But, if the trunk was cut off, can the branches have life? Can live branches come from a dead tree? They cannot, and we all know it.

A Witness: God's Church Has Been Restored

I bear you this witness, that the Bible tells clearly that the true Church of Jesus Christ is the church which recognizes the reality of the apostasy—that Christ's church was to be completely taken off of the earth. But the true church also acknowledges each of the steps of the restoration as they were prophesied in the Bible. We've read the prophecies. Can you give any other explanation for them? There's no other realistic interpretation except that the true Church of Christ is a restored church—The Church of Jesus Christ of Latter-day Saints.

I bear witness to you that this is the Church of Jesus Christ, that we know there was an apostasy, we know there was a restoration, we know what the scriptures tell us and we are founded securely in the scriptures. I know that we have the keys of the kingdom today.

I pray that every one of you will carefully ponder this message, and then act upon it. Recognize that you can't receive God's highest blessings unless you enter in at the strait gate and be baptized into the restored Church of Jesus Christ by one having valid priesthood authority. I pray that you'll come to know that God has placed his power and richest blessings within the restored church and that the church is to grow and fill the whole earth and never be left to another people as Daniel saw in his revelation. I bear you that witness, and I know it's true. in the name of Jesus Christ, Amen.

My brothers and sisters and friends,

It's a pleasure to talk to you on a subject of great importance: Biblical proofs of the Book of Mormon. This topic is exciting to me because it shows the precise handiwork of God. He revealed great insights to his prophets in Old Testament times about the Book of Mormon, and carefully prepared the way so the Bible would bear prophetic witness that the Book of Mormon was also his inspired word. He wanted mankind to know that the Book of Mormon was to stand parallel to the Bible as another witness that Jesus truly is the Christ, our Lord and Savior and Redeemer, and He used Bible prophecy to bear witness that the Book of Mormon is revealed and inspired scripture, and of equal significance with the Bible as a tool to lead us to Christ.

Pray for Guidance—Things of God
Are Revealed by the Spirit of God

My message to you is important, and you'll need to evaluate it carefully and prayerfully. I'd like to ask you to take a few minutes and prepare yourself spiritually for the message I'm going to share with you. I invite you to pray, and ask your Father in Heaven to send the Holy Spirit to be with you while you read to these words and request that his Holy Spirit bear witness to you that my message is true.

Please open your Bible to *1st Corinthians chapter two,* and let's read a very choice passage of scripture together. The passage is 1st Corinthians chapter two, verses 9 through 12. This is what it says:

"Eye hath not seen, nor ear heard, neither have entered into the heart of man, *the things which God hath prepared for them that love him.* But *God hath revealed them unto us by his Spirit:* for the Spirit searcheth all things, yea, the deep things of God. For what man knoweth the things of man, save the spirit of man which is in him? Even so *the things of God knoweth no man, but the Spirit of God.* Now we have received, not the spirit of the world, but the spirit which is of God; *that we might know the things that are freely given to us of God."*

Now my request of you is that you pray, and bring the Holy Spirit into your mind and heart, and through the Spirit discern the intent and importance of this message. God has freely given us important information— that the Bible bears witness that the Book of Mormon is also God's revealed word—I want you to understand that message and know, through the Spirit, that it is true.

A Synopsis of Book of Mormon History

My task is twofold—I need to teach you a little bit of history from the Book of Mormon, and then show how the Bible talks about those historical events. First, the history—

The Book of Mormon is the account of three groups of people who came from the Middle East to the Americas in Old Testament times.

The group which has its history recorded most fully was the Prophet Lehi and his family. They left Jerusalem in 600 B.C., just prior to the fall of that city to the Babylonians under King Nebuchadnezzar. When they left Jerusalem, they traveled to the south, then made their way eastward, eventually coming to the shores of the sea.

They brought with them brass plates which contained much of what is now known as the Old Testament. They had the writings of Isaiah and the words of other Old Testament Prophets. Lehi had four sons at the time: Laman, Lemuel, Sam and Nephi.

As they left Jerusalem, they were joined by another family whose father was named Ishmael. Both families were descendants of Joseph, the son of Jacob, or Israel—that same Joseph who was sold into Egypt, earlier in Old Testament times. These two families intermarried and gave birth to children which eventually became two great nations.

God continually revealed his will to Lehi, and also to his son, Nephi. When they came to the seashore, Nephi was instructed by revelation how to build a ship, and the ship he built eventually carried the two families to the Americas, which they learned by revelation was to be a land of promise. They arrived about 589 B.C. and began to establish their colony. Because of the rebelliousness of Laman and Lemuel, the group broke into two factions following the death of Lehi. The followers of Laman came to be known as Lamanites; the followers of Nephi were known as Nephites. The Lamanites became wicked and warlike; the Nephites were led by prophets—men of God who continually led their followers to prepare for the eventual coming of Jesus Christ into the world. Most of the history of the Book of Mormon tells of the interrelationships between these two groups.

When the two factions separated, the Nephites carried records of their forefathers and the writings of the Old Testament prophets with them, which they studied and applied from day to day in their lives.

About 320 years later, a group of Nephites discovered the city of Zarahemla, which had been founded by another group known as the Mulekites. Mulek fled from Jerusalem about the same time as Lehi, escaping at the time that Zedekiah, king of Judah, was carried away captive into Babylon. His people also journeyed in the wilderness, and were brought by the Lord across the ocean to the Americas. The Mulekites and the Nephites joined together, and the two cultures merged into one.

Over the years various Nephite prophets foretold the coming of the Savior and prophesied of the star which would be the sign of his birth. They saw the star in the Americas and recognized that their Savior had been born. They changed their time system and began numbering their years from the Savior's birth. The Nephites also knew of the Savior's death, and they experienced tremendous volcanic eruptions and other natural calamities at the time of his crucifixion.

One of the most important portions of the Book of Mormon is the record known as Third Nephi, which tells how Jesus came and appeared to the Nephites and Lamanites in the Americas several months after his resurrection. The book stands as a powerful witness of the reality of the Savior's atoning sacrifice, of his conquest over death, and of his love for all mankind.

Following Christ's visit to the Americas, there was peace between the two nations for more than 200 years, as the people lived in righteousness. But as wickedness again began to spread throughout the two cultures, wars broke out between them. The Nephites, who previously had been more righteous than the Lamanites, became more wicked than their brothers. As the Book of Mormon draws to an end, it tells of great wars that took place between the Nephites and the Lamanites, ending in a final battle in 385 A.D. in which all but a handful of the Nephites were destroyed. Prior to this battle, Mormon, the Nephite prophet and leader, was instructed by the Lord to take the numerous metal plates upon which the Nephites had recorded their histories and condensed those histories onto plates of his own called the plates of Mormon. Mormon was one of the few Nephites who survived the last battle. His son Moroni also survived. Mormon gave the plates to Moroni, who eventually buried them so that they could come forth in the last days. Since the plates that comprised the history of the Book of Mormon were abridged by Mormon, the book carries his name today. It is know as the Book of Mormon.

A third group also came to the Americas from the Middle East. They came much earlier—at the time of the Tower of Babel. The Book of Mormon tells of a man named Jared and his followers who were led from the Tower of Babel more than 2,200 years before the birth of Christ. The Jaredites also crossed the oceans to the Americas and settled in approximately the same area where the Nephites and Mulekites would eventually come. The Jaredites had prophets of God among them who led and inspired the people, but as wicked factions sprung up among them, the Jaredites also suffered internal wars which eventually annihilated them as a people. The last survivor of the Jaredites was discovered by the Mulekites more than 1,700 years after the Jaredite civilization began. The history of the Jaredites is summarized in a book of the Book of Mormon known as the book of Ether.

The Book of Mormon, then, tells of three civilizations or cultures which were led by God to the Americas: the Jaredites, the Nephites and the Mulekites. The Book of Mormon tells us that each of these nations prospered so long as it did what was right, but they reaped the wrath of God when they turned to wickedness. All three of them were eventually destroyed when they ceased to worship and obey their Lord and Savior.

We learn much about Jesus Christ from the Book of Mormon as we read the writings of the many prophets whom God inspired to teach the people. The book truly stands as another testament for Christ.

So much for history—now let's consider some of the Bible references which show that the Book of Mormon, like the Bible, truly is a portion of God's revealed word to mankind.

Christ's Prophecy: Other Sheep Shall Hear My Voice

The Lord himself, along with many of the Old Testament prophets, made striking references to the people in the Book of Mormon—powerful allusions which cannot be overlooked by honest truthseekers. About six months before his crucifixion, during his late Judean ministry, Jesus came to attend the Feast of Tabernacles in Jerusalem. While he was there, he was challenged by the Pharisees and debated the points of his doctrine with them. In the *tenth chapter of John* we read how he told them the parable of the good shepherd, saying to them, "He that entereth not by the door into the sheepfold, but climbeth up some other way, the same is a thief and a robber. But he that entereth in by the door is the shepherd of the sheep. To him the porter openeth; and the sheep hear his voice: and he calleth his own sheep by name, and leadeth them out." And then Jesus told them, "Verily, verily, I say unto you, I am the door of the sheep . . . *I am the good shepherd:* the good shepherd giveth his life for the sheep."

In *verse 14 of John 10* we read where he said, "I am the good shepherd, and know my sheep, and am known of mine. As the Father knoweth me, even so know I the Father: and I lay down my life for the sheep." And then, in *John 10:16,* we read that significant verse in which Christ alluded to the people we read about in the Book of Mormon. He said, *"Other sheep I have which are not of this fold: them also I must bring, and they shall hear my voice; and there shall be one fold, and one shepherd."*

In chapter 15 of 3rd Nephi, in the Book of Mormon, we read Christ's words when he visited the Nephites and Lamanites in the Americas following his resurrection. He told the people here that their forefathers had been separated from the house of Judah because of the iniquity of the Jews. He also spoke of the other tribes of the house of Israel which had been taken away from the house of Judah, and said that the iniquity of the Jews kept them from knowing the location of those other tribes also.

Then, in *3rd Nephi chapter 15, verses 21-24,* he explained the passage about the "other sheep" that we read in the 10th chapter of John. He told the people: "Verily I say unto you, that *ye are they of whom I said: Other sheep I have which are not of this fold; them also I must bring, and they shall hear my voice; and there shall be one fold, and one shepherd.* And they understood me not, for they supposed it had been the Gentiles; for they understood not that the Gentiles should be converted through their preaching. And they understood me not that I said they shall hear my voice; and they understood me not that the Gentiles should not at any time hear my voice—that I should not manifest myself unto them save it were by the Holy Ghost. But behold, *ye have both heard my voice, and seen me; and ye are my sheep, and ye are numbered among those whom the Father hath given me.*"

So the Book of Mormon has the explanation for that passage in John 10 that has been so mysterious to Bible scholars for hundreds of years. They have wondered who those other sheep were that weren't the Jews but were still part of Christ's sheepfold. Some of them have said that it was the Gentiles, but Jesus went among the Gentiles only once and said that he wasn't sent to them. We read about it in the 15th chapter of Matthew, where he made a short visit to Tyre and Sidon. When he was approached by a Syrophonecian woman who asked him to heal her daughter, the Savior said, in *Matthew 15:24*, "I am not sent but unto the lost sheep of the House of Israel." Though he healed the woman's daughter, we have no other record to indicate that Jesus ever ministered among the Gentiles. His mission was only to Israel, and the Book of Mormon people were his other sheep.

Jacob's Prophecy: Joseph's Descendants to Come to the Everlasting Hills

Another Bible passage with strong links to the Book of Mormon is found in the 49th Chapter of the Book of Genesis. Let's recall Old Testament history to set the stage for this prophecy. Remember that Abraham was the father of Isaac, and Isaac was the father of Jacob. Jacob was the father of sons who became the heads of the twelve tribes of Israel. Jacob's name was changed to Israel by the Lord Jehovah. Jacob had one son, Joseph, who was particularly outstanding. It was he who was sold into Egypt by his brothers. After he saved the nation of Egypt and all the surrounding nations from the effects of a seven-year-long famine, he became second only to the Pharaoh in power.

At the end of Genesis we read how Jacob, then an old man approaching death, pronounced prophetic blessings upon his sons and upon two of his grandsons. The 49th chapter of Genesis records those prophetic blessings to his descendants. *Genesis chapter 49, verses 22-26,* contains the prophetic words he spoke concerning the descendants of Joseph. Those words describe events which took place in the Book of Mormon account. This is what the passage says:

"Joseph is a fruitful bough, even a fruitful bough by a well; whose branches run over the wall: The archers have sorely grieved him, and shot at him, and hated him: But his bow abode in strength, and the arms of his hands were made strong by the hands of the mighty God of Jacob; (from thence is the shepherd, the stone of Israel:) Even by the God of thy Father, who shall help thee; and by the Almighty, who shall bless thee with blessings of heaven above, blessings of the deep that lieth under, blessings of the breasts, and of the womb: The blessings of thy Father have prevailed above the blessings of my progenitors *unto the utmost bound of the everlasting hills:* they shall be on the head of Joseph, and on the crown *of the head of him that was separate from his brethren."*

Let's go back and analyze this great blessing because there are several phrases here which find application only in the account of Lehi and his people who were descendants of Joseph.

Verse 22 says, "Joseph was a fruitful bough, even a fruitful bough by a well; whose branches run over the wall." Let's see if we can understand that phrase. "Joseph is a fruitful bough" means that he was to have many descendants. He was to be a "fruitful bough by a well," or by a sea, and his branches were to run over the wall. Back in that day, the people of Israel were land people, not seafaring people, and the sea formed a wall to them; yet Jacob's prophecy was that a branch of the house of Joseph was to cross over the wall, or cross over the sea. And that's exactly what happened when Lehi's family constructed a ship and sailed across that wall that was the ocean.

Then there's another phrase that's significant. In verse 26 it says, "The blessings of thy father have prevailed above the blessings of my progenitors unto the utmost bound of the everlasting hills." Now what does that mean? It tells us where those descendants of Joseph went who crossed the great ocean. If you look at a map of the world and find the longest mountain chain on it, you'll discover the everlasting hills. Those everlasting hills are the mountains which come up out of the sea, way up in the north at the very western tip of Alaska. The mountains rise out of the sea, then curve down through Alaska and Canada and the United States and Central

JACOB'S PROPHECY OF THE DESCENDANTS OF JOSEPH

(Genesis 49:22-26)

The ten tribes which made up the nation of Israel were carried into Assyria and later became lost to historians. It is prophesied that they will someday come to the Americas and then return to Palestine. (See D&C 133:25-34, Ezek. 37)

The Wall: The people of Israel were land dwellers and rarely ventured upon the waters.

Lehi and his family, a branch of the house of Joseph, were separated from the rest of Israel when they sailed to the Americas.

America, and continue all the way down to the tip of South America, where they disappear back into the sea. They truly are everlasting hills—with no visible beginning and no visible end. They're the longest mountain range on earth.

It's clear that Jacob knew what would happen to the Book of Mormon colony when he predicted that some of Joseph's branches—not all of Joseph, but some of Joseph's branches—would run over the wall; that his descendants would be greatly blessed, and that those blessings would prevail above the blessings of all his brothers because they would extend to the utmost bound of the everlasting hills as they came to the Americas. He prophesied that those blessings would be on the head of him that was separate from his brethren. That's Lehi, we believe, who came with his people and settled in the Americas.

Now there are those that might not agree with this interpretation, but if they choose to disagree, they should certainly be able to furnish appropriate explanation of, first, who the branches of Joseph were which were to run over the wall; second, where that wall was; third, where is the land of the everlasting hills that those branches were to extend to; and fourth, they should explain who it was that was to be separate from his brethren that was descended from Joseph. That's my challenge to them: provide an adequate explanation of those four statements.

As I read the writings of the Bible scholars, they don't seem to have any answer at all for these questions. They can't identify who the branches were, or what the wall was that they crossed over, or where the land of the everlasting hills was, or who the descendant of Joseph was that was to be separate from his brethren. But we find all of those answers in the Book of Mormon because it truly fulfills biblical prophecy.

Ezekiel's Prophecy: Records of Judah and Joseph to be Joined Together

A prophecy in the 37th chapter of the book of Ezekiel is also significant. Back in the Old Testament days, when people wanted to make a written record, they recorded that record on scrolls. Those scrolls were taken and wound on sticks, so when they would refer to a written record they would call it a stick. In the 37th chapter of Ezekiel we have a prophecy that talks about how there is to be record of Judah, which is the Bible, and also another record, of Joseph. And the prophecy says those records are to be joined together in the last days, and that in the time of their being joined together other events will also occur: the restoring of the house of Israel and the house of Judah to live together in the land of Israel, the building of the Lord's tabernacle or temple there, and the rule of a king by the name of David, who will be their ruler in the last days. This is one of the most significant prophecies concerning last day's events that we have in the Bible.

Let's read the part, though, that talks about the two records, the record of Judah and the record of Joseph. We find it in *Ezekiel, chapter 37, verses 15-20.* It says, "The word of the Lord came again unto me, saying, Moreover, thou son of man, *take thee one stick, and write upon it, For Judah, and for the children of Israel his companions: then take another stick, and write upon it, for Joseph, the stick of Ephraim, and for all the house of Israel his companions: And join them one to another into one stick; and they shall become one in thine hand.* And when the children of thy people shall speak unto thee, saying, Wilt thou not show us what thou meaneth by these? Say unto them, Thus saith the Lord God; Behold, I will take the stick of Joseph, which is in the hand of Ephraim, and the tribes of Israel, his fellows, and will put them with him, even with the stick of Judah, and *make them one stick, and they shalt be one in mine hand.* And the sticks whereon thou writest shall be in thine hand before their eyes."

This, then, is a prophecy that the records of Judah, or the Bible, and the record of Joseph will be brought together. Following that, as the context shows, will come the time when the house of Israel will be reunited, and Judah and Israel will dwell together in the land of Israel.

We know what the stick of Judah is—it's the Bible. But who else but the Latter-day Saints offers any explanation at all for what the stick of Joseph is? We see that the Book of Mormon is a record of Joseph, but no one else even makes any claims at all as to what record fulfills this great prophetic statement.

An interesting prophecy made by Nephi in the Book of Mormon explains the way in which the Lord will bring the records of the various portions of the House of Israel together. Nephi foresaw that there would be a time in the last days when the Book of Mormon would come forth unto men who would complain and challenge its validity, saying, "A Bible! A Bible! We have got a Bible and there cannot be any more Bible!" In chapter 29 of 2nd Nephi, that prophet quoted the words of a revelation from God he had received on this subject, in which the Lord said, *"Know ye not that there are more nations than one?* Know ye not that I, the Lord your God, have created all men, and that I remember those who are upon the isles

EZEKIEL'S PROPHECY OF THE TWO STICKS

(Ezekiel 37:15-28)

The Stick of Judah
(The Bible)

The Stick of Joseph
(The Book of Mormon and the
Records of the Tribes of Israel)

"for Judah, and for the children of Israel his companions . . ."

"the stick of Joseph, which is in the hand of Ephraim, and the tribes of Israel his fellows . . ."

Nephi Prophesied:

And it shall come to pass that the Jews shall have the words of the Nephites, and the Nephites shall have the words of the Jews; and the Nephites and the Jews shall have the words of the lost tribes of Israel; and the lost tribes of Israel shall have the words of the Nephites and the Jews.

And it shall come to pass that my people, which are of the house of Israel, shall be gathered home unto the lands of their possessions; and my word also shall be gathered in one. (2 Ne. 29:13-14)

Ezekiel said his prophecy would receive final fulfillment when:

1. The children of Israel will be gathered from among the heathen and restored to the land of Palestine.

2. The two kingdoms, Judah and Israel, will have combined and will have been established as one nation in that land.

3. They shall be ruled by a King.

4. The Lord will have cleansed them from sin.

5. Their king shall be named David.

6. The Lord's sanctuary will have been built in the land of Palestine.

7. The heathen nations will have been taught that God sanctifies and protects Israel.

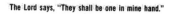

The Lord says, "They shall be one in mine hand."

Latter-day Saints see the beginning of the fulfillment of Ezekiel's prophecy in the coming forth of the <u>Book of Mormon</u>, which represents a portion of the record of the tribes of Israel which were separated from Judah.

of the sea; and that I rule in the heavens above and in the earth beneath; and *I bring forth my word unto the children of men, yea, even upon all the nations of the earth?* Wherefore murmur ye, because that ye receive more of my word? *Know ye not that the testimony of two nations is a witness unto you that I am God, that I remember one nation like unto another?* Wherefore, I speak the same words unto one nation like unto another. And when the two nations shall run together the testimony of the two nations shall run together also. And I do this that I may prove unto many that I am the same yesterday, today and forever; and that I speak forth my words according to mine own pleasure. And *because that I have spoken one word ye need not suppose that I cannot speak another;* for my work is not yet finished; neither shall it be until the end of man, neither from that time henceforth and forever. Wherefore, *because that ye have a Bible ye need not suppose that it contains all my words; neither need ye suppose that I have not caused more to be written.* For I command all men, both in the east and in the west, and in the north, and in the south, and in the islands of the sea, that *they shall write the words which I speak unto them.* For out of the books which shall be written I will judge the world, every man according to their works, according to that which is written. For behold, *I shall speak unto the Jews and they shall write it; and I shall also speak unto the Nephites and they shall write it;* and I shall also speak unto the other tribes of the house of Israel, which I have led away, and they shall write it; and I shall also speak unto all nations of the earth and they shall write it. And it shall come to pass that *the Jews shall have the words of the Nephites, and the Nephites shall have the words of the Jews;* and the Nephites and Jews shall have the words of the lost tribes of Israel; and the lost tribes of Israel shall have the words of the Nephites and the Jews. And it shall come to pass that my people, which are of the House of Israel, shall be gathered home unto the lands of their possessions; and *my word also shall be gathered in one.* And I will show unto them that fight against my word and against my people, who are of the House of Israel, that I am God, and that I covenanted with Abraham that I would remember his seed forever."

So Nephi's prophecy that the records of the different portions of the House of Israel would be gathered together, and that Israel then would be gathered back to the lands of its inheritance, runs parallel to Ezekiel's prophecy, in Ezekiel 37, that the Lord would join the sticks of Judah and the sticks of Joseph together, and then he would gather the people of Judah and Israel together and make them one in the land upon the mountains of Israel. The Bible and the Book of Mormon serve as parallel witnesses of God's works in the last days.

The Psalmist's Prophecy: Truth Shall Spring Out of the Earth

Other Bible prophecies speak of the Book of Mormon. Several of them in particular allude to the way in which the Book of Mormon was to come forth. To be able to understand those prophecies you need to know more of how the Book of Mormon was restored to the earth in these latter days. In 1823, on the night of September 21st, a young man named Joseph Smith was visited in his room in Manchester, New York, by an angelic being who identified himself as Moroni. This was the same Moroni, son of Mormon, who had buried the plates of Mormon more than 1,400 years previous, following that final battle in which most of the Nephite people were destroyed. Now a resurrected being, Moroni had returned to prepare the way for the restoration of this important record to the earth. Three times on the night of September 21st Moroni visited Joseph Smith, told him of the mission he was to perform, and showed him in vision where the plates had been buried so he could obtain them. Then once a year for four years Moroni met with Joseph at the site where the plates had been buried, and taught and prepared him to bring the plates forth and to translate them into modern language through the gift and power of God. Finally, on September 22nd, 1827, Joseph again uncovered the plates which had been placed by Moroni in a hill near Joseph's home. As Moroni stood and watched, Joseph took the plates from the earth and prepared to remove them to his home for safekeeping.

There's an interesting allusion to this event in the *85th Psalm, verse 11,* that says, *"Truth shall spring out of the earth; and righteousness shall look down from heaven."* What other event is there in the history of mankind where we know that an angelic being gazed down from heaven as the words of God were taken from the earth? History records no other event that specifically fulfills this prophetic statement. Again, the answer to Bible prophecy is found only in the Book of Mormon.

Isaiah's Prophecy: The Restoration and Coming Forth of the Book of Mormon

One of the most significant Bible prophecies of all relates not only to events in the Book of Mormon, but to the coming forth of the Book of

Mormon in the last days. Again, to understand the prophecy, one needs to know the history of how the Book of Mormon came forth. The first vision which God granted to Joseph Smith was when Joseph was a young man less than 15 years of age, in the spring of 1820. Because he was very concerned about which church he should join, Joseph went into the woods near his home in upper New York State. There he was visited by two heavenly personages.

As he recorded his vision Joseph wrote, "I saw two Personages, whose brightness and glory defy all description, standing above me in the air. One of them spake unto me, calling me by name and said, pointing to the other—This is My Beloved Son. Hear Him! My object in going to inquire of the Lord was to know which of all the sects was right, that I might know which to join. No sooner, therefore, did I get possession of myself, so as to be able to speak, than I asked the Personages who stood above me in the light, which of all the sects was right . . . and which I should join. I was answered that I must join none of them, for they were all wrong; and the Personage who addressed me said that all their creeds were an abomination in his sight; that those professors were all corrupt; that: 'They draw near to me with their lips, but their hearts are far from me, they teach for doctrines the commandments of men, having a form of godliness, but they deny the power thereof.' He again forbade me to join with any of them; and many other things did he say unto me, which I cannot write at this time." *(Joseph Smith—History 1:17-20)*

I've already briefly described the second series of manifestations which he received, which went from September 1823 thru September 1827, when the plates were finally given into his care. What came next was the translating of those plates under the gift and power of God. When he received them, he found that two thirds of the plates were sealed, and that he wasn't allowed to open or examine the sealed portion. In the days that followed, however, he began to translate using translating tools which had been buried with the plates, called Urim and Thummim.

As Joseph began the translating process, he was requested by a friend who had helped him, Martin Harris, to give him a copy of the characters and some of the translation he had made, so that Martin could take those characters to scholars in New York City and get their opinion as to the translation's validity. Martin obtained a copy of the characters and went to New York to visit Professor Charles Anthon. He showed Professor Anthon the characters, and received from that scholar a certificate indicating that the characters were Egyptian, Chaldaic, Assyriac, and Arabic, that they were true characters, and that the translation of such of them as had been translated was also correct.

As Martin Harris turned to leave, Dr. Anthon called him back, and asked him how the young man found out that there were gold plates in the place where he had found them. Martin replied that an angel of God had revealed it unto him. Dr. Anthon then said to him, "Let me see that certificate." When Martin returned it to him, he took it and tore it in pieces, and expressed his opinion that there was no such thing now as the ministering of angels. Then Dr. Anthon told Martin that if he would bring the plates to him, he would translate them. When Martin informed him that part of the plates were sealed and that he was forbidden to bring them, Dr. Anthon replied, with words which were the fulfillment of prophecy, "I cannot read a sealed book."

Martin Harris then went and visited with a Dr. Mitchell, who sanctioned what Professor Anthon had said respecting both the characters and the translation.

One of the most exciting passages in all the Old Testament is Isaiah 29, which refers in detail to these incidents. Let me read for you *Isaiah 29, verses 11-14,* where Isaiah said, *"The vision of all is become unto you as the words of a book that is sealed,* which men deliver to one that is learned, saying, Read this, I pray thee: and he saith, *I cannot; for it is sealed:* And the book is delivered to him that is not learned, saying, Read this, I pray thee: and he saith, I am not learned. Wherefore the Lord said, Forasmuch as *this people draw near me with their mouth, and with their lips do honour me, but have removed their heart far from me,* and their fear toward me is taught by *the precept of men:* Therefore, behold, I will proceed to do a *marvelous work among this people, even a marvelous work and a wonder:* for the wisdom of their wise men shall perish, and the understanding of their prudent men shall be hid."

What a powerful prophecy this is! It refers not only to Joseph Smith's first vision in which he was visited by both God the Father and his Son, the Lord Jesus Christ, but also to the incident where Martin Harris took the Book of Mormon characters and showed them to Dr. Anthon.

Let's examine it in detail. It says, *"The vision of all* is become unto you as the words of a *book that is sealed."* That's really a significant statement as to the scope of the Book of Mormon, isn't it? The vision of all!

And note that the book that was to fulfill the prophecy was to be a sealed book. Bible scholars have struggled with that phrase for years. And the prophecy tells that the words of the book were to be delivered to one that is learned saying, "Read this," and he was to reply, "I cannot; for it is sealed," and those were almost exactly the words of the learned Dr. Anthon. The prophecy also tells how the book was to be given to one that was not well educated, and he would reply, "I am not learned." We believe that individual was Joseph Smith himself, who was deeply concerned about his lack of academic preparation, but who was given the ability to translate the Book of Mormon through the gift and power of God.

And then the prophecy in Isaiah 29 gives in detail almost the exact words that Joseph heard from the lips of the Savior himself: "This people draw near me with their mouth, and with their lips do honour me, but have removed their heart far from me, and their fear toward me is taught by the precept of men." And because men were fearing God only because it was a precept of men, the Lord promised through Isaiah that he would do a marvelous work among the people, even "a marvelous work and a wonder," and that he would make the wisdom of their wise men perish and the understanding of their prudent men to be hidden. And that's exactly what we have with this passage, for instance. Much to their consternation, Bible scholars for centuries have been unable to explain, in even general terms, what this passage in the 29th chapter of Isaiah means. And yet Latter-day Saints, with their knowledge of the Book of Mormon and how it came forth through Joseph Smith, recognize in detail the fulfillment of prophecy.

A few verses later, in *Isaiah 29:18,* it says, "In that day shall the deaf hear the words of the book, and the eyes of the blind shall see out of obscurity, and out of darkness." We see, then, that this book that was sealed was to be heard and seen by those that are deaf and blind, and we recognize that that prophecy has been fulfilled through modern recording equipment and technology which the Church has utilized, and through braille editions which are now available for them.

The prophecy in Isaiah 29 is detailed, and specific, and has literal fulfillment—not some imagined fulfillment, but word-by-word, step-by-step fulfillment that is clear and easily identified. If critics of Mormonism doubt the interpretation of this prophecy, challenge them to offer a valid explanation of each of the details of this prophecy. Ask them to explain what book was sealed, and how it was "The vision of all." Ask them to explain who was the educated man who said, "I cannot read a sealed book." And have them tell you why the Lord's statement that men would draw near to him with their mouth and know him with their lips while their hearts are far from him has any significance in this context. And have them explain how the part of the prophecy concerning the deaf and the blind receiving the words of the book has been fulfilled. They have no coherent answer, but your Mormon friends understand every phrase of the prophecy in detail. Pray for discernment in the matter!

Isaiah's Prophecy: The Fall of the Nephite Nation

But there is far more in Isaiah chapter 29 than this portion of prophecy that deals with the coming forth of the Book of Mormon. There's also an extensive prophecy which refers to the final battle between the Nephites and Lamanites and to other events that took place in the Book of Mormon.

Let's review those events before we explain the prophecy. The final battle between the Nephites and the Lamanites took place on a large hill known in the Book of Mormon as the Hill Cumorah. The Nephites had gathered their people from throughout the land onto the top of the hill to await the final challenge of the Lamanites. The Lamanites came and gathered around the hill and camped against them, trapping the Nephites there so that they couldn't flee away. And then, in one mighty day-long struggle they charged them, brought them down and slew more than 230,000 Nephite men, plus all their women and children. All that took place in one day, suddenly. The Nephite records had been buried in the hill and were taken out of their hiding place after the conflict was over by Moroni, one of the few Nephites who escaped with his life.

In the 29th Chapter of Isaiah that great prophet compared the fall of the Nephites to the fall of Jerusalem, which he also knew was going to take place. It's significant to read how that comparison is made as the different events are listed in detail. Let's read together, beginning with the *first verse of Isaiah 29.* It says, "Woe to Ariel, to Ariel, the city where David dwelt!" Ariel is another name for Jerusalem, and that city was David's capitol. The passage continues, "I will distress Ariel, and there shall be heaviness and sorrow," and then begins a comparison which says, "and *it* shall be unto me *as* Ariel." So now we're not talking about the fall of Jerusalem any more, we're talking about something else Isaiah refers to as "it" that's being compared to the fall of Jerusalem. *"It* shall be unto me *as* Ariel."

And then the Lord gives through Isaiah four characteristics of this battle which was to take place. He said, *"I will camp against thee round about,* and will lay seige against thee with a mount, and I will raise forts against thee." That's the first characteristic; to camp round about, or to surround. "And *thou shalt be brought down,"* or defeated—that's the second characteristic of the battle Isaiah foretells. And the third is (thou) *"shalt speak out of the ground,* and thy speech shall be low out of the dust, and thy voice shall be, as of one that hath a familiar spirit, out of the ground, and thy speech shall whisper out of the dust." And then Isaiah prophesies the fourth identifying characteristic of the battle: "It shall be *at an instant suddenly."*

Let's summarize the four prophetic characteristics of this battle. Number 1, "I will camp against thee round about," or surround the base of the hill. Two, "thou shalt be brought down," or defeated. Third, "thou shalt speak out of the ground"—the account of the battle would be taken from the earth in some manner. And fourth, "it shall be at an instant suddenly," or happen in a very short period of time.

In this battle, as the Nephites were gathered atop the Hill Cumorah, the Lamanites did surround them and camp against them round about. Secondly, the Nephites were brought down and defeated. Third, their records came forth out of the ground to tell of the outcome of the conflict. And fourth, it did happen at an instant, suddenly, with approximately a million of the Nephites being slain in just one day. Do you realize how many people that is? That's more than the total loss of American lives in the combined Revolutionary War, War of 1812, Mexican War, Civil War, Spanish American War, World War I and a portion of the Second World War. That was tremendous conflict, and it all happened suddenly, in just one day!

But as Isaiah spoke of this "it" place that he was comparing to Jerusalem, he told of more characteristics which were to identify it. He said in *Isaiah 29, verse six,* "Thou shalt be visited of the Lord of hosts with thunder, and with earthquake, and great noise, with storm and tempest, and the flame of devouring fire." An entire chapter of *3rd Nephi* in the Book of Mormon, *chapter 8,* describes in detail the fulfillment of this prophecy, telling of the terrible destructions which occurred at the time of Christ's crucifixion. Surely there was specific fulfillment of this prophecy which Isaiah made concerning the "it" place he was comparing to Jerusalem.

Isaiah's Prophecy: Revelation Withheld During the Great Apostasy

Verses 9 and 10 of Isaiah 29 tell of another event which took place among the Book of Mormon people—that "it" place or civilization he was com-

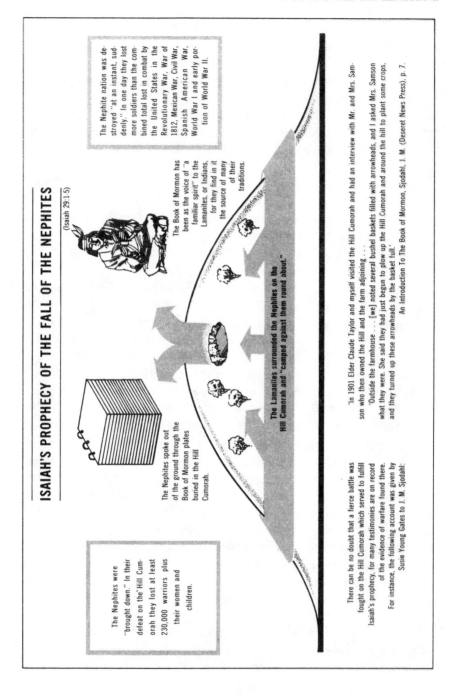

ISAIAH'S PROPHECY OF THE FALL OF THE NEPHITES

(Isaiah 29:1-5)

The Nephite nation was destroyed "at an instant, suddenly." In one day they lost more soldiers than the combined total lost in combat by the United States in the Revolutionary War, War of 1812, Mexican War, Civil War, Spanish American War, World War I and early portion of World War II.

The Book of Mormon has been as the voice of "a familiar spirit" to the Lamanites, or Indians, for they find in it the source of many of their traditions.

The Nephites spoke out of the ground through the Book of Mormon plates buried in the Hill Cumorah.

The Lamanites surrounded the Nephites on the Hill Cumorah and "camped against them round about."

The Nephites were "brought down." In their defeat on the Hill Cumorah they lost at least 230,000 warriors plus their women and children.

There can be no doubt that a fierce battle was fought on the Hill Cumorah which served to fulfill Isaiah's prophecy, for many testimonies are on record of the evidence of warfare found there. For instance, the following account was given by Susie Young Gates to J. M. Sjodahl:

"In 1901 Elder Claude Taylor and myself visited the Hill Cumorah and had an interview with Mr. and Mrs. Samson who then owned the Hill and the farm adjoining . . .
"Outside the farmhouse . . . [we] noted several bushel baskets filled with arrowheads; and I asked Mrs. Samson what they were. She said they had just begun to plow up the Hill Cumorah and around the hill to plant some crops, and they turned up these arrowheads by the basket full."

An Introduction To The Book of Mormon, Sjodahl, J. M. (Deseret News Press), p. 7.

paring with Jerusalem. He said, "Stay yourselves, and wonder; cry ye out, and cry: they are drunken, but not with wine; they stagger, but not with strong drink. For *the Lord hath poured out upon you the spirit of deep sleep, and hath closed your eyes: the prophets and your rulers, the seers hath he covered."*

That's what took place in the Americas as the Nephites were destroyed and their prophets were taken from among the people. This great destruction in the Americas caused a famine from hearing the words of the Lord, and they went for more than 1,400 years without the blessing of being taught and directed by their prophets and rulers and seers. The restoration of the Book of Mormon, the record and witness of God's dealings with his people in the Americas, began the process of removing the great spiritual darkness which had occurred. As we already read in *verse 11,* "The *vision of all* is become unto you as the words of a book that is sealed. . . ."

Let's summarize, then, the many specific prophecies which are fulfilled through the Book of Mormon and its restoration, as found in Isaiah 29. As the chapter begins Isaiah compares the fall of Jerusalem to someplace he calls "it", and that "it" has reference to the fall of the Nephites in the Americas. He said, "I will camp against thee round about"—that *first* point was fulfilled as the Lamanites attacked the Nephites around the Hill Cumorah. "Thou shalt be brought down," the *second* point, was fulfilled when the Nephites were destroyed. *Third,* "thou shalt speak out of the ground" was fulfilled as the Book of Mormon record came forth from being buried in the hill. And *fourth,* "it shall be at an instant suddenly" —that's how the final destruction of the Nephite nation took place, in just one day.

Fifth, "thou shalt be visited with thunder and earthquake and great noise and storm and tempest and the flame of devouring fire." The Book of Mormon records many specific cataclysmic events which took place following the crucifixion of Jesus Christ in fulfillment of this portion of the prophecy. *Sixth,* the prophets and seers would be covered—prophets ceased to function in the Americas following the destruction of the Nephites. *Seventh,* "the vision of all is become unto you as the words of a book that is sealed," —two thirds of the Book of Mormon plates were sealed, and Joseph Smith wasn't permitted to translate them.

Eighth, words from that book were to be given to a learned man who, when asked to read it would say, "I cannot, for it is sealed." That's what Charles Anthon expressed when he was visited by Martin Harris. *Ninth,*

Isaiah's prophecy records the words exactly which the Lord spoke to Joseph Smith in his first vision when he said, "This people draw near me with their mouth, and with their lips do honour me, but have removed their hearts far from me." *Tenth,* Isaiah prophesied that the Lord would do a marvelous work among the people which would cause the wisdom of wise men to perish and understanding of self-sufficient prudent men to be hid. Bible scholars for years have lacked the ability to understand these prophecies which have reference to the Book of Mormon because they haven't known of the manner of their fulfillment. And finally, *eleventh,* in that day the deaf shall hear the words of the book and the eyes of the blind shall see out of obscurity and out of darkness. The Book of Mormon has been made available to both the deaf and the blind through modern recording and braille technology.

It's obvious that there are specific, literal fulfillments to this broad spectrum of prophecy made by the prophet Isaiah. It's clear that the Bible makes very specific references to the Book of Mormon and to the way it would be restored through Joseph Smith.

If there were those who would deny that the Book of Mormon fulfills this prophecy, then they should be prepared to explain just how each of these events was otherwise fulfilled. There's no way they can do that, for there is no other valid explanation and fulfillment.

A Summary: Biblical Proofs of the Book of Mormon

Let's summarize, then, as we conclude our consideration of these Biblical prophecies of the Book of Mormon. We referred to John chapter 10, verse 16, where the Lord spoke of other sheep not of that fold which were to hear his voice, so there could be one fold and one shepherd. We showed how that was literally fulfilled when he came and appeared to the Nephites following his resurrection. And we showed how the interpretation that he had reference to the Gentiles was incorrect as we read Matthew 15:24 where the Lord said, "I am not sent but unto the lost sheep of the house of Israel."

Then we talked about Jacob's blessing upon his son Joseph in Genesis 49, in which he prophesied that Joseph's branches—not all of the house of Joseph, but just his branches—would run over the wall, and his blessings would extend unto the utmost bound of the everlasting hills, and would be upon the head of those that were separate from their brethren. We discussed how this was fulfilled literally when Lehi and his family were brought across the ocean to the Americas, the land of the everlasting hills, and were separated from their brethren.

Then we quoted from the 37th chapter of Ezekiel the prophecy of the two sticks in which the records of Judah and the records of Joseph were to be combined so that they could be held together in a person's hand. We saw that this was a last day's event that was to shortly precede the gathering of Israel, in which the tribes of Israel and the tribe of Judah would be restored and be together upon the mountains of Israel. We see that this is being fulfilled as the Book of Mormon and the Bible are combined together as a dual witness that Jesus is the Christ and that he is remembering his covenant which he has made unto the descendants of Abraham.

Then we cited Psalms chapter 85, verse 11, that says that truth will spring out of the earth and righteousness will look down from heaven, and saw how that was literally fulfilled when Joseph Smith received the plates to the Book of Mormon as the Angel Moroni stood nearby and observed his actions.

And then we analyzed Isaiah 29, with its numerous references to the Book of Mormon events, as it prophesied the fall of the Nephites and compared that event to the fall of Jerusalem: as it foretold the period of the great apostasy when the seers and prophets would be covered, and said that the "vision of all" would be through the restoration of the book that is sealed. We spoke of how direct reference was made to the first vision given to Joseph Smith in which the Lord told him that men would draw near to him with their lips but their hearts were far from him because they were teaching the precepts of men, and then we considered how Martin Harris took characters from the Book of Mormon plates to Dr. Charles Anthon who fulfilled Isaiah's prophecy when he said, "I cannot read a sealed book." We listed a total of eleven specific items of prophecy from Isaiah 29 which had been literally fulfilled through the Book of Mormon and its restoration.

Now, with all that detailed Bible prophecy which finds its fulfillment in the Book of Mormon, can you possibly deny the Bible clearly indicates that the Book of Mormon is also God's revealed word and another witness that Jesus is the Christ? If you truly invited the Holy Spirit in your heart, I believe that He will testify to you that this message is true.

You Can Gain a Revealed Testimony the Book of Mormon Is God's Word

As I share this message with you, I'm fully aware that you'll eventually have to make a judgment concerning the Book of Mormon. You'll either accept this message that the Bible offers significant evidence that the Book of Mormon is truly part of God's revealed word, and you'll obtain a Book of Mormon, and read it, and let it touch your life for good. Or else you'll reject this message and discard it, and put the Book of Mormon out of your mind. We all have to make that judgment.

You know Moroni, the last prophet to write in the Book of Mormon, and that same being who came back and restored the Nephite records to Joseph Smith, wrote something very significant about that judgment process. We read about it in the Book of Mormon in *Moroni, chapter 7, verses 13 through 16.* He said:

"*That which is of God inviteth and enticeth to do good continually;* wherefore, every thing which inviteth and enticeth to do good, and to love God, and to serve him, is *inspired of God.* Wherefore, take heed, my beloved brethren, that ye *do not judge that which is evil to be of God, or that which is good and of God to be of the devil.* For behold, my brethren, it is given unto you to judge, that ye may know good from evil; and the way to judge is as plain, that ye may know with a perfect knowledge, as the daylight is from the dark night. For behold, *the Spirit of Christ is given to every man, that he may know good from evil;* wherefore, I show unto you the way to judge; for *every thing which inviteth to do good, and to persuade to believe in Christ, is sent forth by the power and gift of Christ; wherefore ye may know with a perfect knowledge it is of God.*"

Nephi, an earlier prophet in the Book of Mormon, bore witness to the writings he left. His witness is typical of the writings of all the Book of Mormon prophets. He said, in *2nd Nephi chapter 33, verses 10 and 11:*

"And now, my beloved brethren, and also Jew, and all ye ends of the earth, *hearken unto these words and believe in Christ;* and if ye believe not in these words believe in Christ. And *if ye shall believe in Christ ye will believe in these words, for they are the words of Christ,* and he hath given them unto me; and *they teach all men that they should do good.* And if they are not the words of Christ, judge ye—for *Christ will show unto you, with power and great glory, that they are his words, at the last day;* and you and I shall stand face to face before his bar; and ye shall know that I have been commanded of him to write these things. . . ."

That's a testimony you need to ponder carefully. Someday, at the great judgment bar of God, we'll all know for sure that the Book of Mormon is God's revealed word. But you can know, for sure, long before that. You can know in a matter of days, like many thousands of others have done.

How? Read the Book of Mormon, and as you read it, ask God in prayer to open your mind and heart, and let you know if the book truly is his word. He'll tell you! I bear witness to that. He did it for me. I've seen Him do it for others in hundreds of situations. That's a fact! It's true! And the book is true, too.

Moroni's Promise: Ask God with Real Intent

Did you know that Moroni actually wrote a promise to that effect right in the book? That promise has been read and applied by millions of people over the last century and a half, and you can do it, too. You'll find it in *Moroni, chapter 10, verses 4 and 5.* This is what the promise says:

"When ye shall receive these things, I would exhort you that ye would *ask God, the Eternal Father, in the name of Christ, if these things are not true;* and if ye shall *ask with a sincere heart, with real intent, having faith in Christ, he will manifest the truth of it unto you,* by the power of the Holy Ghost. And *by the power of the Holy Ghost ye may know the truth of all things.*"

That's the promise of the Book of Mormon. Please read the book and apply it. It's a choice experience to receive guidance and revelation from God, and this is the best way I know of to bring that blessing into your life. Paul taught us in *1st Thessalonians 5:21* to *"Prove all things,"* and then to *"hold fast that which is good."* Apply that counsel here. Read and study the book, and seek God's revealed witness that the book is truly his word and that you should accept it and apply it in your life. You'll receive an answer if you truly ask with a sincere heart, with real intent and desire to know, and with true faith in Christ. And the testimony you gain will be one of the most treasured blessings which will ever come into your life.

I pray that you will seek that testimony and apply Moroni's promise, and learn for yourself that the Book of Mormon is truly the word of God, and I ask that blessing of our Heavenly Father in the worthy name of his Son Jesus Christ, our Lord and Savior and Redeemer, amen.

God
Speaks
Through
Prophets
Today

Duane S. Crowther

C-60
Cassette

The Bible is important to me. It is a record of God's dealings with his people for almost four thousand years, and it serves as a pattern for us now, showing how God plans to deal with us in our day.

In the Old Testament we have many indications concerning the nature of God. In *Malachi 3:6,* as he is talking to Malachi, the Lord says, *"I am the Lord, I change not."* I believe that statement expresses an important principle: How God was in Biblical times is how he is today. In Hebrews 13:8 in the New Testament, Paul expressed the same concept: *"Jesus Christ the same yesterday, and to day, and for ever."*

The Psalmist, back in his day, talked about God and His great creations. He observed that the earth and work of God's hands would perish, but expressed to God his knowledge "that thou shalt endure." And then he said to God, *"Thou art the same, and thy years shalt have no end."* That passage is in *Psalms 102:25-27.* In the New Testament Paul alluded to that same Psalm and wrote these words, in *Hebrews 1:10-12:* "Thou, Lord, in the beginning hast laid the foundation of the earth; and the heavens are the works of thine hands: They shalt perish; but thou remainst; and they all shall wax old as doth a garment; And as a vesture shalt thou fold them up, and they shall be changed: but *thou art the same, and thy years shall not fail.*"

So the Bible teaches repeatedly that God is unchanging in his nature and attitudes. I want to apply this principle and show that understanding the nature of God, as he dealt with people in Old and New Testament times, helps us recognize how he is going to deal with mankind today.

Two Key Questions Asked by a Thoughtful Seeker of Truth

I have in my possession a letter from a lady whom I believe is an honest seeker after truth. She asks questions that are important for every thoughtful Christian to ponder.

First, she asks whether prophets are functioning and needed on the earth today. Her church has no prophets, and it preaches that God no longer speaks to men. She's concerned because she feels she has a need for God's revealed guidance in the affairs of men and nations today, and she believes that it would be unfair for God to reveal His will in other eras but to refuse to speak to the world today. Reason tells her there is a need for prophets to serve as God's spokesmen now, as they did in Biblical times, but that conflicts with the views of her church.

Her **second question** concerns the many churches which exist today. She wonders if participation in a church is really necessary. **Is a church merely a social organization which Christians may attend or not, as they choose, or are there vital ordinances provided through the church which are essential to one's eternal well-being?** And if these ordinances are essential, can people in any church perform them, or is there only one church in which resides the authority to act in the name of Jesus Christ? In short, are the ordinances of the church necessary for salvation, and is there only one true church of Jesus Christ which holds the priesthood power and authority to act in the name of God?

God Ministered to His People Through
Prophets in Old Testament Times

Let's consider the question about prophets first, and turn to some passages of scripture that tell us that God's plan down through the ages was to talk to His people, and all the people of the earth, through prophets.

I want to show you that God said that He would minister to his people through prophets, that He did so during Old Testament times, that He did so in New Testament times, and that He also plans to minister to His people in these last days through prophets. The Bible tells us about all these prophets. There are literally hundreds of scriptural passages that teach us about prophets. Though there is no way that we can consider them all, let's examine quite a number of them that convey these messages clearly.

Please turn, first of all, to *Amos 3:7.* In that passage the prophet Amos expressed his assurance that, *"Surely the Lord God will do nothing, but he revealeth his secret unto his servants the prophets."* This passage teaches us that God uses prophets to tell the people of the earth what He intends to do.

Another passage with similar meaning is in *Hosea 12:10.* In this passage the Lord says, *"I have also spoken by the prophets, and I have multiplied visions, and used similitudes, by the ministry of the prophets."*

As early as the time of Moses, the Lord clearly instructed His people that he would teach and deal with them through prophets. Turn back to *Deuteronomy 18* and let's read several verses of an extensive passage on prophets. *Verse 15* says, *"The Lord thy God will raise up unto thee a Prophet* from the midst of thee, of thy brethren, like unto me: *unto him ye shall hearken."* Then, in *verses 18 and 19* He said, "I will raise them up a Prophet from among their brethren, like unto thee, and will *put my words in his mouth;* and *he shall speak unto them all that I shall command him.* And it shall come to pass, that *whosoever will not hearken unto my words which he shall speak my name, I will require it of him."*

Here the Lord is telling us that He will place prophets upon the earth, that He will speak to the people through prophets, and that He will expect people to obey those prophets. And if they fail to obey the prophets, He will require that disobedience of them.

The **principle of a prophet functioning in behalf of the people** was made known even earlier than that time. Back in the book of *Genesis,* in the 20th chapter, we read the story of Abraham. He was traveling southward and came into the domain of Abimelech, the king of Gerar. Abimelech, not knowing that Sarah was Abraham's wife, took her to make her his wife. We read in *chapter 20, verse 7,* that the Lord came and spoke to Abimelech in a night dream, and said concerning Abraham, "Now therefore restore the man his wife; for *he is a prophet, and he shall pray for thee, and thou shalt live:* and if thou restore her not, know thou that thou shalt surely die, thou, and all that are thine." And so, because Abraham was a prophet, he had the power to pray for Abimelech and have Abimelech be spared. The Lord in his wisdom and mercy saw fit to talk to Abimelech and tell him that he must respect the role of the prophet, and that he must respect the wife of that prophet also.

One of the most interesting accounts in all of the Old Testament is the story of Jehoshaphat, a king of Judah, and his dealing with the problems of his day. On one occasion Jehoshaphat wanted to know what God's will was going to be concerning his people. We read of this instance in *2 Kings 3:11.* Since he sought to know what God would say in a certain situation, Jehoshaphat said, *"Is there not here a prophet of the Lord, that we may enquire of the Lord by him?"* And one of the king of Israel's servants answered and said, "Here is Elisha the son of Shaphat."

It was that same Jehoshaphat that we read about in *2 Chronicles 20:20,* who said, *"Believe in the Lord* your God, so shall ye established; *Believe his prophets, so shall ye prosper."*

We learn more about the role of a prophet by reading of Samuel, who was called as a young boy to be a servant of the Lord. Turn back to *1 Samuel 3:19-21,* and lets see what the Lord said about how one serves as a prophet. The passage says that, "Samuel grew, and the Lord was with him, and did let none of his words fall to the ground. And all Israel from Dan even to Beer-sheba *knew that Samuel was established to be a prophet of the Lord.* And the Lord appeared again in Shiloh; for *the Lord revealed himself to Samuel in Shiloh by the word of the Lord."* We can see, then, that a prophet was held in great respect because he was accepted as God's spokesman to God's people throughout the world.

Prophets speak the word of God to his people, and represent His will unto them. Yet they often are not accepted by the people. An interesting passage which tells us these principles is found in the book of *Judges, chapter 6, verses 8-10.* The passage says "That the Lord sent a prophet unto the children of Israel, which said unto them, Thus saith the Lord God of Israel, I brought you up from Egypt, and brought you forth out of the house of bondage; And I delivered you out of the hand of the Egyptians, and out of the hand of all that oppressed you, and drove them out from before you, and gave you their land; and I said unto you, I am the Lord your God; fear not the gods of the Amorites, in whose land ye dwell: but ye have not obeyed my voice."

Not only does **a prophet** serve to testify of the existence of God and to bear his word to the people, he also sometimes **testifies against the people in the name of God.** We see a passage where this is happening in the Old Testament, in *2 Kings 17:13-14,* which says that *"The Lord testified against Israel, and against Judah, by all the prophets, and by all the seers,* saying, Turn ye from your evil ways, and keep my commandments and my statutes, according to all the law which I commanded your fathers, and *which I sent to you by my servants the prophets.* Notwithstanding they would not bear, but hardened their necks, like to the neck of their fathers, that did not believe in the Lord their God."

The prophet Daniel taught us another principle concerning prophets, that **a prophet sets the laws of God before the people.** In *Daniel 9:10,* we read Daniel's prayer confessing the sins and the weaknesses of the people, when he acknowledged that "Neither have we obeyed the voice of our Lord our God, to walk in his *laws, which he set before us by his servants the prophets."* Prophets are men called of God and chosen to be his spokesmen.

An interesting passage tells us about Jeremiah, a prophet who was chosen by God even before he was born upon the earth, and was instructed, even though he was timid and afraid, that he was to speak whatever God commanded. Let's read in *Jeremiah 1:5-7* where the Lord told Jeremiah, *"Before I formed thee in the belly I knew thee;* and before thou camest forth out of the womb *I sanctified thee,* and *I ordained thee a prophet unto the nations.* Then said I, Ah, Lord God! behold, I cannot speak: for I am a child. But the Lord said unto me, Say not, I am a child; for *thou shalt go to all that I shall send thee, and whatsoever I command thee thou shalt speak."*

It was Jeremiah that taught us that **God calls people to repentance through his prophets, and God also gives them dire warnings of things to come if they will not be obedient.** Lets read two passages in Jeremiah, chapters 25 and 26. Turn first to *Jeremiah 25:4-7.* It says, *"The Lord hath sent unto you all his servants the prophets,* rising early and sending them; but ye have not hearkened, nor inclined your ear to hear. *They said, Turn ye again now every one from his evil way, and from the evil of your doings,* and dwell in the land that the Lord hath given unto you and to your fathers for ever and ever: And go not after other gods to serve them, and to worship them, and provoke me not to anger with the works of your hands; and I will do you no hurt. Yet ye have not hearkened unto me, saith the

Lord: that ye might provoke me to anger with the works of your hands to your own hurt."

And the second passage, in *Jeremiah 26:4-6,* reads, "Thou shalt say unto them, Thus saith the Lord; *If ye will not hearken to me, to walk in my law,* which I have set before you, *To hearken to the words of my servants the prophets, whom I sent unto you,* both rising up early, and sending them, but ye have not hearkened; Then will I make this house like Shiloh, and will make this city a curse to all the nations of the earth."

In the 42nd Chapter of *Jeremiah* we learn how **a prophet inquires of the Lord in behalf of the people.** *Chapter 42, verses 4-6* says, "Then Jeremiah the prophet said unto them, I have heard you; behold, *I will pray unto the Lord your God according to your words;* and it shall come to pass, that *whatsoever thing the Lord shall answer you, I will declare it unto you; I will keep nothing back from you.* Then they said to Jeremiah, the Lord be a true and faithful witness between us, if we do not even according to all things for the which the Lord thy God shall send thee to us. Whether it be good, or whether it be evil, we will obey the voice of the Lord our God, to whom we send thee; that it may be well with us, when we obey the voice of the Lord our God." So Jeremiah, then, went and prayed to the Lord in behalf of the people who were inquiring Him through Jeremiah."

Several passages tell us that **when people become wicked, God withdraws His prophets from among them** and does not allow prophets to preach or prophesy to them. One such passage is Isaiah 29:9-10, in which the warning was given that the people would lose the visions of the prophets. The warning said, "Stay yourselves, and wonder; cry ye out, and cry: They are drunken, but not with wine; they stagger, but not with strong drink. For the *Lord hath poured out upon you the spirit of deep sleep, and hath closed your eyes: the prophets and your rulers, the seers hath he covered."*

Ezekiel spoke of the same kind of trouble in his day. In *chapter 7, verses 25-26 of Ezekiel* we read, "Destruction cometh; and they shall seek peace, and there shall be none. Mischief shall come upon mischief, and rumour shall be upon rumour; *then shall they seek a vision of the prophet;* but the law shall perish from the priest, and counsel from the ancients."

To be an authorized prophet of the Lord requires a special calling from God. Just as God told Jeremiah that he had ordained him to be a prophet we read of others also being given authority to be prophets from God. *1 Samuel, chapter 10* tells us of how Samuel annointed Saul to be a king and also gave him the power to be a prophet for God. In *verses*

5 through 7 we read of Samuel's instructions to Saul saying, "After that thou shalt come to the hill of God, where is the garrison of the Philistines: and it shall come to pass, when thou art come thither to the city, that thou shalt meet a *company of prophets* coming down from the high place with a psaltery, and tabret, and a pipe, and a harp before them: and *they shall prophesy; And the Spirit of the Lord will come upon thee, and thou shalt prophesy with them, and shalt be turned into another man.* And let it be, when these signs are come unto thee, that thou do as occasion serve thee; for *God is with thee."*

And then, in *verses 9 and 10* we read, "And it was so, that when he had turned his back to go from Samuel, *God gave him another heart:* and all those signs came to pass that day. And when they came thither to the hill, behold, a company of prophets met him; and the *Spirit of God came upon him, and he prophesied among them."* And when the people started to be aware that Saul had received the prophetic calling, they asked the question, "Is Saul also among the prophets?"

Much earlier in the Old Testament, we read of others being given the responsibility to serve as prophets of God. Moses, for instance, was heavily burdened, and didn't have enough time to properly minister to all the people of Israel. In the eleventh chapter of Numbers we read how the Lord instructed him to call out 70 men to serve as other leaders to the people. In *verse 17 of Numbers 11* the Lord said, "I will come down and talk with thee there: and *I will take the spirit which is upon thee, and will put it upon them;* and they shall bear the burden of the people with thee, that thou bear it not thyself alone." And then he poured out His spirit upon them. And in *verse 25* it says that "The Lord came down in a cloud, and spake unto him, and *took of the spirit that was upon him, and gave it unto the seventy elders:* and it came to pass, that, *when the spirit rested upon them, they prophesied, and did not cease."*

But two of the men that were prophesying were outside of the camp. This concerned Joshua, and he suggested to Moses that he should forbid these two men to prophesy, but Moses disagreed with Joshua. In *verse 29* we read his response: "Enviest thou for my sake? *Would God that all the Lord's people were prophets, and that the Lord would put his spirit upon them!"* So we see how the Lord chose to delegate to others the role of prophet, and gave to them, as well as to Moses, the power to speak in His name. Those servants who were authorized to be prophets received power from God to function in His behalf, and God manifested to Israel that those men were His authorized servants and prophets.

Another interesting experience is recorded in the days of Elijah, when he challenged 450 of the priests of Baal on Mt. Carmel. Remember, these other priests laid their wood and tried to call down fire from heaven, but couldn't do so. And then Elijah laid his materials, and sought to call down fire from heaven to burn the sacrifice and prove that he was a prophet of the true and living God. *1 Kings chapter 18* tells the story of this experience, and *verses 36 to 38* relate exactly what happened. "And it came to pass at the time of the offering of the evening sacrifice, that Elijah the prophet came near, and said, Lord God of Abraham, Isaac, and of Israel, let it be known this day that thou art God in Israel, *and that I am thy servant, and that I have done all these things at thy word."* And he continued to pray, "Hear me, O Lord, hear me, that this people may know that thou art the Lord God, and that thou hast turned their heart back again. *Then the fire of the Lord fell, and consumed the burnt sacrifice, and the wood, and the stones, and the dust, and licked up the water* that was in the trench. And when all the people saw it, they fell on their faces: and they said, *The Lord, he is the God; the Lord, he is the God."* So the proof that Jehovah, the pre-mortal Jesus Christ, was truly God, also proved that Elijah was His servant, and that his actions were truly authorized of God.

Now I have quoted more than 20 passages from the Old Testament showing how God operated through prophets in that time. There are hundreds more, and one only has to look under the word prophet in a concordance, and examine the passages listed, to see that in instance after instance, God operated through his servants the prophets, to bear witness to the people of His divinity, to call them to repentance, to give them laws, to provide them a channel through which they could inquire of God's will through the prophet, and to instruct the people and lead them to righteousness.

Perhaps we can summarize all these passages by repeating what Jehoshaphat said in *2 Chronicles 20:20, "Believe in the Lord your God, so shall ye be established; believe his prophets, so shall ye prosper."*

God Ministered to His People Through Prophets in New Testament Times

In the New Testament we also learn much about prophets. Jesus Christ gave authority to his twelve apostles that they could be both prophets and apostles. We read of his comment concerning the authority he granted unto them in *John 15:15-16*, where he told those twelve, "Henceforth I call you not servants; for the servant knoweth not what his lord doeth: but I have called you friends; for all things that I have heard of my Father I have made known unto you. *Ye have not chosen me, but I have chosen you, and ordained you, that ye should go and bring forth fruit,* and that your fruit should remain: that whatsoever ye shall ask of the Father in my name, he may give it you."

Matthew, chapter 10, tells how the Lord sent out his twelve and instructed them that they were to use the power of the priesthood and the prophetic calling which was theirs. And then, after giving them much instruction, he told them of their role as prophets, and explained how they should be received by the people. In *verses 40 and 41 of Matthew, chapter 10,* he said, *"He that receiveth you receiveth me,* and he that receiveth me receiveth him that sent me. *He that receiveth a prophet in the name of a prophet shall receive a prophet's reward;* and he that receiveth a righteous man in the name of a righteous man shall receive a righteous man's reward." So those prophets and apostles were instructed to reward those who would receive them, and to allow them to partake of the rich blessings which would come from accepting God's chosen prophets.

Jesus knew the tremendous suffering his prophets would have to endure. In *Matthew 23, verses 34, 35, and 37,* we read how Christ spoke of the prophets He had sent out and said, "Wherefore, behold, *I send unto you prophets,* and wise men, and scribes: and *some of them ye will kill* and crucify; and some of them shall ye scourge in your synagogues, and persecute them from city to city: That upon you may come all the righteous blood shed upon the earth." And then He said, "O Jerusalem, Jerusalem, *thou that killest the prophets, and stonest them which are sent unto thee,* how often would I have gathered thy children together, even as a hen gathereth her chickens under her wings, and ye would not!"

Shortly after the day of Pentecost Peter made a profound statement concerning prophets and the role that they were to play. We read about this in *Acts 3:18-24.* Peter had just healed a man who was lame and then was talking to the people there in Jerusalem as he uttered these words, "But *those things, which God before had shewed by the mouth of all his prophets,* that Christ should suffer, *he hath so fulfilled.* Repent ye therefore, and be converted, that your sins may be blotted out, when the times of refreshing shall come from the presence of the Lord; And he shall send Jesus Christ, which before was preached unto you: Whom the heaven must receive until the times of restitution of all things, *which God hath spoken by the mouth of all his holy prophets since the world began.* For Moses truly said unto the fathers, *A prophet shall the Lord your God raise up unto you of your brethren, like unto me; him shall ye hear in all things whatsoever he shall say unto you.* And it shall come to pass, that every soul, which will not hear that prophet, shall be destroyed from among the people. Yea, and *all the prophets from Samuel and those that follow after, as many as have spoken, have likewise foretold of these days."*

And Paul, when he wrote to the Ephesians, stressed the importance of prophets in the church and the kingdom of God. He compared the church to a building and said it was built upon the foundation of the apostles and prophets. The passage is found in *Ephesians 2:19-20,* "Now therefore ye are no more strangers and foreigners, but fellowcitizens with the saints, and of the household of God; And *are built upon the foundation of the apostles and prophets,* Jesus Christ himself being the chief corner stone."

If apostles and prophets were the foundation of the church in that day, wouldn't they be an indispensible part of God's program? He goes on to tell how the entire organization of the church was essential in the next verse, saying, "In whom all the building fitly framed together groweth unto an holy temple unto the Lord." Could the church be an holy temple if it were not complete? Could it grow unto the Lord if it did not have the foundation of the apostles and prophets? And can a church be God's true Church today if it lacks the foundation of apostles and prophets?

The Bible Prophesies of Future Prophets Who Will Minister in the Last Days

And finally, let's consider Biblical allusions to prophets who are to function in the last days—in a time yet future. The book of Revelation has several such references. One tells about a terrible time of sorrow and strife which will exist in connection with the battle of Armageddon. In *chapter 11* of the book of *Revelation* we read of two prophets who will serve as witnesses of God in the city of Jerusalem just as that battle is about to take place. *Verses 3, 5, and 6* say, *"I will give power unto my two witnesses, and they shall prophesy* a thousand two hundred and threescore days, clothed in sackcloth. . . . And if any man will hurt them, *fire proceedeth out of their mouth,* and devoureth their enemies: and if any man will hurt them, he must in this manner be killed. *These have power to shut heaven, that it rain not in the days of their prophecy: and have power over waters* to turn them to blood, *and to smite the earth* with all plagues, as often as they will."

Here's a passage that tells us of the tremendous god-given power that will be held by prophets as they function in that future period. Later in *chapter 11* we read of that which is to be said in heaven after these prophets are taken from the earth. *Verses 17 and 18* tell us that there is to be a group of 24 elders who will give thanks unto God and say, "Thy wrath is come, and the time of the dead, that they should be judged, and that *thou shouldst give reward unto thy servants the prophets.*"

And in chapter 18 in the book of Revelation we read of the future destruction of a terrible city that will be the center of wickedness. We learn that at that time there will be apostles and prophets who will rejoice because of the fall of that wicked city. *Revelation 18:20* says that after the city is fallen the time will come to "Rejoice over her, thou heaven, and *ye holy apostles and prophets; for God hath avenged you on her.*"

So we read in the Bible of prophets which are to exist in a time yet future. We see a clear pattern, that Jesus Christ, the same yesterday, today and forever, guided his people through prophets in Old Testament times. He directed his church through prophets in New Testament times. And those prophets foretold that there would be prophets in these last days.

These, then, are some of the passages that lead us to firmly believe that God operates among men through prophets, and that he uses them as his servants to bear witness of his works and his word and to warn the people and to prepare them, and that he reveals his will to his Church and to all the people of the world through prophets.

We believe that the existence and acceptance of prophets is a test whereby one can evaluate whether a church is truly the Church of Jesus Christ today. The true Church of Jesus Christ will accept this broad Biblical doctrine that prophets are to function in the name of God. The true Church of Jesus Christ in this day will have prophets to lead and guide it and to speak to all the world. The true believer in Christ will accept his prophets, recognize them as God's authorized spokesmen and give diligent heed to their inspired message.

There are some who reject the vast array of Biblical passages that show that God reveals His will to his people and to the world through prophets. Their churches don't have prophets so they say that prophets are not necessary. Their churches don't receive revelation so they say they don't believe God reveals his will to man anymore.

Truly their acknowledgment that they do not have prophets and that they do not receive revelation is a direct result of the great apostasy which occurred shortly after the death of Christ's apostles and prophets in New Testament times. The power and authority to act in the name of God was lost from the earth, and all that remained were the churches of men. Certainly, if those men lacked the authority to speak in the name of God they would not receive revelation from Him. No wonder they soon reached the uninspired conclusions that prophets were no longer necessary, and that God no longer revealed his will to man.

Revelation 22:18-19 Refers Only to the Book of Revelation, Not the Entire Bible

During the Protestant Reformation, as the reformers sought to counteract the power and control of Catholicism, they began to preach that the Bible is a closed book and that no new revelation or doctrine can be added to it. They didn't have any solid scriptural backing for this teaching. All they knew was that there were no authorized prophets among them and that they weren't receiving any revelation.

They finally hit upon one passage of scripture which they began to quote, in *Revelation chapter 22, verses 18 and 19*. Their interpretation was so superficial and so transparently contradictory to fact and to reason that it really doesn't deserve comment. But since this passage and its rationale is still offered as a rebuttal to the hundreds of passages telling how God speaks through prophets, let's consider it briefly here. The verses they quote come right near the end of the last chapter of the book of Revelation. Unthinking people sometimes read it and then say, "See, there's not supposed to be any other revelation or scripture besides what's in the Bible. Those verses end it all." This is what the passage says: "I testify unto every man that heareth the words of the prophecy of this book, If any man should add unto these things, God shall add unto him the plagues that are written in this book: And if *any* man shall take away from the *words of the book of this prophecy,* God shall take away his part out of the book of life, and out of the holy city, and from the things which are written in *this book."*

Let me share with you four reasons that show that this line of thinking is incorrect. It's nothing more than sloppy interpretation based on false

premises, and to express this scriptural objection should be an embarrassment to any knowledgeable student of the Bible. It's quite obvious that the
passage in Revelation chapter 22 refers only to the book of Revelation, not
the entire Bible. First, you should know that when John wrote the book
of Revelation in about 96 A.D., there was no Bible. The various epistles
and accounts of the New Testament were not formally canonized until the
Third Council of Carthage in 397 A.D. There was no way that John's clos-
ing statement could have been intended to apply to the entire Bible he did
not even know that the New Testament books would be collected, nor that
his book would be placed as the final book in the collection when he wrote
his book of prophecy.

Second, other New Testament books were written, after Revelation was
written. If Revelation had to be the last book of scripture written then that
logic would require that those other books be excluded from the New Testament and be labeled the false works of men. Eucebius indicates that the
books of 2nd and 3rd John were both written later than John's apocalypse,
and since John was the author of both of these other books, it's clear that
he felt it proper to write them in spite of how he ended the book of
Revelation.

Third, other passages similar to John's occur much earlier in the Bible—
way back in Deuteronomy. If logic says that no more revelation can be
received and recorded after the book of Revelation, that same logic would
require that no more scripture could be added after Deuteronomy. *Deuteronomy 4:2* contains God's commandment that "Ye shall not add unto
the word which I command you, neither shall you diminish ought from
it". *Deuteronomy 12:32* says the same thing. If we acknowledge that God's
warning in Deuteronomy applies only to that book, which we obviously
have to unless we throw out almost the whole Bible, then we likewise have
to acknowledge that John's warning applies only to the book of Revelation. That is, if we are honestly seeking for the truth.

Fourth, John's warning says that if any man should add to these things
God would bring upon him the plagues described in the book of Revelation. The passage doesn't prevent God from sending a revelation; it just
warns that men must not write uninspired words and represent them as
being part of John's book of Revelation.

And new revelations have been given to the world through Latter-day
Saint prophets, and they have been recorded as scripture. If the typical
Protestant interpretation we're discussing were valid and these new revela-

tions were actually uninspired writings dreamed up by men, then most certainly the Latter-day Saints would have been smitten by the plagues spoken of by John during the past 150 years. But those plagues haven't come. What does that fact tell us then about the validity of this weak and faulty interpretation of Revelation 22, and what does it tell us about the unscriptural teaching that there can be no more revelation or scripture besides the Bible? Those who use this shaky and invalid interpretation only show a personal lack of knowledge and lack of desire to discern the truth. They do not seek to add to man's understanding of how God speaks to man.

The Existence and Acceptance of Prophets is a Test by Which One May Identify the True Church of Jesus Christ

Let's turn to our second topic now, and talk about the church that Jesus Christ established. In the *fourth chapter of his epistle to the Ephesians*, Paul compared the church to a human body, and stressed the importance of unity in that body. Beginning with *verse 11*, he said that the Lord "gave some, *apostles;* and some, *prophets*, and some, *evangelists;* and some, *pastors* and *teachers*," and then Paul stated three reasons for the existence of the Church: *"For the perfecting of the saints, for the work of the ministry, for the edifying of the body of Christ."*

Then Paul told how long that Church would be needed: *"Till we all come in the unity of the faith, and of the knowledge of the Son of God, unto a perfect man,* unto the measure of the stature of the fulness of Christ." Have we come to that unity yet? Is there still a need for the one true Church of Jesus Christ? It's obvious that that need is more evident today than ever before. Christianity is not united; it is divided into hundreds of denominations, each with its own beliefs and practices.

Let's read on in *verses 14 and 15*, where Paul explains why we need to find the true Church of Jesus Christ: *"That we henceforth be no more children, tossed to and fro,* and carried about with every wind of doctrine, by the sleight of men, and cunning craftiness, whereby they lie in wait to deceive; But speaking the truth in love, may grow up into him in all things, which is the head, even Christ." Paul knew that the organization of Christ's Church is essential, that it serves to perfect the Saints, and that it shields them from false doctrines and the cunning deceptions of men. He knew also that the ordinances performed by one having priesthood power, and the authority to act in the name of God, were essential for the Saints. Among those ordinances were baptism and the conferring of the gift of the Holy Ghost so that one might have the continual right to the guidance of the Holy Spirit if he were worthy. In one of my other tapes, entitled Biblical Proofs of the Restored Church, the great apostasy that was foretold in the Bible is carefully discussed. That tape explains how the early Christian church leaders were slain, how the chain of priesthood ordination was broken so the authority to act in the name of God was lost, and how the apostles and prophets and revelations were lost from the Church. It tells about counterfeit doctrines that sprang up—how men, because they didn't have the authority to act in the name of God, began to say that authority was not necessary; how men lacking the power and authority to baptize in the name of Jesus Christ began to say that baptism wasn't necessary; how men lacking the authority to confer the gift of the Holy Ghost by the laying on of hands began to say that gift came without the need for that laying on of hands; how men lacking the authority from God began to say that the authorized Church organization was not essential; how the church was merely a social organization that served to unite the people in fellowship; and that one could be saved outside of the church. All of these counterfeit doctrines still linger in the world today, and those counterfeit doctrines, if accepted and believed by people today, can rob them of their salvation.

The Bible Teaches that Baptism Is Essential for Salvation and Must Be Administered by Authorized Priesthood Bearers

Let's examine a few of the Biblical passages that tell us about one of those essential ordinances—baptism. In the third chapter of John we read how a ruler of the Jews named Nicodemus came to Christ at night and asked the Lord what he should do. Jesus told him, beginning in *verse 3 of John chapter 3, "Except a man be born again, he cannot see the kingdom of God."* Nicodemus didn't understand, and asked if a man then had to go back into his mother's womb and be born. Jesus answered, "Verily, verily, I say unto thee, *Except a man be born of water and of the Spirit, he cannot enter into the kingdom of God."*

Baptism by immersion for the remission of sins, by one holding authority to perform that baptism, is an essential ordinance in the plan of salvation which God has revealed. Jesus Christ served as our example. Though he was without sin, yet he was baptized to show us the way. *Matthew chapter 3, verses 13-15,* tells of that baptism: "Them cometh Jesus from Galilee to Jordan unto John, to be baptized of him. But John forbad him, saying,

I have need to be baptized of thee, and comest thou to me? And Jesus answering said unto him, Suffer it to be so now: for *thus it becometh us to fulfill all righteousness."* John performed that baptism, though Christ was without sin.

If the Savior, who was without sin, was baptized to fulfill all righteousness, how much more need do we have, with all our personal weaknesses, to be baptized by one having authority, that we may fulfill all righteousness also?

John 4:1-2 tells us Jesus required that his disciples be baptized. If we believe Jesus is the same yesterday, today, and forever, and we know that he required his disciples to be baptized in that day, shouldn't we recognize that baptism performed by one having proper priesthood authority is equally necessary today? Jesus sent his disciples, who had authority to baptize, to go forth and perform that ordinance. *Matthew 28:18-19* tells us the commandment Jesus gave to his disciples at the close of his mortal ministry. He said, "All power is given unto me in heaven and in earth. Go ye therefore, and teach all nations, *baptizing them* in the name of the Father, and of the Son, and of the Holy Ghost."

In Mark's recording of this final directive he adds a significant phrase to it. In *Mark chapter 16, verses 15 and 16* we read that Jesus said unto them, "Go ye unto all the world, and preach the gospel to every creature. *He that believeth and is baptized shall be saved; but he that believeth not shall be damned."* Here the Savior made it clear that baptism was the necessary result of true belief and faith in Christ. And He linked belief and baptism inseparably together.

The apostle Peter knew very well the necessity for those who believe on Christ to be baptized by one having authority. When he preached his great sermon on the day of Pentecost the people who heard him were touched in their hearts and said, "Men and brethren, what shall we do?" *Acts 2:38 and 41* tells us Peter's answer. He said, *"Repent, and be baptized every one of you in the name of Jesus Christ for the remission of sins,* and ye shall receive the gift of the Holy Ghost. . . . Then they that gladly received his word *were baptized:* and the same day there were added unto them about three thousand souls."

Have you ever pondered the physical exertion involved in immersing three thousand people? If baptism was not a necessary ordinance, would they have gone to all that effort? Of course not! But Peter and his companions knew that baptism by immersion, by an authorized priesthood holder, was an essential ordinance their converts had to receive if they were to be able to fulfill all righteousness. So they performed that sacred ordinance three thousand times.

And it was Peter who received that great experience with Cornelius. The Holy Ghost was poured out upon Cornelius and his household as a sign to Peter that the Gentiles could also receive the gospel. But though that great sign was manifested through them, Peter still knew that Cornelius and his household needed to be baptized by one holding authority. *Acts 10, verses 47 and 48* contains Peter's instruction to Cornelius in which he said, *"Can any man forbid water, that these should not be baptized,* which have received the Holy Ghost as well as we? And *he commanded them to be baptized* in the name of the Lord."

In *1st Peter 3:21,* Peter tells us that baptism is essential as the means by which we become eligible to receive salvation and reap the benefit of the atonement and resurrection of Jesus Christ, by giving us the great blessing of a conscience free from sin. He said, "Baptism doth also now save us (not the putting away of the filth of the flesh, but the answer of a good conscience toward God,) by the resurrection of Jesus Christ." He knew that baptism by one holding authority to perform it was an essential ordinance for men to be eligible to be saved in the kingdom of God.

The apostle Paul saw the risen Jesus Christ on the road to Damascus. Certainly, if baptism was not a necessary requirement of Christ's gospel plan, that great vision would have sufficed to make Paul eligible for salvation. But the Lord still sent Ananias, his authorized servant, to Paul. Ananias laid his hands upon Paul's head and healed him of his blindness, and then under Ananias's direction Paul was baptized. We read in *Acts 9:18* that following Paul's reception of Ananias' healing ministration, "Immediately there fell from his eyes as it had been scales: and he received sight forthwith, and arose, and *was baptized."*

In his preaching Paul continually connected the doctrine of baptism by authority to the principle of believing in Christ for salvation. During his second missionary journey, for instance, when Paul was in Macedonia, he and his companion were imprisoned. An earthquake was sent by the Lord that allowed them to be freed. The jailer came and pled with them, thinking that he was about to be slain by the prisoners. We read about it in *Acts chapter 16, verses 30 through 33.* The jailer brought them out and said, "Sirs, what must I do to be saved? And they said, Believe on the Lord Jesus Christ, and thou shalt be saved, and thy house. And they spake unto him the word of the Lord, and to all that were in his house. And he took them the same hour of the night, and washed their stripes; and *was baptized, he and all his, straightway."*

Paul taught that baptism is the act whereby a man puts on Christ. We read Paul's teaching in *Galatians 3:27* that *"As many of you as have been baptized unto Christ have put on Christ."* Paul continues this theme in his epistle to the *Romans,* saying in *chapter 6, verses 3 and 4,* "Know ye not, that *so many of us as were baptized into Jesus Christ were baptized into his death?* Therefore *we are buried with him by baptism* into death: that like as Christ was raised up from the dead by the glory of the Father, even so we also should walk in newness of life."

Paul continually emphasized that there was only one true Church of Jesus Christ and only one valid baptism. He taught that the saints would have to come into that church and be unified in it to be eligible for salvation through Christ. In *Ephesians 4:3 through 5* Paul wrote that the saints should be "Endeavoring to keep the unity of the Spirit in the bond of peace. There is one body, and one Spirit, even as ye are called in one hope of your calling; *One Lord, one faith, one baptism."*

Acts 19:1 through 6 tells of an important event that occurred during Paul's third missionary journey. Paul found a group of people who had been baptized, but they had not been baptized into the Church of Jesus Christ, but only into John's baptism. Paul knew John's baptism did not allow them to receive the gift of the Holy Ghost so he insisted that they needed to be rebaptized. Let's read the account together. "It came to pass, that, while Apollos was at Corinth, Paul having passed through the upper coasts came to Ephesus: and finding certain disciples, He said unto them, *Have ye received the Holy Ghost since ye believed?* And they said unto him, *We have not so much as heard whether there be any Holy Ghost.* And he said unto them, Unto what then were ye baptized? And they said, Unto John's baptism. Then said Paul, John verily baptized with the baptism of repentance, saying unto the people, that they should believe on him which should come after him, that is, on Christ Jesus. When they heard this, *they were baptized in the name of the Lord Jesus. And when Paul had laid his hands upon them, the Holy Ghost came on them;* and they spake with tongues, and prophesied." Here, then, was a group of people who had received baptism without proper authority, and without proper instruction and preparation. They were not baptized into the true Church of Jesus Christ. Paul knew that it was necessary for them to be rebaptized by one having the authority of an authorized representative of the Church of Jesus Christ. He baptized them with that authority and then laid his hands upon them so that they could properly receive the gift of the Holy Ghost.

True Priesthood Authority is Necessary for Men to Perform Ordinances Which Are Acceptable to God

Let's review some of those Biblical passages that tells us of the need for authority to labor in Christ's ministry. Remember what the book of *Hebrews* tells us in *chapter 5, verse 4: "No man taketh this honour unto himself,* but he that is called of God, as was Aaron." The *28th chapter of Exodus* tells how Aaron was called to the ministry with *verse 41* of that chapter telling how he was given the authority of the priesthood.

Note the implications of the commandment in *Hebrew 5:4* that no man can take the authority of the priesthood unto himself but instead must be ordained by one who already possesses that authority, just as Aaron had to be ordained by Moses. For instance, a man can't just decide that he will go to theological school and just because he's attended school automatically become an authorized minister of the gospel of Jesus Christ. Instead, he has to receive that ordination from one who already holds the priesthood and has the authority to act in the name of God. That power is only found in the Church of Jesus Christ—it's not available in the theological schools of the world today.

Recall what Paul told Timothy as he wrote in *1st Timothy 4:14,* "Neglect not the gift that is in thee, which was given thee *by prophecy,* with *the laying on of the hands of the presbytery."* Paul knew that ordination to the priesthood was a sacred and necessary ordinance that was not to be taken lightly. He told Timothy in *chapter 5, verse 22 of 1st Timothy,* "Lay hands suddenly on no man . . . " In *2nd Timothy 1:6* Paul reminded his disciple of the need to use his priesthood power carefully and effectively, saying, "Wherefore I put thee in remembrance that thou stir up the gift of God, *which is in thee by the putting on of my hands."* So Timothy had been ordained by Paul. He had received the authority to act in the name of God from one who previously had held that power—that's the only way priesthood power is obtained. It's not received as a by-product of graduation from ministerial school.

The book of Acts tells us of several instances where men who did not hold priesthood authority attempted to use the power of God and were severely rebuked because of their unauthorized abuse. *Acts 19:13 through 16,* for instance, tells us of the seven sons of Sceva: "Then certain of the vagabond Jews, exorcists, *took upon them to call over them which had evil spirits the name of the Lord Jesus, saying,* We adjure you by Jesus whom Paul preacheth. And there were seven sons of one Sceva, a Jew, and chief of the priests, which did so. And the evil spirit answered and said, *Jesus I know, and Paul I know; but who are ye?* And the man in whom the evil spirit was leaped on them, and overcame them, and prevailed against them, so that they fled out of that house naked and wounded."

The eighth chapter in the book of Acts tells us about Simon, who previously had been a sorcerer but was converted to the church. The account tells us he was a member but did not yet hold the priesthood. When Simon saw two of the apostles come to Samaria, and watched them lay hands upon the heads of the people to confer upon them the gift of the Holy Ghost, he very much wanted to be able to do that himself. Simon offered them money and attempted to purchase priesthood power. The account of how he was rebuked by Peter starts with *Acts 8, verse 18,* and says, "When Simon saw that through laying on of the apostles' hands the Holy Ghost was given, he offered them money, Saying, Give me also this power, that on whomsoever I lay hands, he may receive the Holy Ghost. But Peter said unto him, Thy money perish with thee, because thou hast thought that the gift of God may be purchased with money. Thou hast neither part nor lot in this matter: for thy heart is not right in the sight of God. Repent therefore of this thy wickedness, and pray God, if perhaps the thought of thine heart may be forgiven thee. For I perceive that thou art in the gall of bitterness, and in the bond of iniquity." Simon, then, thought that he could pay money and obtain the privilege of being an authorized laborer in the ministry in that way. But we learned from this account that is not the way the priesthood is awarded unto men.

The Lord Jesus Christ taught that there would be many who would attempt to function in his name without proper priesthood authority, and he warned that they would not be accepted at the last day. *Matthew 7:21-23* contains the warning that *"Not every one that saith unto me, Lord, Lord, shall enter into the kingdom of heaven; but he that doeth the will of my Father* which is in heaven. Many will say to me in that day, Lord, Lord, have we not prophesied in thy name? and in thy name have cast out devils? and in thy name done many wonderful works? And then will I profess unto them, *I never knew you: depart from me, ye that work iniquity."*

Luke 13:23 through 28 tells how Jesus met with some of his adversaries. They baited and tempted him saying, "Lord, are there few that be saved? And he said unto them, *Strive to enter in at the strait gate: for many, I say unto you, will seek to enter in, and shall not be able.* When once the master of the house is risen up, and hath shut to the door, and ye begin to stand without, and to knock at the door, saying, Lord, Lord, open unto us; and he shall answer and say unto you, *I know you not whence ye are:* Then shall ye begin to say, We have eaten and drunk in thy presence, and thou hast taught in our streets. But he shall say, I tell you, *I know you not whence ye are; depart from me, all ye workers of iniquity.* There shall be weeping and wailing and gnashing of teeth, when ye shall see Abraham, and Isaac, and Jacob, and *all the prophets, in the kingdom of God, and you yourselves thrust out."*

As we have clearly seen, the Lord has said that the only way one enters into his sheepfold, meaning his Church, is by baptism performed by one holding valid priesthood authority. And the way that one becomes authorized to labor in Christ's ministry and becomes the possessor of priesthood authority to act in the name of God is through ordination to the priesthood by one already holding that authority.

In *John 10:1 through 5,* the Lord said, "Verily, verily, I say unto you, *He that entereth not by the door into the sheepfold, but climbeth up some other way, the same is a thief and a robber.* But he that entereth in by the door is the shepherd of the sheep. To him the porter openeth; and the sheep hear his voice: and he calleth his own sheep . . . he goeth before them, and the sheep follow him: for they know his voice. And *a stranger will they not follow, but will flee from him:* for they know not the voice of strangers."

Hebrews 13:8 tells us that Jesus Christ is the same "yesterday, to day and for ever." We also can go back into Old Testament times and learn how God feels about unauthorized ministrations by those who attempt to labor in his name but do not have authority. The *16th chapter of Numbers* tells us of the rebellion of Korah and 250 of his followers. They gathered against Moses and Aaron and said, "Ye take too much upon you, seeing all the congregation are holy, every one of them, and the Lord is among them: wherefore then lift ye up yourselves before the congregation of the Lord?" Moses directed them to come and challenge his power. He had all the followers of Korah gather themselves together in the camp, and all the rest of the people of Israel assembled to watch. And then *verses 32 and 33* tell us that *"the earth opened her mouth, and swallowed them up, and their houses, and all the men that appertained unto Korah, and all their goods.* They, and all that appertained to them, went down alive into the pit, and the earth closed upon them: and they perished from among the congregation." And it goes on to tell that "there came out a fire from the Lord, and consumed the two hundred and fifty men that offered incense." So the Lord clearly established Moses as his authorized representative and did away with those who rebelled against his priesthood power.

First Chronicles 13:10 tells of what happened to Uzza, who attempted to steady the ark of the covenant. When the oxen stumbled as the ark was being transported Uzza, who lacked authority to do so, reached up and held the ark "And the anger of the Lord was kindled against Uzza, and he smote him, because he put his hand to the ark: and there he died before God." You'll remember that in *Numbers 4:15* the Lord had warned his people that "They shall not touch any holy thing, lest they die." Uzza, who lacked authority from God, broke that sacred commandment.

Chapter 13 of 1st Samuel tells how Saul, who had been anointed king over Israel, usurped priesthood authority and performed a burnt offering ritual for which he was not authorized. *Verses 13 and 14* tell us that Samuel rebuked Saul because he did that saying, *"Thou hast done foolishly: thou hast not kept the commandment of the Lord thy God,* which he commanded thee: for now would the Lord have established thy kingdom upon Israel for ever. But now thy kingdom shall not continue: the Lord hath sought him a man after his own heart, and the Lord hath commanded him to be captain over his people, because thou hast not kept that which the Lord commanded thee." So Saul fell from his position as king because he usurped priesthood authority.

2nd Chronicles 26 tells of Uzziah the king of Judah who was a valiant king but was stricken by the Lord with leprosy because he attempted to officiate in priesthood ordinances without authorization. The account begins in *verse 16* and says, "But when he was strong, his heart was lifted up to his destruction: for *he transgressed against the Lord his God, and went into the temple of the Lord to burn incense upon the altar of incense.* And Azariah the priest went in after him, and with him fourscore priests of the Lord, that were valiant men: And they withstood Uzziah the king, and said unto him, *It appertaineth not unto thee, Uzziah, to burn incense unto the Lord, but to the priests the sons of Aaron, that are consecrated to burn incense:* go out of the sanctuary; for thou hast trespassed; neither shall it be for thine honour from the Lord God. Then Uzziah was wroth, and had a censer in his hand to burn incense: and while he was wroth with the priests, the *leprosy even rose up in his forehead* before the priests in the house of the Lord, from beside the incense altar. And Azariah the chief priest, and all the priests, looked upon him, and, behold, he was leprous in his forehead, and they thrust him out from thence; yea, himself hasted also to go out, because *the Lord had smitten him.* And Uzziah the king was a leper unto the day of his death, and dwelt in a several house, being a leper; for he was cut off from the house of the Lord: and Jotham his son was over the king's house, judging the people of the land."

Here, then, is another instance that shows those who attempt to labor in priesthood functions, but without proper authorization of God, are not acceptable in God's sight. Just as it was in Old Testament times and just as it was in New Testament times, it is today. And though there be many who profess to be preachers or ministers or laborers in the cause of God, yet, if they do not have priesthood and have not been ordained by one who already holds that priesthood authority, they are usurpers and are not going to be received in the kingdom of God at the last day. And they are not authorized nor able to properly interpret the scriptures nor correctly teach people the true doctrines of God—to give them their salvation.

Perhaps my message can best be summarized by quoting the words of the Lord Jesus Christ in the Sermon on the Mount where He spoke of those who would function without authority. He admonished the people to enter in at the strait gate, the narrow gate that leads to life eternal. He said, beginning with *verse 13 of Matthew chapter 7, "Enter ye in at the strait gate:* for wide is the gate, and broad is the way, that leadeth to destruction, and many there be which go in thereat: Because strait is the gate and narrow is the way, which leadeth unto life, and few there be that find it. *Beware of false prophets,* which come to you in sheep's clothing, but *inwardly they are ravening wolves. Ye shall know them by their fruits.* Do men gather grapes from thorns, or figs of thistles? Even so every good tree bringeth forth good fruit; but *a corrupt tree bringeth forth evil fruit.* A good tree cannot bring forth evil fruit, neither can a corrupt tree bring forth good fruit. *Every tree that bringeth not forth good fruit is hewn down, and cast into the fire. Wherefore by their fruits ye shall know them."*

In another tape, Biblical Proofs of the Restored Church, I cited a broad pattern of scriptural prophecies showing that there was to be an apostasy, a falling away in which the authority to act in the name of God would be taken from the earth. I showed that the taking of the authority from the earth was to be complete, and that the only way that authority to act in God's name could be here in these last days was for it to be restored. And then I showed a broad pattern of Biblical prophecy going step-by-step through the events of the restoration. I showed how that restoration had taken place in these last days, and that only The Church of Jesus Christ of Latter-day Saints had that priesthood power restored and now has the authority to act in the name of God.

My Invitation: Enter In at the Strait Gate that Leads to Eternal Life

We've talked at length about the need for authority and for the need to find the Church of Jesus Christ. Those sacred ordinances performed in it are necessary for all men to receive if they are to come and dwell in Christ's kingdom. I hope that you will seriously consider the many scriptural passages we've talked about. Ponder your need to receive those essential ordinances from men who have the power and authority to minister in the name of God.

Beware of the many counterfeits which have been put forth. Beware of men who have no authority. They say that authority is not necessary, that one doesn't need to be baptized by one holding authority, and that it isn't necessary to receive the laying on of hands for the gift of the Holy Ghost by a person who holds the authority of the priesthood. These are counterfeit doctrines that can rob you of salvation. And be careful of that apostate doctrine which says that the church is not essential, that the church is only a social organization, and that there are many churches which are acceptable to Christ. Paul said *"One* Lord, *one* faith, *one* baptism." And he was truly stating the actual doctrine of the Lord Jesus Christ.

Ponder in depth the words that I have spoken. Consider them carefully and fully. Pray about them, and seek guidance so that you will understand that they are true, and apply them in your own life. Seek out those who hold the authority to act in the name of God—that priesthood which is so often spoken of in the scriptures.

I bear you this witness, that the priesthood is found in the authorized representatives of The Church of Jesus Christ of Latter-day Saints. If you will let them guide you and direct you, you will find that salvation which you so much desire and seek. Of this I testify in the name of our Lord and Savior, Jesus Christ. Amen.

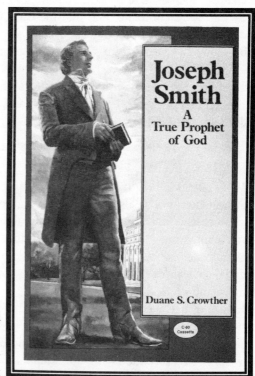

Joseph
Smith
A
True Prophet
of God

Duane S. Crowther

C-60
Cassette

Brothers and sisters and friends,

I appreciate this opportunity to tell you about a great man, and to explain the accomplishments in his life which show that God led and directed him and used him as a prophet to guide the people of the earth in these latter days.

That man was Joseph Smith, the Mormon prophet. His life was snuffed out by assassins when he was only thirty eight and one-half years of age. Yet during his time on earth he accomplished far more than most of us would do in a dozen lifetimes.

Joseph Smith—A Man of Significant
Accomplishment and Influence

Let me begin by briefly summarizing some of his accomplishments for you. They were outstanding, and extended to seventeen different fields.

First, Latter-day Saints regard Joseph Smith as a **Prophet, Seer, and Revelator.** This was his greatest calling. My purpose tonight is to give evidence and testimony that he truly was a prophet, and God's spokesman here on the earth.

Second, Joseph was a **Church Organizer and Religious Leader.** He organized The Church of Jesus Christ of Latter-day Saints. He was a capable administrator who cared for both the spiritual and the temporal needs of his people. The ecclesiastical organization he established has long been regarded as a model of efficiency, and still functions effectively in leading the Church after 150 years. The Church he founded now numbers over six million members and is one of the fastest growing Churches in the world today.

Third, Joseph was an **Educator.** Though he received only a grade-school education in the public schools, Joseph Smith was self-educated and knew the importance of proper schooling. He established schools for the youth of the Church in Ohio, Missouri and Illinois. He pioneered the adult education movement in the United States and established America's first school for adults. He studied Hebrew and procurred an instructor to teach that language to the other leaders of the Church. When the charter was being prepared for the City of Nauvoo, Illinois, he caused that provisions be made for the establishing of a University there, saying that "the University of the City of Nauvoo will enable us to teach our children wisdom, to instruct them in all the knowledge and learning, in the arts, sciences, and learned professions." Joseph constantly sought for his people to be better educated in both the things of God and the things of man, and warned that "It is impossible for a man to be saved in ignorance."

Fourth, Joseph Smith was an **Author.** As the inspired servant of the Lord, Joseph brought forth the *Book of Mormon,* the *Doctrine and Covenants,* and the *Pearl of Great Price.* He also wrote an accurate and comprehensive history of the Church which encompasses well over 3,000 pages in printed form, and wrote numerous articles for early Church periodicals. While some men have produced a greater quantity of written material, there is no literature written which can surpass the greatness or profundity of the material penned by the Prophet.

Fifth, Joseph Smith was an **Editor** of the Church's periodical, the *Times and Seasons,* for nearly a year, commencing in February of 1842. He continued in this position until the heavy demands of Church business caused him to relinquish his position. During Joseph's tenure as editor, the periodical made several important contributions to the history and doctrine of the Church, including the first publication of the Book of Abraham, the Wentworth letter, the beginning of the *History of the Church,* etc.

Sixth, Joseph Smith was an **Historian.** During his mature life, Joseph was extremely careful to keep an accurate history of both his personal activities and the undertakings of the Church. His published testimony comprises six lengthy volumes and has been found to be extremely accurate. Not only did he keep careful records himself but he saw to it that others were appointed as historians for the Church. Through his study of the *Book of Mormon* Joseph also became an authority on the history of ancient America. The findings of archaeologists during recent decades have clearly supported the historical assertations made by Joseph Smith over a century ago.

Seventh, Joseph Smith was a **Translator.** Through inspiration given through the Urim and Thummim, Joseph translated the *Book of Mormon.* He also translated the *Book of Abraham* from ancient papyri and the *Record of Joseph.* Another important contribution made by Joseph Smith was his *Inspired Revision* of the Holy Bible. The translations which he made are invaluable contributions to the field of theology and religious understanding.

Eighth, Joseph Smith was a **Bible Scholar.** His understanding of the Bible was profound. He repeatedly gave detailed explanations and exegesis of scriptural passages, and was well able to handle himself in debates with ministers. He learned the Hebrew language and was qualified to draw the original meanings of the passages as found in ancient manuscripts. It appears that he was also intimately acquainted with many of the Biblical personalities because they had appeared to him in visions. He left record of communications with such awesome individuals as Adam, Seth, Abraham, Elijah, Elias, John the Baptist, Peter, James, John, Paul, and all of Jesus's twelve disciples. Is it small wonder that he was a capable Bible scholar with such sources as these?

Ninth, Joseph Smith was a great **Teacher.** The effectiveness of a teacher can often be judged by the type of men who follow him and adhere to his teachings. Joseph was followed by great scholars such as Sidney Rigdon, Orson Pratt, John Taylor, and Willard Richards; great leaders such as Brigham Young, Heber C. Kimball, and Charles C. Rich; and great teachers and theologians such as Wilford Woodruff and Parley P. Pratt. Common people also followed him, and they clung to his every saying. Few teachers have ever had such a host of followers who carefully recorded their mentor's comments and teachings as Joseph Smith had. He was a powerful speaker as well as a teacher, and was able to hold his audiences spellbound for long periods of time—to move them to tears or to laughter—but most of all, to motivate them and to change their lives.

Tenth, Joseph Smith was a **Philosopher.** With the exception of the Savior, no man has ever done more to provide humanity with an accurate and realistic answer to life's great questions than has Joseph Smith. He defined for the world the nature of God, and in contrast, the nature and actuality of Satan. He gave to mankind a clear understanding of the pre-mortal life, the purpose of earth life, the nature of death, and the nature of the resurrection and after-life. He defined man's relationship with God and told of the possibilities for mankind in the life to come. He answered the ages-old question "What is truth?" and revealed those qualities which will bring man the greatest good and allow him to perform the greatest good for others. He was the spokesman for God, and in that capacity he brought forth the solutions to problems which have been debated by countless philosophers over the centuries. His contribution to the field of philosophy was immense.

Eleventh, Joseph Smith was a **City Planner.** In 1833 Joseph drew a plan for the proposed City of Zion. His plan featured wide streets, square blocks with the roads running towards the four points of the compass, careful provision for business and church facilities within a few blocks of every home, the restricting of unsightly farm buildings to the outlying areas, and deep home lots with large back yards for gardens and other domestic needs. The Prophet's plan was used as the basis for Nauvoo, Illinois, "the city beautiful." His plan also served as a model for many of the western cities established by the Saints.

Twelfth, Joseph Smith was an **Architect.** It was Joseph who made the preliminary designs and plans for the Kirtland, Nauvoo, and Jackson County Temples. He also oversaw most of the construction work for the temples built during his lifetime. Again, it was a work done through inspiration, for Joseph told how he had seen the Nauvoo Temple in vision and insisted that the building be constructed in the manner shown him by revelation.

Thirteenth, Joseph Smith was a **Civic and Political Leader.** Joseph was named as mayor of Nauvoo in 1842 and developed that city into the largest city in Illinois. The charter he devised for the city was a monumental work which served to protect his people and to foster the city's rapid growth.

In 1844 he became a candidate for the presidency of the United States. At this time, the Saints were unable to find a presidential candidate from whom they could expect fair treatment. They were also in a difficult position in local politics: because of their large numbers they held sufficient voting power to elect or defeat either party in state politics, but they knew that to support one party would bring harsh treatment and persecution from those they chose not to support. Because of this situation, and because it would give national publicity which would serve to further the Church's missionary efforts, Joseph ran for the office of President of the United States. His far-sighted platform included prison reforms, a plan for the abolition of slavery, revision of the methods for treating deserters from the army, a national banking system, the annexation of Oregon and Texas, presidential power to supress mobs, greater economy in government, and the reduction of Congress and congressional pay scales. His untimely death came during the campaign and prevented him from carrying his case to the polls.

Fourteenth, Joseph Smith was a **Military Leader.** Joseph was responsible for two great military undertakings. The first was in 1834 when he led a group of two hundred five Mormon soldiers in a 1,000-mile march from Kirtland, Ohio to Independence, Missouri. This group, known as Zion's Camp, sought the re-establishment of the Saints in their homes from which they had been driven by mobs. Later the Prophet became a general in the Illinois state militia and commander of the Nauvoo Legion. Under his direction the legion became a highly-trained and capable unit which was the pride of the state militia.

Fifteenth, Joseph Smith was an **Economist.** He made several contributions in the field of economics. He established the United Order—a communal living plan which functioned in Thompson, Ohio and other communities in 1831. In 1836 he devised a special banking system based on promissory notes which helped for a time to solve the needs of the Saints rapidly expanding economy in Kirtland, Ohio. when the Saints began to build the city of Nauvoo, Joseph directed them in their industry. They established communal farms, stores and manufacturing enterprises to foster the community's growth. Joseph saw the importance of manufacturing and emphasized that it was to be the means of preventing poverty and unemployment in Nauvoo. The Prophet understood matters of finance, and was able to apply economic principles for the good of his people.

Sixteenth, Joseph was a **Scientist.** He was interested in astronomy, and revealed much concerning various planets, the system of revolutions which governed their time, and the nature of light. He understood the nature of the creation of the earth and spoke of the eternal nature of the elements. He brought forth numerous teachings concerning early American cultures and the existence of metals, cement, and animals such as the horse and elephants which have later been substantiated by archaeologists and anthropologists. The Word of Wisdom, Mormondom's code of health, was also a scientific contribution of the prophet Joseph Smith.

Seventeenth, Joseph was a great **Humanitarian.** Joseph Smith continually sought the well-being of all mankind. In his political platform he asked for reforms which would bring pardons for convicts and which would make the penitentiaries "seminaries of learning." His plan called for the paying of slaveholders by the government for their slaves so that they could become free. He sought for the elimination of social classes and held that the government should "make less distinction among the people." Joseph's plea was that the government should "give every man his constitutional freedom." His humanitarian ideals were expressed in other ways besides his political platform. For instance, he was an advocate of women's rights, and his organization, on March 1, 1842, of the Female Relief Society of Nauvoo was an act which far preceded other movements for the betterment of womankind in the United States.

What Historical American Has Exerted the Most Powerful Influence Upon His Countrymen?

Truly Joseph Smith was a remarkable man—an individual of amazing accomplishments, who did more in his brief life than the rest of us will probably achieve, by far. A non-Mormon contemporary, Josiah Quincy, wrote the following about the Mormon Prophet just a month-and-a-half before Joseph's death:

"May 15, 1844

It is by no means improbable that some future textbook, for the use of generations yet unborn, will contain a question something like this: *What historical American of the nineteenth century has exerted the most powerful influence upon the destinies of his countrymen?* And it is by no means impossible that the answer to that interrogatory may be thus written: *Joseph Smith, the Mormon Prophet.* And the reply, absurd as it doubtless seems to most men now living, may be an obvious commonplace to their descendants. History deals in surprises and paradoxes quite as startling as this.¹"

---

1. *Church News,* December 29, 1962, p. 6, as cited in the author's book *The Prophecies of Joseph Smith* (Bountiful, Utah: Horizon Publishers, 1963), pp. 37-38. Further references to this source will be indicated as PJS.

But today I'm here to talk to you not just of the significant accomplishments made by this remarkable man in the fields of temporal learning and endeavor, but to bear you my witness that Joseph Smith was truly a prophet of God—God's spokesman here upon the earth called to convey divine instructions to the people of the world.

My desire is to share with you some of the prophesies made by Joseph Smith which have been fulfilled, and to tell you some of the remarkable experiences which took place during his life time that show that God was truly guiding and directing him.

Prophetic Fulfillment—the Test of a Prophet

But let me read you, first, something that I wrote in the beginning of my book *The Prophecies of Joseph Smith* that talks about how we know a prophet is truly a prophet of God.

Two men stood in the house of the Lord before a large congregation of intent listeners. The moment was dramatically tense, for each of the two was giving important counsel on a matter of national importance. The Jewish listeners knew the two both claimed to be prophets—spokesmen for the Lord God of Israel. Yet their messages were opposite. One, named Hananiah, spoke of peace and promised that within two years the oppression they then suffered from a northern enemy would be ended. The other, Jeremiah, challenged his words and said that the oppression would continue. Which message was true? It was obvious that one of the two men was not a servant of God but rather a hireling prophet—a political stooge planted to deceive people. How would the congregation know whom to follow and obey? Then Jeremiah proposed the profound test:

"When the word of the prophet shall come to pass, then shall the prophet be known, that the Lord hath truly sent him."[2]

Thus a servant of God clearly set forth the test which will identify a true prophet of the Lord—**those things he prophesies will come to pass.** How simple a test this is, and it is God's will that we apply it, for the Lord had previously revealed this counsel on true and false prophets:

"But *the prophet, which shall presume to speak a word in my name, which I have not commanded him to speak,* or that shall speak in the name of other gods, even that prophet shall die.

---

2. *Jeremiah* 28:9

"And if thou say in thine heart, How shall we know the word which the Lord hath not spoken?

"When a prophet speaketh in the name of the Lord, *if the thing follow not, nor come to pass, that is the thing which the Lord hath not spoken, but the prophet hath spoken it presumptuously:* thou shalt not be afraid of him."[3]

And so, as I tell you of some of the prophecies made by Joseph Smith, I invite you to apply the test of fulfillment which the Bible sets forth.

The Hidden Thoughts of Oliver Cowdery Revealed Through Joseph

Let me begin with three incidents which show how God drew men to Joseph, and helped them to recognize that Joseph was truly the Lord's authorized servant here upon the earth, with an inspired commission to restore the true Church of Jesus Christ and spread forth Christ's gospel to all the world.

In the Spring of 1829, Joseph was in Harmony, Pennsylvania, working on the translation of the Book of Mormon. Back in Joseph's hometown, Palmyra, New York, the trustees of the community saw fit to hire a new schoolteacher for the district school by the name of Oliver Cowdery. As was the custom in those days, the schoolteacher would board in the homes of the school children. Since Joseph's room was vacant, Oliver came to board at the Smith home. Almost immediately he began hearing rumors from the neighbors and children concerning the gold plates and the translating Joseph was doing. He asked the Smith family for further information about Joseph's activities, but for several days they declined to give it to him. Finally Joseph's father gave him a brief explanation of the nature of the plates and of Joseph's work. Following father Smith's explanation, Oliver began receiving promptings from above which completely changed the course of his life. This is what the history records about Oliver:

"Shortly after receiving this information, he told Mr. Smith that he was highly delighted with what he had heard, that he had been in a deep study upon the subject all day, and that *it was impressed upon his mind, that he should yet have the privilege of writing for Joseph.* Furthermore, that he had determined to pay him a visit at the close of the school, which he was then teaching.

---

3. *Deuteronomy* 18:20-22

"On coming in on the following day, he said, *'The subject upon which we were yesterday conversing seems working in my very bones, and I cannot, for a moment, get it out of my mind;* finally, I have resolved on what I will do. Samuel, I understand, is going down to Pennsylvania to spend the spring with Joseph; I shall make my arrangements to be ready to accompany him thither, by the time he recovers his health; for *I have made it a subject of prayer, and I firmly believe that it is the will of the Lord that I should go.* If there is a work for me to do in this thing, I am determined to attend to it.' "

Father Smith told Oliver that if God did have a work for him to do he could seek and gain a testimony of the mission he was to perform from the Lord. Accordingly, Oliver went to the Lord in prayer and received a witness of the Spirit. He apparently told no one of this witness, but his behavior immediately changed and "From this time, Oliver was so completely absorbed in the subject of the Record, that it seemed impossible for him to think or converse about anything else."[4]

Oliver served as a Palmyra schoolteacher for less than a month before he left his work to go to Harmony to meet Joseph. He was accompanied by Samuel Smith, Joseph's twenty-one-year-old brother.

They hiked the long distance from Palmyra, New York to Harmony, Pennsylvania in April, when the weather was wet and disagreeable—raining and freezing and thawing, alternately, leaving roads almost completely impassable. No communication was made with Joseph that Oliver was coming. Yet Joseph *knew* that a scribe was being sent him. Joseph had called upon the Lord, three days prior to the arrival of Samuel and Oliver, to send him a scribe, and he was informed that help should be forthcoming in a few days. So when Oliver introduced himself and told Joseph of the business that he'd come upon Joseph was not surprised. It wasn't until several days later, however, that Oliver believed without reservation that Joseph was a prophet. Oliver asked Joseph to inquire, and determine the will of the Lord concerning himself. In the revelation Joseph received in behalf of Oliver, the Lord said:

"*I tell thee these things as a witness unto thee— that the words or the work which thou hast been writing are true.* Verily, verily, I say unto you, if you desire a further witness, *cast your mind upon the night that you cried unto me in your heart, that you might know concerning the truth of these*

---

4. *History of Joseph Smith By His Mother, Lucy Mack Smith* (Salt Lake City: Bookcraft, 1958), p. 139; cited in PJS, p. 104.

things. Did I not speak peace to your mind concerning the matter? What greater witness can you have than from God?

And now, behold, you have received a witness; for *if I have told you things which no man knoweth, have you not received a witness?"*[5] You can read the rest of the revelation in the *Doctrine and Covenants,* in *section 6.*

Joseph later recorded Oliver's testimony to him on the matter:

"After we had received this revelation, Oliver Cowdery stated to me that after he had gone to my father's to board, and after the family had communicated to him concerning my having obtained the plates, that one night after he had retired to bed he called upon the Lord to know if these things were so, and the Lord manifested to him that they were true, but he had kept the circumstance entirely secret, and had mentioned it to no one; so that after this revelation was given, he knew that the work was true, because *no being living knew of the thing alluded to in the revelation,* but God and himself."[6]

Joseph Foretells David Whitmer's Movements

Let me tell you of another experience that followed about two months later. During those two months while Oliver was assisting Joseph as his scribe, they saw opposition from some of the religionists of the Harmony area change to persecution. One day, in late May of 1829, as Joseph was translating the Book of Mormon by means of the Urim and Thummim, he received, instead of the translation words, a commandment and warning from the Lord. The commandment was to write a letter to a man by the name of David Whitmer, who lived in Waterloo, New York, requesting him to come immediately with his team and wagon, to convey Joseph and Oliver to his own residence, because evil designing people were seeking to take Joseph's life. Joseph didn't know David Whitmer, but Oliver had met him briefly. David had expressed an interest in the work that Joseph was doing and Oliver had agreed to write him about it.

You can imagine how Joseph's letter must have been received by the Whitmer family. His request was to make a round trip of 275 miles, pick up Joseph, Oliver and Joseph's wife, Emma, take them and board them for an indefinite period of time at the Whitmer home, and to participate in

---

5. *Doctrine & Covenants* 6:17, 22-24.
6. *History of the Church,* vol. 1, p. 35; cited in PJS, p. 106.

a work they knew nothing about except for the many rumors that were circulating throughout the area. David Whitmer's father suggested to David that he shouldn't go unless he could get a witness from God that it was absolutely necessary. Let me recount for you the events that followed during the next several days, as David received his witness from God:

"This suggestion pleased David, and he asked the Lord for a testimony concerning his going for Joseph, and *was told by the voice of the Spirit to go as soon as his wheat was harrowed in.* The next morning, David went to the field, and found that he had two heavy day's work before him. *He then said to himself that, if he should be enabled, by any means, to do this work sooner than the same had ever been done on the farm before, he would receive it as an evidence, that it was the will of God, that he should do all in his power to assist Joseph Smith in the work in which he was engaged.* He then fastened his horses to the harrow, and instead of dividing the field into what is, by farmers, usually termed lands, drove around the whole of it, continuing this till noon, when, on stopping for dinner, he looked around, and discovered to his surprise, that he had harrowed in full half the wheat. After dinner he went on as before, and by evening he finished the whole two days' work.

"His father, on going into the field the same evening, saw what had been done, and he exclaimed, *'There must be an overruling hand in this, and I think you would better go down to Pennsylvania as soon as your plaster of paris is sown.'*

"The next morning, David took a wooden measure under his arm and went out to sow the plaster, which he had left, two days previous, in heaps near his sister's house, but, on coming to the place, he discovered that it was gone! He then ran to his sister, and inquired of her if she knew what had become of it. Being surprised she said, 'Why do you ask me? was it not all sown yesterday?'

"Not to my knowledge,' answered David.

" 'I am astonished at that,' replied his sister, 'for the children came to me in the forenoon, and begged of me to go out and see the men sow plaster in the field, saying that they never saw anybody sow plaster so fast in their lives. I accordingly went, and saw three men at work in the field, as the children said, but, supposing that you had hired some help, on account of your hurry, I went immediately into the house, and gave the subject no further attention.'

"David made considerable inquiry in regard to the matter, both among his relatives and neighbors, but was not able to learn who had done it. However, the family was convinced that there was an exertion of super-natural power connected with this strange occurrence.

"David immediately set out for Pennsylvania, and arrived there in two days, without injuring his horses in the least, though the distance was one hundred and thirty-five miles. When he arrived, he was under the necessi-ty of introducing himself to Joseph, as this was the first time that they had ever met."[7]

In spite of the accelerated pace in which David prepared for his journey and traveled to Harmony, his unannounced coming was anticipated by the Prophet. To his surprise, David found Joseph and Oliver waiting for him some distance from the town. He was even more astounded to discover that the Prophet had foretold the movements he would make to his scribe. He later told of their meeting to other members of the Church, saying:

"When I arrived at Harmony, Joseph and Oliver were coming toward me, and met me some distance from the house. Oliver told me that Joseph had informed him when I started from home, where I had stopped the first night, how I read the sign at the tavern, where I stopped the next night, etc., and that I would be there that day before dinner, and this was why they had come out to meet me; all of which was exactly as Joseph had told Oliver, at which I was greatly astonished."[8]

After Joseph, Emma and Oliver came to the Whitmer home, the work on the Book of Mormon translation proceeded at an even greater pace, and it was completed during the summer of 1829. The book was soon pub-lished, and the Church was restored according to the commandment of the Lord on April 6, 1830.

A Lawyer Prompted to Deliver "The Lord's Anointed"

Missionary work began immediately, and one of the earliest branches to be founded was back in the area near Harmony, Pennsylvania in a little town called Colesville. Joseph, along with several others, visited Coles-ville on several occasions. They taught the gospel there and won converts. In June, 1830, they came to Colesville to hold a baptismal meeting. A stream

---

7. History of Joseph Smith, *op. cit.*, pp. 147-49; cited in PJS, pp. 125-26.
8. *Millennial Star*, 1878, vol. 40, no. 49, p. 772; cited in PJS, pp. 126-27.

was dammed up, but persecution led by sectarian ministers had increased as converts began to be won in the area, and a mob broke up the dam.

Two days later, a constable came and arrested Joseph on the charge of disorderly conduct for building the dam, and bound him over for trial. In those days if a person wanted to hinder another's activities an easy way to do it was to swear out legal charges. The legal machinery was so slow and cumbersome that an individual could be detained for days before being found innocent of the charges being made against him. This tactic was quite frequently used against Joseph Smith, though time after time he was found innocent when the trial was finally held.

On this occasion Joseph Knight, a friend of the prophet Joseph, sought legal aid from his neighbor who was well acquainted with the law—John Reed. Mr. Reed was reluctant to come to the aid of the prophet, whom he did not even know, but he received a revealed witness that it was important for him to do so. This is what he recorded concerning it:

"I was so busy at that time, when Mr. Smith sent for me, that it was almost impossible for me to attend the case, and never having seen Mr. Smith, I determined to decline going. But soon after coming to this conclusion, I thought I heard someone say to me, *'You must go, and deliver the Lord's Anointed!'* Supposing it was the man who came after me, I replied, 'The Lord's Anointed?' He was surprised at being accosted in this manner, and replied, 'What do you mean, sir? I said nothing about the Lord's Anointed.' I was convinced that he told the truth, for these few words filled my mind with peculiar feelings, such as I had never before experienced; and I immediately hastened to the place of trial. Whilst I was engaged in the case, these emotions increased, and when I came to speak upon it, *I was inspired with an eloquence which was altogether new to me, and which was overpowering and irresistible.'*"[9]

Once again the Holy Spirit had testified of the divine calling of Joseph Smith.

Orson Hyde to Go to Jerusalem

A prophet sometimes can foretell the future actions of his friends and associates. Joseph Smith did that on several occasions, prophesying events that happened many years after his words were spoken, even to men he didn't previously know.

---

9. *History of Joseph Smith, op. cit.*, pp. 176-77; cited in PJS, p. 204.

Early in 1831, Joseph moved to the area of Kirtland, Ohio. It was in the fall of 1831 that a convert was baptized, for instance, whose name was Orson Hyde. Joseph Smith confirmed him a member of the church and pronounced a blessing upon him in which he said:

"In due time *thou shalt go to Jerusalem,* the land of thy fathers, and be a watchman unto the house of Israel; and by thy hand shall the Most High do a great work, which shall *prepare the way and greatly facilitate the gathering together of that people.*"[10]

Orson Hyde rose rapidly in the ranks of the Church, and was one of the original Quorum of the Twelve Apostles. He filled missions to New York, Canada and England.

During the April, 1840, conference in Nauvoo, Orson Hyde was called on a mission to Palestine. He made his way to the Eastern States and labored there trying to obtain funds to go. His missionary companion left him, and Orson found himself in the difficult situation of being alone, and still without funds to make the journey. His passage across the ocean was made possible by a stranger who walked up to him one day and gave him a bag of gold. On October 24, 1841 Orson Hyde stood on the Mount of Olives and dedicated the land of Palestine for the gathering of Judah's scattered remnants.[11] Those Latter-day Saints who have studied the history of Israel mark that event as the beginning of the return of the Jews to what has become the nation of Israel today.

Recently I watched on television a program showing the October 24, 1979 dedication of the Orson Hyde Memorial in Jerusalem, and there on television I saw the mayor of Jerusalem participating and commenting that everyone who knew the history of Israel was well acquainted with Orson Hyde's dedication of the land and prophecy of the return of the Jews. So we see the literal fulfillment of Joseph's 1831 prophecy that Orson would do a great work which would prepare the way and greatly facilitate the gathering together of that people.

Brigham Young to Preside Over the Church

In the Spring of 1832, back in the area of Mendon, New York, new converts were being won. Three of them were Brigham Young, his brother,

---

10. *History of the Church,* vol.4, p. xxxi; cited in PJS, p. 219.

11. Jenson, Andrew, *Latter-day Saint Biographical Encyclopedia* (Salt Lake City: the *Deseret News,* 1901), vol. 1, p. 81; cited in PJS, p. 220.

Joseph Young, and Heber C. Kimball. In the fall of that year the three of them decided that they wanted to become personally acquainted with the prophet Joseph, so they travelled westward in a horse-drawn wagon and arrived in Kirtland, Ohio in September of 1832. On the way they stopped at the home of one of the church members in Connfret, N.Y. and there, during the evening, Brigham Young spoke in tongues—one of the first times we know of that someone within the church spoke in tongues in this dispensation.

When they finally arrived in Kirtland, the three found that Joseph and his brothers were out chopping and hauling wood. They went out and introduced themselves, and Joseph invited them to come to a meeting that evening. It was Brigham Young who recorded the events of the meeting in these words:

"In the evening a few of the brethren came in, and we conversed upon the things of the kingdom. He called upon me to pray; *in my prayer I spoke in tongues.* As soon as we arose from our knees, the brethren flocked around him, and asked his opinion concerning the gift of tongues that was upon me. *He told them it was the pure Adamic language.* Some said to him they expected he would condemn the gift Brother Brigham had, but he said, *'No, it is of God, and the time will come when Brigham Young will preside over this church.'* "[12]

Students of history know that Brigham Young was the president of the Quorum of the Twelve Apostles when Joseph was martyred, and that it was he who followed as the second leader and the second president of The Church of Jesus Christ of Latter-day Saints, in fulfillment of Joseph's prophecy.

Joseph's Prophecies of the U.S. Civil War and Future Wars

Prophets of God have the power to foresee major political upheavals and events of nature—things which they have no power to influence or control. Joseph Smith foresaw such events—happenings which took place long after his death. For instance, on Christmas day, 1832, Joseph prophecied in detail the beginning of the U.S. Civil War. The revelation which contains this prophecy is known as Doctrine and Covenants section 87, and it begins with these words:

---

12. *Comprehensive History of the Church*, vol. 1, p. 289; cited in PJS, p. 227.

"Verily, thus saith the Lord concerning the *wars that will shortly come to pass, beginning at the rebellion of South Carolina, which will eventually terminate in the death and misery of many souls;* And the time will come that *war will be poured out upon all nations,* beginning at this place. For behold, the *Southern States shall be divided against the Northern States,* and the *Southern States will call on other nations, even the nation of Great Britain,* as it is called, and *they shall also call upon other nations;* and *then war shall be poured out upon all nations.*"[13]

The prophecy is too detailed to be considered here in depth, but that which is important is that here, 29-and-a-half years prior to the beginning of the Civil War, Joseph prophecied its beginning, and correctly indicated that it would begin with the secession of the state of South Carolina, and that Great Britain would participate in the war on the side of the Southern states.

Joseph's prophecy was again referred to in a statement he recorded on September 6, 1842. He wrote: "I prophesy, in the name of the Lord God, that the *commencement of the difficulties* which will cause much bloodshed previous to the coming of the Son of Man *will be in South Carolina.* It may probably arise through the slave question. *This a voice declared to me,* while I was praying earnestly on the subject, December 25th, 1832."[14]

Certainly here are two of the most significant of the many prophecies made by the prophet Joseph.

The Falling of the Stars Foretold

Let me share with you another prophecy made by Joseph concerning one of the most memorable nights in history. It was in the fall of 1833, while Joseph was preaching at a meeting in Kirtland, that he made this statement: *"Forty days shall not pass and the stars shall fall from heaven."*

One man present was not a member of the church and was skeptical of the prophecy, so he wrote it down and kept careful track of the days. It happened that 39 days after the utterance of that prophecy, a brother in the church by the name of Joseph Hancock was out hunting game and got lost. He and a companion wandered around until night, when they found themselves at the home of this unbeliever. The man produced his notes about Joseph's prophecy and asked Brother Hancock what he thought of

13. *Doctrine and Covenants* 87:1-3.
14. *Doctrine and Covenants* 130:12-13.

his prophet now that 39 days had passed and the prophecy was not yet fulfilled. Brother Hancock was unmoved and quietly remarked, "There is one night left of the time and *if Joseph said so, the stars will certainly fall tonight. This prophecy will all be fulfilled."* The matter weighed upon the mind of Brother Hancock, who watched that night, and it proved to be the historical one known in all the world as 'the night of falling stars."

The whole heavens were lit up with the falling meteors, and the countenance of the skeptic as he viewed the spectacle was plainly seen and closely watched by Brother Hancock, who said that he turned pale as death and spoke not a word.[15]

That great shower of falling stars was so extensive that it was visible throughout the entire United States, and took place on November 12, 1833, but Joseph had prophesied its coming 40 days earlier.

Prophecies and Pentecostal Days in the Kirtland Temple

One of the most interesting periods in church history occurred in early 1836, as the Kirtland Temple neared completion. The Saints sacrificed greatly to build it, and received rich blessings in return. Joseph prophesied to the apostles that great blessings would be poured out upon the Church, saying, "If we are faithful, and live by every word that proceeds forth from the mouth of God, *I will venture to prophesy that we shall get a blessing that will be worth remembering, if we should live as long as John the Revelator;* our blessings will be such as we have not realized before, nor received in this generation."[16]

The fulfillment of this prophecy was a literal outpouring of heavenly manifestations upon the leaders and members of the Church that lasted for over three months. On seven different occasions, for instance, they saw visions of the Savior. Of the first of these occasions, Joseph wrote that

"The heavens were opened upon us, and *I beheld the celestial kingdom of God, and the glory thereof,* whether in the body or out I cannot tell. I saw the transcendent beauty of *the gate through which the heirs of that kingdom will enter,* which was like unto circling flames of fire; also the blazing *throne of God,* whereon was seated *the Father and the Son.* I saw the *beautiful streets* of that kingdom, which had the appearance of being

15. Parry, Edwin F., *Stories About Joseph Smith the Prophet* (Salt Lake City: The Deseret News Press, 1934), pp. 67-69; cited in PJS, pp. 239-40.

16. *History of the Church,* vol. 2, p. 309; cited in PJS, p. 260.

paved with gold. I saw Fathers *Adam* and *Abraham*, and my father and mother, my brother, Alvin that has long since slept, . . . "[17]

Visions of angels and the ministrations of those heavenly beings were also received on numerous occasions. They received the gift of speaking in foreign tongues and recorded that on several occasions "the *gift of tongues fell upon* us in mighty power, *angels mingled their voices with ours,* while their presence was in our midst, and unceasing praises swelled our bosoms."[18] One of the brethren saw a pillar of fire rest down and abide upon the heads of the presidents of Seventy. Many prophesied.

On Sunday, March 27, 1836, the temple was dedicated. Perhaps the greatest outpouring of the Spirit came during a meeting for Church authorities on the night of the building's dedication. Joseph had given various instructions concerning the spirit of prophecy and then called on them to use their prophetic gifts, saying, "Do not quench the Spirit, for *the first one that opens his mouth shall receive the Spirit of prophecy.*"[19] Suddenly the Spirit was poured out as it had been on the day of Pentecost in New Testament times. Joseph recorded:

"Brother George A. Smith arose and began to prophesy, when a noise was heard like the *sound of a rushing mighty wind,* which filled the Temple, and all the congregation simultaneously arose, being moved upon by an invisible power; *many began to speak in tongues and prophesy;* others saw glorious visions; and I beheld *the Temple was filled with angels,* which fact I declared to the congregation. The people of the neighborhood came running together (hearing *an unusual sound within, and seeing a bright light like a pillar of fire resting upon the Temple),* and were astonished at what was taking place."[20]

A description of this event left by Lorenzo Snow said:

"Father Smith presided over the meeting in the northwest section of the Temple, and after the meeting was opened by singing, he was mouth in prayer, and in course of supplication he very earnestly prayed that the Spirit of God might be poured out as on the day of Pentecost—that it might come 'as a rushing mighty wind.' Some time after in the midst of the exercises of the forenoon, it did come; and whether Father Smith had forgotten what

---

17. *History of the Church*, vol. 2, p. 380; cited in PJS, p. 261.

18. *History of the Church*, vol. 2, p. 383 (see also pp. 392, 428); cited in PJS, p. 261.

19. *History of the Church*, vol. 2, p. 428; cited in PJS, p. 261.

20. *History of the Church*, vol. 2, p. 428; cited in PJS, pp. 261-62.

he had prayed for or whether, in the fervency of his heart, when praying he did not realize what he prayed for, I never ascertained, but when the sound came and filled the house, with an expression of great astonishment he raised his eyes, exclaiming, 'What! Is the house on fire?' But presently he comprehended the cause of his alarm, and was filled with unspeakable joy."[21]

The climax to this glorious period of blessings and spiritual endowment came on the first Sunday after the temple was dedicated. During the afternoon service, just after the Lord's supper had been administered to those present, Joseph and Oliver Cowdery went behind the curtain which separated the congregation from the pulpit. There they kneeled in silent prayer, and when they arose, they were suddenly granted an interview with the Savior, as is recorded in the Doctrine and Covenants, section 110:

"The veil was taken from our minds, and the eyes of our understanding were opened.

"We saw the Lord standing upon the breastwork of the pulpit, before us; and under his feet was a paved work of pure gold, in color like amber.

"His eyes were as a flame of fire; the hair of his head was white like the pure snow; his countenance shone above the brightness of the sun; and his voice was as the sound of the rushing of great waters, even the voice of Jehovah, saying:

"I am the first and the last; I am he who liveth, I am he who was slain; I am your advocate with the Father.

"Behold, your sins are forgiven you; you are clean before me; therefore, lift up your heads and rejoice.

"Let the hearts of your brethren rejoice, and let the hearts of all *my people* rejoice, who have, with their might, built this house to my name.

"For behold, I have accepted this house, and my name shall be here; and *I will manifest myself to my people in mercy in this house.*

"Yea, *I will appear unto my servants, and speak unto them with mine own voice,* if my people will keep my commandments, and do not pollute this holy house.

"Yea the hearts of thousands and tens of thousands shall greatly rejoice in consequence of the blessings which shall be poured out, and the endowment with which my servants have been endowed in this house.

21. Smith, Eliza R. Snow, *Biography and Family Record of Lorenzo Snow* (Salt Lake City: Deseret News Co., 1884), pp. 12-143; cited in PJS, p. 262.

"And the fame of this house shall spread to foreign lands; and this is the beginning of the blessing which shall be poured out upon the heads of my people. Even so. Amen."[22]

And thus ended the period of endowment of which Joseph had prophesied. And with its conclusion he uttered another prophecy which is finding its fulfillment in numerous records such as this one:

The brethren continued exhorting, prophesying, and speaking in tongues until five o'clock in the morning. *The Savior made His appearance to some, while angels ministered to others,* and it was a Pentecost and an endowment indeed, long to be remembered, for *the sound shall go forth from this place into all the world, and the occurrences of this day shall be handed down upon the pages of sacred history,* to all generations; as the day of Pentecost."[23]

Jackson County to be Visited by Fire and Sword

As the church grew, opposition against it mounted rapidly, led primarily by ministers of other faiths. In the fall of 1838, Joseph and other leaders of the church were arrested and held during the winter of 1838-39 in a jail at Liberty, Missouri without any indictment being made against them. The Saints had previously been bitterly persecuted and driven by force out of Jackson County, Missouri. Joseph hired Alexander Doniphan, a lawyer, as his legal counsel.

On one occasion Joseph had been brought to Doniphan's office, and was there as a man came in to pay a debt to the lawyer. The man wanted to give a tract of land in Jackson County to Doniphan in payment for his debt. After the man left, Joseph turned to Doniphan and made this significant prophecy:

"Doniphan, I advise you not to take Jackson county land in payment of the debt. God's wrath hangs over Jackson county. God's people have been ruthlessly driven from it, and you will live to see the day when *it will be visited by fire and sword. The Lord of Hosts will sweep it with the besom of destruction. The fields and farms and houses will be destroyed, and only the chimneys will be left to mark the desolation.*"[24]

---

22. *Doctrine and Covenants* 110:1-10.
23. *History of the Church,* vol. 2, pp. 432-33; cited in PJS, p. 263.
24. *Comprehensive History of the Church,* vol. 1, p. 538; cited in PJS, pp. 326-27.

The Civil War occasioned the fulfillment of this prophecy. When the war began, Missouri was the only slave state above the Mason-Dixon line and was surrounded on three sides by free states. Continual skirmishes were fought between the communities in Kansas and Missouri over the question of slavery. Although it had been a slave state, Missouri entered the war as a free state to protect itself from the conquest it knew would be forthcoming. A large group of Southern guerilla fighters, however, established themselves in western Missouri and especially in the Jackson County area. Aided by the pro-South citizens they harassed the union army from their hideouts. A state of continual warfare existed in western Missouri.

Finally, the Union army issued the famous "Order Number 11," which commanded the residents of Cass, Jackson, and Bates Counties to evacuate their homes so the guerrillas could be wiped out. The Union soldiers, when they saw that their order was not heeded by most of the residents, swept down upon the area killing animals, burning homes and fields, and molesting the inhabitants. The brutal order was ruthlessly carried out, and became but a re-enactment, on a larger scale, of what had happened to the Saints there thirty years before.

This action in Jackson County and its surrounding area was regarded by many historians of the Civil War as the action that caused more suffering than any other conflict during the War. A soldier who came into the area in 1864 recorded this: "I went down the Blue river, we found houses, barns, outbuildings, nearly all burned down, and *nothing left standing but the chimneys* which had, according to the fashion of the time, been built on the outside of the buildings. I remember very well that *the country looked a veritable desolation.*"[25] Thus we see the literal fulfillment of Joseph's prophecy made more than two decades earlier.

Martin Van Buren Not to Be Elected Again

Joseph Smith made several prophecies of great significance concerning politics. In October and November of 1839, he and several others travelled to our nation's capitol to lay the grievances of the Saints before the Congress and before President Martin Van Buren. They met President Van Buren, who heard their plea for redress for sufferings of the Saints, but the president's reply was politically motivated as he said, *"What can I do?*

---

25. Letter from A. Saxey to Junius Wells, *Improvement Era*, November, 1902, vol. vi, p. 10; cited in PJS, p. 328.

I can do nothing for you! If I do anything, I shall come in contact with the whole state of Missouri."[26]

Because of Van Buren's unwillingness to help the Saints, Joseph Smith made this prophecy: *"May he never be elected again to any office of trust or power, by which he may abuse the innocent and let the guilty go free."*[27]

Joseph's prophecy was fulfilled. Martin Van Buren served only one term—from 1837 to 1841. In the presidential election of 1840 he was nominated once again by the Democratic Party, but was defeated by William Henry Harrison, the Whig candidate. His other attempts at gaining political office also failed. He was defeated for the Democratic nomination in 1844 and in 1848 was the candidate for president of the Free- Soil party but also was defeated. He died a broken man in July of 1862.

Stephen A. Douglas to Seek the Presidency of the United States

Joseph made another political prophecy of significance in May of 1843. At that time, as he was mayor of Nauvoo, Ill., he was visited by Stephen A. Douglas, a judge of the Illinois court. They enjoyed a pleasant dinner together and discussed many of the sufferings of the Saints which had occurred in the Missouri area.

As Joseph concluded his remarks, he turned to Judge Douglas and made this prophetic statement about him: *"Judge, you will aspire to the presidency of the United States; and if you ever turn your hand against me or the Latterday Saints, you will feel the weight of the hand of the Almighty upon you; and you will live to see and know that I have testified the truth to you; for the conversation of this day will stick to you through life."*[28]

Although Stephen A. Douglas manifested a friendly spirit toward the Prophet at that time, a few years later he entered into national politics and followed the popular trend of denouncing the Mormons. On June 12, 1857, he gave a speech in Springfield, Ill. in which he called the Saints a "disgusting cancer" and spoke a number of untruths about them. This speech was printed in the Missouri Republican of June 18, 1857, and found its way to Utah where a review of it was printed in the Deseret News. Accompanying the review was a copy of William Clayton's account of Joseph's prophecy, plus an editorial statement proclaiming to Douglas that *"by your*

---

26. *History of the Church*, vol. 4, p. 40; cited in PJS, p. 335.

27. *History of the Church*, vol. 4, p. 89; cited in PJS, p. 335.

28. *Comprehensive History of the Church*, vol. 2, p. 183; cited in PJS, p. 336.

own choice you have closed your chance for the Presidential chair, through disobeying the Council of Joseph. . . ." A copy of the editorial was sent to the Judge.

But Douglas was popular, and a renowned orator! In all America's history there have been few elections when the candidate seemed so likely to win the presidency. Stephen A. Douglas was a Democrat and that party was the predominant party in national politics at the time. His Republican opponent was a relatively unknown man who had lost a number of elections and was not considered a strong contender. Yet when the elections came, Douglas felt the weight of the hand of the Almighty upon him. His party was divided, and his Republican opponent, the little-known Abraham Lincoln, carried the election, with Douglas receiving the electoral votes of only two states—Missouri and New Jersey. Again a prophecy by Joseph Smith had foretold the events of the future in great detail.

This Church Will Fill the Rocky Mountains and North and South America

Joseph Smith made several significant prophecies concerning the settlement of the Mormon pioneers in the Rocky Mountain area. On April 26, 1834, he made a statement at Kirtland, Ohio concerning that westward expansion. He said this:

"I want to say to you before the Lord, that you know no more concerning the destinies of this Church and Kingdom than a babe upon its mother's lap. You don't comprehend it. It is only a little handful of Priesthood you see here tonight, but *this Church will fill North and South America—it will fill the world. It will fill the Rocky Mountains. There will be tens of thousands of Latter-day Saints who will be gathered in the Rocky Mountains and there they will open the door for the establishing of the Gospel among the Lamanites. . . . This people will go into the Rocky Mountains; they will there build temples to the Most High.*"[29]

The Saints Will Be Driven to the Rocky Mountains

And on August 6, 1842, Joseph made this statement in Montrose, Iowa:
"*I prophesied that the saints would continue to suffer much affliction and would be driven to the Rocky Mountains,* many would apostatize, others

---

29. *Conference Report,* April 8, 1898, p. 57; cited in PJS, p. 365.

would be put to death by our persecutors, or lose their lives in consequence of exposure or disease; and some of you will live to go and assist in making settlements and build cities and *see the saints become a mighty people in the midst of the Rocky Mountains.*"[30]

Anyone who has visited the Utah area has seen the literal fulfillment of these prophecies. We have built the temples, and we have become a mighty people in the midst of the Rocky Mountains, in fulfillment of Joseph's prophecies.

Joseph's Work to Be Accomplished Before His Death

Even in the last days of his life, prophecies made by Joseph Smith had significance concerning his future and concerning the future of others around him.

On October 15, 1843 at the Nauvoo Temple, Joseph commented on the enemies who were seeking to take his life and said, "I prophesy that *they will never have power to kill me till my work is accomplished* and I am ready to die."[31]

Joseph continued his ministry, yet he knew when he had completed his work. Shortly before his death there came the time when he announced that his life's work was completed. In a meeting of the leaders of the Church shortly before his passing, Joseph said, *"In the name of the Lord, I now shake from my shoulders the responsibility of bearing the Kingdom of God to all the world, and here and now I place that responsibility, with all the keys, powers and privileges pertaining thereto, upon the shoulders of you, the Twelve Apostles."*[32]

Joseph Prophesied That His Death Was Near

Persecution against the saints in Nauvoo, Illinois grew intense during the early summer of 1844. Joseph was mayor of the city and defended the rights of the saints. Incidents in the Mormon city such as the removal of the anti-Mormon newspaper, the Nauvoo Expositor, by the Nauvoo City council, caused the attacks against Joseph to increase. A warrant was sworn out by the mobocrats for Joseph's arrest because of the Expositor's

---

30. *Comprehensive History of the Church*, vol. 2, p. 181; cited in PJS p. 364.

31. *History of the Church*, vol. 7, p. 58; cited in PJS, p. 370.

32. Letter of Benjamin F. Johnson to John H. Gibbs, p. 10; cited in PJS, p. 371.

destruction. Joseph knew that if he were ever taken into custody that he would be assassinated. He told a friend, for instance, *"That if I and Hyrum were ever taken again we should be massacred, or I was not a prophet of God."*[33]

And yet he went to Carthage, Illinois to answer the demands of the law. As they were riding towards Carthage the party encountered sixty mounted militiamen on their way to Nauvoo. As he saw them coming Joseph commented, *"I am going like a lamb to the slaughter; But I am calm as a summer's morning; I have a conscience void of offense towards God, and towards all men. I shall die innocent, and it shall yet be said of me—he was murdered in cold blood."*[34]

The sixty militiamen were headed for Nauvoo to disarm the Nauvoo Legion. They prevailed upon Joseph to return to Nauvoo to help them, in exchange for which they would guarantee him protection as he entered the mob-infested area of Carthage. They went back, collected the arms, and started back to Carthage about six in the evening. As the group passed his farm, Joseph turned several times to gaze at it. This raised some comment from his friends, to which he replied, "If you had such a farm, and *knew you would not see it any more* you would want to take a good look at it *for the last time.*"[35]

Mobocrats to Face the Cannon's Mouth from an Unanticipated Source

Joseph and his party arrived in Carthage about midnight on June 24th, 1844. A number of the mobocrats were present and they began yelling and cursing and becoming abusive. Governor Thomas Ford, the governor of Illinois, had come to Carthage and was also housed in the Hamilton House where Joseph was to spend the night. Disturbed by the cries of the mob, he called out the window to quiet them and promised them he would have the Prophet pass through the troops of the Illinois Militia on the square the next morning so they could all see him.

True to his promise, the Governor invited President Smith and his party to pass among the troops early the next day, after which they returned to

33. *History of the Church*, vol. 6, p. 546; cited in PJS, p. 381.
34. *Comprehensive History of the Church*, vol. 2, p. 249; cited in PJS, p. 381.
35. *Comprehensive History of the Church*, vol. 2, p. 250; cited in PJS, p. 381.

Hamilton House. When the troops were dismissed, many of them followed the Prophet into the hotel where they engaged him in heated conversation and questioned the good intentions of the brethren. While talking to them, Joseph made this prophecy:

"I can see what is in your hearts, and will tell you what I see. I can see that you thirst for blood, and nothing but my blood will satisfy you. It is not for crime of any description that I and my brethren are thus continually persecuted and harassed by our enemies, but there are other motives, and some of them I have expressed, so far as relates to myself, and inasmuch as you and the people thirst for blood, *I prophesy, in the name of the Lord, that you shall witness scenes of blood and sorrow to your entire satisfaction. Your souls shall be perfectly satiated with blood, and many of you who are now present shall have an opportunity to face the cannon's mouth from sources you think not of. . . ."*[36]

It was almost three years later when this prophecy saw its fulfillment in the Mexican War. Illinois was asked to furnish four regiments of volunteers, and these men of western Illinois were quick to volunteer. A large number of them were among the 3,720 Illinois recruits who fought in northeastern and central Mexico. On February 22 and 23, 1847, two of the Illinois regiments, along with a regiment from Kentucky, engaged 17,000 of the soldiers in Santa Ana's army in the battle of Buena Vista.

Although outnumbered almost four-to-one, the American soldiers held their own the first day. On the morning of the second day they seemed to gain the advantage on the left flank of the Mexicans, and led a wild charge against the retreating enemy. Suddenly they discovered that they had been led into a trap as they were charged by 12,000 of Santa Ana's regulars. The Americans retreated into a narrow gorge in the Mexican territory where the sides were so steep and covered with loose pebbles that they were hardly able to stand up. The Mexican army surrounded the top of the gorge and saturated the terrain with their gunfire. Suddenly American cannons began to fire from behind the American lines and cleared the Mexican calvary from the north of the gorge. The Mexicans then made a wild bayonet charge down the sides of the gorge, and to escape their attack the Americans had to retreat directly into the cannon fire of their own troops at the mouth of the gorge. Thus many of them died from their own artillery fire, in fulfillment of Joseph's statement to them three years before, that their

---

36. *Comprehensive History of the Church,* vol. 2, pp. 271-72; cited in PJS, p. 384.

"souls shall be perfectly satiated with blood," and that many of them who
were present would have to *"face the cannon's mouth"* from sources they
had not anticipated—their own artillery.

Dan Jones to Live to Fulfill a Mission to Wales

During the night before he was martyred, the Prophet was confined with
his friends in the debtor's apartment of the Carthage jail. Sometime after
midnight, because of a gunshot fired outside near the prison, Joseph left
his bed and stretched out on a mattress between John Fullmer and Dan
Jones. After a brief conversation with them, Joseph turned to Dan Jones
in the darkness and asked, "Are you afraid to die?" He was answered by
a question: "Has the time come, think you? Engaged in such a cause, I
do not think death would have many terrors." Then the Prophet said to
him, *"You will yet see Wales, and fulfill the mission appointed you before
you die."*[37]

The following morning Dan Jones was sent by the Prophet on an errand
to Governor Ford. When he returned to the jail he was refused readmis-
sion by the mobocrats. After trying unsuccessfully to gain access to the
prison his life was threatened by the rabble in the street, and he was forced
to flee for his life to Quincy. Thus he escaped the peril of the mob's attack
on June 27, 1844.

Elder Dan Jones, who had come from Wales just a few years before,
saw the fulfillment of this prophecy just two months later. On August 28,
1844, he left on his mission to Wales in the company of Wilford Woodruff.
During his mission he was asked to preside over the Welsh district. He
filled a second mission to Wales from 1852 to 1856. During his missions
in Wales 2,000 souls entered the waters of baptism. So successful were
these two missions and so beloved was Elder Jones among the converts
in Wales that more than 700 Saints accompanied him when he returned
to America, and they made their homes in the valleys of the Rocky
Mountains.

Williard Richards' Life Would Be Preserved
While Friends Would Fall Around Him

It was about 5:30 p.m. on the night of June 27, 1844, when the mob
with painted faces attacked Carthage jail. At this time Joseph and his brother

37. *History of the Church,* vol. 6, p. 601; cited in PJS, p. 385.

Hyrum, together with Willard Richards and John Taylor, were in the jailer's apartment upstairs. The mob encircled the building. Some of them rushed up the stairs and began firing through the door into the room where the prisoners were located. Others commenced firing through the windows. The four prisoners sprang against the door to hold it closed, but when the first bullet came through they immediately went to the side of the door. Joseph, John Taylor and Dr. Richards were to the left of the door. Hyrum tried to cross in front of the door to join them and was hit in the face by a bullet which came through the door. Three other bullets hit him. Joseph had a six-shooter which he fired through the door, while Elder Taylor tried to parry the guns with a cane. Elder Taylor then tried to jump out the window but was shot in the thigh. He rolled under the bed but was shot once again. One of the bullets fired at John Taylor hit his watch, which prevented the bullet from penetrating his body. Since the watch was in a pocket which covered Elder Taylor's heart, the watch in all probability saved his life. Joseph also attempted to leap from the window, but was hit by two balls in the back, and he fell outside into the mob. But of Willard Richards the History of the Church records:

"Dr. Richard's escape was miraculous; he being a very large man, and in the midst of a shower of balls, yet he stood unscathed, with the exception of a ball which grazed the tip end of the lower part of his left ear. His escape fulfilled literally a prophecy which Joseph made over a year previously, that *the time would come that the balls would fly around him like hail, and he should see his friends fall on the right and on the left, but that there should not be a hole in his garment.*"[38]

And thus the life of God's prophet was ended, with his prophecies being fulfilled by his death and also with the preservation of the lives of those around him.

A Tribute to Joseph: Praise to the Man Who Communed with Jehovah

Many are the tributes spoken in honor of the memory of Joseph Smith, but perhaps the greatest is that composed by the hymn-maker, William W. Phelps:

---

38. *History of the Church*, vol 6., p. 619; cited in PJS, pp. 386-87.

Praise to the man who communed with Jehovah!
Jesus annointed that Prophet and Seer.
Blessed to open the last dispensation,
Kings shall extol him, and nations revere.

Praise to his memory, he died as a martyr;
Honored and blest be his ever great name!
Long shall his blood, which was shed by assassins,
Plead unto heaven while earth lauds his fame.

Great is his glory and endless his priesthood.
Ever and ever the keys he will hold.
Faithful and true, he will enter his kingdom,
Crowned in the midst of the prophets of old.

Sacrifice brings forth the blessings of heaven;
Earth must atone for the blood of that man.
Wake up the world for the conflict of justice.
Millions shall know "brother Joseph" again.

Hail to the Prophet, ascended to heaven!
Traitors and tyrants now fight him in vain.
Mingling with Gods, he can plan for his brethren;
Death cannot conquer the hero again.

Now I've shared with you dozens of prophecies made by Joseph Smith that have seen literal fulfillment. In my research I've documented hundreds of prophecies by him, and about him, which have come to pass. I have no doubts about the divinely inspired mission fulfilled by this great man.

As I began this talk, I quoted Jeremiah's revealed test that "when the word of the prophet shall come to pass, then shall the prophet be known, that the Lord hath truly sent him." Now I invite you to apply that test to Joseph Smith. I have shared just a few of his many fulfilled prophecies. He revealed the hidden thoughts and the travels of his contemporaries. He foretold the identity of his successor the first time they met. He foretold significant events in future wars, on both the national and international scene. He predicted the falling of the stars, the Civil War destruction of Jackson county, the political fall of Martin Van Buren and the election failure of

Stephen A. Douglas. He foresaw the establishment of the Saints as a mighty people in the Rocky Mountains. He prophesied his enemies would face the cannon's mouth during the Mexican War. And he predicted many events connected with his martyrdom. Was he a true prophet of God? The evidence is overwhelming—there can be no doubt.

I bear you my witness that I know that Joseph Smith was truly a prophet of God, and that the Church restored through him is the true Church of Jesus Christ upon the earth today. That Church holds God's authorization to preach and serve in Christ's name. That Church alone can open the door to the highest blessings God has provided for his children upon the earth today.

I pray that you will gain a personal, burning testimony that God restored his Church and gospel through this great prophet, just as I have, in the name of Jesus Christ, amen.

Note:

The Prophecies of Joseph Smith, the author's book from which the above historical incidents are cited, is available from Horizon Publishers & Distributors, Inc., P.O. Box 490, Bountiful, Utah 84010-0490.

The 413-page book is the most comprehensive listing and analysis of Joseph Smith's fulfilled prophecies in print. Four appendices to the book list and summarize the following:

- 184 Scriptural Prophecies about the Restoration Cited in the Book.
- 141 Prophecies Made or Recorded by Joseph Smith Cited in the Book.
- 40 Prophecies Made by Others About Joseph Smith Cited in the Book.
- 52 Other Supernatural Experiences Cited in the Book.

The Prophecies of Joseph Smith also contains fourteen maps which cover in detail the major events in early LDS history until the death of the Prophet, with references correlating the historical events to major LDS historical sources. Numerous other chapters and photographs are also included which make the book a useful study guide to early Latter-day Saint history.

$\mathbf{H}$ello! My name is Duane Crowther. I'm going to discuss a very important subject—the nature of God. My message is important, and I ask you to consider it carefully, and prayerfully, with an open and inquiring mind.

Life Eternal Requires Knowing The Truth About God

How important is it? Our Savior taught that the blessing of eternal life requires that we know the truth *about God,* and that we truly *know him.* On the last day of his mortal life, Jesus Christ said in a prayer to his Father in Heaven, "This is *life eternal, that they might know thee the only true God, and Jesus Christ,* whom thou hast sent." You'll find that in *John, chapter 17, verse 3.*

If your potential to attain eternal life requires a true knowledge of God, then this subject is worth deep, penetrating study, and prayerful consideration which will allow you to receive God's answer to your prayers, bearing witness if you've come to a correct understanding. I testify to you that

He will grant you that witness if you pray sincerely with faith, honest interest, and desire to know the truth.

My Motive For Preparing These Comments

Before I begin, let me briefly tell you about myself by asking and answering a few questions. First, *who am I?* I'm a lay member of The Church of Jesus Christ of Latter-day Saints. I'm not a Church authority, nor an official spokesman for the Church.

Why did I prepare these comments? Because I believe the Lord expects his followers to speak out in defense of truth, and to testify to others concerning knowledge which has been granted to them through their study and through their answers to personal prayer.

Am I qualified to speak on this subject? Very much so. I graduated with high honors with a Masters Degree in Old and New Testament. I have spent over twenty-five years writing on theological subjects, with over thirty-five books and tapes produced and more than a quarter million copies in print. I also spent almost fifteen years fulfilling part- and full-time missionary callings in Guatemala, Panama, Virginia, Idaho and Utah. I spent four years as a Latter-day Saint Seminary teacher, and I've taught religion courses on a college level.

What motivated me to prepare this lecture? Over the years, but particularly during the past decade, opponents of The Church of Jesus Christ of Latter-day Saints have become increasingly vocal in their attacks against the Church. I've been deeply offended as I've observed the vicious falsehoods circulated against my people. I've seen us slandered and fallaciously represented by people calling themselves "born again" Christians, who somehow have the mistaken notion they're doing God's will when they fabricate and spread such falsehoods.

For more than twenty years my personal approach was to turn the other cheek to such misconduct and to overlook it or to bear it quietly. But critics of Mormonism have grown bolder in their attacks, more sophisticated in their spreading of falsehoods through the media, and they are circulating more and more false concepts about who we Mormons are and what we believe. It reached the point that I drew the line and resolved to take a personal stand for what I know to be true, and good, and acceptable to God.

False Logic—the Source of Anti-Mormon
Teachings that Mormons Are Not Christians

One widely circulated falsehood I find to be particularly offensive is the assertation that Latter- day Saints are not Christians. When the name of our Church is literally "The *Church of Jesus Christ* of Latter-day Saints," that allegation is hard to believe, but it now appears in almost every anti-Mormon tract, or article, or film that these critics circulate.

Where do they get such a notion? It comes from a seriously-flawed line of logic these critics have concocted. That so-called logic circulated by these critics goes like this:

1. *We* are Christians.

2. *Our creeds* say that God is only a formless spirit and that there is only *one* God, a trinity composed of three persons.

3. The Mormons don't believe *our creeds*.

4. They say that God has a tangible body, and that God the Father, Jesus Christ, and the Holy Spirit are separate individuals, and that each of them is a God.

5. Therefore, the critics have drawn the conclusion that we Mormons aren't Christians because Mormon doctrine doesn't *conform to the creeds of their critics*.

Now the fallacy to this so-called logic is easy to see—these critics make the assumption that their creeds are a valid statement of Christian beliefs. In reality, *those creeds are in direct opposition to what the Bible teaches*. One needs to compare both Mormon theology and the creeds of other churches with the Bible, and evaluate which is the true doctrine of Christianity.

Your Task—Serve as Judge and Jury
as These Doctrines Are Compared

I'm going to ask you to serve as the judge and jury in a trial. I'm going to review the teachings of those creeds and compare them to what the Bible teaches. And I'm going to ask you to *make a decision and declare a verdict*—to determine in your mind whether those creeds are true statements of Christian belief or whether they are falsehoods which lead away from a true understanding of God.

You're both the judge and jury. But remember, you're also responsible before God to act upon your own decision. If you find, deep in your heart, that those creeds are not true and that truth is found in the Latter-day Saint concept of God, you'll have an obligation to yourself to follow after truth, wherever that may lead you.

The Creeds Reflect an Eight-Step Doctrinal Evolution Concerning the Nature of God

Let's begin by discussing the creedal statements utilized by today's churches. You need to know that they show a definite, eight-step evolution of doctrine concerning the nature of God. I'm going to invite you to do your homework and actually read those creeds we'll discuss. They're available in various encyclopedias and reference books. I found them all compiled in chronological order in a useful book entitled *Creeds of the Churches—A Reader in Christian Doctrine From the Bible to the Present*, published in 1963 by Anchor Books, a division of Doubleday.

What intrigued me about the book was the ease in which its chronological arrangement allows one to trace the formation and evolution of doctrinal concepts. You can easily follow how an idea was introduced in one situation, then developed and amplified in later statements. Concepts which weren't even mentioned in early creeds became foundations of later creedal statements as the evolutionary process unfolded.

Step One. The book traces creedal statements of early apostolic fathers like Ignatius of Antioch, Justin Martyr, Iranaeus, Tertullian, Hippolytus, Marcellus, Rufinus, and others, all of which made clear references to *three distinct members of the Godhead: God the Father, Jesus Christ his Son, and the Holy Ghost, and regarded them as separate, distinct beings.*

Step two. The book then examines changes which began to creep in at the *Council of Nicaea*, in 325 A.D. On page 28, the book describes what happened there: "Nicaea is sufficiently different from anything that had gone before to represent *a new epoch in creed-making.* The occasion was the dispute concerning the theology of Arius, which raised in acute form the question of the real meaning and significance of Jesus Christ. The Christian community had been accustomed to regard his as God as well as man. *Arian theology forced the Christian Church to say in what sense he was God."*

The book focused on a new concept introduced at that council—a line from the creed it formulated said that Jesus Christ was *"of the same essence as the Father,"* and the book explained how for fifty years after the council the Church debated the meaning of that line. It told how various other phrases were proposed in its place when the *Second Creed of Antioch* was being formulated sixteen years later, in 341 A.D., and in other meetings which followed thereafter. Phrases were suggested to replace the "same essence" concept because many of the early church leaders recognized that it was misleading and dangerous—phrases such as, *"Like the Father who begot Him according to the scriptures,"* and *"Like the Father in all things,"* and *"Of like essence with the Father,"* and *"Exact image of the Godhead."* (pp. 29-34) But after 50 years, the creed adopted at Constantinople in 381 A.D. retained the phrase which said that Jesus was *"of the same essence as the Father,"* and the doctrinal evolution concerning the nature of God began in earnest.

Step three. By 553 A.D., at the *Second Council of Constantinople,* the idea that the Father and the Son were of the same essence had evolved to the point that the Father and the Son and the Holy Ghost were losing their separate identities, and *being referred to as constituting the same person.* That creed said, "If anyone does not confess that the Father and the Son and the Holy Spirit are one nature or essence, one power or authority, *worshipped as a trinity of the same essence, one deity in three hypostases or persons,* let him be anathema." (p. 46)

Step four. By 1215 A.D., when the *Fourth Lateran Council* was held, the idea that the three members of the Godhead were one and the same person had evolved still further. This council set forth the belief which became the doctrine of medieval Catholicism. It said, "We firmly believe and openly confess that *there is only one true God, eternal, beyond measure* and unchangeable, *incomprehensible,* omnipotent and ineffable, the Father, the Son, and the Holy Spirit: *Three persons but a single essence, substance, or nature that is wholly one; . . . "* (p. 57)

Step five. The *Protestant Reformation* came, and began a whole new era of creed-making. The *Augsburg Confession* was written in 1530 by Philip Melanchthon, and stated *fundamental Lutheran doctrines which went another step further* in the evolutionary process. In this creed, the three members of the Godhead were not just called "one essence," but the new concept was added that they were also to be *"without division."* The creed began explaining away the belief that they were somehow separate persons. (pp. 67-68)

Step six. Then came still other creeds, which evolved the concept of God even further. The "Reformed" churches that had their source in the work of Zwingli and Calvin produced the *Westminster Confession of Faith in*

1646. In this creed, they not only *took away God's body, but they made him a spirit,* and they also *took away his visibility and body parts and feelings and locality,* stretching him throughout space. This creed said, "There is but one only living and true God, who is infinite in being and perfection, a most pure spirit, *invisible, without body, parts, or passions,* immutable, *immense,* eternal, *incomprehensible, . . . "* (p. 197)

Step seven. The Reformation spread to England, and they repeated the same theme in the *Thirty-Nine Articles of Religion* formulated seventeen years later, in 1563. Their creed said, "There is but one living and true God, everlasting, *without body, parts, or passions;* of infinite power, wisdom, and goodness; the Maker, and Preserver of all things both visible and invisible. And in unity of this Godhead *there be three Persons, of one substance,* power, and eternity: the Father, the Son, and the Holy Ghost." (pp. 266-267)

Two centuries later, John Wesley found himself caught between two factions: Classic Protestantism, and the Liberal Protestantism of his day. His followers adopted The *Twenty-Five Articles of Religion* at a Methodist conference held in Baltimore in 1784. Their creed taught that "There is *but one living and true God,* everlasting, *without body or parts,* of infinite power, wisdom, and goodness; the Maker and Preserver of all things, visible and invisible. And in *unity of this Godhead there are three persons, of one substance,* power, and eternity—the Father, the Son, and the Holy Ghost." (p. 354)

And finally, *Step eight.* the *depersonification of God continued* even further as the Reformation spread to America. The Baptists drew up *The New Hampshire Confession* in 1833, and reduced the members of the Godhead down even farther, from "Persons" to what they called *"relative distinctions."* Their creed said, "There is *one, and only one,* living and true God, whose name is *JEHOVAH,* the Maker and Supreme Ruler of heaven and earth; inexpressibly glorious in holiness; worthy of all possible honor, confidence, and love; *revealed under the personal and relative distinctions of the Father, the Son, and the Holy Spirit;* equal in divine perfection, . . . " (p. 335)

Now this has been a very brief explanation of a very complex process which stretched over fifteen centuries. But my point is this: the doctrine of the nature of God *evolved* in these creeds. Before it began the Father, Son and Holy Ghost were *three separate beings,* with their own individual forms, identities, and personalities. *As the creeds evolved they were first rationalized into being only one person; then they lost their body parts and passions and were represented as being only spirits; then they were stretched throughout space and became immense, shapeless blobs who weren't even persons, but only relative distinctions.*

As we compare the teachings that evolved in these creeds with the Bible, you be the judge. Decide for yourself if those creeds are profound statements of truth, or *a conglomeration of confusion and contradictions which lead people away from God.*

Many Protestants and Catholics Don't Understand or Fully Accept Their Church's Creeds

Now the next item I'll ask you to consider is the premise that many Protestants and Catholics don't believe in the creeds of their own churches. Many more, though they profess belief, readily admit they can't reconcile the contradictions expressed in their creeds.

I have no way of evaluating the extent of belief or disbelief which exists among the Protestant and Catholic congregations today, but every sign I see tells me that *there is major doctrinal discontent.* Sometimes it's kept below the surface to keep peace in the churches, but its very clearly there. How do I know? I spent several years as a guide on Temple Square, in Salt Lake City, where each week I'd explain a series of exhibits portraying Mormon beliefs. After the tours, there was time to talk with the visitors on a one-to-one basis. I've had literally thousands express their unsolicited but quite vocal discontent with their church's creeds and teachings about the nature of God. They can't understand their own creeds, and when they would see the Mormon doctrine of God laid out in its simplicity *they frequently said that the Mormon teachings were what they truly believed,* rather than the teachings of their own churches.

But you non-Mormons go to Protestant Sunday Schools and Bible Study groups. Answer for yourself—what do you see in your churches? *Do your church members continually struggle, as they read their Bibles, with the creeds' contradictions that the Father and the Son and the Holy Spirit are the same person, and all three of them are gods but there is only one God, and that God isn't in any particular place but fills the immensity of space?*

One thing is evident in the writings of Protestant scholars. Time after time in their explanations, they observe that their churches' creeds just don't make sense, even to themselves.

Let me share a few examples from their writings showing their frustrations with their creeds. J. I. Packer, in his 1983 book *The Apostles' Creed,* published by Tyndale House, said on pages 19 and 20, "The three persons together constitute one God. Here we face *the most dizzying and unfathomable truth* of all, the truth of the Trinity, . . . What should we make of it? In itself, *the divine tri-unity is a mystery, a transcendant fact which passes our understanding. . . .*How the *one eternal God is eternally both singular and plural,* how *Father, Son and Spirit are personally distinct yet essentially one* (so that *tritheism,* belief in three gods who are not one, and Unitarianism, belief in one God who is not three, are both wrong), is more than we can know, and *any attempt to 'explain' it—to dispell the mystery by reasoning,* as distinct from confessing it from Scripture—is *bound to falsify it.* Here, as elsewhere, our God is too big for his creatures' little minds."

Another example: Paul E. Little, in his book *Know What You Believe,* a 1970 volume from Victor books, says on pages 34 and 35, "At the heart of the Christian view of God is the concept of the Trinity. Rather than being *'excess baggage,'* as former Episcopal Bishop James A. Pike called it, this truth is central to an understanding of biblical revelation and the Christian Gospel. *Departure from the doctrine of the Trinity has been and is one of the major sources of heresy in the Christian Church. The Trinity is a difficult concept,* not fully susceptible to human explanation, because *it involves categories which our finite mental powers cannot grasp.*"

Charles C. Ryrie, in his book *A Survey of Bible Doctrine,* published by Moody Press in 1972, commented several times on the difficulties of understanding and accepting the Protestant doctrine of the Trinity. Let me briefly cite a few of his comments drawn from pages 30 through 33: "You have probably heard lessons on the Trinity in which you were taught only the results: that the one God exists in three Persons. Then *you asked for illustrations and got none that were satisfying.* Can the Trinity be illustrated? *Not perfectly, nor probably very well,* because most illustrations cannot include the idea that the three fully possess all the qualities of the one equally and without separation. . . .*It is no wonder that a difficult doctrine like this has been the focal point of many errors throughout church history.*"

Walter Martin is another Protestant who publicly admits that the three-in-one concept of God just doesn't add up. He says, on page 75 of his book *The Maze of Mormonism,* published by Vision House Publishers, "There can be no doubt that the New Testament sets forth the thesis that there are three separate Persons in the Deity, known as the Father, the Son, and the Holy Spirit, and each of these is affirmed to be Eternal God (2 Pet. 1:17; John 1:1; Acts 5:3,4). At the same time, the New Testament declares that there is only one God. (1 Timothy 2:5) *We are led inexorably to the conclusion that the three distinct Persons are the one God, though the finite mind of man may not be able to grasp the depth of this revelation of the divine character."*

Another example: *The Utah Evangel,* a Protestant newspaper, said on page 4 of its May-June 1986 issue, "To a Christian, the term 'deity of Christ' means that Jesus is God (John 1:1, Philip 2:6, Heb. 1:8). The Godhead consists of three Persons—the Father, the Son, and the Holy Ghost. While none of these Persons is to be confused with another (for example the Father is *not* the Son) they are all equally God—not three gods, but one God. Jesus is the same God as the Father is, and is just as much God as the Father is. *This is admittedly impossible to understand . . . "*

One other example ought to be enough to firmly establish that *though modern Christian churches give lip service to their creeds, their members don't necessarily understand them, nor accept them fully.* Richard J. Coleman, in his book *Issues of Theological Conflict—Evangelicals and Liberals,* published in 1972 by Eerdmans, presents on pages 59 and 60 an interesting dialogue he has concocted representing the differences between evangelical and liberal factions of modern Protestantism in their views of the nature of God:

"Liberal: I might be able to agree with you if we were talking about a living person, someone I can talk with and see, but we're talking about the historical person Jesus who lived nearly two thousand years ago."

"Evangelical: Don't you believe in the Resurrection?"

"Liberal: Yes, but I don't see how that makes any difference. I believe that Jesus appeared to the disciples and others after his crucifixion *in some form of a 'spiritual body,'* but then his appearances ended except for an occasional appearance to a saint in a vision."

"Evangelical: So you don't believe that *Christ is still present with us as a living Spirit?"*

"Liberal: He may be present, but not in such a way that I can enter into a personal relationship with him."

"Evangelical: But you don't understand. My relationship with Jesus is not as if I enter communion with a *formless spirit floating around some*

place. The Spirit of Jesus has a personality, a character, even an individuality, which we know from the New Testament."

His dialogue continues, but that is enough to demonstrate that *distinctly different views on the nature of God and Christ exist within modern Christianity,* and that present-day Christians are *by no means united in acceptance of their churches' creeds on the nature of God and the Trinity.*

My Challenge: The Creeds of Christianity Are in Error Concerning the Nature of God

Why is there continuing, wide-spread dissension, misunderstanding and frustration with the Protestant and Catholic doctrine concerning the nature of God?

Let me suggest this reason: *I believe those creeds are in error. They contradict themselves. They embrace false principles.* I believe that ancient theologians, during the time of the Great Apostasy so often predicted in the New Testament, labored without the guidance of the Holy Ghost and hammered out *man-made explanations of the nature of God which are riddled with errors* and which have *drawn false conclusions.*

I believe that modern Protestantism and Catholicism have an immense millstone hanging around their necks— a millstone of false doctrine concerning the nature of God. I believe the formulators of those erroneous creeds reasoned wrong when they decided that God the Father, and God the Son, and God the Holy Ghost were the same person. I believe they reasoned wrong when they decided that God the Father and God the Son are only spirits, without glorified bodies.

And I believe they reasoned wrong when *they counted and said that one, plus one, plus one, equals only one.* I believe that the answer to "How many Gods are God the Father, plus God the Son, plus God the Holy Ghost, is *three,* not one. I believe they coined the word *"trinity"—a word not even found in the Bible,* and made it the heart of their doctrine.

I believe those who promulgate these incorrect creeds have chosen to intentionally overlook and reject broad patterns of Biblical scripture and doctrine because those Bible teachings don't harmonize with the erroneous notions they've embraced.

Let me give you some examples of Biblical truths which they've bypassed because those truths don't harmonize with their man-made creeds. You're the judge and jury—you must discern where is truth: in the creeds of main-

stream Christianity, or in the Bible verses I'll point out to you which contradict those creeds.

Issue Number One: Mainline Christianity Has Rejected the Literal Resurrection of Jesus Christ

That dialogue I quoted earlier between Evangelicals and Liberals used
phrases which characterize the typical Protestant understanding of the
resurrection—that Jesus appeared after his crucifixion in some form of a
"spirit body," and that he's now a "formless spirit floating around someplace." But that's not what the Bible teaches. Let's review the key scriptures together.

First of all, we know that Jesus, through his mother Mary, received a
mortal body of flesh and bones, and that body became united with his eternal
Spirit at birth. *That's what birth is: the clothing of a spirit with a physical
body of flesh and bones.*

He lived through his ministry, and culminated his great mission with
death on the cross, when he gave his life for the salvation of mankind.
Luke 23:46 tells us that his last words on the cross were, "Father, into
thy hands *I commend my spirit,"* and that having said this, *"he gave up
the ghost." Matthew 27:50, Mark 15:37,* and *John 19:30* all repeat the teaching that at death, his body "gave up the ghost." That means his spirit left
his body. *That's what death is—the separation of the spirit from the body.*

We know from each of the four gospels that Christ's body was taken and
placed in a tomb owned by Joseph of Arimathaea. But what did he do as
a spirit while his body was in the tomb? *Luke 23:43* records his promise
to the thief on the cross that "To day shalt thou be with me in paradise."
1st Peter 3:18 and 19 tells us that his spirit was alive and functioning while
his body lay in the tomb. It says, "Christ also hath once suffered for sins,
the just for the unjust, that he might bring us to God, *being put to death
in the flesh, but quickened by the Spirit: by which also he went and preached
unto the spirits in prison."*

Then, after fulfilling his mission among the spirits of those who had
previously died, we learn the next part of the glorious story from the 24th
chapter of Luke. The women came to the tomb, and "found not the body
of Jesus." Instead they saw two angels. *Luke 24:5 through 7* tells us their
message: "Why seek ye the living among the dead? He is not here, but
is risen: remember how he spake unto you when he was yet in Galilee,

Saying, The Son of man must be delivered into the hands of sinful men, and be crucified, and the third day rise again."

Now what is the resurrection process? The spirit of an individual returns to its own body. *Resurrection is the reunion of body and spirit.* Did Jesus take up his own body of flesh and bones? Of course he did. One of the most central themes of Christianity is that he rose again—his same body came forth out of the tomb. It wasn't some other body, or someone else's body—it was the body of Jesus Christ, and it was the tangible body of flesh and bones which had been laid there three days before.

John chapter 20 tells the next part of the story. Early in the morning of that first Easter Jesus appeared to Mary Magdalene near the site of the tomb where his body had been buried. It appears that Mary reached out to him, but Jesus told her, "Touch me not; for *I am not yet ascended to my Father:* but go to my brethren, and say unto them, *I ascend unto my Father, and your Father; and to my God, and your God." (John 20:17)*

But did Jesus have a tangible body that literally could be touched, even though he didn't let Mary touch him at that moment? Luke makes it overwhelmingly clear that his resurrected body was touchable, and tangible, and still a body of flesh and bones. *Luke 24:36 through 43* tells us what happened in a room in Jerusalem that very evening, when ten of his disciples were gathered. "As they thus spake, Jesus himself stood in the midst of them, and saith unto them, Peace be unto you. But they were terrified and affrighted, and supposed that they had seen a spirit. And he said unto them, Why are ye troubled? and why do thoughts arise in your hearts? *Behold my hands and my feet, that it is I myself: handle me, and see; for a spirit hath not flesh and bones, as ye see me have.* And when he had thus spoken, *he shewed them his hands and his feet.* And while they yet believed not for joy, and wondered, he said unto them, Have ye here any meat? And they gave him a piece of a broiled fish, and of an honeycomb. And he took it, and *did eat before them."*

Now let me emphasize several points about this passage. First of all, it's clear that Jesus's resurrected body was his same body. There's no doubt about that. *John 20:24 through 29* tells us how the Savior appeared a week later in the same room to the same men, but this time Thomas was with them—the same Thomas who said, in *John 20:25,* "Except I shall see in his hands the print of the nails, and put my finger into the print of the nails, and thrust my hand into his side, I will not believe." And Jesus told

Thomas, in *John 20:27, "Reach hither thy finger, and behold my hands; and reach hither thy hand, and thrust it into my side: and be not faithless, but believing."*

Now did Jesus have his own body? Of course he did. The wounds in his hands and in his side from his crucifixion were still in it. There's no way that this was some formless spiritual blob.

And here's another point that must be emphasized: was Jesus trying to clearly teach them concerning the nature of a resurrected body—that it still has a head and hands and sides and all its bodily parts, and that a resurrected being can eat and digest? Or was he deceiving them? Is it possible that he was leading them astray, showing them his body and teaching them that's what a resurrected body is like, when a resurrected body really is a formless blob? *No,* he wasn't deceiving them! It's the creed-makers who think that a resurrected body is a formless blob that are deceived, and who are deceiving others.

And what about that important passage in *Matthew 27:52 and 53,* that tells about others who were resurrected after Jesus was raised from the dead? Were those people shapeless blobs floating around the city and filling the immensity of space, or were they literal bodies, with arms and legs and feet and hands, and body parts and passions? The scripture says, "The graves were opened; and *many bodies of the saints which slept arose,* And came out of the graves after his resurrection, and went into the holy city, and appeared unto many." I don't find anything there that says that a resurrected being is only a spirit, or is only a shapeless blob that floats around and fills the immensity of space, do you?

Now let me ask an essential question: could Jesus take up his body from the grave, and then shed it later? That is what some mainline believers seem to teach. Does that make sense, and is it scriptural?

It doesn't make a bit of sense, and it runs directly counter to the Bible. Look at *Romans 6:9* with me. What does it say? *"Christ being raised from the dead dieth no more;* death hath no more dominion over him." Now what is death, once again? It's the separation of the body from the spirit. This passage in Romans is telling us that when Christ's spirit went back into his body, it was there to stay. For how long? Forever—death hath *no more* dominion over him.

Do other passages say the same thing? *Revelation 1:18* records his testimony that "I am he that liveth, and was dead; and behold, *I am alive for evermore."* Now did Jesus really mean that, or was he deceiving the apostle John? He meant it! It's true! It's Bible doctrine. Jesus has a resurrected body of flesh and bones and spirit today.

Luke 20:36 also teaches about those who have been resurrected. It says, *"Neither can they die any more: for they are equal unto the angels; and are the children of God, being the children of the resurrection."*

But let's learn from the Bible that a resurrected body has a lot of powers that a mortal body doesn't have. It has the power to pass through walls or doors, and to suddenly appear in a closed room. That's what Jesus's resurrected body did, according to *John 20:19 and 26,* when he appeared to his apostles and told them to handle him and see that he had a tangible body.

And a resurrected body has the power to suddenly vanish from out of the sight of people talking to him face to face. That's what *Luke 24:31* tells us Jesus did after he walked with the two disciples on the road to Emmaus.

A resurrected body has the power to travel rapidly through space, and go up into heaven, and ascend unto God the Father. That's what *Luke 24:50 and 51,* and *Mark 16:19,* and *John 20:17* tell us.

Jesus has a resurrected body that is "glorious," according to *Philippians 3:21,* far more advanced than a mortal body. Paul called the mortal body only a "vile body" when compared to the "glorious body" of the resurrected Lord.

And we know that Christ's body will still be like ours when he comes in glory. *1st John 3:2* tells us, "Beloved, now are we the sons of God, and it doth not yet appear what we shall be: but we know that, *when he shall appear, we shall be like him;* for we shall see him as he is." That certainly doesn't sound like he'll return in his second coming as a formless blob, does it?

Now let's go on with the account of his resurrection and ascension. After he had been with his disciples for forty days following his resurrection, Jesus went out with his disciples onto the Mount of Olives, on the way to Bethany. *Acts 1, verses 9 through 11* tells what happened as he ascended into heaven. "When he had spoken these things, *while they beheld, he was taken up; and a cloud received him out of their sight.* And while they looked steadfastly toward heaven as he went up, behold, two men stood by them in white apparel; which also said, Ye men of Galilee, why stand ye gazing up into heaven? this same Jesus, which is taken up from you into heaven, *shall so come in like manner as ye have seen him go into heaven."*

Now, did Jesus lay his body down on a rockpile and ascend into heaven as only a spirit? My Bible doesn't say that and neither does yours. His glorified, resurrected body that will never die, and will never have his spirit separated from it, went up into heaven while his disciples stood and watched in awe. And what was the promise of the angels who appeared to them? That Jesus will some day come in the same way as they saw him go into heaven. Will he have his body? If his spirit is never to leave his body again, as the Bible clearly teaches, then he'll have his body when he comes, and he has a glorified body of flesh and bones and spirit in the heavens today.

The prophet Zechariah proclaimed that in the last days Jesus will appear on the Mount of Olives, and *Zechariah 13, verse 6* says that at that day, "One shall say unto him, *What are these wounds in thine hands?* Then he shall answer, *Those with which I was wounded in the house of my friends.*" So, will Jesus still have his same body at that future day? The Bible says so.

Now *you* are the judge and jury. *Does* the Bible teach that Jesus Christ has a tangible, resurrected body of flesh and bones and spirit in the heavens today? I've presented the evidence. The case is yours to decide.

Issue Number Two: Christian Theologians Have Adopted an Unscriptural and Erroneous Definition of What a Spirit Is

These people teach that God is only a spirit, and they have made up an unscriptural definition which assumes a spirit is a formless blob that fills the immensity of space, rather than being in the shape and form of a human being. I challenge them to validify their definition of what a spirit looks like from the Bible. They can't do it, because their definition is incorrect!

Let me tell you what the Bible says about a spirit. Do you think Christ's apostles knew what a spirit looks like? If anyone knew, they would be the most likely candidates, don't you think? The Bible tells us their understanding of the matter. We've already read one of the key passages on the subject. It's *Luke 24:36 through 39.* Here's what it says, once again: "As they thus spake, Jesus himself stood in the midst of them, and saith unto them, Peace be unto you. But they were terrified and affrighted, and *supposed that they had seen a spirit.*" Now they were seeing the resurrected Lord standing in front of them in bodily form, and yet they thought that he was only a spirit.

What does that teach us about what a spirit looks like? The answer is obvious—*they knew a spirit looks just like a person does. They could not distinguish between a spirit being and a person with a tangible body.*

Jesus had to have them handle him, so they could understand that he wasn't only a spirit.

There's a similar example in *Mark 6:49.* You remember the incident where the Lord walked on the water as he came to join his disciples in a ship on the Sea of Galilee. The account says that "When they saw him walking upon the sea, *they supposed it had been a spirit,* and cried out." Now they saw a form in the shape of a man, and they saw it walking, which means they observed that it had legs, and the apostles thought it was a spirit. What does this tell us about the size and shape and appearance of a spirit being? It means that a *spirit looks like a human being.*

The other Bible passages on the subject all indicate that spirit beings have the same attributes and shape which characterize man. *1st Kings 22:21* records that "There came forth a spirit, and *stood* before the Lord," and the same passage says that the spirit talked with the Lord. *2nd Chronicles 18:20* says the same thing. In *Job 4:15 through 17* Job tells how a spirit passed before him and talked to him. Now spirits don't stand without having legs, and they don't talk without have a speech apparatus. *Mark 9:25* tells how Jesus rebuked and cast out a spirit that was deaf and dumb, which again indicates that a spirit being has hearing and speaking apparatus just like a human being.

But more important, it becomes obvious from a host of Biblical passages on the subject that every person has a spirit. Or better put, every person *is* a spirit, with a body of flesh and bones fitting over the spirit like a glove. *James 2:26* says that a body without a spirit is dead, so we learn that every living individual has a spirit. *Job 32:8* says *"there is a spirit in man:* and the inspiration of the Almighty giveth them understanding."

In *Numbers 27:16* Moses taught us that the Lord is "the God of *the spirits of all flesh." 1st Corinthians 2:11* asks, "What man knoweth the things of a man, save the *spirit of man* which is in him?" And *1st Corinthians 6:20* tells the church to "glorify God in your body, and *in your spirit,* which are God's." *1st Corinthians 7:34* says that a women cares for the things of the Lord so "that she may be holy *both in body and in spirit."* And *Philippians 3:3* says, "We are the circumcision, which *worship God in the spirit,* and rejoice in Christ Jesus...."

Now what am I leading up to? There are two points which the scriptures make abundantly clear. First *a spirit has a bodily form.* There is no evidence from the Bible, at all, that a spirit is a big, shapeless blob which fills the immensity of space. That concept has no scriptural foundation what-soever. It's false!

Second, *every individual on earth is possessor of both a spirit body and a physical body.* Man is a spirit, but that in no way implies that he does not have a tangible body. *God is a spirit too, but that in no way implies that he does not have a tangible body either.*

Again, you are the judge and jury. Are spirits formless entities floating around in space, or are they individuals in the shape and form of human beings? You've heard the scriptural evidence. The case is yours to decide.

Issue Number Three: Passages Which Teach That God Is a Spirit Are Misinterpreted to Imply He Doesn't Also Have a Tangible Body

Let's take another look at that frequently quoted and more frequently misinterpreted scripture in *John 4:24* which talks about God being a spirit. It says, *"God is a Spirit:* and they that worship him must *worship him in spirit* and in truth."* I'm sure we all agree that mortal man is supposed to worship God, and this passage, like *Philippians 3:3,* tells us that it is man's spirit that worships God. But man still has a physical body, even though he has a spirit; and there's absolutely nothing in this passage which indi-cates that God does not have a body either. That belief is sheer assump-tion and sloppy interpretation on the part of those who frequently abuse the passage.

I challenge those who delight in using this verse to prove, in any way from the Bible, that it means that God doesn't have a tangible body. They can't do it! And I challenge them to prove from the Bible that there is any validity for their assumption that something which is spiritual cannot also be tangible. They can't do that either, because that assumption also is a falsehood.

Paul taught in *1st Corinthians 6:17* that "He that is joined unto the Lord *is one spirit."* We are spirits in the same sense John had in mind when he said that "God is a spirit."

Paul also teaches us concerning the resurrection, and shows those who attempt to contrast physical bodies with spirit don't understand the term "spirit." We've already examined in depth the broad pattern of Biblical pas-sages that show Jesus Christ has a tangible body—a glorious resurrected body of flesh and bones which are joined with his spirit for all eternity. *1st Corinthians 15:44 through 47* tells us that Christ's tangible body of flesh and bones is a spiritual body. It says, "It is sown a natural body; it is raised *a spiritual body. There is a natural body, and there is a spiritual body.* And so it is written, the first man Adam was made a living soul; the last Adam was made a quickening spirit. Howbeit that was not first which is spiritual, but that which is natural; and afterward that which is spiritual. The first man is of the earth, earthy: *the second man is the Lord from heaven.*"

What does that mean? It means that Jesus Christ, the last Adam that passage is talking about, *has a resurrected body that is spiritual, and its that same body that Thomas touched*—the same body that ate broiled fish and honeycomb in front of the disciples.

There's no doctrinal conflict here at all. There's just the realization that those who have interpreted the term "spirit" to mean "without form or shape or tangible nature" have made a *wrong* definition of the term, and fouled up a whole lot of theology for their churches in the process.

Again, you are the judge and jury. Is there strong scriptural evidence a spirit can have a tangible body? The issue is yours to decide.

Issue Number Four: God the Father Also Has a Tangible Body

As I read Protestant and Catholic explanations of their creeds, I'm amazed at how *they consistently avoid key Bible passages,* particularly those that show God the Father also has a tangible, glorified body like his firstborn son, Jesus.

Let me point out, as I begin to discuss this subject, that his having a body is the logical conclusion one would draw even before studying the matter, isn't it? *If a son has a body, it's natural to assume that his father also has one.* We all know the truth of the proverb, "Like father, like son."

So let's discuss what the Bible tells us about God the Father. Are the creeds correct in their assertion that He is a nebulous blob, without shape or form? Is He really so large He fills the immensity of space? Is He really without body parts and passions, as the creeds announced? I want to tell your very clearly, that's not what I believe, and most certainly that's not what the Bible teaches about Him.

The Genesis account of the creation of man gives us the first clue concerning what kind of being He is. That account tells us that *more than one God was involved in the creation of this earth,* and makes it clear that mankind is patterned after the physical appearance, and image, and likeness, of those divine Beings.

Genesis chapter 1, verses 26 and 27, is the reference I've turned to. Notice that the first of these two verses records a conversation, with one individual speaking to another. We'll discover from other passages that the two participants in the conversation are God the Father and His Son, Jesus Christ. Now *if those two were actually the same person, then one wouldn't speak to the other,* would he? So those who assert that the Father and the Son are all one person—only one God and being—are teaching directly counter to the Bible, aren't they?

Anyway, the passage states, "God said, Let *us* make man in *our image, after our likeness. . . ."* Notice two things, now. First, the statement clearly indicates that more than one being is involved in the conversation—it uses the words "us" and "our." Very clearly the passage is recording the presence and involvement of more than one God in the creation process.

The second important item in the passage is that one God declared to another God that man was to look like, and be like, them—man was to be created in their "image," and in their "likeness." Now what, exactly, did that mean? Let's review our understanding of what kinds of beings the Father and the Son were at that time, as we'll soon establish from the Bible. Latter- day Saints believe that God the Father at that time had already attained a glorified, eternal body—a physical body, with arms and legs and hands and feet, and that physical body housed his spirit body, which has the same appearance. He was and is a tangible, physical being, with his physical body and his spirit body eternally united, just as Jesus Christ's body and spirit were eternally united through His resurrection.

But at that time, Jesus had not yet been born on the earth. He was still a spirit being and had not yet entered mortality, nor received his glorious resurrected body. But *his spirit body had the same appearance as his physical body would have,* so God was able to say, "Let us make man in our image, after our likeness." And the next verse verifies that what God said was brought to pass. It ways, *"God created man in his own image, in the image of God created he him."*

Now I don't believe there are many Bible verses for which so many attempts to explain away their meaning have been made, as have been made for these two verses. For centuries Bible scholars have tried to perform the impossible task of reconciling the clear meaning of those verses to the confused, erroneous, and completely different teachings of the creeds of Christiandom. They've twisted, and turned, and squirmed, and hedged, but they still haven't been able to hide the three central messages of the passage: first, that *more than one God participated* in the creation of this earth and its inhabitants; second, that *they are separate, distinct beings* who spoke of themselves with the pronoun "us" and "our"; and third, that *the spiritual and physical bodies of man are in exactly the same form and image of those Divine Beings!*

Now some have weaseled on the meaning of the words "image" and "likeness," trying to make them appear allegorical and mythical, or as they say, "spiritualized." But the Bible just won't let them do it, because it uses those same words several other times in the early chapters of Genesis to show that those terms meant tangible, physical, touchable, in- only-one-place-at-one-time, human-shaped people.

Genesis chapter 5, verses 1 through 3, says, "In the day that God created man, in the likeness of God made he him; Male and female created he them, and blessed them, and called their name Adam, in the day when they were created. And Adam lived an hundred and thirty years, and *begat a son in his own likeness, after his image;* and called his name Seth."

Let's focus on several key insights in this passage too. First, notice that *Seth is in the likeness and image of Adam in the same way Adam and Eve were in the likeness and image of God.* Now was Seth a formless, shapeless blob without body parts and passions, or was he a tangible person with arms and legs and all the body parts that characterize human form? And could Seth be seen and touched, or was he invisible and untouchable? The answer is obvious, and that same clarity which shows that God the Father and Jesus look like man just as clearly refutes the false concept that God is a formless blob floating around in the immensity of space.

A second insight: note now that more than one God was present as man's physical form was created, but that only one of them performed the creation process. And there are several passages which indicate that the God which created man was Jesus Christ. (See, for instance, *Colossians 1:15-16; Ephesians 3:9; Hebrews 1:2;* and *Revelation 14:6-7)* These passages show that Jesus actually was the creator, acting under the direction of God the Father. And numerous passages show that Jesus Christ was assigned by His Father to be the God of this earth: its creator, its redeemer, its savior, its ruler, and its king.

But let's not stray from the concept that *man is made in the actual, physical image of God.* That principle was reiterated by God once again in the days of Noah. God gave Noah commandments, and one of them concerned murder and the preservation of human life. *Genesis 9, verse 6,* uses the word "image" again, and in the very tangible, physical sense. The passage says, "Whoso sheddeth man's blood, by man shall his blood be shed: for *in the image of God made he man.*" In other words, don't destroy man's body, because it is made in the image of God's body. There's just no way that these passages concerning God creating man in his image can mean anything else than actual, tangible, touchable, physical form.

There are some who, in spite of these very explicit passages, assert that man is made only in what they have called the "spiritual image of God." That's a fancy theory, but it's completely without Biblical backing. It's a doctrinal "cop out"—a theory which can't be substantiated from the scriptures. And it's a philosophical theory which is completely refuted by the Bible.

For instance, *James 3:8 and 9,* clearly links man's being in the likeness of God to man's temporal body. The passage is talking about the troubles caused by man's unruly speech. It says, "The tongue can no man tame; it is an unruly evil, full of deadly poison. Therewith bless we God, even the Father; and therewith curse we *men, which are made after the similitude of God.*" Here in the same sentence James links man's physical body, including its unruly tongue, with man's being made in the similitude or likeness of God. Does that passage sound like we are only in God's spiritual image? It's obvious James is talking about physical characteristics.

Now let's look at another passage that provides us a host of very clear insights about the nature of both God the Father and his Son, Jesus Christ. That passage is *Hebrews 1, verses 1 through 3.*

"God, who at sundry times and in divers manners spake in time past unto the fathers by the prophets, Hath in these last days spoken unto us by his Son, *whom he hath appointed heir* of all things, *by whom also he made the worlds;* Who being the brightness of his glory, and the *express image of his person,* and upholding all things by the word of his power, when he had *by himself* purged our sins, *sat down on the right hand of the Majesty on high.*"

Isn't that a powerful passage? and one loaded with information! Let's analyze its teachings. First, it makes it very clear that God the Father and Jesus Christ are two separate, distinct beings. They are not the same person. They are not the same God. It says God the Father spoke to us "by his Son," not by himself directly. It says God the Father "appointed" his Son "heir of all things." If the Father and the Son were the same person, that wouldn't make sense. God wouldn't appoint himself the heir of anything because he already possessed all things: all power, all knowledge, and vast creations. And the passage clearly asserts that Jesus Christ is the *Son* of God the Father, as well as being his heir.

Now I don't believe the Bible is deceiving us when it tells us, in dozens of places, that Jesus was the actual Son of God. And no being is a son of himself. *To say that the Father and the Son are actually the same person is in direct contradiction to the scriptures, as well to as reason.* And the passage goes on to say that God made the worlds through his Son. If they were the same person that phrase, and that relationship, just would not make sense. But if we recognize that the Father and the Son are two separate persons, both of them Gods so they are two separate Gods, then the passage is easily understood: the Father directed the creation process, but His Son Jesus actually did the work of creation.

And the passage tells us even more: it describes the physical relationship of the Father and Son. It says Jesus is "the express image" of his Father's "person," and that after he had died for our sins he went back up to heaven and "sat down on the right hand of the Majesty on high." *If the resurrected, glorified body of Jesus is the express image of his Father's person, does that indicate God the Father is a shapeless blob, or that he has a tangible body just like Jesus Christ?* The answer is inescapable—he has a tangible body. And could Jesus sit down to the right of God the Father if God the Father was shapeless and everywhere at one time? Again, that's impossible. And by the same token, could Jesus sit to the right of the Father if the two were actually the same person? *Can anyone sit down beside himself?* Once again, that's impossible. *The Bible is clearly telling us the Father has the same kind of appearance and form as his Son—just like any father and son—and that they, in their tangible, physical bodies, are able to sit side by side.*

Now other passages also stress that Jesus Christ is a separate being from God the Father, but that they look alike because they both have tangible, glorified bodies. *2nd Corinthians 4:4 through 6* says that Christ "is the image of God," and says that God the Father reveals the light of knowledge "in the face of Jesus Christ." Again, that passage wouldn't make sense if God the Father and the Son were the same being.

Colossians 1:15 through 18 gives us the same relationship. It says that Christ is "The *image of the invisible God,* the *firstborn* of every creature," and that Christ is the head of the church, "For *it pleased the Father that in him should all fulness dwell.*" Once again, Jesus is depicted as being in the image of his Father, yet he was here on earth so he was visible, but the Father was not on earth so he was called "invisible"—*could they be the same person if one was visible and the other wasn't?* No, of course not. And would it make sense to say that it pleased the Father to make Jesus the head of the church and give him the fulness of power if they were one and the same God? The interpretation that they are the same being doesn't make sense in this context either, does it?

John 14:8 and 9 gives us another indication that the Father and the Son are the same kinds of beings. In this passage the disciple Philip asked Jesus to let them see God the Father. He said, "Shew us the Father, and it sufficeth us." Now before you read the next verse, let me make two observations about Philip's request. First, it's obvious that Philip and the disciples realized that Jesus and God the Father were two separate, distinct persons, and they knew they had not yet seen God the Father even though they had labored daily with Jesus for several years. Second, Philip obviously thought that God the Father had a tangible form and could be seen, or he wouldn't have asked Jesus to show the Father to them. Right? Right!

But the next verse records Jesus's answer in which he asserted his physical likeness to his Father in heaven. He told his disciple, "Have I been so long time with you, and yet hast thou not known me, Philip? *he that hath seen me hath seen the Father;* and how sayest thou then, Shew us the Father?" Here Jesus was saying that he and his father were similar in appearance—like father, like son.

I once heard a man assert that this verse meant Jesus actually was his Father, rather than that they had similar appearances. But anyone who reads that whole chapter would easily recognize his interpretation as grossly erroneous. *Verse 12* records Jesus's statement that *"I go unto my Father."* That wouldn't make any sense at all if Jesus and the Father were the same person. *Verse 13* contains Jesus's expression of intent "that the Father may be *glorified in the Son."* Again, that wouldn't make sense if they were the same being. *Verse 16* contains Christ's statement that *"I will pray the Father,* and he shall give you another Comforter." Here the Son, the Father, and the Holy Ghost are clearly depicted as three separate beings.

In *verse 23* Jesus again indicated that he and his Father are a plurality, not the same person. He said, "If a man love me, he will keep my words: and my Father will love him, and *we* will come unto him, and make *our* abode with him." Here Jesus clearly indicates that he and his Father are two separate, individual beings when he uses the words "we" and "our."

Verse 24: Christ said, *"The word which ye hear is not mine, but the Father's which sent me."* Now, if those creeds are correct in their assertion that Christ and the Father are the same being, then that verse would have to be branded an absolute falsehood. It's message is completely opposite to the creedal teaching.

And don't forget *verse 28,* where Jesus said, "If ye loved me, ye would rejoice, because I said, *I go unto the Father:* for my Father is *greater* than I." Here again Jesus shows himself to be an entirely different individual than the Father. If the creed-based interpretation that asserts God the Father is everywhere were correct, there is no way Jesus could go to him, because the Father would already be there. And *how could the Father be greater than the son if they are the same Being?*

Read the whole gospel of John—there are dozens of significant statements which clearly indicate that the Father, the Son, and the Holy Ghost are three separate, individual beings. And *if they're separate, and if each of them is a God, then there are three Gods that have influence on this earth! That's the message of the Bible, and to escape it literally hundreds of passages have to be explained away, twisted out of context or completely avoided.*

Objection Answered: Man in God's Image Debases God

Let's talk about an objection sometimes raised to the Biblical doctrine that God has a physical body. As an editor, I am alert to situations where people play with words, and this objection is tainted with a touch of that editorial trickery in its phraseology. It is an objection, also, which is offered without scriptural support—just emotionalism and faulty logic. The critics say, "It debases God to be in man's image." Notice how they have reversed the roles as they play with words. God is not in man's image—man is in God's image. They are asserting that God's creation—man—is a debasement of God because the Gods created man in their image. What nonsense!

They should go back to the first chapter of Genesis and read what God said at the end of the sixth day— the day in which he created man. *Genesis 1:31* tells us how God felt about creating man in his image. It says that "God saw every thing that he had made, and, behold, *it was very good."* Certainly God did not feel he was debased to have created mankind in his image.

Those who have concocted the false notion that man's being in the image of God somehow debases God should remember what the scriptures say about man as one of God's creations. Paul tells us in *Ephesians 2:10* that "We are his workmanship, created in Christ Jesus unto good works." And John tells us in *Revelation 4:11* that those before the throne of God will tell him, "Thou art worthy, O Lord, to receive glory and honour and power: for *thou hast created all things,* and for *thy pleasure* they are and were created."

And is man inherently a low and debased creature? I believe fundamentalists have hammered away on the concept that all men are sinners to the point they've lost sight of man's true status before God. The Psalmist reminded us of how God views man. *Psalm 8:4 and 5* says, "What is man, that thou art mindful of him? and the son of man, that thou visitest him? For *thou hast made him a little lower than the angels, and hast crowned him with glory and honour.*"

Objection Answered: No Man Has Seen God

And while we're on this subject, I'd like to comment on a proof text that's frequently quoted in support of the theory that God has no form or shape or bodily parts. Some individuals take great delight in quoting *John 1:18,* that says, "No man hath seen God at any time." But if that passage is taken at face value, it contradicts a multitude of other Bible passages, some of which refer to people seeing God the Father, and some referring to seeing the pre-mortal or post-mortal Jesus Christ. If this passage is taken only at face value, without the insights added by other Bible verses, it stands in serious conflict with a multitude of scriptures.

For instance, in *Acts 7:55-56* Stephen testifies that he sees both God the Father and Jesus Christ at the same time. He says, "Behold, *I see the heavens opened, and the Son of man standing on the right hand of God.*"

Genesis 32:30 records Jacob's testimony that *"I have seen God face to face,* and my life is preserved," and the experience is so significant for him that he names the place where it happened Peniel, which means *"The Face of God."*

In *Exodus 24:9 through 11* we're told that Moses and Aaron and seventy-two leaders of Israel *"Saw the God of Israel:* and there was under *his feet* as it were a paved work of sapphire stone, and as it were the body of heaven in his clearness. And upon the nobles of Israel he laid not *his hand:* also *they saw God,* and did eat and drink."

Exodus 33:9 to 11 tells us that *"The Lord spake unto Moses face to face,* as a man speaketh unto his friend." In *Isaiah 6:1 through 4,* the prophet

Isaiah bears his witness of God, saying, *"I saw also the Lord sitting upon a throne,* high and lifted up, and his train filled the temple." In *Revelation 1:10 through 20,* the apostle John recorded seeing the risen Christ, saying that he saw "One like unto the Son of man, clothed with a garment down to *the foot,* and girt about *the paps* with a golden girdle. *His head* and *his hairs* were white like wool, as white as snow; and *his eyes* were as a flame of fire; And *his feet* like unto fine brass, as if they burned in a furnace; and *his voice* as the sound of many waters."

1st John 3:1 to 3 contains the promise that "Now are we the sons of God, and it doth not yet appear what we shall be: but we know that, when he shall appear, *we shall be like him; for we shall see him as he is."*

And Revelation 22:3 and 4 promises concerning the future, "There shall be no more curse: but *the throne of God and of the Lamb* shall be in it; and his servants shall serve him: And *they shall see his face; . . . "*

When a passage of scripture is apparently in contradiction with a broad pattern of scriptures, as John 1:18's statement that no man has seen God is with these and other scriptural accounts, we need to look for other passages which will clarify the situation, and there are several which explain this seeming contradiction quite clearly. Turn over to *John 6, verse 46,* where it says, "Not that any man hath seen the Father, *save he which is of God, he hath seen the Father."* It's obvious that the privilege of seeing God is a very rare experience, but Jesus taught that an individual who is "of God"—one who has drawn near to the divine, can have that privilege.

More light on the subject is given in *Matthew 11:27,* where Jesus says, "All things are delivered unto me of my Father: and no man knoweth the Son, but the Father; neither knoweth any man the Father, save the Son, *and he to whomsoever the Son will reveal him."* The same teaching is recorded in *Luke 10:22.*

So its obvious that John 1:18 doesn't tell the full story when it says that no man has seen God, because passages in the Bible, like those I've quoted, record instances where *people do see God, and when they see him, they record that he is in a specific place, and that he has a specific form and shape like a man, with bodily parts.* And that applies both to those who have seen God the Father and to those who have seen the pre-mortal Christ—the Jehovah of the Old Testament.

Objection Answered: Passages Showing
the Nature of God Are Anthromorphisms

And while I'm covering objections that are occasionally raised, let's address the issue of *anthropomorphism*. Anti-Mormon tracts frequently try to sidestep the many passages which talk in great detail about God having a tangible body and the shape of a man by quoting one or two verses and then nonchalantly asserting or implying that the passages Mormons typically quote are figurative expressions rather than passages with literal meaning. A typical treatment is to quote some scholarly opinion that a particular verse is anthropomorphism—that it is figurative rather than literal—and then make a hasty exit from the subject, leaving the impression that the hundreds of passages which make reference to the tangible nature of God's being are all figures of speech: anthropomorphisms. They allude to a small handful of verses which obviously are figures of speech, and attempt to leave the impression that all the rest of them are too. *That's deception, not gospel scholarship.*

A typical presentation of the anthropomorphism theme is found in the booklet *What Every Mormon Should Know,* by Edmond C. Gruss, from Accent Books, on pages 22 and 23: "You may ask, 'Don't the expressions which attribute bodily members (face, ears, eyes, hands, arms, etc.) and physical movements to God prove that He has a literal body?' It must be admitted that the Bible often describes God in this way. But these expressions are metaphors which are very common in the Old Testament. The specific kind of metaphor under examination here is anthropomorphism, the describing of God 'in the form of a man.' The expressions are not meant to be taken literally. Such figurative language is necessary to convey truth which is beyond man's experience. It expresses God's concern and relationship to man. To take other figurative language literally would be absurd. For example, one could demonstrate that God is a 'bird' because in the Psalms reference is made to 'feathers' and 'wings.' In Deuteronomy God is referred to as 'a consuming fire' and in Jeremiah He refers to Himself as 'the fountain of living waters.' Are these to be understood literally? Obviously not. Space does not allow a further discussion of the points raised. . . ."

But the truthseeker will do well to look hard at the hundreds of passages that describe the nature of God, and try to discern whether figures of speech are involved. That's not very difficult for anyone who paid attention in junior high school English. Just be aware that most passages about the nature of God are not figures of speech, and should be interpreted literally unless a broad pattern of scripture indicates otherwise.

Issue Number Five: God the Father is Father of the Spirits of All Mankind

There is another erroneous concept that lurks beneath the false logic I mentioned earlier—that logic which asserts that God is somehow debased because man is in his image. That erroneous concept appears again in the area of man's inherent relationship with God the Father. Typical Protestant doctrine sees men only as creations of God, and asserts that men become children of God only if they accept the gospel of Christ, and at that acceptance are adopted into the church. But this doctrine excludes a host of Bible passages that tell us that *men are actually the children of God— his spirit children born before the creation of this earth.*

Back in the days of King David—hundreds of years before there was a church of Christ to adopt converts, the Psalmist taught in *Psalm 82, verse 6: "Ye are gods; and all of you are children of the most High."* Other Old Testament passages also talk about the children of God, long before there was a New Testament church to adopt them. *Job 1:6* says that "There was a day when *the sons of God came to present themselves before the Lord."* And *Job 38:4 through 7* alludes to the creation of this earth, and says that at the time, "All the sons of God shouted for joy."

The New Testament also affirms that all men are the spirit children of God the Father. *Hebrews 12:9* tells us that we should "Be in subjection unto the *Father of spirits." Romans 8:16 and 17* tells us that "The Spirit itself beareth witness with *our spirit, that we are the children of God: And if children, then heirs; heirs of God, and joint-heirs with Christ."* And *verse 29* of the same chapter, *Romans 8,* tells us that Christ was the *"firstborn among many brethren,"* and that those whom God foreknew before this earth life he sent to receive a body like Christ's, or as Paul expressed it, God the Father sent them "To be conformed to the image of his Son."

And Paul, in his great sermon on Mars Hill recorded in *Acts 17:28 and 29,* twice taught that "We are the offspring of God." The *third chapter of Luke* traces Jesus's mortal lineage all the way back to Adam, and then teaches in *verse 38* that *Adam "Was the son of God."*

Probably the best know passage of all scripture is the Lord's Prayer, which Jesus taught to a multitude who were mostly non-members of his Church.

Yet *Matthew 6:9* tells us he taught them to pray, *"Our Father which art in heaven."* Why would he teach them to pray to God the Father if he was not literally the father of their spirits? That would be the ultimate deception, for Christ to teach them they had a heavenly father to whom they should pray, and whom they should address as Father, if he wasn't truly their father! I don't believe Christ deceived them—*they truly were, and are, spirit children of our Father in heaven.*

And remember what Jesus said to Mary when she encountered him near the tomb, on that first Easter Sunday. *John 20:17* records his words to her: "Go to my brethren, and say unto them, *I ascend unto my Father, and your Father;* and to my God, and your God."

Before I leave this subject, let me observe that the basic reason why God the Father had Christ create man's physical body in their image was so that his children would be able to obtain a resurrected body which would allow them to regain his presence and dwell with him for eternity there. *It's not demeaning to have man's physical body created in the image of God—it's glorious!*

But what is demeaning is that some theologians deny that all mortal beings are spirit children of their Heavenly Father. *There are few things I can conceive of which would offend God more than for man to deny his Fatherhood, yet that denial is a basic tenant of modern so-called Christianity.*

Issue Number Six: The Father, Son and Holy Ghost Are Three Separate Beings

The Bible frequently talks about members of the Godhead being *different places at the same time.* Now there's no problem with that as long as you recognize that the Father, and the Son, and the Holy Ghost are separate, distinct beings. *But those passages pose horrendous problems if you're trying to support the theory that somehow they're the same person.*

Let's start with the stoning of Stephen, in the *seventh chapter of Acts, verses 55 and 56.* Stephen, you'll recall, bore a powerful testimony to the Jewish Sanhedrin but they rejected his words when he told them of the glorious appearance of both the Father and the Son to him. The passage says that "He," meaning Stephen, "being full of the Holy Ghost," so the Holy Ghost was there on the ground with him, "looked up stedfastly into heaven, and *saw the glory of God, and Jesus standing on the right hand of God,* And said, Behold, I see the heavens opened, and *the Son of man standing on the right hand of God."* So Stephen, with the Holy Ghost there on the ground with him, looked into heaven and saw both God the Father and God the Son, standing side by side, with Jesus on the right hand of the Father!

Now here the three members of the Godhead were in three different places at the same time. Is there any possible way a rational observer could conclude from this passage that those three persons are actually the same being? No way! Either the Bible passage is a lie, or the belief that the three divine beings are the same essence, or being, or substance, is an error. *Which is it that's wrong—the Bible or the creed?* The answer is obvious.

There's another situation where God the Father, God the Son, and God the Holy Ghost were all in different places at the same time. It also shows that they are not the same person, or being, or essence, or substance. It's recorded in *Luke, chapter 3, verses 21 and 22.* This, you'll recognize, is the account of the baptism of Jesus. It says, "Now when all the people were baptized, it came to pass, that Jesus also being baptized, and praying, the heaven was opened, And the *Holy Ghost descended in a bodily shape* like a dove upon him, and a *voice came from heaven,* which said, *Thou art my beloved Son; in thee I am well pleased."*

Now there was Jesus, God the Son, in the water being baptized by John the Baptist. God the Father spoke from up in heaven, and the Holy Ghost, assuming the form of a dove to make his presence known, was descending to earth when the Father spoke from heaven. Is there any possible way an unbiased observer could conclude that the three are the same being, or that there was actually only one divine being involved? Again, no way!

Another instance: in the last week of the Savior's mortal life, just after he made his triumphal entry into Jerusalem on a colt, God the Father spoke to Jesus from heaven while Jesus was on the earth. *John 12, verse 28,* records part of Jesus's prayer to his Father in which he said, "Father, glorify thy name. Then came there a voice from heaven, saying, I have both glorified it, and will glorify it again."

Now if God the Father and Jesus Christ were the same person. would this instance have taken place? *Would Jesus have prayed to himself? And would he have played the role of ventriloquist, projecting his voice so it would sound like it was coming from heaven to deceive the people?* Of course not! Jesus and the Father are two separate beings, and those creeds that say they're the same person, or substance, or essence, are in error.

Another instance in which God the Father, God the Son, and God the Holy Ghost are clearly shown to be three distinct personages is recorded in the words of Jesus in *John 14, verse 16.* The Savior told his disciples, "I will pray the Father, and he shall give you another Comforter, that he may abide with you for ever." And *verse 26* continues in the same manner: "But the Comforter, which is the *Holy Ghost, whom the Father will send in my name,* he shall teach you all things, . . . "

Here Jesus said that he would pray to the Father. *Would he deceive his disciples by praying to himself?* That's the inevitable conclusion one must draw if he accepts the creed that says they're the same substance or essence. And would the Father send the Holy Ghost if He and Jesus and the Holy Ghost were actually the same being or essence? That would mean that the Father wouldn't send the Holy Ghost, because Jesus was the Holy Ghost and he was already there. That interpretation turns into a mixed up mess in a hurry, doesn't it? No, the Father, and the Son, and the Holy Ghost are three separate and distinct beings—they're not the same person.

So you be the judge and jury. Are the creeds correct when they assert that there is only one God? Does one, plus one, plus one, really add up to only one? Or does the Bible repeatedly show that the Father, the Son, and the Holy Ghost are three separate beings, each of them Gods who have been seen or heard in different places at the same time?

Issue Number Seven: The Trinity Are United in Purpose But Three Separate Beings

Now I've cited a lot of passages which quite clearly indicate that God the Father, his Son Jesus Christ, and the Holy Ghost are three separate, distinct beings. But there are passages which speak of them as being "one." Again the question looms, does this mean they are somehow the same person, or does it mean that they are three separate beings who are united in purpose and intent?

The *seventeenth chapter of John* gives one of the best answers in scripture to that question. This records Christ's prayer to his Father the evening before he was taken and crucified. The entire chapter merits careful, prayer-inspired reading, but let me comment on several key verses.

Jesus began by saying, in *verse 1,* "Father, the hour is come; *glorify thy Son, that thy Son also may glorify thee."* Now again, let me emphasize that he wasn't praying to himself—he was praying to his Father, a separate being whom he sought to obey and to glorify. In *verse 4* he told his his Father, *"I have finished the work which thou gavest me to do."* Again, a being doesn't give work to himself, and he doesn't pray to himself, nor report his accomplishments to himself. Christ was praying to a separate being, located in a different place.

In *verse 5* Christ said, "O Father, glorify thou me with thine own self with the *glory which I had with thee before the world was."* Again he spoke of his pre-mortal relationship with his Father, and asserted that he was with God the Father in a definite location at that time.

And then Jesus began to pray for those whom his Father had entrusted into his keeping here on earth. In *verse 6* he said, *"I have manifested thy name* unto the *men which thou gavest me* out of the world: thine they were, and thou gavest them me; and they have kept thy word."* He spoke at some length concerning the disciples who had labored with him in his ministry, but then he broadened the scope of his prayer, and in doing so he carefully defined his relationship with his Father. In *verses 20 through 24* he said,

"Neither pray I for these alone, but for them also which shall believe on me through their word; *That they all may be one; as thou, Father, art in me, and I in thee, that they also may be one in us:* that the world may believe that thou hast sent me. And the *glory which thou gavest me* I have given them; that they may be one, even *as we are one:* I in them, and thou in me, that they may be made perfect in one; and that the world may know that *thou hast sent me,* and hast loved them, as thou hast loved me. Father, I will that they also, *whom thou hast given me,* be with me where I am; that they may behold *my glory, which thou hast given me:* for *thou lovedst me before the foundation of the world."*

Now let's examine the two doctrinal alternatives in the light of this passage. If God the Father and Jesus and the Holy Spirit are all the same person—some huge, shapless blob without body parts and passions, then what Jesus was requesting here was that his disciples could also become part of that blob. He was very explicit about it—he wanted them to be one in the same way as he and the Father were one, and he wanted them to be one *"in us,"* he said. He prayed "that they may be one, *even as we are one: I in them, and thou in me,* that they may be made perfect in one." So the "one God" theory would lead to the conclusion that Jesus wanted his disciples to become part of that huge, shapeless god-being blob. A valid interpretation? That doesn't sound too realistic, does it?

So let's try the other interpretation again—that the Father and Son and Holy Ghost are three separate beings—each one holding the power and glory and authority of Godhood. Each of them have separate roles to fulfill and duties to perform, but *they are united in purpose and ultimate*

objective: the perfection of mankind. Jesus wanted his disciples to be united in that common cause, and to be one in effort and respect and service
and loyalty, in the same manner as he and his father are united. Is that
better doctrine? With that interpretation, everything falls into place—the
passage makes sense! And the hundreds of other passages that are in absolute conflict with the impossible-to-understand "three in one God" suddenly make sense, and are in harmony with the teaching.

It makes clear such significant passages as *1st John 5:7,* which testifies,
*"There are three that bear record in heaven, the Father, the Word, and
the Holy Ghost: and these three are one."*

And since we understand that the three members of the Godhead are
not the same person, and that the Father and the Son have tangible, glorified bodies that will never again be separated from their spirits, and that
the members of the Godhead are firmly united in purpose and intent, we
are able to grasp the true meaning of the Savior's instruction in *Matthew
28:19 and 20,* "Go ye therefore, and teach all nations, *baptizing them in
the name of the Father,* and *of the Son,* and *of the Holy Ghost:* Teaching
them to observe all things whatsoever I have commanded you: and lo, I
am with you alway, even unto the end of the world. Amen."

A Modern Witness of the Nature of God: Joseph Smith

But there is another witness of the nature of God—a modern witness—
with penetrating first-hand knowledge of who God is, and how God regards
the teachings embodied in the creeds of the churches.

After refraining from revealing themselves to man for almost eighteen
hundred years, God the Father and his Son Jesus Christ appeared to a young
seeker of truth in the spring of 1820. They revealed themselves to him,
and prepared him to restore vital principles of their gospel which had been
lost to mankind during the great apostasy and the dark ages. That young
man was Joseph Smith, who left this description of that glorious
manifestation:

"I saw a pillar of light exactly over my head, above the brightness of
the sun, which descended gradually until it fell upon me. . . .When the
light rested upon me *I saw two Personages,* whose brightness and glory
defy all description, standing above me in the air. One of them spake unto
me, calling me by name and said, pointing to the other—*This is My Beloved Son. Hear Him!" (Joseph Smith—History,* 1:16-17)

This was the first of several glorious experiences when Joseph Smith was privileged to see God. On this occasion, in his first vision, he saw as Stephen saw: God the Father and His Son, Jesus Christ, standing side by side. Suddenly the doubt and confusion concerning the nature of God which had spread across the earth was penetrated. Joseph saw them, and could bear personal witness that they are separate, individual beings, with glorious, tangible bodies. He learned, in that moment, profound truths which had been lost to scholars and theologians for centuries.

But he learned even more than what his eyes beheld. His purpose in seeking God had been to discover which of the churches of his day he should join. To his surprise, he was instructed to join none of them, and he learned a significant insight concerning the creeds that had warped the understanding of men for centuries. His testimony was that "The Personage who addressed me said that *all their creeds were an abomination in his sight.*"

More than a century and a half have passed since the Father and the Son first revealed themselves to man in these latter days. The Church restored through Joseph Smith has spread throughout much of the earth, and is growing rapidly, while many other churches are declining. Filled with zeal based on the sure knowledge of latter-day revelation, over thirty thousand missionaries—more than the missionary force of almost all other Christian churches combined—are laboring to teach man that it truly means life eternal to correctly understand the nature of God so they can truly come to know both the Father and the Son, and be personally guided and inspired by the Holy Spirit.

Their labors have excited the jealousy and antagonism of some who have chosen to fight against the Lord's work rather than to render obedience to the gospel of their Savior. Perhaps it was they of whom the Savior spoke when he warned Joseph of their creeds which were an abomination in his sight. He said, "They draw near to me with their lips, but their hearts are far from me, *they teach for doctrines the commandments of men,* having a form of godliness, but *they deny the power thereof.*"

Now you have heard the evidence, though not all of it by any means, but enough that you can evaluate many of the key scriptures in the Bible that teach you about the true nature of God the Father, our Lord Jesus Christ, and the Holy Spirit. You truly are both the judge and the jury. It is you who must arrive at the verdict—one which will influence the course of your own life for all eternity. You must decide if the creeds are correct, or if the Godhead is composed of separate, tangible beings who are united in purpose and intent, seeking to bring about the salvation and exaltation of mankind.

And if you find those ancient creeds in error and based on contradictions which are impossible to reconcile, then seek for those who can give you further understanding of the truths of eternity. I testify to you that you will find those who can teach you those truths, and who hold authority from God to do so, in The Church of Jesus Christ of Latter-day Saints.

And now, thank you for studying these principles with me. I sincerely hope that I have touched your life for good. May *"the grace of the Lord Jesus Christ, and the love of God, and the communion of the Holy Ghost, be with you all. Amen." (2 Cor. 13:14)*

DOCTRINAL EVIDENCES
that
MORMONS ARE
CHRISTIANS

A Refutation of Misleading
Statements Circulated by
Anti-Mormon Critics

Duane S. Crowther

C-90
Cassette

Down through the ages, in all the eras of Christianity, there have been those who have fought against the growth and progress of God's work by spreading falsehoods and malicious rumors. Many religious faiths have suffered this type of misrepresentation and persecution. But in recent years there have been those who have attempted to circulate what I regard as the *"ultimate falsehood"*: the gross fabrication that Mormons—members of The Church of Jesus Christ of Latter-day Saints—are not Christians. These anti-Mormon critics have attempted to circulate the concept that Latter-day Saints somehow don't believe in the Jesus Christ taught of in the Bible, and that's *deception in the extreme!*

False Assertions of Mormon Doctrine
Are Advanced by Anti-Mormon Critics

Anti-Mormon critics have advanced all sorts of variations on this theme. Some have tried to make Mormons appear as pagans or attempted to link them with the Hindus and other oriental religions. Others have put forth their false thesis that Mormonism is somehow linked with the occult. Still others have been even more absurd, attempting to tie Mormon doctrine to science fiction creations and works of pure fiction. Yet others have taken still another false approach, asserting that Latter-day Saints have followed some other Christ, which isn't the Jesus Christ portrayed in the New Testament at all but a different Jesus.

As a member of The Church of Jesus Christ of Latter-day Saints, I'm highly offended by these false allegations, just as I believe Baptists, or Methodists, or Lutherans, or Pentecostals, or members of any other Christian denomination would be offended if someone suddenly alleged that their religion didn't believe in the Lord Jesus Christ.

Why This Discussion Was Prepared

Let me introduce myself and tell you my motivation for preparing this discussion. My name is Duane S. Crowther. I live in Bountiful, Utah. I've been a Latter-day Saint all my life though I've had ample opportunity to associate with people of many different Christian faiths. I was raised in Arlington, Virginia and was one of only twenty Mormons in a high school of 2,700 students, so many of my friends were of other faiths.

Three decades have passed since that time, and I am now the owner of a book publishing firm and vinyl products manufacturing company. We make an attractive line of Bible cases which we sell to Christian bookstores across the nation. Six times a year I attend sales conventions where I meet many hundreds of good Christian people—Bible and religious bookstore owners whom I regard as fine individuals and people who generally are trying to serve the Lord to the best of their ability. I sell my wares conscientiously, but I keep to myself and usually avoid talking doctrine with them unless they come to me with questions; I'm content to just conduct my business in an honorable manner and enjoy my association with them. But I'm in a position to see the continuing flow of new books from major Protestant publishing houses, and I am vividly aware that up to a dozen new anti-Mormon books hit the market each year.

More and more of these books are pushing the misconception that Mormons are not Christians. Now I'm not a Mormon Church leader nor an official spokesman for the Mormon faith, but I'm a lay member who believes that it's my responsibility to be valiant in the testimony of Jesus Christ. And I'm a person who believes in setting the record straight when I see people misrepresenting the truth. I also have a firm belief that the Christian man on the street is an individual who wants to know the truth, and I believe it's appropriate that I do what little I can to set the record straight on this matter.

Critics Intentionally Avoid Scriptural Passages Which State Mormon Doctrines

In this discussion I'm responding to misconceptions advanced in such anti-Mormon books as Gordon Fraser's *Is Mormonism Christian?*, published by Moody Press; Dave Hunt's *The Cult Explosion,* published by Harvest House; Walter Martin's *The Maze of Mormonism,* produced by Vision House; and Ed Decker's and Dave Hunt's *The God Makers,* another publication by Harvest House. These are representative of a number of heavily biased or weakly researched and poorly written books which pursue the same erroneous theme: that the Mormon belief concerning Jesus Christ is different than that which is set forth in the Bible.

Every one of these books intentionally overlooks the hundreds of scriptural passages which make the LDS position concerning Jesus Christ abundantly clear, and substitutes a hodgepodge of nonsense which any informed Latter-day Saint would immediately identify as being a full 180 degrees opposite from the doctrine of Mormonism. The authors of those books are intentionally obscuring the truth and substituting fabrications in its place.

Book of Mormon Passages State Latter-day Saint Doctrines Concerning Christ

Rather than argue the scriptures, I'd rather make my point by presenting to you more than seventy doctrinal statements about Jesus Christ which informed Latter-day Saints regard as revealed truth. These statements are taken from a volume Latter-day Saints regard as scripture—the Book of Mormon. Now I realize that some of you non-Mormon friends probably don't believe as we do, that the Book of Mormon is God's revealed word. Nevertheless, what I will quote to you should be ample evidence that Mormons believe very firmly that Jesus is the Christ, and that he is the same Jesus Christ you read about in your Bible.

Now let me point out four things before I begin. *First,* I have chosen to quote a broad range of doctrinal items rather than to treat just a few in depth. Of necessity this means that I will only cite one or two passages as evidence for the doctrine. I want you to have the opportunity to know more about those doctrines, so I've listed other references in the footnotes.

I've also listed several Bible verses for each teaching, so you can compare and discover that the Book of Mormon and Bible both serve as witnesses of the very same doctrinal principles.

Second, in the interest of time and space, I've condensed many of the passages I'll quote, eliminating a lot of phrases referring to other themes. I invite you to obtain a copy of the *Book of Mormon* and read the passages in their entirety so you can know for sure that I have quoted them properly and accurately even though they are condensed. And I hope you'll also take time to read the other references I've suggested for your consideration.

Third, I've been very careful to identify doctrinal concepts which are generally accepted by Latter-day Saints. Mormons believe that our doctrines are found in the scriptures where there is a broad pattern of scripture asserting the same message. In every case the scriptures I'll be citing are part of a broad doctrinal pattern which is well substantiated in Mormon scripture.

And *fourth,* since the purpose of this discussion is to refute a malicious error which is being circulated, and to help you discern what is true, I would invite you to pray and ask the Holy Spirit to help you discern whether the things I will cite to you are true or not. That's one blessing we can all enjoy—we can be guided into increased understanding of the truth by the Holy Ghost. Please pray as you study, and open your minds and hearts so you can be receptive to truth!

Seventy-Two Doctrinal Teachings
About Christ in Mormon Theology

The *Book of Mormon* was first printed in the spring of 1830, so the doctrines expressed have been the basic beliefs of Mormonism for over a century and a half. You'll observe that they are so clearly stated that no honest investigator could attempt to assert that Mormons don't believe in Christ—the same Christ we read about in the New Testament. I'll also quote, occasionally, from two other volumes Latter-day Saints regard as scripture: the *Doctrine and Covenants* and the *Pearl of Great Price.* They both date back over a hundred years. And occasionally I'll quote from the *King James Version of the Bible.* But since my purpose is to show that a belief in Christ is inherent to the faith of the Latter-day Saints, of necessity most of my sources will obviously be from Mormon scriptures rather than from the Bible.

Doctrinal Evidence *Number 1:* It's the clearly stated doctrine of The Church of Jesus Christ of Latter-day Saints that **we believe in the Father, the Son, and the Holy Ghost.** Early in the Church's history, a list of basic doctrines was prepared which is known as the "Articles of Faith." The very first among the thirteen doctrinal statements was the Article which states, *"We believe in God, the Eternal Father, and in His Son, Jesus Christ, and in the Holy Ghost."*[1]

Number 2: It is Mormon doctrine that **Jesus Christ is the Son of God the Father.** Many dozens of passages in Latter-day Saint scripture assert this basic tenet of our faith. For instance, *3rd Nephi, chapter 9, verse 15* contains the words of Jesus recorded when he appeared in the Americas, following his resurrection. As he introduced himself to the people he said, "Behold, *I am Jesus Christ the Son of God."* About 150 years prior to the Savior's appearance, a group of believers responded to the teachings of King Benjamin with these words recorded in *Mosiah 4:2:* "O have mercy, and apply the atoning blood of Christ that we may receive forgiveness of our sins, and our hearts may be purified; for *we believe in Jesus Christ, the Son of God,* who created heaven and earth, and all things; who shall come down among the children of men."

That Jesus is the Son of God the Father is also taught in many dozens of passages in the New Testament. Based on erroneous interpretations of *Matthew 1:20* and *Luke 1:35,* there are some who mistakenly assert that Jesus is the son of the Holy Ghost. The passage in Luke records the words of the angel to Mary in which the angel explained that "The Holy Ghost shall come upon thee, and *the power of the Highest shall overshadow thee:* therefore also that holy thing which shall be born of thee shall be called the *Son of God."*

The interpretation that that passage means the Savior was the Son of the Holy Ghost rather than the Son of the Highest, or God the Father, is easily shown to be erroneous when compared with accounts such as Mark's report of the baptism of Jesus, in *Mark 1, verses 9 through 11:* "Jesus came from Nazareth of Galilee, and was baptized of John in Jordan. And straightway coming up out of the water, he saw the heavens opened, and the Spirit like a dove descending upon him: And *there came a voice from heaven, saying, Thou art my beloved Son, in whom I am well pleased."* So in this instance, while the Holy Ghost was descending on the Lord in the form

---

1. B of M: 3 Ne. 11:25; 3 Ne. 11:32-36.

of a dove, his Father was still in heaven. It's obvious, then, that the Holy Ghost is not Jesus's father. And there are many dozens of Biblical passages which clearly show that God the Father, not the Holy Ghost is the father of Jesus Christ.[2]

Evidence *Number 3:* Latter-day Saints believe that **Jesus is the Only Begotten Son in mortality of God the Father.** In *Alma 9, verses 26 through 28,* we read the words of the great prophet Alma who taught, "Not many days hence the Son of God shall come in his glory; and *his glory shall be the glory of the Only Begotten of the Father,* full of grace, equity, and truth, full of patience, mercy, and long-suffering, quick to hear the cries of his people and to answer their prayers. And behold, *he cometh to redeem those who will baptized unto repentance, through faith* on his name. Therefore, prepare ye the way of the Lord, . . . "

And the Book of Mormon also contains the prophecy of Nephi, in *2nd Nephi 25:12 and 13,* which says, "When the day cometh that the *Only Begotten of the Father,* yea, even the Father of heaven and of earth, shall manifest himself unto them in the flesh, behold, they will reject him, because of their iniquities, and the hardness of their hearts, and the stiffness of their necks. Behold, they will crucify him; and after he is laid in a sepulchre for the space of three days *he shall rise from the dead,* with healing in his wings; and *all those who believe on his name shall be saved in the kingdom of God.* Wherefore, my soul delighteth to prophesy concerning him, for I have seen his day, and my heart doth magnify his holy name."[3]

Doctrinal Evidence *Number 4:* We believe that **the mortal mother of Jesus Christ was the virgin, Mary.** The Book of Mormon, in *Alma 7:10,* contains Alma's prophecy, made about 83 B.C., concerning Jesus' birth which proclaims, *"He shall be born of Mary, . . . she being a virgin, a precious and chosen vessel,* who shall . . . bring forth a son, yea, even the Son of God." And in *2nd Nephi 17, verse 14,* the great prophecy of Isaiah is cited which says, "Therefore the Lord himself shall give you a sign—*Behold, a virgin shall conceive, and shall bear a son,* and shall call his name Immanuel."[4]

2. B of M: Morm. 9:29; 1 Ne. 13:40. Bible: Rom. 15:6; John 17:1-3; John 8:42; John 20:17; Acts 13:33.
3. B of M: Alma 9:26-28; 2 Ne. 2:12-13; Jacob 4:11-12; Alma 12:33-34. Bible: John 1:14, 18; John 3:16, 18; 1 John 4:9.
4. B of M: Alma 7:10; 2 Ne. 17:14; Mosiah 3:8. Bible: Matt. 1:16; 18-25; Luke 1;26-38; Luke 2:4-21.

The next seven evidences I'll mention all refer to names and titles of Jesus Christ used both in the Book of Mormon and in the Bible. I have a special reason for presenting them in this order. I'll explain that reason after I've referred to each of the seven.

Doctrinal Principle *Number 5:* **Jesus Christ is the Savior.** In *1st Nephi 10, verse 4* it tells of Nephi's prophecy that "Yea, even six hundred years from the time that my father left Jerusalem, a prophet would the Lord God raise up among the Jews—*even a Messiah, or in other words, a Savior of the world.*"

In *3rd Nephi 5:20* Mormon exclaimed, *"I have reason to bless my God and my Savior Jesus Christ,* that he brought our fathers out of the land of Jerusalem." I'll say much more about Jesus being our Savior later.[5]

Principle *Number 6:* Mormons believe that **Jesus Christ is the Redeemer** who releases the recipients of his redemption from death and hell. The prophet Lehi explained this role of the Savior in *2nd Nephi 2, verses 6 through 8* when he said, *"Redemption cometh in and through the Holy Messiah; for he is full of grace and truth. Behold, he offereth himself a sacrifice for sin,* to answer the ends of the law, unto all those who have a broken heart and a contrite spirit; and unto none else can the ends of the law be answered. Wherefore, how great the importance to make these things known unto the inhabitants of the earth, that they may know that there is no flesh that can dwell in the presence of God, *save it be through the merits, and mercy, and grace of the Holy Messiah,* who layeth down his life according to the flesh, and taketh it again by the power of the Spirit, that he may *bring to pass the resurrection of the dead, being the first that should rise."*[6]

Doctrinal Evidence *Number 7:* Another title for **Jesus Christ is the King of all the earth and heaven.** Alma the younger recorded the promptings which he received on this theme in *Alma 5, verse 50.* He wrote, "Thus saith the Spirit: Repent, all ye ends of the earth, for the kingdom of heaven is soon at hand; yea, the *Son of God cometh in his glory, in his might, majesty, power, and dominion.* Yea, my beloved brethren, I say uno you, that the Spirit saith: *Behold the glory of the King of all the earth; and also the King of heaven* shall very soon shine forth among all the children of men."

---

5. B of M: 1 Ne. 10:4; 3 Ne. 5:20; 1 Ne. 13:40; 2 Ne. 31:13; Morm. 3:14. Bible: Luke 2:11; John 4:42; Acts 13:23; Titus 1:3-4, 3:6; 2 Pet. 3:18; Philip 3:20.

6. B of M: 2 Ne. 2:6-8; Enos 26-27; 3 Ne. 9:21-22; 3 Ne. 10:10. Bible: Gal. 3:13; Titus 2:13-14; Rom. 3:22-24; Heb. 9:11-15.

As you can easily recognize, these titles are also frequently used in the Bible as titles of the Lord Jesus Christ.[7]

Number 8: Still another title—**Jesus Christ is known as the first and the last.** In *Alma 11:39* Amulek answered the question of an antagonist by saying that the Son of God "Is the *beginning and the end, the first and the last.*" Nephi quotes the same title of the Lord in *1st Nephi 20:12,* when he cited these words from Isaiah: "Hearken unto me, O Jacob, and Israel my called, for I am he; *I am the first and I am also the last.*"[8]

Evidence *Number 9:* We believe that **Jesus Christ is the God of Israel** and is identified by the title **Holy One of Israel.** In *1st Nephi 19, verses 13 through 17,* Nephi quotes teachings of the former prophet Zenos when he says, "As for those who are at Jerusalem, saith the prophet, they shall be scourged by all people, because *they crucify the God of Israel,* and turn their hearts aside, rejecting signs and wonders, and *the power and glory of the God of Israel.* And because they turn their hearts aside, . . . and have *despised the Holy One of Israel,* they shall wander in the flesh, and perish, and . . . be hated among all nations. Nevertheless, when that day cometh, . . . that they *no more turn aside their hearts against the Holy One of Israel,* then will he remember the covenants which he made to their fathers. . . .Then will he remember the isles of the sea; yea, and all the people who are of the house of Israel, will I gather in, saith the Lord. . . .Yea, and all the earth shall see the salvation of the Lord, . . . every nation, kindred, tongue and people."[9]

Doctrinal Principle *Number 10:* It is Mormon doctrine that **Jesus Christ is the creator of this earth and all that is in it.** *3rd Nephi 9:15,* for instance, contains the witness of the Lord that he truly is the creator of the earth. He said, "Behold, I am Jesus Christ the Son of God. *I created the heavens and the earth, and all things that in them are.* I was with the Father from the beginning . . . and in me hath the Father glorified his name."

Jacob taught the same principle in *Jacob 4, verses 6 through 9,* when he said, "We search the prophets, and we have many revelations and the spirit of prophecy; and having all these witnesses we obtain a hope, and our faith becometh unshaken, insomuch that we truly can command in the

---

7. B of M: Alma 5:50; 2 Ne. 10:14; Mosiah 2:19-20; 2 Ne. 29:7; 3 Ne. 11:14. Bible: 1 Tim. 6:14-15; Rev. 17:14; Luke 1:31-33; Isa. 33:22.
8. B of M: Alma 11:39; 1 Ne. 20:12; 3 Ne. 9:15-18. Bible: Rev. 22:13-16; Rev. 1:1-11; Rev. 21:6-7.
9. B of M: 1 Ne. 19:13-17; 2 Ne. 6:15; 2 Ne. 6:9; Omni 25-26; 2 Ne. 25:29. Bible: Compare Isa. 41:14, Isa. 43:11, & Isa. 48:17 with Gal. 3:13 & Rev. 5:9.

name of Jesus and the very trees obey us, or the mountains, or the waves of the sea . . . behold, *by the power of his word man came upon the face of the earth, which earth was created by the power of his word.* Wherefore, *if God being able to speak and the world was, and to speak and man was created,* O then, why not able to command the earth, or the workmanship of his hands upon the face of it, according to his will and pleasure?"[10]

Principle *Number 11:* Another title used for Jesus Christ in Latter-day Saint scripture is Jehovah. In the final verse of the Book of Mormon, *Moroni 10:34,* Moroni concluded with these words which focus on that title: "I soon go to rest in the paradise of God, until my spirit and body shall again reunite, and I am brought forth triumphant through the air, to meet you before *the pleasing bar of the great Jehovah, the Eternal Judge* of both the quick and the dead. Amen."

And a modern revelation reporting an appearance of the Lord Jesus Christ also identifies him as being Jehovah. It's found in *Doctrine and Covenants 110, verses 2 through 4:* "We saw the Lord standing upon the breastwork of the pulpit, before us; and under his feet was a paved work of pure gold, in color like amber. His eyes were as a flame of fire; the hair of his head was white like the pure snow; his countenance shone above the brightness of the sun; and his voice was as the sound of the rushing of great waters, *even the voice of Jehovah,* saying: *I am the first and the last; I am he who liveth, I am he who was slain; I am your advocate with the Father."*

Now in these last few paragraphs I have listed seven titles of the Lord Jesus Christ. Let me review them: Savior, Redeemer, King, first and last, Holy One of Israel, Creator, and Jehovah. If you know your Bible, you know that these titles are also used in the New Testament as references to Jesus Christ. Why did I choose these titles to comment upon? Because every one of them also has reference to the God of the Old Testament. The fact that these titles refer to both Jesus Christ and to Jehovah lead to an unescapable conclusion, that *Jehovah, the God of the Old Testament, and Jesus Christ of the New Testament, are the same person—the same divine being!*

Let me cite four brief passages from the Old Testament prophet, Isaiah, to show you what I mean. But first, I need to explain about the word LORD,

---

10. B of M: 3 Ne. 9:15; Jacob 4:6-9; Mosiah 3:8; Mosiah 4:2, 9; 2 Ne. 9:5; Ether 3:15-16. Bible: John 1:1-3, 14; Col. 1:12-17; Heb. 1:1-2; Heb. 2:9-10; Eph. 2:10, 3:9.

L-O-R-D, written in all capitals, as it is used in the Old Testament. That word is used to represent what is called the tetragrammation—the sacred name of God consisting, in the Hebrew consonantal script, of the four letters Y-H-W-H. The Jews in ancient times refused to pronounce the name because it was so sacred. Refusal to pronounce the name has gone on for so long that no one now knows for sure what vowels were intended to be used with those four consonants, though scholars think the name of God was pronounced Yahweh.

The word Jehovah first appeared in medieval times. Jehovah was adopted as an attempt to pronounce the vowels written under the letters by the scribes, but those vowels were never intended to be combined with the consonants of this word. What we need to remember is that the word LORD, written in all capital letters, stands for the name of the God of the Old Testament people often referred to as Jehovah.

With that much explanation let me cite these four brief passsages about the God of the Old Testament from the book of Isaiah. That great Biblical prophet uses every one of those titles of the Lord Jesus Christ as titles for the Old Testament God.

Isaiah 43:10 through 12: "Ye are my witnesses, saith the LORD, and my servant whom I have chosen: that ye may know and believe me, and understand that I am he: before me there was no God formed, neither shall there be after me. *I, even I, am the LORD; and beside me there is no saviour.* I have declared, and have saved, and I have shewed, when there was no strange god among you: therefore ye are my witnesses, saith the LORD, that I am God."

That passage says that the God of the Old Testament is the savior.

Isaiah 43:14-15: Thus saith the LORD, your redeemer, the Holy One of Israel; For your sake I have sent to Babylon, and have brought down all their nobles, and the Chaldeans, whose cry is in the ships. *I am the LORD, your Holy One, the creator of Israel, your king."*

In the previous passage four more of the seven titles are used: redeemer, Holy One of Israel, creator, and King.

Isaiah 44:6: "Thus saith the *LORD the King of Israel, and his redeemer* the LORD of hosts; *I am the first, and I am the last;* and beside me there is no God."

Here again the titles King, redeemer, and the first and the last are used.

Isaiah 44:24: Thus saith the LORD, *thy redeemer,* and he that *formed thee from the womb,* I am the LORD that *maketh all things;* that stretcheth forth the heavens alone; that spreadeth abroad the earth by myself."

Here the God of the Old Testament again depicts himself in two of the seven roles: as redeemer and as creator.

There are many more verse comparisons that can be made to show that Jesus Christ of the New Testament is also Jehovah of the Old Testament, though there is no room to make them in this context. But Latter-day Saints believe that Jesus Christ is the God spoken of in the *6th chapter of Deuteronomy, verses 4 and 5* which say, "Hear, O Israel; the LORD our God is one LORD: And *thou shalt love the LORD thy God* with all thine heart, and with all thy soul, and with all thy might."

We also believe that he is the God who gave the ten commandments found in *Exodus 20, 2-3,* and said, "I am the LORD thy God, . . . Thou shalt have no other gods before me."

Before we leave this subject let me at least give you a brief list of scriptures to compare. In each case you'll find that the Old Testament passage says *Jehovah* does something, the New Testament passage says that *Christ* is the one that does it. Here's the list: compare *Genesis 17:1* with *Revelation 1:8* (The Almighty); *Exodus 3:14* with *John 8:55 through 58* (I AM); *Deuteronomy 1:32 and 33* with *1st Corinthians 10:1 through 4* (went before Israel in a cloud); *Psalm 96:13* with *John 5:22 and 23* (the judge); *Isaiah 44:6* with *Revelation 1:17* (the first and the last); *Isaiah 45:11 and 12* with *John 1:1 through 3* (the creator); *Isaiah 45:23* with *Romans 14:10 and 11* (every knee shall bow, and every tongue confess); *Hosea 13:4* with *Acts 4:12* (the only saviour); and *Zechariah 14:5* with *1st Thessalonians 3:13* (shall come with his saints). That's not all the passages, by any means, but that should be enough to convince you that Jesus Christ is Jehovah.[11]

Principle *Number 12,* then, is the conclusion that **the New Testament Jesus Christ is the Jehovah of the Old Testament.**

But the Old Testament verses I cited leave some challenging questions unanswered. They talk about there being only one god, they and seem to be in direct contradiction to literally hundreds of Bible verses that talk about the existence of a God the Father, a God the Son, and a God the Holy Ghost. Catholic and Protestant theologians have struggled with that

---

11. B of M: Moro. 10:34; D&C 110:2-4, D&C 109:68. PGP: Abr. 2:7-9. Bible: see number 12.

contradiction for almost nineteen centuries and still they haven't come up with an answer that satisfies them nor the world at large. They've formulated theories and creeds, engaged in countless arguments and debates, and created hundreds of new churches based on their conclusions, and the debates still continue. Critics of Mormonism who accept their theories as fact stand on very shaky ground, for their fellow theologians continue to be in disagreement on what the true nature of God is.

But I'm digressing from my intended purpose, to show from Latter-day Saint scripture and doctrine that Mormons are truly Christians. But as I report further principles, let me suggest that the answers to the dilemma are found in those principles.[12]

Doctrinal Evidence *Number 13:* Let's focus a bit longer on the creation. Latter-day Saints believe that **Jesus Christ was the creator of not just this earth, but of worlds** (plural). The book of *Hebrews, chapter 1, verses 1 and 2,* helps us to understand this principle: "God, who at sundry times and in divers manners spake in time past unto the fathers by the prophets, Hath in these last days spoken unto us by *his Son, whom he hath appointed heir of all things, by whom also he made the worlds."* Notice that last word: worlds, plural. And we read the same thing in *Hebrews 11:3:* "Through faith we understand that *the worlds* (plural) *were framed by the word of God. . . ."*

A passage in Latter-day Saint scripture, *Moses, chapter 1, verses 32 through 35,* gives us much more understanding about this concept: *"By the word of my power, have I created them, which is mine Only Begotten Son,* who is full of grace and truth. And *worlds without number have I created;* and I also created them for mine own purpose; and *by the Son I created them,* which is mine Only Begotten. And the first man of all men have I called Adam, which is many. *But only an account of this earth, and the inhabitants thereof, give I unto you.* For behold, there are *many worlds that have passed away by the word of my power.* And there are many that now stand, and innumerable are they unto man, but all things are numbered unto me, for they are mine and I know them."

And then the next verse, *verse 36,* contains a request which I personally believe holds the key to the dilemma I mentioned earlier: the question of is there more than one God for this earth? The request was, "Be merciful unto thy servant, O God, and *tell me concerning this earth, and the*

---

12. Bible: Isa. 43:10-12; Isa. 43:14-15; Isa. 44:6; Isa. 44:24. See Deut. 6:4-5, Ex. 20:2-3.

inhabitants thereof, and also the heavens, and then thy servant will be content." I think an important key to understanding the scriptures is that *God usually tells us only about this earth,* while only occasionally giving us a glimpse concerning the eternities before this earth was created, and the future after the millennium.

Both the Bible and Latter-day Saint scriptures tell us emphatically that *there is only one God for this earth, and that God is the Jehovah of the Old Testament, who is Jesus Christ of the New Testament.* But they both give us a little extra information that shows that Jehovah was God the Son, and that he has a father who is also functioning as a Diety.[13]

Principle 14: **Jesus Christ worked under the direction of God the Father when he created the earth and when he came here in his mortal ministry.** We already read *Hebrews 1:2,* which says that God made the worlds by his Son. If I can make a comparison, I'd like to suggest that the relationship of God the Father and God the Son is a bit like a corporate structure today. God the Father is the Chairman of the Board; God the Son, the Lord Jesus Christ, is the General Manager. The Chairman of the Board said to create the world; the General Manager obeyed that instruction and created it. So the General Manager, Jesus Christ, is the creator of the earth, but God the Father told him to do it.

Mormon scripture goes further in explaining that Jesus Christ functioned under the direction of God the Father during his ministry here on earth. *3rd Nephi 27, verses 13 through 15* contain these words of the Savior: *"I came into the world to do the will of my Father, because my Father sent me.* And my Father sent me that I might be lifted up upon the cross; and after that I had been lifted up upon the cross, that I might draw all men unto me, that as I have been lifted up by men even so should men be lifted up by the Father, to stand before me, to be judged of their works, whether they be good or whether they be evil—And for this cause have I been lifted up; therefore, *according to the power of the Father I will draw all men unto me, that they may be judged according to their works."*[14]

Principle 15: **God the Father has given complete responsibility for creating, governing, redeeming and judging this earth to his son Jesus Christ.** This is Biblical doctrine. *John 3:35* says, "The Father loveth the

---

13. Bible: Heb. 1:2; Heb. 11:3. D&C 76:23-24; 93:7-11. PGP: Moses 1:32-36. In the scriptures, God is usually speaking only about this earth.

14. B of M: 3 Ne. 27: 13-15; 3 Ne. 18:27; Mosiah 15:6-9. D&C 93:1-5; D&C 76: 41-43. Bible: Heb. 1:2; Eph. 3:9; Col. 1:12-18; John 1:1-14.

Son, and *hath given all things unto his hand." John 13:3* says "Jesus knowing that *the Father had given all things into his hands,* and that he was come from God, and went to God, . . . " In *Luke 10:22* Jesus said, *"All things are delivered to me of my Father."* *Colossians 1:15 through 19* describes Jesus as the firstborn of every creature, and says, "By him were all things created, that are in heaven, and that are in earth, visible and invisible, whether they be thrones, or dominions, or principalities, or powers: *all things were created by him, and for him: And he is before all things, and by him all things consist.* And he is the head of the body, the church: who is the beginning, the firstborn from the dead; that in all things he might have the preeminence. *For it pleased the Father that in him should all ful- ness dwell." In John 5:22 and 23* Jesus said concerning the judgment: "The Father judgeth no man, but hath committed all judgment unto the Son: That all men should honour the Son, even as they honour the Father. He that honoureth not the Son honoureth not the Father which hath sent him." And *verses 26 and 27* add, "As the Father hath life in himself; *so hath he given to the Son to have life in himself; And hath given him authority to execute judgment* also, because he is the Son of Man."[15]

Doctrinal Evidence *Number 16:* Jesus Christ is a God, and rules as the God of this earth. When he came to the Americas, according to *3rd Nephi 11:14,* Jesus told the people, "Arise and come forth unto me, that ye may thrust your hands into my side, and also that ye may feel the prints of the nails in my hands and in my feet, that ye may know that *I am the God of Israel, and the God of the whole earth,* and have been slain for the sins of the world." In *2nd Nephi 29, verse 7* the Lord says, "Know ye not that there are more nations than one? Know ye not that I, the Lord your God, have created all men, and that I remember those who are upon the isles of the sea; and that *I rule in the heavens above and in the earth beneath;* and I bring forth my word unto the children of men, yea, even upon all the nations of the earth?"

So we can say that God the Father has given Jesus Christ complete pow- er and responsibility for governing this world. In that sense Jesus is the God of this earth and the only God with responsibility to function here.

---

15. Bible: John 3:35; John 13:3; Luke 10:22; Col 1:15-19; John 5:22-23, 26-27. B of M: Mosiah 15:1-9; 3 Ne. 28:7. D&C 93:1-5.

He is sometimes assisted by God the Father and the Holy Ghost, but Jesus is the God responsible for this earth.[16]

Principle *Number 17:* Jesus Christ will inherit this earth and all things he has created. *Hebrews 2:9 and 10* speaks of Jesus being "crowned with glory and honour, . . . *For whom are all things,* and by whom are all things."* He will deliver his kingdom spotless to God the Father, who will then give it back to Jesus and permit him to reign over it forever. *Doctrine and Covenants 76, verses 106 through 108* reads, "Christ shall have subdued all enemies under his feet, and shall have perfected his work; When *he shall deliver up the kingdom, and present it unto the Father,* spotless, saying: I have overcome and have trodden the wine-press alone, even the wine-press of the fierceness of the wrath of the Almighty God. *Then shall he be crowned with the crown of his glory, to sit on the throne of his power to reign forever and ever.*"[17]

Doctrinal Evidence *Number 18:* We need to understand that Jesus Christ and God the Father are not in competition with each other. **God the Father glorifies his name through Jesus Christ.** We've already read *3rd Nephi 9, verse 15* where the Lord explained, "I was with the Father from the beginning . . . and *in me hath the Father glorified his name." John 13:31* records Jesus' comment just prior to his crucifixion that "Now is the Son of man glorified, and *God is glorified in him.*" With that scripture in mind let's return to our corporate comparison: when the General Manager performs a specific assignment well, it adds to the stature of the corporation and to the prestige of the Chairman of the Board.[18]

Insight *Number 19:* Jesus Christ, like his Father, has a throne, and he sits at the right hand of God the Father. *Moroni 9:26* says, "May the grace of God the Father, whose throne is high in the heavens, and our Lord *Jesus Christ, who sitteth on the right hand of his power,* until all things shall become subject unto him, be, and abide with you forever." That's the same message as *Hebrews chapter 1, verse 3.* Talking about the Son, through whom the Father made the worlds, the scripture says, "Who

16. B of M: 3 Ne. 11:14; 2 Ne. 29:7; Mosiah 13:33-35; Mosiah 5:15; 2 Ne. 6:15; Mosiah 15:1; Morm. 3:21; Mosiah 27:31; Alma 26:7-37; 1 Ne. 13:40-42. Bible: Matt. 1:23; 1 Tim. 1:15-17; 2:3; Titus 1:3; 2:10; 3:4; Heb. 12:23. Compare John 5:22-23.
17. D&C 76:106-108; D&C 132:22-24; D&C 45:56-59; D&C 84:99-102. Bible: Heb. 2:9-10; John 14:2-3; Rev. 21:1-7; Rev. 22:1-7; Ps. 24:1-5.
18. B of M: 3 Ne. 9:15; 3 Ne. 23:9. D&C 132:31; D&C 19:17-19. Bible: John 13:31; John 14:13; John 17:1-5; 1 Pet. 4:11.

being the brightness of his glory, and the express image of his person, and upholding all things by the word of his power, when he had by himself purged our sins, *sat down on the right hand of the Majesty on high."* And *Hebrews 8:1* says, "We have such an high priest, who is *set on the right hand of the throne of the Majesty* in the heavens."[19]

Principle *Number 20:* Jesus Christ and God the Father are separate, distinct individuals. Some of the creeds of Christendom have asserted that Jesus Christ and God the Father are the same person. That statement is in direct contradiction to hundreds of passages of scripture both in the Bible and in Latter-day Saint scriptures. A person just doesn't sit beside himself as in the passages I've just quoted.

3rd Nephi 11, verse 7 records the words of God the Father, who spoke to the people from the heavens while Jesus Christ was on the earth among the people, saying "Behold *my Beloved Son,* in whom I am well pleased, *in whom I have glorified my name*—hear ye him." A person just isn't in two places at the same time, and Jesus isn't the Beloved Son of God the Father if they both are the same person.

The vision of Stephen, recorded in *Acts 7:55 and 56,* clearly shows that the Father, Jesus Christ and the Holy Ghost are three separate and distinct beings. While the Holy Ghost was on earth, with Stephen, he saw Jesus standing beside God the Father in the heavens. The passage says, "But he, *being full of the Holy Ghost,* looked up steadfastly into heaven, and *saw the glory of God, and Jesus standing on the right hand of God,* And said, Behold, I see the heavens opened, and *the Son of man standing on the right hand of God."*

In *John 16, verses 26 through 28,* Jesus said, "I will pray the Father for you: For the Father himself loveth you, because ye have loved me, and have believed that *I came out from God. I came forth from the Father,* and am come into the world: again, *I leave the world, and go to the Father."* Now Jesus didn't pray to himself, and he didn't leave himself when he came into the world, and he didn't go back to himself when he returned to heaven. The interpretation that Jesus Christ and God the Father are the same person just doesn't make sense. They're two separate persons, and those creeds that say they are the same person are in direct contradiction to hundreds of passages of scripture.

---

19. B of M: Moro. 9:26; Moro. 7:27. D&C 76:19-24, D&C 49:6. Bible: Heb. 1:3, 8:1; Luke 22:69; Mark 16:19; Acts 7:55-56; Col. 3:1; 1 Pet. 3:22.

But anti-Mormon critics try to accuse Mormons of not being Christian and of being polytheistic because of this very point. Traditional Christianity, they say, insists that there can be only one God. Since they believe the Father, Son and Holy Ghost are all Gods, the deduction is made that they have to be the same person. This deduction doesn't make sense, and thoughtful Christians know it doesn't, but they don't have the answer to their dilemma.

Let me give you an example of their struggle. This is what Walter Martin wrote on page 75 in his anti-Mormon diatribe, *The Maze of Mormonism*. Note carefully what he says and his acknowledgment of inability to resolve the problem: "There can be no doubt that the New Testament sets forth the thesis that there are three separate Persons in the Deity, known as the Father, the Son, and the Holy Spirit, and each of these is affirmed to be Eternal God (2 Peter 1:17; John 1:1; Acts 5:3, 4). At the same time, the New Testament declares that there is only one God (1 Timothy 2:5) *We are led inexorably to the conclusion that the three distinct Persons are the one God, though the finite mind of man may not be able to grasp the depth of this revelation of the divine character.*"

I'll tell you why the finite mind of man can't grasp the idea that the Father, The Son and the Holy Ghost are only one God, and hence the same person— because the idea's false! They are separate, distinct individuals. They are not all assigned to govern this earth—there is only one God assigned to this earth, and that God is the Old Testament Jehovah, who is the New Testament Jesus Christ.

You know, when someone calls me on the telephone and gets my name wrong or confuses me with someone else, I get a little bit irritated. I correct them. I believe that's typical behavior and that a normal person would feel and do the same. Most of Christianity seems confused, and many say God and Jesus Christ are the same person and have said it for hundreds of years; so I can't help but wonder if God the Father and Jesus Christ feel the same irritation at having their names confused.[20]

Doctrinal Evidence *Number 21:* Jesus Christ is one with his disciples in the same way that he is one with God the Father—they are united in purpose and objectives, but they are not the same person. A prayer offered by Jesus for his disciples, while he was among the people in the Americas, makes this relationship very clear. It's found in *3rd Nephi 19,*

20. B of M: 3 Ne. 11:7; 3 Ne. 18:27. D&C 76: 19-24; D&C 130:22. Bible: Acts 7:55-56; John 16:26-28; John 17:1-3; Heb. 1:1-3.

23 through 29: "And now, Father, I pray unto thee for them, and also for all those who shall believe on their words, that they may believe in me, *that I may be in them as thou, Father, art in me, that we may be one.* . . .Father, I thank thee that thou hast purified those whom I have chosen, because of their faith, and I pray for them, and also for them who shall believe on their words, that they may be purified in me, through faith on their words, even as they are purified in me. Father, I pray not for the world, but for those whom thou hast given me out of the world, because of their faith, that they may be purified in me, *that I may be in them as thou, Father, art in me, that we may be one, that I may be glorified in them."*

There's a very similar prayer offered by Jesus in *John 17, verses 20 through 23.* In these scriptures Jesus was also praying for unity among his disciples. He said, "Neither pray I for these alone, but for them also which shall believe on me through their word; *That they all may be one; as thou, Father, art in me, and I in thee, that they also may be one in us:* that the world may believe that thou hast sent me. And the glory which thou gavest me I have given them; *that they may be one, even as we are one: I in them, and thou in me, that they may be made perfect in one;* and that the world may know that thou hast sent me, and hast loved them, as thou hast loved me."

Now what is the logical interpretation of these two prayers? Did Jesus want himself and his disciples and their converts and God the Father to all be combined in some type of undefined, shapeless, everywhere-but-nowhere blob? Or did he want them all to be unified in the same harmonious objectives? Obviously, it is the latter concept that makes sense. The passage is not saying that the disciples and Jesus are the same person any more than Jesus and God the Father are the same person. They are separate, distinct individuals but unified in purpose.[21]

Number 22: It is Mormon doctrine that **Jesus Christ is a Mediator—an intermediary between man and God the Father.** He serves as our advocate, making intercession with the Father in behalf of men. *2nd Nephi 2:9* records the teachings of Lehi who taught, "Wherefore, he is the first-fruits unto God, inasmuch as *he shall make intercessions for all the children of men;* and they that believe in him shall be saved." *Verse 28* of the same chapter records his admonition to his sons in which he says, "I would

21. B of M: 3 Ne. 19:23-29; 3 Ne. 11:32-36; 3 Ne. 11:27-30; 3 Ne. 28:11. Bible: John 17:20-23; John 17:9-11; 1 John 5:7-8; Gal. 3:26-28.

that ye would *look to the great Mediator,* and hearken unto his great commandments; and be faithful unto his words, and choose eternal life, according to the will of his Holy Spirit."[22]

Evidence *Number 23:* Jesus Christ is the object of our praise. The Book of Mormon prophet Jacob taught, in *2nd Nephi 10:25,* "Wherefore, may God raise you from death by the power of the resurrection, and also from everlasting death by the power of the atonement, *that ye may be received unto the eternal kingdom of God, that ye may praise him through grace divine."* And *3rd Nephi 10:10* records the praise rendered to Jesus at the end of the great destruction which occurred in the Americas during the meridian of time: "And the earth did cleave together again, that it stood; and the mourning, and the weeping, and the wailing of the people who were spared alive did cease; and their mourning was turned into joy, and *their lamentations into the praise and thanksgiving unto the Lord Jesus Christ, their Redeemer."*[23]

Number 24: It is Latter-day Saint doctrine that **we worship Jesus Christ.** In *2nd Nephi 25, verses 28 and 29,* for instance, Nephi wrote: "I have spoken plainly unto you, that ye cannot misunderstand. And the words which I have spoken . . . are sufficient to teach any man the right way; for *the right way is to believe in Christ and deny him not;* for by denying him ye also deny the prophets and the law. And now behold, I say unto you that the right way is to believe in Christ, and deny him not; and Christ is the Holy One of Israel; wherefore *ye must bow down before him, and worship him with all your might, mind and strength,* and your whole soul; and if ye do this ye shall in nowise be cast out."[24]

Doctrinal Evidence *Number 25:* We believe that, as a God, **Jesus Christ is omnipotent—he is all powerful.** Ammon, a great missionary whose words were recorded in the Book of Mormon, said in *Alma 26, verses 35 and 36,* "My joy is carried away, even unto boasting in my God; for *he has all power, all wisdom, and all understanding; he comprehendeth all things,* and he is a merciful Being, even unto salvation, to those who repent and believe on his name....This is my life and my light, my joy and my

22. B of M: 2 Ne. 2:9; 2:28; Mosiah 14:12; 3 Ne. 27:16; Moro. 7:27-28; Mosiah 15:8. Bible: 1 John 2:1; Heb. 8:6; 9:15; 12:24.
23. B of M: 2 Ne. 10:25; 3 Ne. 10:10; Alma 26:36; 1 Ne. 15:15; 18:16; 2 Ne. 4:30; 9:49; Mosiah 18:30. Bible: Rev. 14:6-7; 19:5; Ps. 150:1-6; Ps. 148:1-5.
24. B of M: 2 Ne. 25:28-29; 1 Ne. 11:24; 3 Ne. 11:17; 4 Ne. 37. D&C 101:22-23; 115:8; 133:38-39; 76:20-21. Bible: Matt. 2:1-2; 8:2; 9:18; 14:33; 28:9, 16-17; Heb. 1:6; Rev. 4:10-11.

salvation, and my redemption from everlasting wo. Yea, blessed is the name of my God, who has been mindful of this people."

And in *1st Nephi 9:6* Nephi wrote that "The *Lord knoweth all things from the beginning;* wherefore, he prepareth a way to accomplish all his works among the children of men; for behold, *he hath all power unto the fulfilling of all his words.*"[25]

Number 26: We believe that **Jesus Christ is omniscient—that he knows all things.** The Book of Mormon prophet Jacob, about 550 B.C., said these words which are recorded in *2nd Nephi 9:20 and 21:* "O how great the holiness of our God! For *he knoweth all things, and there is not anything save he knows it.* And he cometh into the world that he may save all men if they will hearken unto his voice; for behold, he suffereth the pains of all men, yea, the pains of every living creature, both men, women, and children, who belong to the family of Adam."[26]

Doctrinal Evidence *Number 27:* We believe that **Jesus Christ is a God of miracles,** and that those miracles are manifest among men unless they are unrighteous or unbelieving. Moroni, the final prophet of the Book of Mormon, wrote these words in *Mormon chapter 9, verses 16 through 20:* "Behold, are not the things that God hath wrought marvelous in our eyes? Yea, and who can comprehend the marvelous works of God? *Who shall say that it was not a miracle that by his word the heaven and the earth should be;* and by the power of his word man was created of the dust of the earth; and *by the power of his word have miracles been wrought? And who shall say that Jesus Christ did not many mighty miracles?* And there were many mighty miracles wrought by the hands of the apostles. And if there were miracles wrought then, why has God ceased to be a God of miracles and yet be an unchangeable Being? And behold, I say unto you he changeth not; if so he would cease to be God; and *he ceaseth not to be God, and is a God of miracles.* And the reason why he ceaseth to do miracles among the children of men is because that they dwindle in unbelief, and depart from the right way, and know not the God in whom they should trust."[27]

---

25. B of M: Alma 26:35-36; 1 Ne. 9:6; Mosiah 3:5, 18; Mosiah 4:6-9; Mosiah 5:15. Bible: Matt. 28:18; Rev. 19:1-10; Eph. 1:20-22; Rom. 1:20.

26. B of M: 2 Ne. 9:20-21; 1 Ne. 9:6; Mosiah 4:9; Alma 26:35; Morm. 8:17. D&C 88:41. Bible: Matt. 9:4; John 2:24-25; John 18:4; Acts 15:8.

27. B of M: Morm. 9:16-20; 3 Ne. 29:5-7; 2 Ne. 27:23; Morm. 9:8-12. Bible: Mark 16:17-18; John 2:23; John 12:37.

Evidence *Number 28:* We believe that **Jesus Christ is a God of mercy.** In *1st Nephi 1:20* we read, "Behold, I, Nephi, will show unto you that *the tender mercies of the Lord are over all those whom he hath chosen, because of their faith,* to make them mighty even unto the power of deliverance." And Alma testified of Christ's great mercy when he told of his great conversion experience in *Alma 38:8:* "I was three days and three nights in the most bitter pain and anguish of soul; and *never, until I did cry out unto the Lord Jesus Christ for mercy, did I receive a remission of my sins. But behold, I did cry to him and I did find peace to my soul.*"[28]

Number 29: Latter-day Saints believe that **Jesus Christ is the source of all good** here upon the earth. In *Moroni 7, verses 11-14,* the final prophet of the Book of Mormon wrote these words: "Behold, a bitter fountain cannot bring forth good water; neither can a good fountain bring forth bitter water; wherefore, a man being a servant of the devil cannot follow Christ; and if he follow Christ he cannot be a servant of the devil. Wherefore, *all things which are good cometh of God;* and that which is evil cometh of the devil; for the devil is an enemy unto God, and fighteth against him continually, and inviteth and enticeth to sin, and to do that which is evil continually. But behold, *that which is of God inviteth and enticeth to do good continually; wherefore, every thing which inviteth and enticeth to do good, and to love God, and to serve him, is inspired of God.* Wherefore, take heed, my beloved brethren, that ye do *not judge that which is evil to be of God, or that which is good and of God to be of the devil.*"[29]

Doctrinal Evidence *Number 30:* We believe that **Jesus Christ is the source of all spiritual gifts,** and that those gifts or signs are found among those who believe in him. As Moroni taught, in *Moroni 10:18 and 19,* "I would exhort you, my beloved brethren, that ye remember that *every good gift cometh of Christ.* . . .Remember that he is the same yesterday, today, and forever, and that *all these gifts of which I have spoken, which are spiritual, never will be done away,* even as long as the world shall stand, only according to the unbelief of the children of men."[30]

---

28. B of M: 1 Ne. 1:20; Alma 38:8; Hel. 3:27-28; Alma 26:35-36; Alma 36:17-21. Bible: Matt. 9:12-13; Luke 23:24; Matt. 5:7; Luke 7:12-15; John 8:3-11.

29. B of M: Moro. 7:11-19; Omni 25; Ether 4:11-12; Moro. 7:22-24; Alma 5:38-40. Bible: Gen. 1:31; 1 Tim. 4:4; Hab. 1:12-13; Ps. 122:9; Acts 14:15-17.

30. B of M: Moro. 10:18-19; Morm. 9:24-25; Omni 25, 26; Alma 9:19-23; Moro. 10:8-17. Bible: Mark 16:16-20; Acts 2:43; 1 Cor. 12:1-31; 1 Cor. 13:1-13.

Evidence *Number 31:* Latter-day Saints believe that **Jesus Christ is the Father of heaven and earth, in the sense that he created them.** In *Helaman chapter 14, verses 12 and 13,* Samuel the Lamanite called Jesus the Father, meaning he created them, when he told the people he wanted them to "Know of the coming of *Jesus Christ, the Son of God, the Father of heaven and of earth, the Creator of all things from the beginning;* and that ye might know of the signs of his coming, to the intent that ye might believe on his name. And if ye believe on his name ye will repent of all your sins, that thereby ye may have a remission of them through his merits."

In *Ether 4:7,* the Lord also refers to himself as Father and Creator saying, "In that day that they shall exercise faith in me, . . . that they may become sanctified in me, then will I manifest unto them the things which the brother of Jared saw, even to the unfolding unto them all my revelations, saith *Jesus Christ, the Son of God, the Father of the heavens and of the earth, and all things that in them are.*"[31]

Doctrinal Principle *Number 32:* We believe that **man is created in the image of the pre-mortal Jesus Christ.** You remember the account from *Genesis in chapter 1, verses 26 and 27:* "God said, Let us make man in our image, after our likeness: . . . So *God created man in his own image, in the image of God created he him.*" And *Genesis 5:1* tells us that "In the day that God created man, *in the likeness of God made he him.*"

The Book of Mormon gives us more details. *Ether chapter 3, verses 15 and 16,* tells of how Jesus appeared to the brother of Jared several thousand years before he was born in the flesh, and the brother of Jared saw the body of the spirit of Christ and learned that his spirit body was the model after which man's temporal body was created. In the message, the Lord told him, "Seest thou that ye are created after mine own image? Yea, even all men were created in the beginning after mine own image. Behold *this body, which ye now behold, is the body of my spirit; and man have I created after the body of my spirit;* and even as I appear unto thee to be in the spirit will I appear unto my people in the flesh."

Mosiah chapter 7, verses 26 and 27, also teaches that man was created in the form of Christ's pre-mortal spirit body. The passage tells us of the preaching of the prophet Abinadi, saying that he "Prophesied of many things which are to come, yea, even the coming of Christ. And because he said

31. B of M: Hel. 14:12-13; Ether 4:7; Mosiah 3:8; Alma 11:38-40; Mosiah 7:27. Bible: Mal. 2:10; Acts 17:24-29; Isa. 9:6.

unto them that *Christ was the God, the Father of all things,* and said that *he should take upon him the image of man, and it should be the image after which man was created in the beginning;* or in other words, he said that *man was created after the image of God,* and that God should come down among the children of men, and take upon him flesh and blood, and go forth upon the face of the earth."[32]

Doctrinal Evidence *Number 33:* Mormon doctrine asserts that **Jesus Christ was prepared from the foundation of the world to redeem his people.** *Ether, chapter 3, verse 14* records a manifestation given to the brother of Jared in which the Lord said, *"I am he who was prepared from the foundation of the world to redeem my people. Behold, I am Jesus Christ. . . . In me shall all mankind have light, and that eternally, even they who shall believe on my name."*[33]

Number 34: We believe that it is **Jesus Christ who will restore the descendants of Jacob, known as the house of Israel, to their homeland in Israel and to their former glory in the last days.** *3rd Nephi chapter 5, verses 20 through 26,* reports these comments from the prophet Mormon: "I have reason to bless my God and my Savior Jesus Christ, that he brought our fathers out of the land of Jerusalem, . . . and that he hath given me and my people so much knowledge unto the salvation of our souls. . . . And he hath covenanted with all the house of Jacob, even so shall the covenant wherewith he hath covenanted with the house of Jacob be fulfilled in his own due time, *unto the restoring all the house of Jacob unto the knowledge of the covenant that he hath covenanted with them. And then shall they know their Redeemer, who is Jesus Christ, the Son of God; and them shall they be gathered in from the four quarters of the earth unto their own lands."*[34]

Principle *Number 35:* We believe that **it was Jesus Christ who both gave and fulfilled the law of Moses.** *3rd Nephi 15, verses 4 through 9,* reveals that when Jesus appeared in the Americas he taught, "I say unto you that the law is fulfilled that was given unto Moses. Behold, *I am he that gave the law,* and I am he who covenanted with my people Israel; therefore, *the law in me is fulfilled, for I have come to fulfill the law;* there-

---

32. B of M: Ether 3:15-16; Mosiah 7:26-27; Alma 18:34; Alma 22:12. Bible: Gen. 1:26-27; Gen. 5:1-3; Col. 3:10; Rom. 8:29.

33. B of M: Ether 3:14; Mosiah 15:18-20; Mosiah 4:6-7; Mosiah 18:13; Alma 22:13. Bible: 1 Pet. 1:19-20; Acts 2:23; Luke 22:22; Rev. 13:8; John 17:4-5.

34. B of M: 3 Ne. 5:20-26; 2 Ne. 25:16-17; 2 Ne. 30:7-8. Bible: Ezek. 37:21-22; Isa. 51:11; Isa. 35:1-10.

fore it hath an end. . . .Behold, the covenant which I have made with my people is not all fulfilled; *but the law which was given unto Moses hath an end in me. Behold, I am the law,* and the light. Look unto me, and endure to the end, and ye shall live; for unto him that endureth to the end will I give eternal life."

Almost six centuries before Christ came in the flesh Nephi was already anticipating that Jesus would fulfill the law of Moses. We read in *2nd Nephi 25:24 through 26,* "Notwithstanding we believe in Christ, we keep the law of Moses, and look forward with steadfastness unto Christ, *until the law shall be fulfilled.* For, for this end was the law given; wherefore *the law hath become dead unto us, and we are made alive in Christ because of our faith;* yet we keep the law because of the commandments. And *we talk of Christ, we rejoice in Christ, we preach of Christ, we prophesy of Christ,* and we write according to our prophecies, that our children may know to what source they may look for a remission of their sins."[35]

Number 36: We believe that **salvation is only available to mankind through Jesus Christ.** *2nd Nephi 25:20* records Nephi's profound testimony that, "As the Lord God liveth, there is *none other name given under heaven save it be this Jesus Christ,* of which I have spoken, *whereby man can be saved.*"

And King Benjamin said, in *Mosiah 3:16 through 18,* "*There shall be no other name given nor any other way nor means whereby salvation can come unto the children of men, only in and through the name of Christ,* the Lord Omnipotent. . . .Men drink damnation to their souls except they humble themselves and become as little children, and believe that *salvation was, and is, and is to come, in and through the atoning blood of Christ, the Lord Omnipotent.*"[36]

Doctrinal Evidence *Number 37:* It is Latter-day Saint doctrine that **Jesus Christ offers his salvation to all mankind**—he is no respecter of persons. As Nephi wrote, in *2nd Nephi chapter 26, verses 23 through 28,* "The Lord God worketh not in darkness. He doeth not anything save it be for the benefit of the world; for he loveth the world, even that he layeth down his own life that he may draw all men unto him. Wherefore, *he commandeth none that they shall not partake of his salvation. . . .He hath given*

---

35. B of M: 3 Ne. 15:4-9; 2 Ne. 25:24-26; 3 Ne. 9:15-17; Moro. 8:8. Bible: Compare Ex. 17:5-6 & 1 Cor. 10:1-4; Matt. 5:17-18; Rom. 10:4; Isa. 33:22.
36. B of M: 2 Ne. 25:20; Mosiah 3:16-18; 2 Ne. 31:20-21; Mosiah 5:8-9; Hel. 5:9-12. Bible: Acts 4:10-12; Acts 2:21; 1 Thes. 5:9; Matt. 1:21.

it free for all men; and he hath commanded his people that they should persuade all men to repentance. Behold, hath the Lord commanded any that they should not partake of his goodness? Behold I say unto you, Nay; but *all men are privileged the one like unto the other, and none are forbidden.*"[37]

Doctrinal Evidence *Number 38:* We believe that **Jesus Christ broke the bands of death, and made it possible for mankind to live again after death.** In *Mosiah 16:7 and 8* Abinadi teaches, "If Christ had not risen from the dead, or have *broken the bands of death that the grave should have no victory, and that death should have no sting, there could have been no resurrection. But there is a resurrection, therefore the grave hath no victory, and the sting of death is swallowed up in Christ.*"[38]

Evidence *Number 39:* Latter-day Saint doctrine asserts that **Jesus Christ took the sins of all the world upon himself and paid for the transgressions of mankind.** *Mosiah 26:22 through 24* records the words of the Lord to Alma in which he said, "This is my church; whosoever is baptized shall be baptized unto repentance. And whomsoever ye receive shall believe in my name; and him will I freely forgive. For *it is I that taketh upon me the sins of the world;* for it is I that hath created them; and it is I that granted unto him that believeth unto the end a place at my right hand. For behold, in my name are they called; and if they know me they shall come forth, and shall have a place at my right hand."

As Jacob explained, in *2nd Nephi 9:20 through 22:* "O how great the holiness of our God! For he knoweth all things, and there is not anything save he knows it. And he cometh into the world that he may save all men if they will hearken unto his voice; for behold, *he suffereth the pains of all men, yea, the pains of every living creature, both men, women, and children, who belong to the family of Adam.* And he suffereth this that the resurrection might pass upon all men, that all might stand before him at the great and judgment day."[39]

Number 40: We believe that **the sacrifice and death of Jesus Christ began the resurrection process,** and that Jesus was the "firstfruits"

---

37. B of M: 2 Ne. 26:23-28; 2 Ne. 26:33; Hel. 3:27-30; Alma 41:6-8; Hel. 14:29-31. Bible: 1 Tim. 4:10; 1 John 4:14; Acts 10:34-35; Rom. 1:16; 1 Cor. 15:21-22.

38. B of M: Mosiah 16:7-8; Mosiah 15:21-27; Alma 11:42-43; Hel. 14:15-17; Morm. 7:5-7; Alma 22:13-14. Bible: 1 Cor. 15:22; 2 Tim. 1:10; Rom. 6:8-11; John 11:25-26.

39. B of M: Mosiah 26:22-24; 2 Ne. 9:20-22; Mosiah 15:6-9; Alma 7:11-13; Alma 11:40-45. Bible: John 1:29; 1 Pet. 3:18; 1 Pet. 2:21-24; Isa. 53:4-5.

of the resurrection. *Helaman chapter 14, verses 15 through 17,* contain the words of Samuel the Lamanite on the subject: "He surely must die that salvation may come; yea, it behooveth him and becometh *expedient that he dieth, to bring to pass the resurrection of the dead, that thereby men may be brought unto the presence of the Lord.* Yea, behold, *this death bringeth to pass the resurrection,* and redeemeth all mankind from the first death—that spiritual death; for all mankind, by the fall of Adam being cut off from the presence of the Lord, are considered as dead, both as to things temporal and to things spiritual. But behold, the resurrection of Christ redeemeth mankind, yea, even all mankind, and bringeth them back into the presence of the Lord."[40]

Principle *Number 41:* It is Mormon doctrine that **mankind is saved by the grace of Jesus Christ.** As Nephi explained in *2nd Nephi 25:23,* "We labor diligently to write, to persuade our children, and also our brethren, to believe in Christ, and to be reconciled to God; for *we know that it is by grace that we are saved, after all we can do.*"

And Jacob taught in *2nd Nephi 10:24,* "Wherefore, my beloved brethren, reconcile yourselves to the will of God, and not to the will of the devil and the flesh; and remember, after ye are reconciled unto God, that *it is only in and through the grace of God that ye are saved.*"

Now anti-Mormon critics keep misrepresenting Mormon doctrine on this point, trying to assert that Mormons believe that we are saved by works. What they say is not true! Those passages I've just quoted state our doctrine exactly. After man has done all he can, then the grace of God is still necessary for man to be saved, and without that grace there can be no salvation.

I think a brief comparison is in order. Instead of saying "Man is saved by grace," let's change the statement to be, "Man is graduated by diploma." Now when we go to college, we just do not become a college graduate until that diploma is actually awarded. But it would be foolish to assume that all that must happen is that a diploma be handed to us. We have to go to class, and study diligently, write papers and fulfill every requirement placed by the college before we can be eligible for graduation. When it comes to being saved by the grace of Christ, the same principle applies. Jesus Christ has specified a series of requirements which individuals must meet before he will grant them the gift of his grace—requirements like

---

40. B of M: Hel. 14:15-17; Morm. 9:12-14; 2 Ne. 2:6-9. Bible: Acts 26:23; Col. 1:18; Rev. 1:5.

true faith and complete repentance. We hear our Protestant friends talking a lot about the possibility of being saved by grace, but we wish they would apply themselves a bit more to fulfilling the requirements Jesus has specified that individuals must meet before he will grant them his gift of grace. We need to remember what the Lord said in his Sermon on the Mount. In *Matthew 7:21*, it says, *"Not every one that saith unto me, Lord, Lord, shall enter into the kingdom of heaven; but he that doeth the will of my Father which is in heaven."*

In Mormonism we readily acknowledge that man must have the grace of God to be saved, but we place more emphasis on attempting to do what Jesus says he wants us to do before he will grant his saving grace to us. Those who talk only about being saved by grace, without addressing the need to meet Christ's qualifying requirements, are like college students who talk about getting their diploma while neglecting to go to class and study. And those who talk so much of man's accepting Christ would do well, in our opinion, to *dwell a bit more on the matter of Christ accepting man.* [41]

Number 42: We believe that **man can be redeemed through the blood of Christ** which was shed for them in the Lord's atoning sacrifice. As Alma said in *Alma 5:27,* "Have ye walked, keeping yourselves blameless before God? Could ye say, if ye were called to die at this time, within yourselves, that ye have been sufficiently humble? That *your garments have been cleansed and made white through the blood of Christ,* who will come to redeem his people from their sins?"

In *Mosiah chapter 3, verses 11 and 12,* King Benjamin taught concerning Christ, *"His blood atoneth for the sins of those who have fallen by the transgression of Adam,* who have *died not knowing the will of God* concerning them, or who have *ignorantly sinned.* But wo, wo unto him who knoweth that he rebelleth against God! For salvation cometh to none such except it be through repentance and faith on the Lord Jesus Christ." [42]

Doctrinal Evidence *Number 43:* We believe that **the Book of Mormon was written to persuade men to believe in Jesus Christ,** and we receive constant confirmation from our missionaries that it continues to do so. *Jacob chapter 1, verses 6 through 8,* contains a typical statement,

---

41. B of M: 2 Ne. 25:23; 2 Ne. 10:24; Moro. 10:32; Ether 12:26-27; 2 Ne. 2:6-8; Alma 5:48. Bible: Matt. 7:21; Eph. 2:5-10; Rom. 3:21-24; Acts 15:11.
42. B of M: Alma 5:27; Mosiah 3:11-12; Mosiah 3:16-18; Alma 5:21; Alma 13:11. Bible: 1 Pet. 1:18-19; John 1:7; Col. 1:14; Heb. 9:12.

by an author of the Book of Mormon, concerning his purpose for writing. Jacob said, "We also had many revelations, and the spirit of much prophecy; wherefore, we knew of Christ and his kingdom, which should come. Wherefore we labored diligently among our people, that we might *persuade them to come unto Christ, and partake of the goodness of God,* that they might enter into his rest, lest by any means he should swear in his wrath they should not enter in, as in the provocation in the days of temptation while the children of Israel were in the wilderness. Wherefore, we would to God we could persuade all men not to rebel against God, to provoke him to anger, but that *all men would believe in Christ,* and view his death, and suffer his cross and bear the shame of the world."

And Nephi wrote, in *1st Nephi 6, verse 4,* "The fulness of mine intent is that I may *persuade men to come unto the God* of Abraham, and the God of Isaac, and the God of Jacob, *and be saved.*"[43]

Number 44: We believe that **the Book of Mormon confirms the Bible's witness that Jesus is the Lord.** It is another testament of Jesus Christ.

Nephi, in *1st Nephi 13:40,* recorded the words of an angel who spoke concerning the dual witness of the Bible and the Book of Mormon, in these words: "The angel spake unto me saying: These last records, which thou hast seen among the Gentiles, shall establish the truth of the first, which are of the twelve apostles of the Lamb, and shall make known the plain and precious things which have been taken away from them; and shall make known to all kindreds, tongues, and people, that *the Lamb of God is the Son of the Eternal Father, and the Savior of the world; and that all men must come unto him, or they cannot be saved.*"

And Mormon, whose efforts in abridging the historical records are the reason the book carries his name, wrote in *Mormon 3:20 through 22,* "For this cause I write unto you, that ye may know that *ye must all stand before the judgment-seat of Christ,* yea, every soul who belongs to the whole human family of Adam; and ye must stand to be judged of your works, whether they be good or evil; And also that ye may *believe the gospel of Jesus Christ,* which ye shall have among you; and also that the Jews, the covenant people of the Lord, shall have other witness besides him whom they saw and heard, that *Jesus, whom they slew, was the very Christ and the very God.* And I would that I could persuade all ye ends of the earth to repent and prepare to stand before the judgment-seat of Christ."[44]

---

43. B of M: Jacob 1:6-8; 1 Ne. 6:4; 2 Ne. 33:4-7; Morm. 3:20-22.
44. B of M: 1 Ne. 13:40; Morm. 3:20-22; Morm. 7:8-9; 2 Ne. 29:7-11.

Evidence *Number 45:* Latter-day Saint scriptures counsel and command Church members to study the words of Jesus Christ. Nephi taught in *2nd Nephi chapter 32, verse 3,* "Angels speak by the power of the Holy Ghost; wherefore, they speak the words of Christ. Wherefore, I said unto you, *feast upon the words of Christ; for behold, the words of Christ will tell you all things what ye should do.*"[45]

Principle *Number 46:* Mormon scriptures warn of the danger of denying Jesus Christ and his works. This sharp warning was written by Mormon in *3rd Nephi 29:5 through 7:* "Wo unto him that spurneth at the doings of the Lord; yea, *wo unto him that shall deny the Christ and his works! Yea, wo unto him that shall deny the revelations of the Lord, and that shall say the Lord no longer worketh by revelation, or by prophecy, or by gifts, or by tongues, or by healings, or by the power of the Holy Ghost!* Yea, and wo unto him that shall say at that day, to get gain, that *there can be no miracle wrought by Jesus Christ;* for he that doeth this shall become like unto the son of perdition, for whom there was no mercy, according to the word of Christ!"

And *Jacob chapter 6, verses 8 and 9,* contains this warning: "Behold, will ye *reject these words?* Will ye *reject the words of the prophets;* and will ye *reject all the words which have been spoken concerning Christ,* after so many have spoken concerning him; and *deny the good word of Christ, and the power of God, and the gift of the Holy Ghost, and quench the Holy Spirit,* and make a mock of the great plan of redemption, which hath been laid for you? Know ye not that if ye will do these things, that the power of the redemption and the resurrection, which is in Christ, will bring you to *stand with shame and awful guilt before the bar of God?*"[46]

Evidence *Number 47:* We believe **it is man's responsibility to perform all religious acts in the name of Jesus Christ,** and we carefully strive to fulfill that injunction in our Church meetings and activities. Moroni taught in *Mormon 9:28 and 29,* "Be wise in the days of your probation; strip yourselves of all uncleanness; ask not, that ye may consume it on your lusts, but ask with a firmness unshaken, that ye will yield to no temptation, but that ye will serve the true and living God. See that ye are not baptized unworthily; see that ye partake not of the sacrament of Christ unworthily; but *see that ye do all things in worthiness, and do it in the name of Jesus*

---

45. B of M: 2 Ne. 32:3; 2 Ne. 31:20; Moro. 7:18-19; Jacob 4:3-13; Mosiah 1:6-7.
46. B of M: 3 Ne. 29:5-7; Jacob 6:8-9; 2 Ne. 25:28-29; Alma 30:47; Morm. 9:1-5; Moro. 8:14-21.

Christ, the Son of the living God; and if ye do this, and endure to the end, ye will in nowise be cast out."[47]

Number 48: In obedience to the Lord's commandment **Latter-day Saints pray to God the Father, always in the name of Jesus Christ.** When Jesus visited the Americas following his resurrection, *3rd Nephi 18:19 through 20* records that he taught, "Ye must *always pray unto the Father in my name;* And whatsoever ye shall *ask the Father in my name,* which is right, believing that ye shall receive, behold it shall be given unto you."

And Nephi had previously taught in *2nd Nephi 32:9,* "Ye must pray always, and not faint; ye must not perform any thing unto the Lord save in the first place *ye shall pray unto the Father in the name of Christ, that he will consecrate thy performance unto thee,* that thy performance may be for the welfare of thy soul."[48]

Doctrinal Evidence *Number 49:* Mormons regard themselves and conduct themselves as disciples of the Lord Jesus Christ. The attitude expressed by Mormon in *3rd Nephi chapter 5, verse 13,* is typical: "Behold, *I am a disciple of Jesus Christ,* the Son of God. *I have been called of him to declare his word among his people,* that they might have everlasting life."

In *Moroni 7:30 and 31* the discipleship of Church members was characterized in these words: "For behold, *they are subject unto him, to minister according to the word of his command,* showing themselves unto them of strong faith and a firm mind in every form of godliness. And the office of their ministry is to call men unto repentance, and to fulfill and to do the work of the covenants of the Father, which he hath made unto the children of men, to prepare the way among the children of men, *by declaring the word of Christ unto the chosen vessels of the Lord, that they may bear testimony of him.*"[49]

Number 50: Latter-day Saints believe **man's greatest responsibility during mortal life is to serve Jesus Christ and keep his commandments.** While visiting in the Americas following his resurrection, Jesus stated this

---

47. B of M: Morm. 9:28-29; Jacob 4:6; 3 Ne. 7:15-20; 3 Ne. 26:17-21; 4 Ne. 5. Bible: Col 3:17; Luke 24:47; Acts 2:38, 3:6, 4:7-10, 4:30, 9:27, 16:18, 19:5; Matt. 28:19.

48. B of M: 3 Ne. 18:19-21; 3 Ne. 19:6-8; 3 Ne. 28:25-30; 2 Ne. 32:9; Jacob 4:4-5. Bible: Col 3:17; John 15:16; John 16:23-24.

49. B of M: 3 Ne. 5:13; Moro. 7:30-31; Mosiah 26:20-22; 3 Ne. 15:11-12; Mosiah 2:18-25; 4 Ne. 1. Bible: John 13:34-35; John 8:31-32; John 12:26; Col. 3:24.

responsibility very clearly. We find it in *3rd Nephi 12, 19 and 20: "I have given you the law and the commandments of my Father, that ye shall believe in me,* and that ye shall repent of your sins, and *come unto me* with a broken heart and a contrite spirit. Behold, ye have the commandments before you, and the law is fulfilled. Therefore come unto me and be ye saved; for verily I say unto you, that *except ye shall keep my commandments,* which I have commanded you at this time, *ye shall in no case enter into the kingdom of heaven."*[50]

Principle *Number 51:* Latter-day Saint scripture teaches that **we must put off the natural man by submitting our will to the will of Jesus Christ.** King Benjamin taught this clearly in *Mosiah 3:19:* "The *natural man is an enemy to God,* and has been from the fall of Adam, and will be, forever and ever, unless he yields to the enticings of the Holy Spirit, and *putteth off the natural man and becometh a saint through the atonement of Christ the Lord, and becometh as a child,* submissive, meek, humble, patient, full of love, willing to submit to all things which the Lord seeth fit to inflict upon him, even as a child doth submit to his father."[51]

Principle *Number 52:* We believe that **Jesus Christ requires those who act in his name to be properly authorized and ordained,** and that priesthood power is found in The Church of Jesus Christ of Latter-day Saints. Our *fifth Article of Faith* states, "We believe that *a man must be called of God,* by prophecy, and by the laying on of hands, *by those who are in authority* to preach the Gospel and administer in the ordinances thereof."

We believe that an authorized call from God to serve him comes through those already holding priesthood power and results in a chain of ordinations back to God. Every Latter-day Saint priesthood holder can trace his priesthood authority back to Jesus Christ. My chain of ordinations is typical: I was ordained to the higher priesthood by my father, Don Q. Crowther, who was ordained by Melvin J. Ballard, who was ordained by Heber J. Grant, who was ordained by George Q. Cannon, who was ordained by Brigham Young, who was ordained by Oliver Cowdery, Martin Harris, and David Whitmer, whose priesthood connects back to Joseph Smith, who

---

50. B of M: 3 Ne. 12:19-20; Mosiah 2:18-25; Mosiah 4:6-7; Alma 7:22-24; Alma 37:44-47. Bible: John 14:15; John 15:14; Deut. 10:12-13.

51. B of M: Mosiah 3:19; Alma 19:6; Alma 26:21-22; Mosiah 24:13-16; Alma 7:22-23. Bible: 1 Cor. 2:9-15; 2 Pet. 1:4; Rom. 13:1.

was ordained by Christ's apostles Peter, James and John, who were ordained by Jesus Christ.[52]

Number 53: We believe that **worthy priesthood holders have both the authority and the power to work miracles in the name of Jesus Christ.** *4th Nephi verse 5* records how that power was operating in Book of Mormon times: "There were *great and marvelous works wrought by the disciples of Jesus,* insomuch that they did *heal the sick,* and *raise the dead,* and *cause the lame to walk,* and the *blind to receive their sight,* and the *deaf to hear;* and all manner of miracles did they work among the children of men; and *in nothing did they work miracles save it were in the name of Jesus.*"[53]

Doctrinal Evidence *Number 54:* We believe that **people can be healed through faith in Jesus Christ,** and we are aware of many such experiences among our members. An example of such healing through faith is found in the Book of Mormon when a repentant individual named Zeezrom was made whole. The account is in *Alma 15:6-11: "Alma said unto him, taking him by the hand: Believest thou in the power of Christ unto salvation? And he answered and said: Yea, I believe all the words that thou hast taught. And Alma said, If thou believest in the redemption of Christ thou canst be healed.* And he said: Yea, I believe according to thy words. And then Alma cried unto the Lord, saying: O Lord our God, *have mercy on this man, and heal him according to his faith which is in Christ.* And when Alma had said these words, Zeezrom leaped upon his feet, and began to walk; and this was done to the great astonishment of all the people."[54]

Evidence *Number 55:* **The name of Jesus Christ is included in the name of our Church,** according to the Lord's commandment. *3rd Nephi chapter 27, verses 5 through 8* records the commandment Jesus gave as he visited the Americas following his resurrection. He said, "Have they not read the scriptures, which say *ye must take upon you the name of Christ,* which is my name? For by this name shall ye be called at the last day; And whoso taketh upon him my name, and endureth to the end, the same shall be saved at the last day. Therefore, whatsoever ye shall do, ye shall

---

52. PGP: Fifth Article of Faith. B of M: 1 Ne. 12:6-7; Moro. 8:16; W of M 17; Mosiah 13:5-6; Alma 17:2-3. Bible: John 15:16; Matt. 7:21-23; Matt. 10:1; Mark 13:34; Luke 9:1; Acts 14:23.

53. B of M: 4 Ne. 5; Morm. 8:24; Hel. 10:4-11; Hel. 5:17-19; 4 Ne. 27-34; 3 Ne. 7:16-20. Bible: Mark 16:17-20; Matt. 10:1; James 5:14-15.

54. B of M: Alma 15:6-11; 4 Ne. 5; 3 Ne. 7:22; Morm. 1:13-14; Moro. 10:18-12. Bible: Matt. 8:5-13; Matt. 9:28-30; Acts 14:8-10; James 5:14-15.

do it in my name; therefore *ye shall call the church in my name; and ye shall call upon the Father in my name that he will bless the church for my sake.* And how be it my church save it be called in my name? For if a church be called in Moses' name then it be Moses' church; or if it be called in the name of a man then it be the church of a man; but *if it be called in my name then it is my church, if it so be that they are built upon my gospel."*

The Church of Jesus Christ of Latter-day Saints is one of the few churches today which actually have the name of Jesus Christ as the name of the church.[55]

Doctrinal Evidence *Number 56:* Latter-day Saint Church members partake of the sacrament of the Lord's supper each week in remembrance of the body and blood of Jesus Christ and as a symbolic renewing of our personal covenant with him. We read in *3rd Nephi chapter 18, verses 5 through 10,* of the Lord's instruction in this matter: "Behold there shall one be ordained among you, and to him will I give power that he shall break bread and bless it and give it unto the people of my church, unto all those who shall believe and be baptized in my name. And *this shall ye always observe to do,* even as I have done, even as I have broken bread and blessed it and given it unto you. And *this shall ye do in remembrance of my body,* which I have shown unto you. And *it shall be a testimony unto the Father that ye do always remember me.* And if ye do always remember me ye shall have my Spirit to be with you. . . .Blessed are ye for this thing which ye have done, for *this is fulfilling my commandments, and this doth witness unto the Father that ye are willing to do that which I have commanded you."*[56]

Evidence *Number 57:* As followers and disciples of Jesus Christ, Latter-day saints accept the nickname "Christian" and willingly apply the informal term to ourselves. *Alma 46:13 through 16,* tells how the nickname Christian was adopted in the Americas just as in it was in the Middle East. The account speaks of a righteous military leader named Moroni: "He bowed himself to the earth, and he prayed mightily unto his God for the blessings of liberty to rest upon his brethren, so long as *there should be a band of Christians remain to possess the land—For thus were all the*

---

55. B of M: 3 Ne. 27:5-8; Mosiah 5:8-11. D&C 115:3-4; D&C 18:21-25; D&C 21:11. Bible: Matt. 18:20; Eph. 5:23; Heb. 3:6.
56. B of M: 3 Ne. 18:5-10; Moro. 6:6; Morm. 9:28-29; Moro. 4:1-5:2. Bible; Matt. 26:26-29; John 6:51-58; 1 Cor. 11:23-30.

true believers of Christ, who belonged to the church of God, called by those who did not belong to the church. And those who did belong to the church were faithful; yea, *all those who were true believers in Christ took upon them, gladly, the name of Christ, or Christians as they were called, because of their belief in Christ who should come.* And therefore, at this time, *Moroni prayed that the cause of the Christians,* and the freedom of the land be favored."[57]

Doctrinal Principle *Number 58:* We, on a conscious individual basis, **take the name of Jesus Christ upon ourselves as we become members of his church through baptism.** In the final pages of the Book of Mormon in *Moroni 6, verses 3 and 4,* we read concerning the church of Christ as it functioned almost 400 A.D. The passage says, *"None were received unto baptism save they took upon them the name of Christ, having a determination to serve him to the end.* And after they had been received unto baptism, and were wrought upon and cleansed by the power of the Holy Ghost, they were *numbered among the people of the church of Christ;* and their names were taken, that they might be remembered and nourished by the good word of God, to keep them in the right way, to keep them continually watchful unto prayer, *relying alone upon the merits of Christ, who was the author and the finisher of their faith."*

But the Book of Mormon records, in *Mosiah 5:8,* that this process existed as early as the time of King Benjamin, in 124 B.C. He taught his people, "There is no other name given whereby salvation cometh; therefore, I would that *ye should take upon you the name of Christ,* all you that have entered into the covenant with God that ye should be obedient unto the end of your lives."[58]

Number 59: Latter-day Saint scriptures teach that **Jesus Christ is the example whom we should follow and emulate.** *3rd Nephi chapter 18, verses 14 through 16,* records the words of Jesus when he came to his people in the Americas. He said, *"Blessed are ye if ye shall keep my commandments, which the Father hath commanded me that I should give unto you. Verily, verily, I say unto you, ye must watch and pray always, lest ye be tempted by the devil, and ye be led away captive by him. And as I have prayed among you even so shall ye pray in my church, among my*

---

57. B of M: Alma 46:13-16; Alma 48:10. Bible: Acts 11:26; Acts 26:28; 1 Pet. 4:16.
58. B of M: Moro. 6:3-4; Mosiah 5:8-10; Mosiah 22:35; Mosiah 25:23; Alma 46:21; Moro. 4:3. Bible: Acts 2:38; Gal. 3:27; Rom. 13:14.

people who do repent and are baptized in my name. Behold *I am the light; I have set an example for you.*"⁵⁹

Evidence *Number 60:* Latter-day Saint scriptures record the visits of Jesus Christ to the Americas following his resurrection. These scriptures bear a strong witness to his divine nature. I've already referred several times to the Lord's appearance in the Americas, but let me share with you the actual account of his coming, as recorded in *3rd Nephi chapter 11, verses 8 through 11:*

"It came to pass, . . . they cast their eyes up again towards heaven; and behold, *they saw a Man descending out of heaven;* and he was clothed in a white robe; and he came down and stood in the midst of them; and the eyes of the whole multitude were turned upon him, and they durst not open their mouths, even one to another, and wist not what it meant, for they thought it was an angel that had appeared unto them. And it came to pass that he stretched forth his hand and spake unto the people, saying: *Behold, I am Jesus Christ, whom the prophets testified shall come into the world. And behold, I am the light and the life of the world; and I have drunk out of that bitter cup which the Father hath given me, and have glorified the Father in taking upon me the sins of the world,* in the which I have suffered the will of the Father in all things from the beginning."⁶⁰

Number 61: A strong evidence that Jesus is truly the Christ is **that ancient Book of Mormon prophets accurately foretold his coming,** and revealed numerous details of his ministry, many years before his birth. King Benjamin, for instance, in *Mosiah chapter 3, verses 5 through 10,* shared a prophecy of the minstry of Christ which was to occur more than a century later, indicating that the information was revealed to him by an angel who said:

"The time cometh, and is not far distant, that with power, the Lord Omnipotent who reigneth, who was, and is from all eternity to all eternity, *shall come down from heaven among the children of men,* and shall dwell in a tabernacle of clay, and shall go forth amongst men, *working mighty miracles,* such as healing the sick, raising the dead, causing the lame to walk, the blind to receive their sight, and the deaf to hear, and curing all manner of diseases. And *he shall cast out devils,* or the evil spirits which dwell in the hearts of the children of men. And lo, *he shall suffer temptations*

---

59. B of M: 3 Ne. 18:14-16; Morm. 7:10; 2 Ne. 31:7-16. Bible: John 13:15; 1 Pet. 2:21; Matt. 4:19; Markl 10:21.
60. B of M: 3 Ne. 11:8-11; 3 Ne. 11:12-28:12.

and pain of body, hunger, thirst, and fatigue, even more than man can suffer,
except it be unto death; for behold, *blood cometh from every pore,* so great
shall be his anguish for the wickedness and the abominations of his people. And *he shall be called Jesus Christ, the Son of God,* the Father of
heaven and earth, the Creator of all things from the beginning; and *his
mother shall be called Mary.* And lo, he cometh unto his own, that salvation might come unto the children of men even through faith on his name;
and even after all this they shall consider him a man, and say that he hath
a devil, and *shall scourge him, and shall crucify him.* And *he shall rise
the third day from the dead;* and behold, *he standeth to judge the world;*
and behold, all these things are done that a righteous judgment might come
upon the children of men."[61]

Doctrinal Principle *Number 62:* Mormons believe **Jesus Christ is the
Messiah who will restore Israel in the last days.** A prophecy by Nephi,
for instance, found in *2nd Nephi chapter 25, verses 16 through 18,* says
this concerning the Jews and the Messiah who will come to them in the
last days:

"After they have been scattered, and the Lord God hath scourged them
by other nations for the space of many generations, yea, even down from
generation to generation until they shall be persuaded to believe in Christ,
the Son of God, and the atonement, which is infinite for all mankind—and
*when that day shall come that they shall believe in Christ, and worship
the Father in his name,* with pure hearts and clean hands, and look not
forward any more for another Messiah, then, at that time, the day will come
that it must needs be expedient that they should believe these
things. . . .Wherefore, *he shall bring forth his words unto them, which words
shall judge them at the last day,* for they shall be given them *for the purpose of convincing them of the true Messiah, who was rejected by them;*
and unto the convincing of them that *they need not look forward any more
for a Messiah to come, . . .* for there is save one Messiah spoken of by
the prophets, and *that Messiah is he who should be rejected of the Jews.*"[62]

Doctrinal Evidence *Number 63:* Mormons believe that **Jesus Christ
will again come to the earth, this time in a glorious advent.** We prayerfully watch and strive to be prepared for his second coming. *Doctrine and*

---

61. B of M: Mosiah 3:5-10; Jacob 7:10-12; 1 Ne. 19:8-12; 1 Ne. 1:18-20; 1 Ne. 10:4-11.
62. B of M: 2 Ne. 25:16-18; 1 Ne. 10:4-17; 2 Ne. 2:6-8; 2 Ne. 6:13-15; 2 Ne. 2:26-28. Bible: John 1:41; John 4:25-26;
John 20:31; Acts 18:5.

Covenants chapter 29, verses 9 through 13, is typical of the many passages which foretell his coming in glory:

"The hour is nigh and the day soon at hand when the earth is ripe; and all *the proud and they that do wickedly shall be as stubble; and I will burn them up,* saith the Lord of Hosts, that wickedness shall not be upon the earth; For the hour is nigh, and that which was spoken by mine apostles must be fulfilled; for as they spoke so shall it come to pass; For *I will reveal myself from heaven with power and great glory, with all the hosts thereof, and dwell in righteousness with men on earth a thousand years, and the wicked shall not stand.* And . . . mine apostles, the Twelve which were with me in my ministry at Jerusalem, shall stand at my right hand *at the day of my coming in a pillar of fire,* being clothed with robes of righteousness, with crowns upon their heads, in glory even as I am, to judge the whole house of Israel, even as many as have loved me and kept my commandments, and none else. For *a trump shall sound both long and loud,* even as upon Mount Sinai, and *all the earth shall quake,* and *they shall come forth—yea, even the dead which died in me, to receive a crown of righteousness, and to be clothed upon, even as I am,* to be with me, that we may be one."[63]

Number 64: We believe that Jesus Christ will personally rule and reign here upon the earth during the future period known as the millennium. Our *tenth Article of Faith* states, "We believe . . . that *Christ will reign personally upon the earth;* and, that the earth will be renewed and receive its paradisiacal glory."

Doctrine and Covenants 38, verses 21 and 22, proclaims the Lord's words that "In that time ye shall have no king nor ruler, for *I will be your king and watch over you.* Wherefore, hear my voice and follow me, and you shall be a free people, and *ye shall have no laws but my laws when I come, for I am your lawgiver,* and what can stay my hand?"[64]

Doctrinal Evidence *Number 65:* We believe that Jesus Christ will judge all mankind at the final judgment day. Moroni, the final prophet of the Book of Mormon, taught this clearly in an address to unbelievers who will live in the last days. We read in *Mormon 9:1 through 6:*

---

63. D&C 29:9-13; D&C 88:87-110; D&C 133:41-52; D&C 101:22-38; D&C 133:10-25. Bible: Matt. 16:27; Matt. 24:30; Matt. 26:64; Acts 1:11.
64. PGP: Tenth Article of Faith. D&C 38:17-22; D&C 130:1-2; D&C 63:49-51; D&C 84:98-102. Bible: Rev. 20:4; Rev. 11:15; 1 Cor. 15:23-25; Luke 1:30-33.

"And now, I speak also concerning those who do not believe in Christ. Behold, will ye believe in the day of your visitation—behold, when the Lord shall come, yea, even that great day when the earth shall be rolled together as a scroll, and the elements shall melt with fervent heat, yea, in that great day when *ye shall be brought to stand before the Lamb of God*—then will ye say that there is no God? Then will ye longer deny the Christ, or can ye behold the Lamb of God? Do ye suppose that ye shall dwell with him under a consciousness of your guilt? Do ye suppose that ye could be happy to dwell with that holy Being, when your souls are racked with a consciousness of guilt that ye have ever abused his laws? Behold, I say unto you that ye would be more miserable to dwell with a holy and just God, under a consciousness of your filthiness before him, than ye would to dwell with the damned souls in hell. For behold, *when ye shall be brought to see your nakedness before God, and also the glory of God, and the holiness of Jesus Christ, it will kindle a flame of unquenchable fire upon you.* O then ye unbelieving, turn ye unto the Lord; *cry mightily unto the Father in the name of Jesus, that perhaps ye may be found spotless, pure, fair, and white, having been cleansed by the blood of the Lamb, at that great and last day.*"[65]

Number 66: We believe that **at the last day, every knee shall bow to Jesus,** and every inhabitant of the earth will acknowledge that Jesus is the Christ, the Lord and ruler of this earth. The testimony of Amulek, recorded in *Alma chapter 12, verses 14 and 15,* says:

"*Our words will condemn us, yea, all our works will condemn us; we shall not be found spotless; and our thoughts will also condemn us;* and in this awful state we shall not dare to look up to our God; and we would fain be glad if we could command the rocks and the mountains to fall upon us to hide us from his presence. But this cannot be; *we must come forth and stand before him in his glory,* and in his power, and in his might, majesty, and dominion, and *acknowledge to our everlasting shame that all his judgments are just; that he is just in all his works, and that he is merciful unto the children of men,* and that he has all power to save every man that believeth on his name and bringeth forth fruit meet for repentance."[66]

---

65. B of M: Morm. 9:1-6; Morm. 3:20-22; Morm. 9:12-14; 3 Ne. 27:14-16; Mosiah 3:8-10. Bible: John 5:22-27; Acts 10:40-42; Acts 17:31; Rom. 2:16; 1 Cor. 4:4-5.

66. B of M: Alma 12:14-15; Mosiah 27:30-31; Mosiah 3:20-21; 2 Ne. 33:11-15; Alma 5:15-22. Bible: Philip. 2:9-11; Rom. 14:10-12; Isa. 45:23.

Doctrinal Evidence *Number 67:* It is Mormon doctrine that **faith in the Lord Jesus Christ leads to salvation.** Again, the words of Samuel the Lamanite, in *Helaman 13:5 and 6:* "Behold, I, Samuel, a Lamanite, do speak the words of the Lord which he doth put into my heart; and behold he hath put it into my heart to say unto this people that the sword of justice hangeth over this people; . . . and *nothing can save this people save it be repentance and faith on the Lord Jesus Christ,* who surely shall come into the world, and shall suffer many things and shall be slain for his people."

Moroni, in his final writings, taught about the power of faith in Christ also. In *Moroni 7:25 through 34,* he taught, "Wherefore, by the ministering of angels, and by every word which proceeded forth out of the mouth of God, men began to exercise faith in Christ; and *thus by faith, they did lay hold upon every good thing;* and thus it was until the coming of Christ. And after that he came *men also were saved by faith in his name; and by faith, they become the sons of God.* . . . The Lord God prepareth the way that the *residue of men may have faith in Christ, that the Holy Ghost may have place in their hearts,* according to the power thereof; and after this manner bringeth to pass the Father, the covenants which he hath made unto the children of men. And Christ hath said: *If ye will have faith in me ye shall have power to do whatsoever thing is expedient in me.* And he hath said: Repent all ye ends of the earth, and come unto me, and be baptized in my name, and *have faith in me, that ye may be saved."*[67]

Doctrinal Evidence *Number 68:* Jesus Christ's doctrine of salvation requires faith in him, complete repentance, baptism in his name, reception of the Holy Ghost, and faithfulness to the end. *3rd Nephi chapter 27, verses 18 through 21,* contains the words of Jesus Christ when he appeared in the Americas saying:

"This is the word which he hath given unto the children of men. And for this cause he fulfilleth the words which he hath given, and he lieth not, but fulfilleth all his words. And no *unclean thing can enter into his kingdom; therefore nothing entereth into his rest save it be those who have washed their garments in my blood, because of their faith, and the repentance of all their sins, and their faithfulness unto the end.* Now this is the commandment: *Repent, all ye ends of the earth, and come unto me and be baptized in my name, that ye may be sanctified by the reception of the*

---

67. B of M: Hel. 13:5-6; Moro. 7:25-34; Mosiah 3:12, 20-21; Enos 4-8; Mosiah 4:6-10. Bible: John 3:16; John 6:40; John 11:25; John 20:31; 1 Tim. 4:10.

200

DOCTRINAL DIMENSIONS

Holy Ghost, that ye may stand spotless before me at the last day. Verily, verily, I say unto you, *this is my gospel;* and ye know the things that ye must do in my church; for *the works which ye have seen me do that shall ye also do;* for that which ye have seen me do even that shall ye do."[68]

Number 69: **The redemption of Jesus Christ leads to the process of spiritual birth, or being born again.** Alma the younger taught this principle in *Mosiah chapter 27, verses 24 through 26,* when he told of his own spiritual rebirth. He said, "I have repented of my sins, and have been redeemed of the Lord; behold *I am born of the Spirit.* And the Lord said unto me: Marvel not that *all mankind, yea, men and women, all nations, kindreds, tongues and people, must be born again; yea, born of god, changed from their carnal and fallen state, to a state of righteousness, being redeemed of God, becoming his sons and daughters; And thus they become new creatures;* and unless they do this, they can in nowise inherit the kingdom of God."

Later, that same prophet taught, in *Alma 7, 14 through 16,* "Now I say unto you that *ye must repent, and be born again;* for the Spirit saith *if ye are not born again ye cannot inherit the kingdom of heaven;* therefore come and be baptized unto repentance, that ye may be washed from your sins, that ye may have faith on the Lamb of God, who taketh away the sins of the world, who is mighty to save and to cleanse from all unrighteousness. Yea, I say unto you come and fear not, and lay aside every sin, which easily doth beset you, which doth bind you down to destruction, yea, come and go forth, and *show unto your god that ye are willing to repent of your sins and enter into a covenant with him to keep his commandments, and witness it unto him this day by going into the waters of baptism.* And whosoever doeth this, and keepeth the commandments of God from thenceforth, the same will remember that I say unto him, yea, he will remember that I have said unto him, *he shall have eternal life, according to the testimony of the Holy Spirit, which testifieth in me.*"[69]

Doctrinal Evidence Number 70: It is Latter-day Saint doctrine that **forgiveness of sins comes from Jesus Christ as a result of faith in him.** This is vividly taught in the Book of Mormon in the account of Enos, found in *Enos verses 4 through 8:*

---

68. B of M: 3 Ne. 27:18-21; Mosiah 4:6-10; Alma 7:14-16; 3 Ne. 11:38-40; 3 Ne. 27:16-21. Bible: Acts 2:37-38; Mark 1:4; Mark 16:15-16; John 3:5; Matt. 24:13.
69. B of M: Mosiah 27:24-26; Alma 7:14-16; Mosiah 5:2-9; Alma 36:17-26. Bible: 1 Pet. 1:2-3; 1 Pet. 1:18-23; 1 Cor. 2:9-16.

"My soul hungered; and I kneeled down before my Maker, and I cried unto him in mighty prayer and supplication for mine own soul; and all the day long did I cry unto him; yea, and when the night came I did still raise my voice high that it reached the heavens. And there came a voice unto me, saying: *Enos, thy sins are forgiven thee, and thou shalt be blessed. And I, Enos, knew that God could not lie; wherefore, my guilt was swept away.* And I said: Lord, how is it done? And he said unto me: *Because of thy faith in Christ,* whom thou hast never before heard nor seen. And many years pass away before he shall manifest himself in the flesh; wherefore, go to, thy faith hath made thee whole."[70]

Number 71: Those who are born again through faith on Jesus Christ are considered to be spiritually begotten by him. In the scriptures they are called his children. In this sense he is called the Father of those who accept the gospel. In *Mosiah 5:7,* King Benjamin taught his people:

"*Because of the covenant which ye have made ye shall be called the children of Christ, his sons, and his daughters; for behold, this day he hath spiritually begotten you;* for ye say that your hearts are changed through faith on his name; therefore, *ye are born of him and have become his sons and his daughters.*"

When Jesus appeared in the Americas, he taught the same principle. We read in *3rd Nephi 9, verses 15 through 17,* "Behold, I am Jesus Christ the Son of God. I created the heavens and the earth, and all things that in them are. . . .I came unto my own, and my own received me not. And the scriptures concerning my coming are fulfilled. *And as many as have received me, to them have I given to become the sons of God; and even so will I to as many as shall believe on my name, for behold, by me redemption cometh,* and in me is the law of Moses fulfilled."[71]

Number 72: We believe that **charity is the pure love of Jesus Christ, and that man must have this pure love if he is to gain eternal life.** In *Moroni 7, 44 through 48,* we read, "If a man be meek and lowly in heart, and confesses by the power of the Holy Ghost that *Jesus is the Christ,* he must needs have charity; for if he have not charity he is nothing; . . . Wherefore, *cleave unto charity, which is the greatest of all,* for

70. B of M: Enos 4-8; Mosiah 4:2-3, 10; Alma 38:14-15; Mosiah 27:24-30; Alma 24:8-16. Bible: Matt. 9:6; Luke 5:20-24; Eph. 1:5-7; 1 John 1:7-9; Heb. 8:10-12.
71. B of M: Mosiah 5:7; 3 Ne. 9:15-17; Moro. 7:48; Mosiah 27:24-26. D&C 93:21-22. Bible: 2 Cor. 6:17-18; 1 John 2:28-29; Gal. 4:3-7; Rom. 8:14-16.

all things must fail—but *charity is the pure love of Christ, and it endureth forever; and whoso is found possessed of it at the last day, it shall be well with him.* Wherefore, my beloved brethren, *pray unto the Father with all the energy of heart, that ye may be filled with this love, which he hath bestowed upon all who are true followers of his Son, Jesus Christ;* that ye may become the sons of God; that when he shall appear we shall be like him, for we shall see him as he is; that we may have this hope; that we may be purified even as he is pure."[72]

As I promised, I have presented more than seventy evidences that the Mormons—members of The Church of Jesus Christ of Latter-day Saints—are truly Christians. There are still many others, but these 72 doctrinal principles will suffice. They embrace the heart of Christian doctrine.

These teachings have been in the Book of Mormon and other Latter-day Saint scriptures for over a century. No honest seeker after truth who has studied the doctrines of Mormonism could fail to discover at least some of them. Yet enemies of Mormonism in the shallow, deeply biased diatribes they write, intentionally ignore all, or almost all of these passages and doctrines. As I said in the beginning, they attempt to circulate the "ultimate falsehood" when they assert that Mormons are not Christians. Those who do so are liars—the truth is not in them. You would do well to reject them and the evil falsehoods they teach.

The Invitation of Mormonism: Come Unto Christ and Be Perfected in Him

In conclusion, let me extend to you an invitation. The final summation of the entire Book of Mormon is a call to come unto Jesus Christ, and to be perfected and made holy through his grace and atonement. You'll find in the final chapter of the Book of Mormon, *Moroni 10:32 through 34.* Ponder this invitation, pray about it, and if the Spirit leads you, then accept it with a contrite heart. It was Moroni who wrote it. He said,

"Yea, *come unto Christ, and be perfected in him, and deny yourselves of all ungodliness;* and if ye shall deny yourselves of all ungodliness and love God with all your might, mind and strength, then is his grace sufficient for you, that *by his grace ye may be perfect in Christ;* and if by the

---

72. B of M: Moro. 7:44-48; Mosiah 4:11-15; 2 Ne. 26:30; Moro. 8:17. Bible: John 13:34; John 15:13; 1 Cor. 13:13; 1 Pet. 1:22.

grace of God ye are perfect in Christ, *ye can in nowise deny the power of God*. And again, if ye by the grace of God are perfect in Christ, and deny not his power, *then are ye sanctified in Christ by the grace of God, through the shedding of the blood of Christ, which is in the covenant of the Father unto the remission of your sins, that ye become holy, without spot.* And now I bid unto all, farewell. I soon go to rest in the paradise of God, until my spirit and body shall again reunite, and I am brought forth triumphant through the air, *to meet you before the pleasing bar of the great Jehovah, the Eternal Judge of both quick and dead.* Amen."

Note:

A simplified listing of the seventy-two doctrinal principles presented in this chapter is found in the Table of Contents.

God's Eternal Plan of Salvation

Duane S. Crowther

Of all the principles taught in the Holy Bible, few are more valuable to us than the understanding of God's eternal plan of salvation which has been revealed to us. Hundreds of passages combine to tell us where we came from before our birth into this mortal life, why we are here on earth, and where we are going after death ends our temporal existence. These passages show us that there is a great eternal plan which God has designed for the development and eventual reward of his children who are faithful unto him, and who seek to return to the glory of his presence.

We Are All Spirit Children of God the Father
And Lived Before Our Mortal Birth

For us to understand God's plan of Salvation, the first concept we must grasp is that we are actually children of God. He is our Heavenly father, the Father of our spirits. He loves us, and wants us to be happy. He is concerned about our conduct and our progress, just like our mortal parents feel love and concern for us.

The teaching that God is the father of all mankind is found in many places throughout the Bible. In his Sermon On The Mount the Lord Jesus Christ taught that we are the children of our Heavenly Father, and he did so not just once, but in *eleven* different passages. Turn to Matthew, chapters 5, 6, and 7, and let's consider them briefly together.

In *Matthew 5:16* he said, "Let your light so shine before men, that they may see your good works, and *glorify your Father* which is in heaven." In *Matthew 5:44 and 45* he said, "Love your enemies, bless them that curse you, do good to them that hate you, and pray for them which despitefully use you, and persecute you; That *ye may be the children of your Father which is in heaven:* for he maketh his sun to rise on the evil and on the good, and sendeth rain on the just and on the unjust." And three verses later, in *Matthew 5:48,* He gave that important commandment to "Be ye therefore perfect, even as *your Father which is in heaven* is perfect."

In *Matthew 6:3 through 4,* the Lord said, "When thou doest alms, let not thy left hand know what thy right hand doeth: That thine alms may be in secret: and *thy Father* which seeth in secret himself shall reward thee openly." And in *verse 6,* as He told us how to pray, the Savior said, *"Pray to thy Father* which is in secret; and *thy Father* which seeth in secret shall reward thee openly."

And as he taught his disciples how to pray, our Lord and Savior showed that *He* is also a child of our Heavenly Father, as He instructed them in *verse 9 of Matthew chapter 6,* "After this manner therefore pray ye: *Our Father* which art in heaven, Hallowed be thy name." In *chapter 6, verses 14 and 15,* as he taught about forgiveness, the Lord said, "If ye forgive men their trespasses, *your heavenly Father* will also forgive you: But if ye forgive not men their trespasses, neither will *your Father* forgive your trespasses."

As he instructed men about the principle of fasting, in *verses 17 and 18,* He said, "But thou, when thou fastest, anoint thine head, and wash thy face; That thou appear not unto men to fast, but unto *thy Father, which is in secret:* and *thy Father,* which seeth in secret, shall reward thee openly."

In *verse 26 of Matthew 6,* as the Lord taught men of their great worth in the eyes of God, He said, "Behold the fowls of the air: for they sow not, neither do they reap, nor gather into barns; yet *your Heavenly Father feedeth them.* Are ye not much better than they?"

In *Matthew 6:31 and 32* He said, "Therefore take no thought, saying, What shall we eat? or, What shall we drink? or, Wherewithal shall we be

clothed? (For after all these things do the Gentiles seek:) for *your heavenly Father knoweth* that ye have need of all these things."

In *Matthew, chapter 7, verses 7 thru 11,* as the Savior taught us to ask
of our heavenly Father those things which we need, He said, "Ask, and
it shall be given you; seek, and ye shall find; knock, and it shall be opened
unto you." And then he said, "If ye then, being evil, know how to give
good gifts unto your children, how much more shall *your Father which
is in heaven* give good things to them that ask him?"

So *eleven* times in just His Sermon on the Mount our Lord Jesus taught
that we are all, literally, children of God our Heavenly Father.

Other passages also teach the doctrine that we are the pre-mortal children of our father in heaven with great clarity. *Hebrews chapter 12, verses
7 and 9* says, "If ye endure chastening, God dealeth with you as with *sons;*
for what son is he whom the father chasteneth not?" and then the passage
says, "Furthermore we have had fathers of our flesh which corrected us,
and we gave them reverence: shall we not much rather *be in subjection
unto the Father of spirits,* and live?"

Jeremiah chapter 1, verse 5 tells how God knew that great prophet before he was born here upon the earth and that Jeremiah was assigned his
great missions in his pre-mortal life. The Lord said, "Before I formed thee
in the belly *I knew thee;* and before thou camest forth out of the womb
I sanctified thee, and *I ordained thee a prophet* unto the nations."

Isaiah, another great prophet, apparently had a similar experience. In
Isaiah chapter 49, verse 1, he said, "Listen, O isles, unto me; and heark-
en, ye people, from far; The *Lord hath called me from the womb,* from
the bowels of my mother hath he made mention of my name."

An incident recorded in the Gospel of *John, chapter 9, verses 1 thru
3,* shows that Christ's apostles knew that man lived prior to coming into
mortality. The account says: "As Jesus passed by, he saw a man which was
blind from his birth. And his disciples asked him, saying, Master, *who
did sin, this man, or his parents, that he was born blind?* Jesus answered,
Neither hath this man sinned, nor his parents: but that the works of God
should be made manifest in him."

All these passages combine to show, then, that we are literally the spirit
children of our Heavenly Father, that He loves us, and that mankind lived
as pre-mortal spirits before being born on this earth.

The Pre-Mortal Role of Jesus Christ

Other passages speak specifically of the pre-mortal existence of the Lord Jesus Christ, and tell how He functioned in that life before the creation of this earth. The *first chapter of the gospel of John* tells us of Christ's pre-mortal existence and teaches that He is the only begotten son in the flesh of God he father. *Verses 1 and 2* say, "In the beginning was the Word, and *the Word was with God,* and the Word was God. The same was *in the beginning with God."* And then, in *verse 14,* we are told that the word was Jesus Christ. It says that "The Word was made flesh, and dwelt among us, (and we beheld his glory, the glory *as of the only begotten* of the Father,) full of grace and truth."

John, chapter 17, verses 3 thru 5, contain the great words of the prayer offered by the Savior as he said, "This is life eternal, that they might know thee the only true God, and Jesus Christ, *whom thou hast sent.* I have glorified thee on the earth: I have finished the work which thou gavest me to do. And now, O Father, *glorify thou me with thine own self with the glory which I had with thee before the world was."*

John 16, verses 27 and 28 contain the words of the Savior to his disciples as he told them, "The Father himself loveth you, because ye have loved me, and have believed that *I came out from God.* I came forth from the Father, and am come into the world: again, I leave the world and *go to the Father."*

John 17:24 tells of the Savior's words to his father in prayer in which he said, "Father, I will that they also, whom thou hast given me, be with me where I am; *that they may behold my glory, which thou hast given me: for thou lovedst me before the foundation of the world."*

And we shouldn't overlook the testimony of the apostle Peter concerning Christ's pre-mortal life, in *1st Peter 1:20,* who affirmed that Christ "Verily *was foreordained before the foundation of the world."*

All these passages, then, tells us that mankind existed as spirit children of our father in heaven before the creation of the earth, and that Christ was also a spirit child of our Heavenly Father. They tell us that He had glory and Godhood even before coming here upon this earth. They tell us also that God knew his children, and chose some of them to function as key figures in the furthering of His eternal plan here upon the earth.

The Pre-Mortal Rebellion of Satan and His Followers

As we read more about the eternal plan of salvation, the Bible tells us that Satan existed prior to the formation of this earth and that he played an important role in the pre-mortal events which took place. We read that there came a time when Satan and his hosts rebelled against God the Father and His son Jesus Christ, and that they were eventually cast out of their pre-mortal environment where they lived in close proximity to God.

In *Revelation chapter 12, verses 7 through 10,* John harkened back to the great pre-mortal conflict which transpired and said, "There was war in heaven: Michael and his angels fought against the dragon; and the dragon fought and his angels, And prevailed not; neither was their place found any more in heaven. And the great dragon was cast out, that old serpent, called the Devil, and Satan, which deceiveth the whole world: he was cast out into the earth, and his angels were cast out with him. And I heard a loud voice saying in heaven, *Now* is come salvation and strength, and the kingdom of our God, and the power of his Christ: for *the accuser of our brethren is cast down, which accused them before our God day and night."*

In *Isaiah 14:12-15,* that great prophet raised a taunting song which alluded to the fall of Satan. He said, *"How art thou fallen from heaven, O Lucifer, son of the morning!* how art thou cut down to the ground, which didst weaken the nations! For thou hast said in thine heart, I will ascend into heaven, I will exalt my throne above the stars of God: I will sit also upon the mount of the congregation, in the sides of the north: I will ascend above the heights of the clouds; I will be like the most High. Yet *thou shalt be brought down to hell,* to the sides of the pit."

Jesus mentioned the fall of Satan when he was greeted by the Seventy who returned from their missionary labors. We read in *Luke 10:17-18* that they reported to him, "Lord, even the devils are subject unto us through thy name. And he said unto them, *"I beheld Satan as lightning fall from heaven."*

The book of *Jude, in verse 6,* tells of the fate of those who were cast out with Satan, saying, *"The angels which kept not their first estate,* but left their own habitation, he hath reserved in everlasting chains under darkness unto the judgment of the great day."

In *Revelation 12:4,* as he told of the trememdous impact of this pre-mortal conflict, the apostle John spoke of Satan and said that "His tail drew the *third part of the stars of heaven,* and did cast them to the earth."

All these passages, then, tell us that there was a great pre-mortal conflict in which Satan and his hosts were arrayed against the forces of righteousness. Satan and his followers, a third of all the pre-mortal spirits, were cast out of heaven down to earth. They never received mortal bodies. They are functioning as disembodied spirits, in opposition to God's eternal plan of salvation, trying to tempt mankind and to lead them astray. They want men to share their wickedness and sorrow rather than to reap the joys of obedience to God's eternal plan of salvation.

The Earth Created by Jesus Christ Under the Father's Direction

Now let's consider the next phase of that divine plan. The Bible tells of the creation of the earth and shows that it was a time of great joy for the sons of God who observed it. In *Job 38:4-7* God alludes to His creation, saying, "Where was thou when *I laid the foundations of the earth?* declare, if thou has understanding. Who hath laid the measures thereof, if thou knowest? or who hath stretched the line upon it? Whereupon are the foundations thereof fastened? or who laid the corner stone thereof; When the *morning stars sang together, and all the sons of God shouted for joy?*"

The scriptures tell us that God the Father assigned His son Jesus Christ to be the actual creator of this world. We read in *Hebrews 1:1 and 2* that "God, who at sundry times and in divers manners spake in time past unto the fathers by the prophets, Hath in these last days spoken unto us by his Son, *whom he hath appointed heir of all things, by whom also he made the worlds."*

Colossians, chapter 1, verses 15 thru 19, also tells us that Christ served as the creator of this world in obedience to the direction of His heavenly Father. That passage says that Christ is "The firstborn of every creature: For *by him were all things created,* that are in heaven, and that are in earth, visible and invisible, whether they be thrones, or dominions, or principalities, or powers: *all things were created by him, and for him:* And he is before all things, and *by him all things consist."*

We read in the book of Genesis of the actual creation of man. *Genesis chapter 1, verses 26 and 27* tells us that, "God said, Let us make man in our image, after our likeness: and let them have dominion over the fish of the sea, and over the fowl of the air, and over the cattle, and over all the earth, and over every creeping thing that creepeth upon the earth. So God created man *in his own image,* in the image of God created he him; male and female created he them."

How choice is that passage recorded in *Psalms 8:4-6,* which speaks of the great responsibilities and potential which man enjoys here upon the earth. It says, "What is man, that thou are mindful of him? and the son of man, that thou visitest him? For *thou has made him a little lower than the angels, and hast crowned him with glory and honour.* Thou madest him to have dominion over the works of thy hands; thou hast put all things under his feet."

Ten Tasks to Be Accomplished in Mortal Life

So why are we here living on this earth? What are the tasks we are to accomplish during our mortal life? In the eternal scheme of things, our stay here is but a brief moment. The apostle Peter, in *2nd Peter, chapter 3, verse 8,* commented that a thousand years of man's time is like one day of the Lord's, so our time of testing here upon this earth is but a brief moment, perhaps like an hour-and-a-half or two hours in the eternal scheme of things.

In school when we finish a term and come to the final exam, we take a two-hour test. We close our books, and work as hard as we can during that two hours to do as well on that test as we possibly can—we strive to achieve to the full extent of our potential. Our *mortal life* is an examination period also, and we should be striving to the best of our ability to do and accomplish all those things which God would have us do during this time of probation.

I would like to suggest *ten tasks* the Bible tells us we should strive to accomplish while we are here upon this earth. If we fulfill these ten principles to the best of our ability, we surely will have made good use of our earth life and will have passed our mortal probation.

Be Eligible to Live with God for All Eternity

First, we should *resolve that the most important task in our life is to make ourselves eligible to live with God in His kingdom for all eternity.* We should focus our lives upon the eternal things of God rather than upon the temporal things that surround us. Christ, in his Sermon On the Mount said this in *Matthew 6:33,* "Seek ye *first* the kingdom of God, and his righteousness; and all these things shall be added unto you."

The apostle Paul echoed that teaching in his Epistle to the Colossians. We read in *Colossians 3:1 and 2:* "If ye then be risen with Christ, *seek those things which are above, where Christ sitteth on the right hand of*

God. Set your affection on things above, not on things on the earth." If we apply this principle carefully and fully in our lives, we will recognize that life is a time of preparation and of testing, a time when we must learn and ready ourselves for the future blessings of eternity. Though we still have to earn a living and provide for our temporal needs, that shouldn't be foremost in our goals.

Have Faith in Christ and Partake of His Redeeming Grace

Second, we must *come to Christ and have faith in him.* Jesus Christ is our Savior and Redeemer. We must become full recipients of the benefits of his atoning sacrifice so that it will apply in our behalf, and then we must live the God-like life, based on faith in His power and love, which He has prescribed for us. The Savior described that way of life and invited us to come to him in *Matthew 11:28-30.* He said, "Come unto me, all ye that labour and are heavy laden, and I will give you rest. *Take my yoke upon you, and learn of me;* for I am meek and lowly in heart: and ye shall find rest unto your souls. For my yoke is easy, and my burden is light."

To come unto Christ requires true faith—faith that He is the Son of God, that He is our Savior and Redeemer, and that His way will provide the means through which we can obtain eternal life. Paul, in his Epistle to the *Hebrews,* said in *chapter 11, verse 6,* "But without faith it is *impossible* to please him: for he that cometh to God *must believe that he is, and that he is a rewarder* of them that diligently seek him."

If we have true faith in Jesus Christ, then His grace will serve to cover our sins and will eventually allow us to obtain forgiveness for them. True faith brings the grace of God upon us. Our salvation ultimately comes *through* that faith and the grace which it brings into our lives.

True faith requires *more* than words and professions of belief. True faith is *manifested by works,* and one who will not work in the kingdom of God does not have true faith. *Ephesians 2:8-10* describes that important relationship for us. Paul wrote, "By grace are ye saved through faith; and that not of yourselves: it is the gift of God: Not of works, lest any man should boast. For we are his workmanship, *created in Christ Jesus unto good works, which God hath before ordained that we should walk in them.*"

James, in his Epistle, described this relationship also. We read in *James, chapter 2, verses 14 thru 20* these words: "What doth it profit, my brethren, though a man say he hath faith, and have not works? can faith save him? If a brother or sister be naked, and destitute of daily food, And one of you say unto them, Depart in peace, be ye warmed and filled; notwith-standing ye give them not those things which are needful to the body; what doth it profit? Even so *faith, if it hath not works, is dead, being alone.* Yea, a man may say, Thou hast faith, and I have works: shew me thy faith without thy works, and *I will shew thee my faith by my works.* Thou *believest* that there is one God; thou doest well: the devils also believe, and tremble. But wilt thou know, O vain man, that *faith without works is dead*?"

So faith in the Lord Jesus Christ brings His saving grace upon us, and that *grace, not our works, is what saves us; but* works provide the test which shows whether one's faith is real, and true. He who has true faith will manifest that faith through his deeds and obedience.

The Lord Jesus Christ described this relationship in *Luke 6:46-49* when he said, "Why call ye me, Lord, Lord, and *do not* the things which I say? Whosoever cometh to me, and heareth my sayings, and doeth them, I will shew you to whom he is like: He is like a man which built a house, and digged deep, and laid the foundation on a rock: and when the flood arose, the stream beat vehemently upon that house, and could not shake it: for it was founded upon a rock. But he that heareth, *and doeth not,* is like a man that without a foundation built an house upon the earth; against which the stream did beat vehemently, and immediately it fell; and the ruin of that house was great."

Those who truly seek to come unto Christ will *labor* in his kingdom, and strengthen their faith through those labors which they perform.

Find the True Church of Christ and Make It Your Schoolmaster

Number 3. We must *find the true church* of Jesus Christ and make it our schoolmaster, to teach us the principles of the gospel of Jesus Christ.

In *Romans 10:13-14,* we read questions posed by the apostle Paul which are of profound importance. He said, "Whosoever shall call upon the name of the Lord shall be saved. How then shall they call on him in whom they have not believed? and *how shall they believe in him of whom they have not heard?* and how shall they hear without a preacher?"

In *Ephesians 4:12-14,* Paul told what purpose the church was to serve. He said it was "For the *perfecting* of the saints, for the *work of the ministry,* for the *edifying* of the body of Christ: Till we all come in the unity of the faith, and of the knowledge of the Son of God, unto a perfect man, unto the *measure of the stature of the fulness of Christ:* That we henceforth be no more children, tossed to and fro, and carried about with every wind of doctrine, by the sleight of men, and cunning craftiness, whereby they lie in wait to deceive."

Earlier in that chapter, in *Ephesians 4:4-6,* Paul said, "There is one body, and one Spirit, even as ye are called in one hope of your calling; *One Lord, one faith, one baptism, One God and Father of all,* who is above all, and through all, and in you all." He taught us, then, that we are to seek out that one faith and one baptism which will serve to develop and perfect us.

The Church of Jesus Christ serves to teach us his doctrines and to prepare us to meet God at the last day. If we want to be able to determine whether a church is truly the church of Jesus Christ, then we must pray, and study, and apply the doctrine which that church teaches us, and then allow the Holy Spirit to bear witness whether or not that church and its doctrines are true. In *1st Thessalonians 5:19-21* Paul taught us, "Quench not the Spirit. Despise not prophesyings. *Prove all things; hold fast that which is good.*"

Be Baptized and Receive the Ordinances Required by God

Number 4: We need to be baptized, and partake of the other ordinances administered by the authorized servants of Christ in His Church. In *Mark 16:15-16,* we read Christ's final instructions to his disciples. "He said unto them, Go ye into all the world, and preach the gospel to every creature. *He that believeth and is baptized shall be saved;* but he that believeth not shall be damned." Baptism, performed by one who has divine authority to act in the name of Jesus Christ, is truly necessary for our salvation. It is the direct result of faith in the Lord Jesus Christ.

Paul, in *Galatians, chapter 3, verses 26 and 27* said, "Ye are all the children of God *by faith in Christ Jesus.* For as many of you as have *been baptized into Christ have put on Christ.*" And the opposite is also true: if we have not been baptized by an authorized servant of the Lord, we have not "put on" Jesus Christ.

Another ordinance necessary for our eternal salvation is confirmation, in which the right to have the permanent companionship of the Holy Ghost, if we are worthy, is conferred upon us. The ordinance which gives us this blessing is the laying on of hands to convey the gift of the Holy Ghost, which also must be performed by authorized servants of God. When he wrote his *first Epistle to Timothy, in chapter 4, verse 14,* Paul counseled Timothy, "Neglect not the gift that is in thee, which was given thee by prophecy, with *the laying on of the hands* of the presbytery."

These ordinances are blessings to which every honest believer in Christ is entitled. They come to us through the true church of Jesus Christ, by authorized servants of Christ who hold the power to act in the name of God, called the *Priesthood.*

Another ordinance performed in the church of Jesus Christ is the ordination to the priesthood of worthy men who are chosen to render special service to God. Men don't seek this priesthood of themselves, but rather are chosen of God. Jesus said to his disciples, in *John 15:16,* "Ye have not chosen me, but I have chosen you, and *ordained you,* that ye should go and bring forth fruit, and that your fruit should remain: that whatsoever ye shall ask of the Father in my name, he may give it you."

Be Born Again—Be Cleansed and Changed by the Spirit of God

Number 5: We must be *born again.* In *John 3:3-7* we read of the Savior's instruction to Nicodemus: "Verily, verily, I say unto thee, Except a man be *born again,* he *cannot see* the kingdom of God." Nicodemus didn't understand, so he asked if that meant that a man had to go back into his mother's womb and again experience the birth process. Jesus explained, "Verily, verily, I say unto thee, Except a man be *born of water and of the Spirit,* he cannot *enter* into the kingdom of God. That which is born of the flesh is flesh; and that which is born of the Spirit is spirit. Marvel not that I said unto thee, Ye *must* be born again."

In *1st Peter 1:22-23,* we have an interesting description of the process of being born again. The passage says, "Seeing ye have *purified your souls* in obeying the truth through the Spirit unto unfeigned love of the brethren, see that ye love one another with a pure heart fervently: *Being born again,* not of corruptible seed, *but of incorruptible, by the word of God,* which liveth and abideth forever."

And John the apostle tells us more of the results of being born again, in *1st John 5:4-6.* He says, "Whatsoever is born of God *overcometh the world;* and this is the victory that overcometh the world, even our faith. Who is he that overcometh the world, but *he that believeth that Jesus is the Son of God?* This is he that came by water and blood, even Jesus Christ, not by water only, but by water and blood. And it is *the Spirit that beareth witness,* because the Spirit is truth." And in *chapter 5, verse 18 of 1st John,* that apostle says, "We know that whosoever is *born of God sinneth not;* but he that is begotten of God *keepeth himself,* and that wicked one toucheth him not."

To be born again, then, is to have a mighty change wrought in us where we not longer have a desire to do evil, but we seek to do good and to become Godlike. He who is born again has purified his soul and has overcome the world. He is filled with love, and enjoys the continual witness and guidance of the Holy Spirit.

Keep the Commandments

Number 6. We must *keep God's commandments.* In *1st John 2:3-5,* the Savior told us how we can evaluate our love for Him and our faith in Him. He said, "Hereby we do know that we know him, if we keep his commandments. He that saith, I know him, and keepeth not his commandments, is a liar, and the truth is not in him. But *whosoever keepeth his word, in him verily is the love of God perfected: hereby know we that we are in him."*

We read in *John 14:15* Jesus's words which summarize what he requires of his followers: *"If ye love me, keep my commandments."*

After struggling long to discern what was the duty of man, the writer of Ecclesiastes, in the Old Testament, finally summed up his conclusions in these words in *Ecclesiastes 12:13-14.* "Let us hear the conclusion of the whole matter: *Fear God, and keep his commandments: for this is the whole duty of man.* For God shall bring every work into judgment, with every secret thing, whether it be good, or whether it be evil."

Labor to Do God's Will and Further His Work on Earth

Number 7. We must *do God's will.* As disciples of Christ, we must labor to further His work and to advance His cause upon this earth. Remember the words which the Savior spoke, in his Sermon on the Mount, in *Matthew 7:21:* "Not every one that saith unto me, Lord, Lord, shall enter into the kingdom of heaven; but *he that doeth the will of my Father* which is in heaven." In *James 1:22* we read the inspired counsel to "Be ye *doers* of the word, and not hearers only, deceiving your own selves."

In *Romans 2:13* the apostle Paul wrote, "Not the hearers of the law are just before God, but the *doers of the law* shall be justified." And earlier in the chapter, in *verses 6 thru 11,* Paul wrote that God "Will render to every man according to his *deeds:* To them who by patient continuance in well doing seek for glory and honour and immortality, *eternal life:* But unto them that are contentious, and do not obey the truth, but obey unrighteousness, indignation and wrath, Tribulation and anguish, upon every soul of man that doeth evil, of the Jew first, and also of the Gentile; But glory, honour, and peace, to every man that worketh good, to the Jew first, and also to the Gentile: For there *is no respect of persons* with God." We must involve ourselves in what Paul calls "patient continuance in well doing," striving to further God's purposes and making our world a better place in which to live.

Live So As To Have the Constant Guidance of the Holy Spirit

Number 8. We must *live in the Spirit.* In the *5th chapter of Galatians,* Paul tells us the difference between walking in the Spirit and walking in the flesh. In *verse 5* he says, "We through the Spirit *wait for the hope of righteousness* by faith."

And *beginning with verse 16* he says, *"Walk in the Spirit, and ye shall not fulfil the lust of the flesh.* For the flesh lusteth against the Spirit, and *the Spirit against the flesh:* and these are contrary the one to the other: so that ye cannot do the things that ye would. But if ye be led of the Spirit, ye are not under the law. Now the works of the flesh are manifest, which are these; Adultery, fornication, uncleanness, lasciviousness, Idolatry, witchcraft, hatred, variance, emulations, wrath, strife, seditions, heresies, Envyings, murders, drunkenness, revellings, and such like: of the which I tell you before, as I have also told you in time past, that they which do such things shall not inherit the kingdom of God. But the *fruit of the Spirit is love, joy, peace, longsuffering, gentleness, goodness, faith, Meekness, temperance: against such there is no law. And they that are Christ's have crucified the flesh* with the affections and lusts. If we live in the Spirit let us also walk in the Spirit."

In *Romans 8, verses 5 through 9,* Paul wrote, "They that are after the flesh do mind the things of the flesh; but they that are *after the Spirit the things of the Spirit.* For to be carnally minded is death; but *to be spiritually minded is life and peace.* Because the carnal mind is enmity against God: for it is not subject to the law of God, neither indeed can be. So then they that are in the flesh cannot please God. *But ye are not in the flesh, but in the Spirit, if so be that the Spirit of God dwell in you.* Now if any man have not the Spirit of Christ, he is none of his."

In *Romans 8:14* Paul says, "For as many as are *led by the Spirit of God, they are the sons of God."* And in *Galatians chapter 6, verse 8* Paul summarizes the matter by saying, "He that soweth to his flesh shall of the flesh reap corruption; but *he that soweth to the Spirit shall of the Spirit reap life everlasting."*

Become Godlike—Cultivate the Attributes of the Divine Nature

Number 9. We need to *become Godlike.* In His Sermon on the Mount, in *Matthew 5:48,* the Savior said, "Be ye therefore perfect, even as your Father which is in heaven is perfect." God wants us to become just as He is. He wants it to be "like Father, like son." It's not impossible, or He wouldn't have given us the commandment to do it. God wants us to overcome the world and acquire His divine nature. That's what He expects of those who will someday dwell with Him.

The apostle Peter tells us that we need to be partakers of the Divine Nature. In *2nd Peter 1:3 and 4,* he says that Jesus Christ "Hath *given unto us all things that pertain unto life and godliness,* through the knowledge of him that hath called us to glory and virtue: Whereby are given unto us exceeding great and precious promises: that by these ye might be *partakers of the divine nature."*
Paul, in *Romans 12:1 through 2,* wrote of this same change as he said, "I beseech you therefore, brethren, by the mercies of God, that *ye present your bodies a living sacrifice, holy, acceptable unto God, which is your reasonable service. And be not conformed to this world:* but *be ye transformed by the renewing of your mind,* that ye may prove what is that good, and acceptable, and perfect, will of God."

This life, then, is a time for us to strive to acquire the qualities of love, wisdom, holiness, and all the other attributes of our heavenly Father and our Lord, Jesus Christ. Those who are guided by the Holy Spirit are tutored in this process through His promptings.

Endure in Righteousness to the End

Number 10. We must *endure to the end.* Having taken these other steps and having begun to walk in the path of God's righteousness, we must continue and not turn away from them. The Savior said in *Matthew 24:13,* "He that shall *endure unto the end,* the same shall be saved." He expressed the same teaching in *Matthew 10:22:* "Ye shall be hated of all men for my name's sake: but he that endureth to the end shall be saved."

There are many other principles in the gospel of Jesus Christ which could be added to this list—so many that space doesn't permit discussing them here. But these ten principles embrace much of that which we must accomplish in mortality as we endure the many tests of life and experience the trial of our faith.

Let's summarize these ten principles that provide a pattern for righteous living:

1. We must resolve that the most important task in our life is to make ourselves eligible to live with God in His kingdom for all eternity.

2. We must come to Christ, through faith, and become full recipients of the benefits of His atoning sacrifice.

3. We must find the true Church of Jesus Christ and make it our schoolmaster, to teach us the principles of the gospel of Jesus Christ.

4. We must be baptized and confirmed, and partake of the necessary ordinances administered by authorized servants of Christ in His Church.

5. We must be born again, experiencing that mighty change which purifies our soul, fills us with love, makes us more receptive to the Holy Spirit, and enables us to overcome the world.

6. We must keep God's commandments—all of them.

7. We must do God's will, and labor to further His work here upon the earth.

8. We must live in the Spirit, overcoming our carnal nature and being led and guided by the Holy Ghost.

9. We must become godlike, becoming partakers of His divine nature, and

10. We must endure to the end, holding fast to these principles throughout our lifetime.

If we faithfully live these principles, they will cause us to reach out and embrace all of the precepts of the gospel of Christ. They will help us to overcome the temptations of the evil one. And they will prepare us for eternal life as we return to the presence of God.

Summary: Pre-Mortal and Earth Life

Now before we go further, let's recap those portions of God's eternal plan of salvation we have discussed.

First, we saw from the Bible that all of us—all mankind—are spirit children of our Heavenly Father. Jesus is our older brother—He was the firstborn of God's spirit children, and His Only Begotten Son in the flesh.

Second, we learned that we all lived in God's presence prior to our mortal birth. He knows all his sons and daughters. He loves us, He is concerned about us, and He wants us to be able to return and live with Him through all eternity.

Third, we then learned that Satan is also our brother—one of God's spirit children. He rebelled against God's eternal plan, and was cast out of God's domain, along with a third of all the hosts of heaven, our brothers. He and his followers, disembodied spirits, came to the earth, tempting us and seeking to lead us away from the goodness of God, so we will reap the same eternal sorrow and suffering which is to be their fate.

Fourth, we next spoke of the creation of this earth, and saw that all things were created by Jesus Christ, acting under the direction of our Heavenly Father. We read how man was created in the image of God—we look like Him.

Then, *fifth,* after considering these aspects of our pre-mortal life and our entrance into mortality, we spoke of the purposes of mortal life. We saw that this life is a time of testing, and of preparation for our final reward as we return to the kingdom of our Father. Ten principles were suggested which can be effective guides for our conduct in mortality. If we will live them we will reap eternal joy and will avoid many of the sorrows and trials of earth life.

Now it is time to move forward and consider what lies ahead for us in God's eternal plan of salvation.

Death and the Spirit World

What happens at the end of this life? Just as birth is the entry of a pre-mortal spirit into a mortal body, death is the separation of that spirit from it's temporal body.

The spirit world is not a permanent resting place for man. It is a temporary abode where people, in spirit form, await the resurrection. There are different realms in the spirit world. There is Paradise—a place for the righteous who have accepted Christ and kept His commandments. There is another place called the *spirit prison,* where those who have not yet heard the gospel go to prepare themselves and to have that gospel preached to them. And there is yet another place called *Hell,* which has been prepared for the wicked. Those who are evil are cast down to Hell and are under the influence of Satan. None of these places are "heaven," the final place of reward and glory where God dwells. They are intermediate, temporary areas—places of preparation.

We read in *Luke 23:42 through 43,* of the words of the thief who spoke to Christ when they both hung on the cross. "He said unto Jesus, Lord, remember me when thou comest into thy kingdom. And Jesus said unto him, Verily I say unto thee, *To day shalt thou be with me in paradise."*

You'll remember that three days later, when Christ's body was found missing from the tomb, the Savior appeared to Mary Magdalene in the garden. His words to her, as recorded in *John 20:17* were, "Touch me not; for *I am not yet ascended to my Father;* but go to my brethren, and say unto them, I ascend unto my Father, and your Father; and to my God; and your God."

We see then, that during this interval following his death, Christ had not yet gone to Heaven, to the presence of God the Father. No, He had gone to the spirit world, that intermediate area for spirits who are awaiting their resurrection.

We read about His visit to that area twice in Peter's first epistle. That great apostle explained that Christ, during the interval between his death and his resurrection, went and preached to spirits who were in the spirit prison, preparing the way so that they could hear and accept the Gospel and overcome the imperfections which they had experienced in their mortal lifetime. *1st Peter 3:18-20* says, "Christ also hath once suffered for sins, the just for the unjust, that he might bring us to God, being put to death in the flesh, but quickened by the Spirit: By which also he went and preached unto the spirits in prison; Which sometime were disobedient, when once the longsuffering of God waited in the days of Noah."

In the next chapter, *1st Peter 4:6,* he said, *"For this cause was the gospel preached also to them that are dead,* that they might be judged according to men in the flesh, but live according to God in the spirit."

Vicarious Baptisms Performed for the Dead

There is a process whereby spirits may come out of the spirit prison and enter into that area of the spirit world reserved for the righteous. That process requires the preaching of the gospel to them in the spirit prison, and then their acceptance of vicarious ordinances which are performed for the dead here upon the earth.

Paul talked of that process of vicarious work for the dead in *1st Corinthians 15:29,* where he spoke of baptism for the dead. In that chapter, Paul is explaining the doctrine that all men will be resurrected. He uses baptism for the dead, a practice of which the saints at that time obviously were aware, as an evidence that all men would rise from the grave. He said,

"Else what shall they do which are baptised for the dead if the dead rise not at all? Why are they then *baptised for the dead?"*

The concept of vicarious work, with one person laboring in another's behalf, is not new in the scriptures. Indeed, the atoning sacrifice of Jesus Christ is a vicarious work in which he took the sins of all mankind upon Him.

The same concept existed in Old Testament times. In *Leviticus 16:20 through 22* we read how the sins of Israel were figuratively placed upon the head of a goat and that goat became a "scapegoat." And the *fourth chapter of Leviticus* explains God's commandment to the Israelites to offer a bullock as a sin offering, transferring the sins of the people to the animal which they carried out of the camp to be destroyed.

In summary, preaching the gospel to the dead, as taught by the apostle Peter, and the principle of being vicariously baptized for the dead, as taught by the apostle Paul, comprise God's program for preparing all mankind for judgment on equal terms. They provide the way whereby those who have lived good lives but have not heard of Christ in this life may hear and accept the Savior and His gospel after death, and be judged by the standard of the gospel in the day of judgment. It's a good plan—an inspired plan, that shows God's love and concern for all His children.

Two Resurrections of the Dead and the Final Judgment

Let's move on, now, to the next step in the eternal plan of salvation.

The doctrine of the resurrection of the dead, in which men's physical bodies are restored to their spirit bodies, also was explained by Paul. In *1st Corinthians 15:19 through 23* we read, "If in this life only we have hope in Christ, we are of all men most miserable. But now is *Christ risen from the dead, and become the firstfruits* of them that slept. For since by man came death, by man came also the resurrection of the dead. For as in Adam all die, even so *in Christ shall all be made alive.* But every man in his own order: Christ the firstfruits; afterward they that are Christ's at his coming."

Resurrection is the process of reuniting the body and the spirit. A resurrected person has had his body raised from the grave, recreated if necessary by the power of God, so that it becomes a glorious body like unto the body of God.

In *Job 19:25 and 26,* we read of Job's testimony and faith in the resurrection. He said, "I know that my redeemer liveth, and that he shall stand at the latter day upon the earth: And though after my skin worms destroy this body, *yet in my flesh shall I see God."*

The account of Christ's appearance to his assembled disciples following His resurrection shows us clearly that a resurrected body is a body of flesh and bones plus spirit. In *Luke 24:36-39,* we read of Christ's coming to the disciples gathered in an upper room. It says, "Jesus himself stood in the midst of them, and saith unto them, Peace be unto you. But they were terrified and affrighted, and supposed that they had seen a spirit. And he said unto them, Why are ye troubled? and why do thoughts arise in your hearts? *Behold my hands and my feet, that it is I myself: handle me, and see; for a spirit hath not flesh and bones, as ye see me have."* And so he showed that he was more than just a spirit—his physical body had been reunited with his spirit body. His followers touched him, and felt for sure that he had a tangible, physical body once again. And Jesus sat down and ate fish and honeycomb in front of them.

Once we are resurrected, our physical body can never again separate from our spirit body. Just as death is the separation of the physical body from the spirit, resurrection is the reunion of the physical and spirit bodies inseparably for all eternity. This was the case with Christ, as we read in *Romans 6:9:* "Knowing that Christ being raised from the dead *dieth no more;* death hath no more dominion over him." His body and spirit can never again be separated. And Christ indicated that this principle extends to all men. In *Luke 20:36* He said, concerning those who have been resurrected, *"Neither can they die any more:* for they are equal unto the angels; and are the children of God, being the children of the resurrection."

And we look for our resurrected bodies to be glorious. In *Philippians 3:20 through 21* Paul said, "Our conversation is in heaven, from whence also we look for our Saviour, the Lord Jesus Christ: *Who shall change our vile body, that it may be fashioned like unto his glorious body,* according to the working whereby he is able even to subdue all things unto himself."

Paul taught that there would be different types of resurrected bodies, with varying degrees of glory depending upon the level of final reward which the individuals merit. *1st Corinthians 15:40 through 42* explains this. Paul said, "There are also *celestial bodies,* and *bodies terrestrial:* but the glory of the celestial is one, and the glory of the terrestrial is another. There is one glory of the sun, and another glory of the moon, and another glory of the stars: for one star differeth from another star in glory. *So also is the resurrection of the dead."*

The Bible teaches that there are to be two resurrections: a first resurrection of the righteous, and a second resurrection of the wicked. We read this in *John, chapter 5, verses 25, 28, and 29:* "Verily, verily, I say unto you, The hour is coming, and now is, when the *dead shall hear the voice of the Son of god:* and they that hear shall live. . . .Marvel not at this: for the hour is coming, in the which *all that are in the graves shall hear his voice, And shall come forth;* they that have done good, unto the *resurrection of life;* and they that have done evil, unto the *resurrection of damnation."*

The prophet Daniel also foresaw that there would be two different resurrections, one for the righteous and another for the wicked. In *Daniel 12:2* he said, "Many of them that sleep in the dust of the earth shall awake, *some to everlasting life,* and *some to shame and everlasting contempt."*

It is the apostle Paul who told about the resurrection of the righteous which will take place as the Lord Jesus Christ returns to earth in glory. We read about it in *1st Thessalonians 4, verses 13 through 17:* "I would not have you to be ignorant, brethren, concerning them which are asleep, that ye sorrow not, even as others which have no hope. For if we believe that Jesus died and rose again, even so them also which sleep in Jesus will God bring with him. For this we say unto you by the word of the Lord, that we which are alive and remain unto the coming of the Lord shall not prevent them which are asleep. For the Lord himself shall descend from heaven with a shout, with the voice of the archangel, and with the trump of God: and *the dead in Christ shall rise first: Then we which are alive and remain shall be caught up together with them in the clouds, to meet the Lord in the air:* and so shall we ever be with the Lord."

John the Revelator described the first resurrection, and saw that those who receive their resurrected body at that time will live on the earth and reign with Christ a thousand years. *Revelation 20:4 through 6* records John's vision: "I saw thrones, and they sat upon them, and judgment was given unto them: and I saw the souls of them that were beheaded for the witness of Jesus, and for the word of God, and which had not worshipped the beast, neither his image, neither had received his mark upon their foreheads, or in their hands; and *they lived and reigned with Christ a thousand years.* But the rest of the dead lived not again until the thousand years were finished. *This is the first resurrection. Blessed and holy is he that hath part in the first resurrection:* on such the second death hath no power, but *they shall be priests of God and of Christ, and shall reign with him a thousand years."*

John also described the second resurrection, the resurrection of the wicked which will take place a thousand years later, in *Revelation 20:12 and 13.* He described the judgment-day process too: "I saw the dead, small and great, stand before God; and the books were opened: and another book was opened, which is the book of life: and the dead were judged out of those things which were written in the books, *according to their works.* And the sea gave up the dead which were in it; and death and hell delivered up the dead which were in them: and *they were judged every man according to their works.*"

Thus it is that at the time of our resurrection that we will come and stand before the judgment bar of God. The Savior taught in *John 5:22 and 23* that the process of judgment had been committed to him. He said, *"The Father judgeth no man, but hath committed all judgment unto the Son:* That all men should honour the Son, even as they honour the Father. He that honoureth not the Son honoureth not the Father which hath sent him."

We have several descriptions of the final judgment day given in the Bible. In addition to Revelation 20:12 and 13 which we already considered, we have Paul's statement in *Romans 14:10 through 12:* "But why dost thou judge thy brother? or why dost thou set at nought thy brother? for *we shall all stand before the judgment seat of Christ.* For it is written, As I live, saith the Lord, every knee shall bow to me, and every tongue shall confess to God. So then *every one of us shall give account of himself to God."*

In *2nd Corinthians 5:10,* Paul wrote that *"We must all appear before the judgment seat of Christ;* that every one may receive the things done in his body, according to that he hath done, whether it be good or bad."

The apostle Paul, in *Romans 2:16,* indicated that the gospel of Jesus Christ will be the standard whereby all men are to be judged. He referred to "The day when God shall judge the secrets of men *by Jesus Christ according to my gospel."* And he told how God would reward every man with eternal blessings or misery, according to his acts and conduct here on earth.

In *Romans 2:6 through 11* Paul said God *"Will render to every man according to his deeds:* To them who by patient continuance in well doing seek for glory and honour and immortality, eternal life: but unto them that are contentious, and do not obey the truth, but obey unrighteousness, indignation and wrath, Tribulation and anguish, upon every soul of man that doeth evil, of the Jew first, and also of the Gentile; But *glory, honour, and peace, to every man that worketh good,* to the Jew first, and also to the Gentile: For *there is no respect of persons with God."*

All these passages combine to give us a clear description of the final judgment. Perhaps their message can be best summarized by one phrase spoken by the Master. We read it in *Luke 12:48: "For unto whomsoever much is given, of him shall be much required."*

Many Mansions in New Heavens and a New Earth

At the end of Christ's millennial reign, after the resurrection of the wicked who have finished their stay in hell, and after the final judgment, this earth will undergo a tremendous change. John the Revelator wrote in *Revelation 21:1,* "I saw a *new heaven and a new earth:* for the first heaven and the first earth were passed away; and there was no more sea." The Lord told of this recreated earth through the mouth of his ancient prophet Isaiah, in *Isaiah 65:17:* "For, behold, I create *new heavens and a new earth:* and the former shall not be remembered, nor come into mind."

Paul taught that there would be several different heavens, or kingdoms, in which the righteous would dwell. In *2nd Corinthians 12:2 through 4,* he modestly told of visions he, himself, had received years before, in which visions he had seen even a third heaven, and in which he had also gone into the paradise of the spirit world. He said, "I knew a man in Christ above fourteen years ago, (whether in the body, I cannot tell; or whether out of the body, I cannot tell: God knoweth;) such an *one caught up to the third heaven.* And I knew such a man, (whether in the body or out of the body, I cannot tell: God knoweth;) How that he was *caught up into paradise,* and heard unspeakable words, which it is not lawful for a man to utter."

I commented earlier on Paul's teaching on the resurrection in *1st Corinthians 15:40 through 42,* in which he said that there were celestial bodies and terrestrial bodies. He taught that there will be bodies with glory like the sun, and like the moon, and like the stars, differing in glory one from another, He implied, then, that men will receive different levels of reward, depending upon their conduct here upon the earth.

Jesus also spoke of resurrected bodies, like the sun in their glory, in *Matthew 13:41 through 43:* "The Son of man shall send forth his angels, and they shall gather out of his kingdom all things that offend, and them which do iniquity; and shall cast them into a furnace of fire; there shall be wailing and gnashing of teeth. *Then shall the righteous shine forth as the sun in the kingdom of their Father.* Who hath ears to hear, let him hear."

Jesus also taught that there would be many different locations in which
the righteous would finally abide. In *John 14:2 through 4* the Lord told
his disciples, *"In my Father's house are any mansions:* if it were not so,
I would have told you. *I go to prepare a place for you.* And if I go and
prepare a place for you, I will come again, and receive you unto myself;
that *where I am, there ye may be also.* And whither I go ye know, and
the way ye know."

And *2nd Chronicles 2:6* speaks not only of the heaven, but also the
"heaven of heavens," thus indicating that there is more than one level of
reward in God's eternal dominions. *Job 22:14* tells us that God "walketh
in the *circuit of heaven,"* apparently visiting His various dominions there.

The Epistle to the *Hebrews, in the 12th chapter,* describes the experience
of a portion of the righteous as they will come into their heavenly reward.
It says, *beginning with verse 22,* "Ye are come unto mount Sion, and *unto
the city of the living God, the heavenly Jerusalem,* and to an innumerable
company of angels, *To the general assembly and Church of the firstborn,*
which are written in heaven, and to God the Judge of all, and to the spirits
of just men made perfect, And to Jesus the mediator of the new covenant."

Man Has The Potential to Be "Perfect in Christ Jesus"

And what is the nature of the final reward for those who have done their
best here on earth to "lay up . . . treasures in heaven?" Various scriptural
passages tell us that there is a special reward for those who will strive for
and gain perfection, and rise above the level of salvation. We've already
read the Savior's commandment in *Matthew 5:48* to *"Be ye therefore perfect,* even as your Father which is in heaven is perfect." Paul, in his Epistle to the Colossians, described the perfecting of its members as the labor
of the church, in *Colossians 1:28,* saying, "We preach, warning every man,
and teaching every man in all wisdom; that we may *present every man perfect
in Christ Jesus."*

The Savior alluded to those individuals who will receive the highest of
God's rewards, even sharing the powers and abilities which Christ now
possesses, in the *14th chapter of John, verse 12,* where he said, "Verily,
verily, I say unto you, He that believeth on me, *the works that I do shall
he do also; and greater works than these shall he do;* because I go unto
my Father."

Heirs of God, and Joint-Heirs with Christ

The scriptures tell us that there are some that will be reckoned as joint heirs with Christ and will share his power and glory. Paul wrote, in *Romans 8:16 through 18*, "The Spirit itself beareth witness with our spirit, that we are the children of God: And if children, then heirs; *heirs of God, and joint-heirs with Christ;* if so be that we suffer with him, that we may *be also glorified together.* For I reckon that the sufferings of this present time are not worthy to be compared with the *glory which shall be revealed in us.*"

He expressed the same teaching in the *4th chapter of Galatians, verses 6 and 7,* when he said, "Because ye are sons, God hath sent forth the Spirit of his Son into your hearts, crying, Abba, Father. Wherefore thou art no more a servant, but a son; and *if a son, then and heir of God through Christ.*"

And in *Titus 3:7 through 8,* Paul repeated the teaching once again. While speaking of Jesus Christ he said "That *being justified by his grace, we should be made heirs according to the hope of eternal life.* This is a faithful saying, and these things I will that thou affirm constantly, that they which have believed in God might *be careful to maintain good works.* These things are good and profitable unto men."

This revealed potential to share with Christ the honor and glory of his exaltation, thus partaking of the powers of godhood, has excited God's prophets down through the ages. It was the message of the Psalmist, who wrote in *Psalms 82:6,* "I have said, *Ye are gods;* and all of you are children of the most High." The first verse of that same Psalm says, "God standeth in the *congregation of the mighty; he judgeth among the gods.*"

In the *10th chapter of John, verses 34 and 35,* the Savior made reference to these passages in Psalms and said, "Is it not written in your law, I said, *Ye are gods?*" and then he said that " . . . *He called them gods, unto whom the word of God came, and the scripture cannot be broken.*" The possibility of obtaining this exalted reward is why the Savior instructed us in his Sermon on the Mount to "Be ye therefore perfect," and taught us to "Lay up for yourselves treasures in heaven."

The promise of these glorious blessings was also made by John the Revelator, who quoted the words of the Savior in *Revelation 3:21:* "To him that overcometh will I grant to sit with me in my throne, even as I also overcame, and am set down with my Father in his throne."

And *Revelation 21, verse 7* says, "He that overcometh *shall inherit all things;* and I will be his God, and *he shall be my son.*"

In that exalted relationship we still will render love, allegiance and reverence to God the Father, who is the Father and God of us all, and also to our brother, our Lord Jesus Christ. Paul explained this relationship in *1st Corinthians 8:5 and 6:* "For though there be that are called *gods;* whether *in heaven* or in earth, (as *there be gods many, and lords many,*) But to *us there is but one God, the Father,* of whom are all things, and we in him; and *one Lord Jesus Christ,* by whom are all things, and we by him."

Summary: The Spirit World, Resurrections, and Final Rewards

And now, let's summarize the final section of God's eternal plan of salvation—that portion that answers the question, "Where am I going after this life?"

We learned that death is the separation of the physical body from the spirit body. Though the physical body is consigned to the tomb, the spirit remains conscious, and enters the spirit world where it continues to grow and progress. The spirit world is a temporary abode, and man will reside there only until the day of his resurrection.

There are three general divisions in the spirit world. First, there is *Paradise,* the place where the righteous dwell and progress. These are those who have been "saved" from being cast into Hell through the grace and atonement of Jesus Christ.

Hell, or the domain of Satan, is the second area of the spirit world. It is inhabited by those who were wicked while on earth, and by those who joined with Satan in his rebellion and were cast out from God's presence long ago.

The third area is called the *Spirit Prison.* It is inhabited by those who have not yet heard the gospel. While they are there, righteous spirits will visit and teach them, and eventually all mankind will have the opportunity to hear and accept or reject the gospel.

The Bible speaks of vicarious baptisms being performed here on earth for those who are in the spirit prison. If they choose to accept the baptism performed in their behalf, inhabitants of the spirit prison can leave that area and enter Paradise, the spirit world domain of the righteous, where they can experience greater growth.

We learned that all men will be resurrected, having their physical body restored to house their spirit body for all eternity, never to be separated again. There will be resurrected bodies with various levels of glory—some with glory comparable to the sun, others with an intermediate degree of glory like the moon, and still others with less glory, whom Paul compared to the stars.

The righteous will be called forth in the first resurrection, which will take place as Christ returns to the earth in the glory of His second coming. They will dwell with Christ during His thousand-year reign on the earth. The wicked will be resurrected at the end of the millennium. Since all men will be resurrected, this will end the spirit world, including Hell, but the scriptures indicate that some will again be cast out of the presence of God at the final judgment, and will be condemned to live with Satan for all eternity in misery, in a kingdom of no glory.

All men will come before Christ to be judged for the life they have lived on earth. At that time they will be assigned to the level of eternal reward that they are to receive, though they will already have been resurrected with bodies corresponding to the level of glory they will attain.

At the end of the millennium there will be great changes as the Lord creates new heavens and a new earth. There will be various "heavens," or "mansions" which the righteous will inherit, representing various degrees of glory and eternal rewards. The highest of all the rewards which God has promised is that some may actually become joint-heirs with Christ, sharing His power and glory. It is in preparation for this great blessing that men are commanded to strive to overcome the world and labor to acquire the attributes of God while here on earth.

God's entire plan of salvation is based on the reality that we are all children of our Heavenly Father. He knows us. He loves us. He wants to reward us with the rich blessings of eternal life, and He will do so if we will overcome the temptations which will confront us during our mortal probation. Our Heavenly Father wants to have His children dwell with Him throughout eternity, maintaining our family relationship with Him while enjoying the exquisite joy and blessings of eternal life.

The rewards will be great, and well worth the full dedication of our mortal life to attain them. As Paul wrote in *1st Corinthians 2:9,* "Eye hath not seen, nor ear heard, neither have entered into the heart of man, the things which *God hath prepared for them that love him.*"

May we so live as to gain that great reward, and again share the love and personal companionship of our Father and our God, I pray in the name of Jesus Christ. Amen.

Are
You Saved?

A Mormon's View of Faith, Works,
Grace, and Salvation

Duane S. Crowther

It was late January, 1985. My wife and I were attending a convention in Atlanta, Georgia. The sessions were over for the day, and we set out to walk several blocks back to our hotel. There was some new construction going on so one side of the street was blocked. As we walked along the other sidewalk we approached a man dressed in dirty, tattered clothes, sitting on the curb. The smell of liquor was strong around him. He had thrown up on the sidewalk, and was rocking back and forth in an uncoordinated fashion. It was obvious that he was very, very drunk.

We sensed an unpleasant situation approaching, and I steered my wife into the street to keep him from accosting us. But as we walked by him he remained lost in his drunken reverie. We could hear him mumbling a little chant to himself, over and over again: "Lord, I thank you that I'm saved. Lord, I thank you that I'm saved. Lord, I thank you that I'm saved."

We didn't know the man, and we don't know his background nor his heart, and we certainly aren't his judges. But to all appearances, that man appeared about as unsaved as any individual we had ever seen. Was he really saved, or was he clinging to an illusion?

And how about you? Are **you** saved? And if you think you are saved, what did you do to arrive at that belief? And what are you saved from? And can you ever become unsaved, or are you saved no matter what you do the rest of your life? And what evidence can you show to substantiate that your belief is valid in the sight of God?

I have in front of me a tract, typical of many Protestant tracts on the subject of salvation. It's entitled "Power for Living . . . The First Step." It asks the reader, "Are you going to Heaven when you die?" and it offers a simple solution to the question by saying, "By simply recognizing our need for a divine Savior, and by accepting Christ's payment for our sins and our salvation, the matter of our eternal destiny is immediately resolved. This is the way—the only way—to know for sure that you have eternal life."

And then it asks, "Do you have this assurance?" and says, "If not, you can gain this assurance right here and now." Then it suggests that all you have to do is to be willing to invite Jesus Christ to come in and change your life, and be willing to place all your trust and confidence in him rather than in your own works. And if you feel that way, it suggests that you can get yourself saved, or "complete the transaction" as the tract expresses it, by praying this little prayer:

"Dear God, I know I am a sinner and unable to save myself. But I do believe You love me, and that You sent Your Son, Jesus, to die on the cross for my sins. Right here and now, I ask You to forgive my every sin and give me the gift of eternal life. Thank You, dear God, for hearing and answering my prayer, and for giving me eternal life as You promised You would. Amen."

Wow! Is salvation that easy to obtain? Can you really just say that little prayer, and obtain the promise that you'll go to heaven and have eternal life in the presence of God forever and ever, no matter what you think, or say, or do, all the rest of your life? Apparently there are lots of people who believe that. But I suggest that *you owe yourself a considerable amount of careful, prayerful study of the scriptures before you accept that belief as the true word of God and his final word on the subject.*

Let's examine the scriptures and see what they tell us about the doctrines of salvation, the fall of Adam, the atonement of Jesus Christ, and what happens to man after death. We're dealing with the major doctrines of Christianity, aren't we? These subjects are profound, but they're important, and our eternal future depends on us determining just what Jesus Christ expects us to accept, and think, and believe, and do, if we are to dwell with him in the heavens.

The title of this discussion is "Are You Saved—A Mormon's View of Faith, Works, Grace and Salvation." I'm going to comment on those subjects and present, to the best of my ability, the basic perspective of The Church of Jesus Christ of Latter-day Saints on them. Now I'm just a lay member—I'm not an official spokesman of the Mormon Church. But I'm in a position where I talk to many good Protestant people who ask a lot of questions about what the Mormons believe.

Some of these people have been sold a false bill of goods and a lot of untrue notions about the actual beliefs of the Latter-day Saints by a few professional anti-Mormon critics. It's their intentional misrepresenting of Mormon doctrines, and practices, and history that have raised questions in the minds of honest seekers after truth. I, for one, can't see how *they* can claim to be "saved" and "born again" and yet deal in extensive falsehoods and intentional half-truths—that's not the kind of conduct my Bible tells me should be typical of true followers of Jesus Christ. But that's another subject.

My objective in this discussion is to answer some of the questions raised by honest truth seekers from other churches, and to present, to the best of my ability, what Mormons actually believe on these vital subjects. I'll try to do it by asking a series of fourteen questions, and then answering them. I'll quote from the King James version of the Bible, and also quote from two books Latter-day Saints accept as scriptures: The *Book of Mormon* and the *Doctrine and Covenants*. Now I recognize that you non-Mormon friends may not accept those books as being valid scripture, but it will still help you to understand the Mormon point of view, and will help you to recognize that those books are in complete harmony with the Bible.

If you're knowledgeable in Protestant theology, you'll observe something you may not have known before—that Mormons believe the same as Protestants on many of the key principles of the doctrine of salvation. And they should, because both believe the Bible to be the revealed word of God, and they draw the same doctrinal insights from it.

Man Is Saved Through the Grace of Jesus Christ

So here's the *first question* and it's the big one—the sixty four dollar question: "Do Mormons believe that man is saved by the grace of Jesus Christ?"

The answer is *Yes, absolutely yes!* It is clearly stated in Mormon doctrine that salvation is available to man only through the grace of Christ, and that we can't gain salvation in any other way than by partaking of his grace.

Let me quote you several key passages which make it clear that salvation through the grace of Christ is a fundamental believe of the Mormons. First, from the book of *Ephesians* in the Bible, *chapter 2, verses 8 and 9,* where Paul wrote, *"By grace are ye saved through faith;* and that not of yourselves: it is the gift of God: Not of works, lest any man should boast."

The apostle Peter, in the *15th chapter of Acts, verse 11,* taught the same basic doctrine, that salvation is ultimately achieved through the grace of Christ, when he said, *"We believe that through the grace of the Lord Jesus Christ we shall be saved . . . "*

These are statements of fundamental importance, and are typical of dozens in the Bible. Latter-day Saints believe the Bible to be the word of God, as is clearly stated in our *eighth Article of Faith,* so we firmly accept this teaching as our doctrine.

We find the same doctrine taught in Mormon scriptures also. In *2nd Nephi,* in the Book of Mormon, for instance, in *chapter 25, verse 23,* the prophet Nephi says, "We labor diligently to write, to persuade our children, and also our brethren, to believe in Christ, and to be reconciled to God; for we know that it *is by grace that we are saved, after all we can do."*

Grace is God's Willingness to Bless Mankind with Mercy, Pardon, Gifts and Powers

Question number two: What is "grace," and what is a good definition of the "grace of God" that these scriptures are talking about? *Webster's Dictionary* associates the term grace with words such as mercy, pardon, kindness, favor, approval, acceptance, and asserts the religious meaning of the word to be "unmerited divine assistance given man for his regeneration or sanctification."

The *Cambridge Bible Dictionary* says that "The main idea of the word is the freeness of God's gifts to man, especially to the freeness of his forgiveness."

Millard F. Day, author of *Basic Bible Doctrines,* published by Moody Press, in his article entitled "Grace," defines the term as "the limitless love of God expressed in measureless kindness." He quotes *Titus 3, verse 4,* in his definition, which speaks of "the kindness and love of God our Saviour toward man. . . ."

His definition is typical of those found in many theological explanations. But the term "grace of God" doesn't mean just God's willingness to forgive man's sins, but also his willingness to bless man with gifts and powers and abilities. The Book of Mormon prophet Jacob wrote, for instance, in *Jacob chapter 4, verses 6 and 7,* "We search the prophets, and *we have many revelations and the spirit of prophecy;* and having all these witnesses we obtain a hope, and our faith becometh unshaken, insomuch that we truly can command in the name of Jesus and *the very trees obey us, or the mountains, or the waves of the sea.* Nevertheless, the Lord God showeth us our weakness that we may know that *it is by his grace, and his great condescensions unto the children of men, that we have power to do these things."*

Like almost all believers in Christ, Mormons recognize the doctrinal importance and necessity of the grace of Christ, and the theme appears often in our doctrinal explanations.

All Have Sinned and Are in Need of Christ's Saving Grace

Question 3: Are all men sinners, and does all mankind need the grace of Jesus Christ to be saved?

The scriptures are very emphatic on this subject. *Romans 3:10,* for instance, says that "There is none righteous, no, not one." and *Romans 3:23* says that "All have sinned, and come short of the glory of god." *1st John chapter 1, verse 8,* has the same message: "If we say that we have no sin, we deceive ourselves, and the truth is not in us."

Latter-day Saints clearly believe that they, as well as Protestants, and Catholics, and Buddists, and atheists, and all mankind must be recipients of the redeeming grace of Jesus Christ if they are to be saved.

In a few moments we'll discuss the fall of Adam, that brought sin and death into the world. But there's another kind of fall with which we first must be concerned. Some call it "the fall of me." *The fall of me takes place for each one of us the first time we sin.* Once we have committed even one sin, we become a sinner. We have lost our perfection, and have forfeited our claim to the presence and glory of God—we've personally separated ourselves from Him.

Sin Is Transgression of God's Laws

Question 4: What exactly is sin?

1st John 3, verse 4 tells us that "Sin is the transgression of the law," and *chapter 5, verse 17,* tells us that "All unrighteousness is sin." But the Bible helps us to understand that "Where no law is, there is no transgression," as Paul tells us in *Romans 4, verses 15.*

There are different kinds of laws: man's laws and God's laws. God gave us ancient rules of conduct, such as the Law of Moses. Christ, when he came in the meridian of time, fulfilled the Law of Moses, and revealed new laws and instructions as to how we should conduct ourselves in our daily life.

Latter-day Saints believe that God has revealed even more instructions and guidance and laws in the century and a half since He restored his Church here upon the earth.

Man sins when he knowingly breaks the law. As Paul wrote to the *Romans, in chapter 3, verse 20,* "By the law is the knowledge of sin." And Paul also wrote, in *Romans 5:13,* "Sin is not imputed when there is no law." So a person—for instance, a little child—may break the law, but in God's divine wisdom, his breaking of that law is not counted as sin unless the individual knows that there is a law and that he is willfully breaking it.

The Book of Mormon gives an excellent explanation of the relationship of sin and law in *Alma 42, verses 16 through 21:* "Now, repentance could not come unto men except there were a punishment, which also was eternal as the life of the soul should be, affixed opposite to the plan of happiness, which was as eternal also as the life of the soul. Now, *how could a man repent except he should sin? How could he sin if there was no law? How could there be a law save there was a punishment? Now, there was a punishment affixed, and a just law given, which brought remorse of conscience unto man.* Now, if there was no law given—if a man murdered he should die—would he be afraid he would die if he should murder? And also, if there was no law given against sin men would not be afraid to sin. And *if there was no law given, if men sinned what could justice do, or mercy either, for they would have no claim upon the creature?"*

Sin Results in Spiritual Separation from God

Question 5: What is the inevitable result of sin?

Romans 6:23 says, "The wages of sin is death." *James 1:15* observes that "Sin . . . bringeth forth death." And back in the Old Testament, in *Ezekiel 18, verse 4,* we're also told that "The soul that sinneth, it shall die."

Now what kind of death are the scriptures describing when they speak of the death a sinner must endure? A typical answer given by a Protestant theologian is that expressed by Dr. Curtis Hutson, in his tract, "Salvation Plain and Simple," published by Sword of the Lord Publishers. He wrote, "This infinitely Holy God said sin must be paid for. And the payment for sin is death. This death is more than dying with a gunshot wound or cancer. It is described in the Bible as the second death. *Revelation 20:14,* "And death and hell were cast into the lake of fire. This is the second death." If I pay what I owe as a sinner, I must die, go into Hell and stay there forever and ever. That's the price God demands for my sins."

Latter-day Saints explain the same concept, but with slightly different terminology. We speak of two kinds of death also: physical death and spiritual death. *Physical death* is the separation of the spirit from the body when mortal life comes to an end. That's what the Bible is talking about when it tells us that men "gave up the ghost." When the spirit leaves it, the body is lifeless, and gets put into the grave. We'll talk later about where the spirit goes.

But the scriptures talk of a second kind of death, called *spiritual death,* in which an individual is separated from the presence and influence of God. In the Book of Mormon, in *Alma chapter 42, verse 9,* the prophet Alma taught that "the fall had brought upon all mankind a spiritual death as well as a temporal, that is, *they were cut off from the presence of the Lord."*

We believe that man can experience this spiritual death, this second kind of death, to a limited degree here on earth if he is alienated from God, but it will be much more severe after his physical death if he goes into hell and is completely isolated from the Spirit and guidance of God while he is under the influence of Satan. Amulek, a companion of the Book of Mormon prophet Alma, described this spiritual death in *Alma 12, verses 16 through 18.* He said,

"Now behold, I say unto you then cometh a death, even a *second death, which is a spiritual death;* then is a time that whosoever dieth in his sins, as to a temporal death, shall also die a spiritual death; yea, *he shall die as to things pertaining unto righteousness.* Then is the time when their torments shall be as a lake of fire and brimstone, whose flame ascendeth up forever and ever; and then is the time that they shall be chained down to an everlasting destruction, according to the power and captivity of Satan, he having subjected them according to his will. Then, I say unto you, *they shall be as though there had been no redemption made; for they cannot be redeemed according to God's justice; . . . "*

Adam's Fall Subjected Mankind to Sin, Physical Death and Spiritual Death

Question 6: What were the results of the fall of Adam?

The doctrine of the fall of man, or original sin, as it is often called, involves many ramifications that can't be mentioned here because of lack of space. But the fundamental insight we need to have is that the fall of Adam caused mankind to experience three things: *sin, physical death* at the end of mortal life, and the separation from God I've described as *spiritual death.* In his epistle to the *Romans, chapter 5, verse 12,* Paul said, "By one man sin entered into the world, and death by sin; and so death passed upon all men, for that all have sinned."

Adam's fall brought man into mortality, and made it necessary that man must die. It also separated man from the presence of God so that he has to walk by faith, not by sight. And he also has to undergo the experiences and temptations of mortal life.

Several Book of Mormon passages give us important insights concerning the results of Adam's fall, and in some ways clarify concepts that are very difficult to understand from the Bible. One of those concepts is what would of happened if Adam had not fallen. *2nd Nephi chapter 2, verses 22 through 25,* tells us,

"If *Adam had not transgressed he would not have fallen, but he would have remained in the garden of Eden.* And all things which were created must have remained in the same state in which they were after they were created; and they must have remained forever, and had no end. And they would have had no children; wherefore *they would have remained in a state of innocence, having no joy, for they knew no misery; doing no good, for they knew no sin.* But behold, all things have been done in the wisdom of him who knoweth all things. *Adam fell that men might be; and men are, that they might have joy."*

Another important understanding the Book of Mormon gives us is what would of happened to all mankind because of Adam's fall if there had not been an atonement by Jesus Christ. *2nd Nephi 9, verses 8 through 10,* says:

"O the wisdom of God, his mercy and grace! For behold, *if the flesh should rise no more our spirits must become subject to that angel who fell from before the presence of the Eternal God, and become the devil, to rise no more. And our spirits must have become like unto him, and we become devils, angels to a devil,* to be shut out from the presence of our God, and to remain with the father of lies, in misery, like unto himself; yea, to that being who beguiled our first parents, who transformeth himself nigh unto an angel of light, and stirreth up the children of men unto secret combinations of murder and all manner of secret works of darkness. *O how great the goodness of our God, who prepareth a way for our escape from the grasp of this awful monster;* yea, that monster, death and hell, which I call the death of the body, and also the death of the spirit."

So we can see that if there hadn't been an atonement wrought by Jesus Christ, all mankind would end up as unresurrected spirit beings without bodies, in hell with all its misery, subjected to Satan for all eternity.

An Atonement Was Needed to Overcome Sin, Physical Death, and Separation from God

Question 7: Exactly why was an atonement for mankind necessary?

This is another of those challenging questions that people write whole books attempting to answer, yet no one understands the matter completely. I suppose that we will never understand all the details until we get back to the presence of God and learn them all first hand. There are many passages of scripture that explain the reasons why there had to be an atonement. My favorite is in the Book of Mormon, in *Alma 42:13 through 15.* This is how it explains the need for the atonement:

"According to justice, *the plan of redemption could not be brought about, only on conditions of repentance of men in this probationary state,* yea, this preparatory state; for except it were for these conditions, mercy could not take effect except it should destroy the work of justice. Now *the work of justice could not be destroyed;* if so, God would cease to be God. And thus we see that all mankind were fallen, and they were in the grasp of justice; yea, the justice of God, which consigned them forever to be cut off from his presence. And now, *the plan of mercy could not be brought about except an atonement should be made; therefore God himself atoneth for the sins of the world, to bring about the plan of mercy,* to appease the demands of justice, that God might be a perfect, just God, and a merciful God also."

Now let me try to summarize the need for an atonement in my own words. A brief summary of the basic problem goes something like this:

Before Adam and Eve committed the original sin, they were in the presence of God. They could have lived forever in that state, and they were perfect in the sense that they were sinless. But once they sinned they could no longer stay in the presence of God, they could not live forever, and they were no longer sinless and perfect.

God, who must live by the requirements of perfection because he is God, has to meet the demands of justice which say that sins must be paid for. Since Adam had lost his perfection, he could not pay for his own sin and return himself to his sinless state. The only way that he could eventually be sinless would be to have someone who was perfect pay the debt his fall from perfection had created.

But certain requirements had to be met by the Redeemer who would pay for Adam's sin for that payment to meet the demands of divine justice. *First,* that Redeemer had to be without sin himself. *Second,* he had to have power to break the bands of death and begin the resurrection process so mankind could be resurrected and have the eternal body needed to experience a fulness of eternal joy. And *third,* the Redeemer had to be able to make this atonement, or payment, of his own free will and choice. Only by meeting those three requirements could the Redeemer accomplish the needed atonement.

Only Christ Had the Power to Die and Then Return to Life

Question 8: How did Jesus Christ meet these requirements to perform his atoning sacrifice?

We need to recognize that only Jesus Christ could perform that great sacrifice in our behalf. First, he was able to live on this earth without committing any sin. If he would have committed even one sin, then that sin would have caused him to be fallen, just like Adam. The Bible tells us Christ lived without sin. *1st Peter 1, verse 19,* calls Christ "A lamb without blemish and without spot." *1st Peter 2:22* says that he "Did no sin, neither was guile found in his mouth." And *2nd Corinthians 5:21* says that Christ "Knew no sin" also.

Now to understand Jesus's other qualifications, we have to understand the nature of his birth. Jesus was different than every other person that has ever lived on this earth, because his Father was a God, God the Father, and his mother, the virgin Mary, was a mortal. So combined in Jesus Christ was the power to live forever, drawn from God the Father, and the power to die, drawn from his mortal mother.

Because he had combined within himself the powers of both Godhood and mortality, he could choose to give up his mortal life, and also to reclaim his body after his spirit had left it, and thus begin the resurrection process.

No other being here on earth has ever had that tremendous power of combined Godhood and mortality! That's what Jesus was saying in *John 10, verses 17 and 18:* "Therefore doth my Father love me, because I lay down my life, that I might take it again. *No man taketh it from me, but I lay it down of myself. I have power to lay it down, and I have power to take it again.* This commandment have I received of my Father."

Christ Paid for Our Sins So Man May Attain Eternal Life

What, exactly, was Christ's atoning sacrifice? What did he do for us? In his epistle to the *Galatians, chapter 1, verse 4,* Paul gave us a very basic explanation of the atonement. He wrote that Jesus Christ *"Gave himself for our sins, that he might deliver us from this present evil world,* according to the will of God and our Father." The apostle John explained the atonement in *1st John 2:1 and 2.* He said, "We have an advocate with the Father, Jesus Christ the righteous: And he is the propitiation for our sins: and not for ours only, but also for the sins of the whole world." And in *1st John chapter four, verses 8 through 10,* John wrote: "God is love. In this was manifested the love of God toward us, because that God sent his only begotten Son into the world, that we might live through him. Herein is love, *not that we loved God,* but that *he loved us, and sent his Son to be the propitiation for our sins."*

Jesus Christ, in his atoning sacrifice, took upon himself the sins of mankind. He suffered for all of us as he paid the price for our sins and met the demands of justice. He suffered in the Garden of Gethsemane, and then gave his life in payment for our transgressions through that most horrible of all kinds of death: crucifixion.

In a modern revelation, the Lord described the extent of his great suffering in our behalf. His description is recorded in *Doctrine and Covenants section 19, verses 15 through 19:*

"I command you to repent—repent, lest I smite you by the rod of my mouth, and by my wrath, and by my anger, and your sufferings be sore— how sore you know not, how exquisite you know not, yea, how hard to bear you know not. For behold *I, God, have suffered these things for all, that they might not suffer if they would repent;* But if they would not repent they must suffer even as I; *which suffering caused myself, even God, the greatest of all, to tremble because of pain, and to bleed at every pore, and to suffer both body and spirit*—and would that I might not drink the bitter cup, and shrink—Nevertheless, glory be to the Father, and I partook and finished my preparations unto the children of men."

Christ Began Resurrection for All Mankind and Allows Forgiven Individuals to Regain God's Presence

Question 9: What are the results of our Lord's atoning sacrifice?

You remember that we talked of the results of the fall of Adam—that event introduced two kinds of death into the world: *physical death* and spiritual death. The atonement of Jesus Christ overcame those two deaths. Because of Christ's power to give up his body and then reclaim it, he overcame the power of physical death and began the process of resurrection. Because of his resurrection, all mankind will now be resurrected. The spirits of man will be restored to their bodies at the last day, and mankind will live as resurrected beings for all eternity. This is called *general salvation,* because all men will be resurrected, no matter whether their mortal acts were good or evil. The resurrection is a free gift of Jesus Christ to all mankind.

Jesus also overcame the effects of *spiritual death,* in which man is separated from the presence of God. Because of his atoning sacrifice, he stands as an intermediary between man and God the Father. He has the power, or grace, to forgive an individual's sins, and to allow that forgiven individual to enter once again into the presence of the Father and to dwell with him forever, throughout all eternity.

Jesus overcame the effects of the fall of Adam, so that they will not affect our personal status before God at the last day. This is why the Latter-day Saint *second Article of Faith* says, "We believe that men will be punished for their own sins, and not for Adam's transgression."

And Latter-day Saints believe that the benefits of Christ's atonement extend to every man, woman and child who has ever lived, or ever will live, upon this earth. Our *third Article of Faith* proclaims our faith that "We believe that through the Atonement of Christ, all *mankind may be saved. . . ."*

This overcoming of spiritual death, or separation from God, is on a person-to-person basis. It is called individual salvation, and it's concerned with "the fall of me" that I mentioned before. *Each individual must accept Christ as his Savior, and in turn be accepted by Christ through compliance with the requirements he has established, to gain individual salvation.*

Faith is Personal Commitment to God and Trust in His Power, Promises and Love

Question 10: What is faith?

The scriptures give several classic definitions of faith. *Hebrews 11:1* says, "Faith is the substance of things hoped for, the evidence of things not seen." The Book of Mormon contains a similar definition, in *Alma 32, verse 21:* "Faith is not to have a perfect knowledge of things; therefore if ye have faith ye hope for things which are not seen, which are true."

In *1st Peter 1, verses 7 through 9,* Peter wrote about our faith and how it must be tried and tested. He expressed his desire "That *the trial of your faith,* being much more precious than of gold that perisheth, though it be tried with fire, might be found unto praise and honour and glory at the appearing of Jesus Christ: *Whom having not seen, ye love;* in whom, though now *ye see him not, yet believing, ye rejoice with joy unspeakable* and full of glory: *Receiving the end of your faith, even the salvation of your souls."*

The *Cambridge Bible Dictionary,* in its article on Faith, combines lists of scriptural passages as it defines and explains faith. Let me extract a few of the statements it makes on the subject:

"Faith is that quality in the believer which enables him to grasp the unseen and the future. . . .The object of Faith is a Divine Person; through Faith we enter into fellowship with God, in Christ. . . .Faith requires effort on the part (1) of our intellect, we must understand what it is that we believe, we must grow in the 'knowledge' of God; (2) of our affections, for 'God is love,' and 'he that loveth not knoweth not God'. . . .(3)of our wills, for it must lead to right conduct, 'faith without works is dead'. . . .The effect of Faith is that we gain 'eternal life' . . . we become Christ-like in character as we gain that 'righteousness' which is of God. . . .In fallen man Faith must always be accompanied by Repentance, 'whereby we forsake sin.' "

There's an important insight added in *Hastings' Dictionary of the Bible,* published by Charles Schribner's Sons, in its article on Faith. It begins the article by saying, "It is common in modern English usage to take faith in God to mean something more than belief in God, faith meaning a personal trust and commitment, belief only an intellectual or impersonal acceptance or credence, or a traditional dogmatic statement."

That difference in degree is essential in Christian theology—Protestant commentaries on faith continually dwell on the difference between true faith, which motivates an individual to put his full trust in Christ, to keep his commandments, and to purify his life and become Christlike, as opposed to mere intellectual belief in Christ. Charles C. Ryrie, in his Moody Press book *Understanding Bible Doctrine,* page 174, calls this intellectual acceptance of Christ only a sin-bearer "believism," and comments that this minimal belief level is what allows for the existence of carnal Christians, and he observes that there seems to be plenty of carnal Christians around.

"Works" Are Righteous Deeds Motivated by Faith in God

Question 11: What are "works"?

The term is not clearly defined in scripture, but the term is generally understood to mean righteous acts. The works of the law spoken of in the scriptures would be acts which serve to fulfill the various laws and commandments.

Now the scriptures make two things abundantly clear concerning works: first, *you cannot earn salvation by performing good works,* but second, *one does not have true, saving faith unless he is motivated by his faith to perform good works.* Let's see what the key passages of scripture say on these two points. We'll go back to *Ephesians 2:8 through 10,* and see what it teaches us about works. The passage says, *"By grace are ye saved through faith; and that not of yourselves: it is the gifts of God: Not of works,* lest any man should boast. For we are his workmanship, *created in Christ Jesus unto good works, which God hath before ordained that we should walk in them."*

So the Bible makes it very plain that *we can't earn salvation* by performing good works, but *it is God's design that we should be doing good works continually as the result of our motivating faith.* The epistle of *James* tells us more about how works serve as the evidence that we truly have faith in Christ. In *chapter 2, verses 14 through 26,* it says,

"What doth it profit, my brethren, *though a man say he hath faith, and have not works? can faith save him?* If a brother or sister be naked, and destitute of daily food, And one of you say unto them, Depart in peace, be ye warmed and filled: notwithstanding ye give them not those things which are needful to the body; what doth it profit? Even so *faith, if it hath not works, is dead,* being alone. Yea, a man may say, Thou hast faith, and I have works: shew me thy faith without thy works, and *I will shew thee my faith by my works.* Thou believest that there is one God; thou doest well: the devils also believe, and tremble. But wilt thou know, O vain man, that *faith without works is dead?* Was not Abraham our father justified by works, when he had offered Isaac his son upon the alter? Seest thou how *faith wrought with his works, and by works was faith made perfect?* And the scripture was fulfilled which saith, Abraham believed God, and it was imputed unto him for righteousness: and he was called the Friend of God. Ye see then how that *by works a man is justified, and not by faith only.* Likewise also was not Rahab the harlot justified by works, when she had received the messengers, and had sent them out another way? *For as the body without the spirit is dead, so faith without works is dead also."*

So its obvious that works are an essential result of faith, and that one who claims to have faith in Christ but is not motivated by that faith to keep the Lord's commandments and be anxiously involved in furthering God's work and purposes does not have a moving, saving faith.

But the scriptures constantly remind us that righteous works, themselves, are not what brings us our salvation. Two often quoted passages are in Titus and Galatians. *Titus 3, verses 5 through 7,* says, *"Not by works of righteousness which we have done, but according to his mercy he saved us,* by the washing of regeneration, and renewing of the Holy Ghost; Which he shed on us abundantly through Jesus Christ our Saviour; That *being justified by his grace, we should be made heirs* according to the hope of eternal life."

Galatians 3:10 through 12 is like Ephesians 2 that I just quoted. It tells us that we can't be saved by works, but that those who have true faith will perform good works. It says, "As many as are of the works of the law are under the curse: for it is written, Cursed is every one that continueth not in all things which are written in the book of the law to do them. But that no man is justified by the law in the sight of God, it is evident: for, *the* just shall live by faith. And the law is not of faith: but, *The man that doeth them shall live in them."*

Latter-day Saints are very alert to the Biblical teachings concerning works. We recognize that we can't earn our salvation by performing works and good deeds. But ours is a strong, motivating faith, and we are anxious to serve our God and to be anxiously involved in our Father's business, so the good works of the Christian life are very common among us.

"Justification" Means to Be Declared Free From Sin Before God

Question 12: What is justification?

As Keith Hardman explained in his Tyndale House book, *Ingredients of the Christian Faith,* pages 65 and 66, "To justify is to vindicate, to free from blame, to declare a person righteous. . . .In its simplest definition, justification means "to be declared righteous before God."

Romans 8:33 tells us "It is God that justifieth." Paul, in his great sermon at Antioch, explained that justification means the forgiveness of sins. In *Acts 13, verses 38 and 39,* we read how he preached of Christ, saying "Through this man is preached unto you the forgiveness of sins: And *by him all that believe are justified from all things,* from which ye could not be justified by the law of Moses."

Justification is an important concept in LDS theology, and we recognize the importance of being found free from sin when we come into the presence of our Savior.

"Sanctification" Means To Be Made Clean, Pure and Holy by God

Question 13: What is sanctification?

There is a good definition of this term in the *Zondervan Pictorial Bible Dictionary,* edited by Merrill C. Tenney. Let me draw some of the key ideas from its article entitled "Sanctification." It says, "To sanctify anything is to declare that it belongs to God. It may refer to persons, places, days and seasons, and objects used to worship. . . .*The word "saint" comes from the same root and means "a sanctified one"—one who belongs to Christ.* In an ethical sense sanctification means the progressive conformation of the believer into the image of Christ, or the process by which the life is made morally holy. . . .It is not momentary and instantaneous, but a life-long process, completed only when we see Christ."

Sanctification is the result of the operation of the Holy Ghost in the life of the Christian, and the scriptures make it clear that it is the working of the Spirit within us that brings it to pass. *2nd Thessalonians 2:13 and 14* says, for instance, "God hath from the beginning chosen you to *salvation through sanctification of the Spirit and belief of the truth:* Whereunto he called you by our gospel, to the obtaining of the glory of our Lord Jesus Christ."

In his book *Ingredients of the Christian Faith,* published by Tyndale House, on page 77, Keith Hardman gives this explanation of the sanctification process: "When a person believes in Christ and is regenerated by the Spirit, that person is not thereafter abandoned by him and compelled to grope his way through the Christian life as best he can. Rather, the Holy Spirit makes his home in that believer's heart and offers his power to work the will of the heavenly Father. It is this constant indwelling of the Spirit that gives Christians their hope and power to become more Christlike, which is essentially what sanctification means in the New Testament."

The Book of Mormon describes a group of people who were sanctified, in *Alma 13:12.* The passage says that "They, after being sanctified by the Holy Ghost, *having their garments made white, being pure and spotless before God, could not look upon sin save it were with abhorrence;* and there were many, exceeding great many, who were made pure and entered into the rest of the Lord their God."

And a modern commandment, in *Doctrine and Covenants section 88, verses 74 and 75,* commands the Church to enter into the sanctification process. The Lord says, "Organize yourselves, and prepare yourselves, and *sanctify yourselves; yea, purify your hearts, and cleanse your hands and your feet before me, that I may make you clean;* That I may testify unto your Father, and your God, and my God, that you are clean from the blood of this wicked generation."

"Born Again" Means To Be Personally Changed By the Spirit from a Carnal Disposition to a Righteous-Seeking Disposition

Question 14: What is regeneration, or new birth? What does it mean to be born again?

Jesus taught about being born again when he told Nicodemus, in *John 3, verses 5 through 7,* "Verily, verily, I say unto thee, *Except a man be born of water and of the Spirit, he cannot enter into the kingdom of God.* That which is born of the flesh is flesh; and that which is born of the Spirit is spirit. Marvel not that I said unto thee, *Ye must be born again.*"

In *1st Peter 1:22 and 23,* that great apostle taught about spiritual rebirth. He wrote, "Seeing *ye have purified your souls in obeying the truth through the Spirit* unto unfeigned love of the brethren, see that ye love one another with a pure heart fervently: *Being born again,* not of corruptible seed, but of incorruptible, by the word of god, which liveth and abideth for ever."

In *2nd Corinthians 5:17,* Paul taught that "If any man be in Christ, *he is a new creature:* old things are passed away; behold, all things become new."

The Book of Mormon tells of various groups and individuals who were born again. *Mosiah, chapter 5, verses 2 and 7,* tells of the people of King Benjamin who responded to his great discourse by saying, "Yea, we believe all the words which thou hast spoken unto us; and also, we know of their surety and truth, because of the Spirit of the Lord Omnipotent, *which has wrought a mighty change in us, or in our hearts, that we have no more disposition to do evil, but to do good continually."*

And King Benjamin told them, "Now, because of the covenant which ye have made ye shall be called the children of Christ, his sons and his daughters; for behold, *this day he hath spiritually begotten you; for ye say that your hearts are changed through faith on his name; therefore ye are born of him* and have become his sons and his daughters."

And the *twenty-seventh chapter of Mosiah, verses 24 through 26,* contains the words of Alma, who reported his marvelous experience by saying, "I have repented of my sins, and have been redeemed of the Lord; behold *I am born of the Spirit.* And the Lord said unto me: Marvel not that all mankind, yea, men and women, all nations, kindreds, tongues and people, *must be born again; yea, born of God, changed from their carnal and fallen state, to a state of righteousness,* being redeemed of God, becoming his sons and his daughters; And thus they become new creatures; and unless they do this, than can in nowise inherit the kingdom of God."

So it is very obvious that the doctrine of spiritual rebirth holds a significant place in Latter-day Saint theology.

A Comparison of Protestant and LDS Beliefs on the Fourteen Points of Doctrine

Let's stop, now, and summarize, and note many of the areas in which Protestant theology is in full agreement or closely approximates the beliefs of the Church of Jesus Christ of Latter-day Saints.

Both agree that man is saved by grace—the grace of Jesus Christ, and that man cannot earn his salvation by performing good deeds and doing the works of the law.

Both agree that all have sinned, and come short of the glory of God so they need the atonement of Christ.

Both agree that sin is the transgression of the law, and that where no law is, there is no transgression. Man sins when he knowingly breaks the law.

Both agree that sin brings death: both physical and spiritual death. Because of the fall of Adam, all men must die a physical death. And because of sin, men are separated and alienated from God.

Both agree that without the atonement of Christ, all mankind would have been eternally subject to Satan, separated from God, and without resurrected bodies.

Both Protestants and members of The Church of Jesus Christ of Latter-day Saints agree that Jesus Christ was able to perform his atoning sacrifice because he was without sin, had the abilities of both Godhood and mortality because of his immortal father and mortal mother, and that he had the power to literally give his life for our sins and also the power to take up his body again after his death and thus begin the resurrection process.

Both agree that in his atonement, Jesus paid for the sins of all mankind: past, present and future. He took our sins upon himself and met the demands of justice.

Both agree that because of Christ's atoning sacrifice, the effects of Adam's fall were overcome: all men will be resurrected, and all men will have the opportunity to return to the presence of God if they make themselves eligible to receive the personal benefits of Christ's atonement.

In addition, both accept the basic doctrinal concepts of justification, sanctification, and regeneration, or new birth.

So there are lots of areas of agreement, and many parallels in their basic doctrines. These are major Biblical themes, and both draw their understandings from the same scriptural source on them.

Seven Areas of Doctrinal Disagreement
Between Protestants and Latter-day Saints

But there also are serious differences between Protestants and Latter-day Saints in these doctrinal areas. I wouldn't be fair to you or myself, if I didn't focus your attention on those differences. As a member of The Church of Jesus Christ of Latter-day Saints, I sincerely believe that Protestant doctrine and practice concerning salvation contains some very serious errors and omissions—omissions which prevent many good, Christ-seeking people from partaking of the blessings our Lord would like to bestow upon them. I see places where Protestant logic has been pushed to extremes which conflict with clearly stated Bible doctrines. I see people failing to do all their Lord would have them do because they've accepted a do-nothing approach to salvation which causes them to overlook basic principles which could speed and increase their eternal progress.

I'm going to list my concerns in a series of short, concise statements, and then return and explain them one by one.

First, lack of true repentance. I see potential Protestants being taught to pray a little prayer in which they mention that they are sinners, and then they think they have truly repented of all their sins, when in reality they have not yet begun the true repentance process.

Second, rejection of authorized baptism as an essential step toward salvation. I see Protestants who think that mere expression of their belief in Christ, rather than being baptized by immersion by one holding authority from God, is the way in which one puts on Christ.

Third, presumed guidance of the Holy Ghost. I see Protestants who assume they are being guided by the Holy Ghost because they've accepted unscriptural logic, rather than receiving the laying on of hands by one holding authority for the gift of the Holy Ghost.

Fourth, assumed invulnerability to losing salvation. I see Protestants being taught a line of logic that leads them to believe they're saved and eternally justified, no matter what evil they do or say or think, in direct contradiction to a broad pattern of scripture which warns that they can lose their salvation, justification, sanctification and grace through breaking the commandments of Jesus Christ.

Fifth, assumed freedom from ethical and moral responsibilities. I see some Protestants who have embraced Antinomianism, and have come to believe that so-called saved persons are free from all ethical standards and moral obligations.

Sixth, failure to seek eternal rewards. I see Protestants who are so taken with the idea they've been saved that they do nothing to earn the rewards which lie beyond salvation for those who are diligent in their righteous service and obedience to their Lord and their God.

Seventh, lack of knowledge of after-death events. I see Protestants who have little or no knowledge of what happens after death so they lack understanding of their personal future and potential.

Now, let's go back and analyze each of these concerns, one by one.

Concern #1: Lack of True Repentance

An extremely large percentage of Protestant tracts and theological treatises which deal with salvation follow the custom of printing short prayers which potential Protestants can offer. They do so with the message that if the individual offers the prayer that act, in and of itself, will cause him to be saved, which means that all his sins are eternally forgiven. These prayers typically make brief allusion to sin, but completely sidestep the full process of repentance which God requires.

Here's a typical example, with the language which leads up to it. this is taken from *Answers to Tough Questions,* by Josh McDowell, page 124, published by Here's Life Publishers: "Once a person sees his hopeless condition and realizes that Jesus Christ offers an answer, the next step is to receive that offer personally, for 'the gift of God is eternal life through Jesus Christ our Lord' *(Romans 6:23* KJV). When a person receives Christ as his Savior by accepting God's gift, at that moment he becomes born again. . . .How about you? Have you done this? Have you been born again? If you wish to do it, we offer this prayer that you might pray: 'Lord Jesus, I know that I'm a sinner; I realize that I can't make it on my own. Thank you for dying for me. Right at this moment, the best way I know how, I trust You as my Savior and Lord, in Jesus' name. Amen.' If you prayed sincerely to God, then you have become a Christian!"

I respectfully submit that true repentance requires far more that merely telling the Lord "I know that I'm a sinner." Let me remind you of what the Bible says about repentance.

When his listeners were pricked in their hearts on the day of Pentecost and asked him what they should do, Peter's message was *"Repent, and be baptized every one of you in the name of Jesus Christ for the remission of sins,* and ye shall receive the gift of the Holy Ghost." *(Acts 2:38)*

Paul's message in *2nd Corinthians 7, verse 10,* was that *"Godly sorrow worketh repentance to salvation* not to be repented of: but the sorrow of the world worketh death." In *James 4, verse 8,* James called upon Israel to *"Cleanse your hands,* ye sinners; and *purify your hearts,* ye double minded."

Peter wrote to the church, in *2nd Peter 3:9,* "The Lord is not slack concerning his promise, as some men count slackness; but is longsuffering to us-ward, not willing that any should perish, but that *all should come to repentance."*

John wrote, in *1st John 1, verses 8 and 9,* "If we say that we have no sin, we deceive ourselves, and the truth is not in us. If we confess our sins, he is faithful and just to forgive us our sins, and to cleanse us from all unrighteousness." And certainly confessing our sins involves far more that just saying, "Lord, I'm a sinner."

Let me give you the word of Latter-day scripture, which tells us of the need for repentance even more clearly. *2nd Nephi 2, verse 21,* in the Book of Mormon, says, "The days of the children of men were prolonged, according to the will of God, *that they might repent while in the flesh; wherefore, their state became a state of probation,* and their time was lengthened, according to the commandments which the Lord God gave unto the children of men. For *he gave commandment that all men must repent."*

And in *2nd Nephi 9, verses 23 and 24,* it says, *"He commandeth all men that they must repent, and be baptized in his name,* having perfect faith in the Holy One of Israel, or they cannot be saved in the kingdom of God. And *if they will not repent and believe in his name, and be baptized in his name, and endure to the end, they must be damned;* for the Lord God, the Holy One of Israel, has spoken it."

And the Lord has revealed, in *Doctrine and Covenants section 1, verses 31 through 33, "I the Lord cannot look upon sin with the least degree of allowance;* Nevertheless, he that repents and does the commandments of the Lord shall be forgiven; And *he that repents not, from him shall be taken even the light which he has received;* for my Spirit shall not always strive with man, saith the Lord of Hosts." And finally, from *Doctrine and Covenants section 18, verses 10 through 13,* "Remember the worth of souls is great in the sight of God; For, behold, the Lord your Redeemer suffered death in the flesh; wherefore he suffered the pain of all men, *that all men might repent and come unto him.* And he hath risen again from the dead, that *he might bring all men unto him, on conditions of repentance. And how great is his joy in the soul that repenteth!"*

These passages should be sufficient to show that God expects us to do far more than simply mumble "I'm a sinner." We need to put into practice the five Rs of Repentance: *Recognize, Regret, Resolve, Restore, and Refrain,* and we need to humbly *confess* our sins before our Maker and to those whom we have offended, seeking forgiveness for our wrongdoing.

And I bear solemn witness to you, any teaching concerning how you are saved that doesn't insist on your diligent repentance of all your sins won't save you. That's the message of the scriptures! That's the message of Jesus Christ! And that's the message to which the Holy Spirit bears witness. And that weakness is the first reason why I will not put my trust in the doctrine of salvation as it is taught by my Protestant and Evangelistic friends today.

Concern #2: Rejection of Authorized Baptism as an Essential Step Towards Salvation

I read tracts and books that say all we have to do is believe in Christ to be saved, and that baptism by one having true authority from God isn't necessary, and those teachings come in direct conflict with the scriptures. My Bible, and your Bible, tells us that we must be baptized to put on Christ and enter into his salvation process. Let me remind you of some of those passages:

Remember *Galatians 3:27?* "For as many of you as have *been baptized unto Christ have put on Christ.*" And *1st Peter 3:21?* "Even *baptism doth also now save us* (not the putting away of the filth of the flesh, but the answer of a good conscience toward God,) by the resurrection of Jesus Christ."

And *Romans 6:3 through 6?* "Know ye not, that so many of us as were baptized into Jesus Christ were baptized into his death? Therefore *we are buried with him by baptism into death: that like as Christ was raised up from the dead by the glory of the Father, even so we also should walk in newness of life.* For if we have been planted together in the likeness of his death, we shall be also *in the likeness of his resurrection:* Knowing this, that our old man is crucified with him, that the body of sin might be destroyed, that henceforth we should not serve sin."

I believe we should pay careful heed to what the Lord commanded his disciples in *Mark 16:15 and 16:* "Go ye into all the world, and preach the gospel to every creature. *He that believeth and is baptized shall be saved; but he that believeth not shall be damned.*" Note that the Lord links baptism to believing—baptism is the sign of true belief.

Probably the most quoted passage of all scripture on the subject of salvation is *Acts 16:31.* That's the account of Paul's miraculous deliverance from the jail of Philippi. You remember how an earthquake caused the prison doors to open and the prisoners' bands were loosed. The jailor, knowing that he would be put to death if the prisoners escaped, came to Paul and Silas and said, "Sirs, what must I do to be saved?" And Paul told him, "Believe on the Lord Jesus Christ, and thou shalt be saved, and thy house." But it always makes me cross when I see this verse quoted in Protestant tracts without the next two verses linked with it. They're the verses that show us that baptism is inseparably tied with the act of truly believing on the Savior. *Verse 33* tells us that the jailor and his family, *"The same hour of that night, . . . was baptized, he and all his, straightway."* Now you can't tell me that Paul and Silas would have taken those people and baptized them in the middle of the night, in a tense life-and-death situation, if they didn't know that *baptism was absolutely necessary for the family's eternal salvation!*

And when Peter preached on the day of Pentecost and told the crowd to *"Repent, and be baptized every one of you in the name of Jesus Christ for the remission of sins,* and ye shall receive the gift of the Holy Ghost," as we read in *Acts 2:38,* we read three verses latter, in *verse 41,* that "Then *they that gladly received his word were baptized: and the same day there were added unto them about three thousand souls."*

Can you imagine the work involved in baptizing 3,000 people by immersion? Do you think the apostles would have baptized them all, especially that day when the Holy Ghost had just been poured out like cloven tongues of fire, if they didn't know that baptism was the essential step the people needed to advance in the salvation process?

And what did Jesus tell Nicodemus, in *John 3, verse 5?* "Except a man be *born of water* and of the Spirit, *he cannot enter into the kingdom of God."* I've seen some try to sidestep the obvious meaning of this passage—that a man must be baptized to enter the kingdom of God—by claiming that water meant the living water of Christ's word. But there are too many passages that allude to actual water and washing as part of the salvation and regeneration process for that to be a valid interpretation.

Titus 3, verse 5, for instance, says, "Not by works of righteousness which we have done, but according to his mercy *he saved us, by the washing of regeneration,* and renewing of the Holy Ghost." Note that in this verse baptism—the washing of regeneration—is distinctly separated from the works of righteousness. *Being baptized isn't just a work of righteousness; it's the process of putting on Christ, and accepting his salvation and justification.*

Ephesians 5:26 speaks about the church, saying that Christ "might *sanctify and cleanse it with the washing of water* by the word."

I become very concerned when I see the term "works" interpreted so broadly that it includes repentance, and baptism, and receiving the gift of the Holy Ghost through the laying on of hands. These are not just works—these are basic steps which man must follow to enter into the salvation process. There are those in the ranks of Protestantism who are retarding the growth of others by convincing them that these basic principles of the gospel are simply good deeds, and works of the Law, and not *required steps* in the Lord's plan of salvation.

Do you remember what Jesus told John the Baptist when he came to the River Jordan to be baptized? John forbad him, saying "I have need to be baptized of thee, and comest thou to me? And Jesus answering said unto him, Suffer it to be so now: for *thus it becometh us to fulfill all righteousness*. Then he suffered him. And Jesus, when he was baptized, went up straightway out of the water: and lo, the heavens were opened unto him, and he saw the Spirit of God descending like a dove, and lighting upon him: And lo a voice from heaven, saying, *This is my beloved Son, in whom I am well pleased.*" That account in *Matthew 3:13 through 17* is one of the most significant passages in all the Bible. And when could possibly be a more appropriate time for God the Father to express pleasure in his Son's conduct than when the Only Begotten had just shown that baptism was necessary to fulfill all righteousness?

But just as significant is the commentary made by the Prophet Nephi concerning Christ's baptism in the Book of Mormon, in *2nd Nephi 31, verses 4 through 13.* Nephi wrote, "I would that ye should remember that I have spoken unto you concerning that prophet which the Lord showed unto me, that should baptize the Lamb of God, which should take away the sins of the world. And now, *if the Lamb of God, he being holy, should have need to be baptized by water, to fulfill all righteousness, O then, how much more need have we, being unholy, to be baptized, yea, even by water!* And now, I would ask of you, my beloved brethren, wherein the Lamb of God did fulfill all righteousness in being baptized by water? Know ye not that he was holy? But notwithstanding he being holy, *he showeth unto the children of men that, according to the flesh he humbleth himself before the Father, and witnesseth unto the Father that he would be obedient unto him in keeping his commandments.* Wherefore, after he was baptized with water the Holy Ghost descended upon him in the form of a dove. And again, it showeth unto the children of men *the straightness of the path, and the narrowness of the gate, by which they should enter, he having set the example before them.* And he said unto the children of men: Follow thou me. Wherefore, my beloved brethren, *can we follow Jesus save we shall be willing to keep the commandments of the Father? And the Father said: Repent ye, repent ye, and be baptized in the name of my Beloved Son.* And also, the voice of the Son came unto me, saying: He that is baptized in my name, to him will the Father give the Holy Ghost, like unto me; wherefore, *follow me, and do the things which ye have seen me do.* Wherefore, my beloved brethren, I know that if ye shall follow the Son, with full purpose of heart, acting no hypocrisy and no deception before God, but with real intent, repenting of your sins, *witnessing unto the Father that ye are willing to take upon you the name of Christ, by baptism—yea, by following your Lord and your Savior down into the water,* according to his word, behold, then shall ye receive the Holy Ghost; yea, then cometh the baptism of fire and of the Holy Ghost; and then can ye speak with the tongue of angels, and shout praises unto the Holy One of Israel."

Now there is just one more passage about baptism I want to mention. It's in the *19th chapter of Acts, verses 1 through 6.* It's an extremely important passage because it clearly shows two things: *first,* that baptism is important and necessary, and *second,* that baptism by someone who isn't authorized to perform it is not acceptable in the sight of God.

Paul came to Ephesus and found some disciples who had been baptized by followers of John the Baptist rather than by authorized servants of Jesus Christ. When he found that their baptism wasn't performed by individuals holding the priesthood power of Jesus Christ, he baptized them again, and then laid hands upon them to give them the gift of the Holy Ghost.

Consider this passage carefully, because its message is highly significant. It says, "Paul having passed through the upper coasts came to Ephesus: and finding certain disciples, He said unto them, Have ye received the Holy Ghost since ye believed? And they said unto him, We have not so much as heard whether there be any Holy Ghost. And he said unto them, Unto what then were ye baptized? And they said, *Unto John's baptism.* Then said Paul, John verily baptized with the baptism of repentance, saying unto the people, that they should believe on him which should come after him, that is, on Christ Jesus. When they heard this, *they were baptized in the name of the Lord Jesus. And when Paul had laid his hands on them, the Holy Ghost came on them; and they spake with tongues, and prophesied."*

Now I want to say this, before going on to the next problem area: It is the clear, unmistakeable message of the scriptures that, preceded by belief strong enough to be faith, and by careful and complete repentance, baptism is the gateway to the salvation of Jesus Christ. The Protestant churches today don't stress the importance of the ordinance because they know they don't have the priesthood power of Jesus Christ to perform the ordinance efficaciously.

But I want to bear you this testimony, that the authority to perform the ordinance of baptism is held by priesthood holders of The Church of Jesus Christ of Latter-day Saints.

And this is my counsel to you: before you commit to the faith-alone doctrine of the churches of today, take time to thoroughly examine what the scriptures say about the necessity of baptism in God's eternal plan of salvation.

And take time to examine my claim that authority to baptize you exists today in The Church of Jesus Christ of Latter-day Saints—the Mormons. That investigation will be one of the most important things you do in your entire life!

Concern #3: Presumed Guidance of the Holy Ghost

Many people assume that they have the guidance of the Holy Ghost when in truth they don't have that guidance. I find tract after tract leading Protestants to believe that they automatically receive the Holy Ghost the moment they recite the little prayer found at the end of the tract. But that's not how the scriptures teach us the gift of the Holy Ghost is received.

Paul wrote to Timothy, in *1st Timothy 4:14,* "Neglect not the gift that is in thee, which was given thee by prophecy, with the laying on of the hands of the presbytery." And in *2nd Timothy 1, verse 6* Paul wrote: "I put thee in remembrance that thou stir up *the gift of God, which is in thee by the putting on of my hands."*

The 8th chapter of Acts teaches us very clearly that the gift of the Holy Ghost is conferred by the laying on of hands, and that the ordinance must be performed by one holding proper priesthood power. It tells how Philip had baptized converts in Samaria, including Simon, a former magician. Since Philip apparently did not hold the higher priesthood which has the power to bestow the gift of the Holy Ghost, the apostles Peter and John were sent to give the converts that gift. Starting with *verse 14 of Acts chapter 8,* the account reads: "Now when the apostles which were at Jerusalem heard that Samaria had received the word of God, they sent unto them Peter and John: Who, when they were come down, prayed for them, that they might receive the Holy Ghost: (For as yet he was fallen upon none of them: only they were baptized in the name of the Lord Jesus.) *Then laid they their hands on them, and they received the Holy Ghost.* And when Simon saw that through laying on of the apostles' hands the Holy Ghost was given, he offered them money, Saying, Give me also this power, that on whomsoever I lay hands, he may receive the Holy Ghost. But Peter said unto him, *Thy money perish with thee, because thou hast thought that the gift of God may be purchased with money."*

Now notice another message of this passage: those people in Samaria had already believed in Christ, yet they hadn't received the Holy Ghost. What does that tell us about the teaching that one only has to say a little prayer in which he professes belief in Christ and he will automatically receive the Holy Ghost? It tells us that's not the procedure specified in the scriptures, doesn't it?

I've already mentioned the passage in the nineteenth chapter of Acts where Paul rebaptized believers in Ephesus because they had been baptized by someone who lacked authority. Even though they already believed in Christ, they hadn't received the Holy Ghost either. As *Acts 19:6* tells us, it wasn't until Paul *"laid his hands upon them, the Holy Ghost came on them."*

Now the scriptures teach that occasionally people are visited by the Holy Ghost prior to baptism and receiving the laying on of hands by those holding authority, but those experiences are temporary visits, not the indwelling gift in which the Spirit leads us day-by-day in the Christian walk and into sanctification. As a passage in the *Doctrine and Covenants, section 130, verse 23,* tells us, *"A man may receive the Holy Ghost, and it may descend upon him and not tarry with him."*

Section 76 of the Doctrine and Covenants, verses 50 through 53, describes the process by which the Holy Ghost is received by the true believer. It says: "This is the testimony of the gospel of Christ concerning them who shall come forth in the resurrection of the just—They are they who received the testimony of Jesus, and *believed on his name and were baptized after the manner of his burial, being buried in the water in his name,* and this according to the commandment which he was given—That *by keeping the commandments they might be washed and cleansed from all their sins,* and

receive the Holy Spirit by the laying on of the hands of him who is or-
dained and sealed unto this power; And who overcome by faith, and are
sealed by the Holy Spirit of promise, which the Father sheds forth upon
all those who are just and true."

So it's passages like these that make me feel real concern for those who
assume they have received the gift of the Holy Spirit when all they have
done is spoken one of those little prayers given at the end of those tracts.
I don't believe they have received the constant companionship of the Holy
Spirit at all. Instead, they've been lulled into a false belief which keeps
them from actively seeking that glorious gift.

Concern #4: Assumed Invulnerability to Losing Salvation

Some are being taught that once they've professed a belief in Christ, they
are guaranteed salvation, no matter what evil they commit. They think they
are saved, and justified, and sanctified because of Christ's redemption. That
belief is based on a lie of logic that clearly contradicts the scriptures.

Christ's atonement paid for the fall of Adam, and will pay for their sins
too, but only if they have faith, and repent of their sins, and are baptized,
and receive the Holy Ghost, and then endure in righteousness until the
end. If they return to sin, and fail to repent of it, then they forfeit the benefits
of the atonement wrought in their behalf. Let me remind you of several
key scriptural passages on this subject.

Hebrews 10, verses 26 through 29, says, *"If we sin wilfully after that
we have received the knowledge of the truth, there remaineth no more
sacrifice for sins,* But a certain fearful looking for of judgment and fiery
indignation, which shall devour the adversaries. . . .Of how much sorer
punishment, suppose ye, shall he be thought worthy, *who hath trodden under
foot the Son of God, and hath counted the blood of the covenant, wherewith he was sanctified, an unholy thing,* and hath done despite unto the
Spirit of grace?"

And *Hebrews 6, verses 4 through 6,* tells us, "It is impossible for those
who were once enlightened, and have tasted of the heavenly gift, and were
made partakers of the Holy Ghost, And have tasted the good word of God,
and the powers of the world to come, *If they shall fall away, to renew them
again unto repentance; seeing they crucify to themselves the Son of God
afresh, and put him to an open shame."*

In *Galatians 5, 1 to 4,* Paul entreated the believers to "Stand fast therefore in the liberty wherewith Christ hath made us free, and be not entan-

gled again with the yoke of bondage." And he warned that if they become again entangled with sins against the law, *"Christ is become of no effect unto you, . . . ye are fallen from grace."*

The prophet Ezekiel taught that the gift of salvation functions in two ways. If a sinner repents, all his sins will be forgiven and forgotten. But by the same rule, if a righteous man returns to sin, then his righteous deeds are forgotten and he is held guilty of all his sins. *Ezekiel 18, verses 21 through 24* says, "If the wicked will turn from all his sins that he hath committed, and keep all my statutes, and do that which is lawful and right, he shall surely live, he shall not die. All his transgressions that he hath committed, they shall not be mentioned unto him: in his righteousness that he hath done he shall live. Have I any pleasure at all that the wicked should die? saith the Lord God: and not that he should return from his ways, and live? *But when the righteous turneth away from his righteousness, and committeth iniquity,* and doeth according to all the abominations that the wicked man doeth, shall he live? *All his righteousness that he hath done shall not be mentioned: in his trespass that he hath trespassed, and in his sin that he hath sinned, in them shall he die."*

A passage in *section 20 of the Doctrine and Covenants, verses 30 through 34,* contains this warning: "We know that *justification* through the grace of our Lord and Savior Jesus Christ is just and true; And we know also, that *sanctification* through the grace of our Lord and Savior Jesus Christ is just and true, to all those who love and serve God with all their mights, minds, and strength. *But there is a possibility that man may fall from grace and depart from the living God; Therefore let the church take heed and pray always, lest they fall into temptation;* Yea, and even let those who are sanctified take heed also."

I am deeply troubled when I encounter those who flaunt their belief that, no matter what they do, they are unalterably saved and justified. They sometimes make derisive statements about Latter-day Saints, who are far more aware of the message of the scriptures on this subject, and know that anyone can become entangled in sin and loose the personal benefits of Christ's atonement, and the higher you climb on the mountain, the stronger the winds of temptation may blow.

Concern #5: Antinomianism—Assumed Release from Ethical and Moral Responsibilities

Some Protestants have become involved in Antinomianism—the belief that since they are unalterably saved, they no longer must be responsible for ethical conduct, moral responsibilities, and obedience to the laws of God. Included in this group, it appears, are some who have become strong critics of Mormonism, and have little concern for the truth as they circulate falsehoods against us. Yes, there is room for honest differences in belief, but some have gone far beyond the limits of ethical and moral conduct in their attacks on not only Mormons, but also members of other faiths. They make their livings, and enjoy personal popularity and power by spreading falsehoods and half truths and slander and innuendo.

How do we recognize those who are truly in Christ? The Savior taught, in *John 14, verses 15 and 21,* "If ye love me, keep my commandments. . . .*He that hath my commandments, and keepeth them, he it is that loveth me;* and he that loveth me shall be loved of my Father, and I will love him, and will manifest myself to him."

And the Lord's teaching in his sermon on the mount, *Matthew 7, verses 16 through 21,* gives us insight on this subject: *"Ye shall know them by their fruits.* Do men gather grapes of thorns, or figs of thistles? Even so every good tree bringeth forth good fruit; but a corrupt tree bringeth forth evil fruit. A good tree cannot bring forth evil fruit, *neither can a corrupt tree bring forth good fruit.* Every tree that bringeth not forth good fruit is hewn down, and cast into the fire. *Wherefore by their fruits ye shall know them. Not everyone that saith unto me, Lord, Lord, shall enter into the kingdom of heaven; but he that doeth the will of my Father which is in heaven."*

In *Luke 6:46,* the poignant question of the Savior is posed, *"Why call ye me, Lord, Lord, and do not the things which I say?"* That question deserves deep consideration by every so-called Christian who thinks he is saved and that his supposed salvation is license to defy the commandments and ethical responsibilities found in the teachings of Jesus Christ.

Concern #6: Failure to Grow and Seek Eternal Rewards

I'm not about to minimize the importance of being saved, but salvation is not the final goal for mankind. It is an intermediate step, related to the spirit world experience prior to the resurrection and final judgment. A person who is saved is spared from going to hell at the time of death, and goes instead into the paradise of the righteous or into another area instead of hell where he is taught the gospel of Jesus Christ. But by the time of the second resurrection, at the end of Christ's millennial reign, salvation is mostly a concern of the past, and man's eternal reward will be based on his deeds of righteousness. *No, works can't earn salvation, but yes, works and personal righteousness and achievement do determine our ultimate position and status and responsibility for all eternity.*

If I can make a comparison, life is like going out for the high school football team. Being saved is like surviving the first cut when the team is being chosen. But the final reward is far beyond that stage, when the team develops and matures and goes on to win the state championship. The coach's grace let you get onto the team, but your personal skill and determination, under the coach's direction, is what makes you, personally, an all-star player.

In the time frame of the final judgment, the emphasis will have shifted from the concept of salvation to that of reward based on man's works, and passage after passage of scripture makes that plain. *Matthew 16:27* says that "The Son of man shall come in the glory of his Father with his angels; and *then he shall reward every man according to his works."*

Revelation 20, verses 12 and 13, describes the final judgment, and makes it clear that the deeds mankind will have performed, or failed to perform, will be the basis for that judgment. John wrote, "I saw the dead, small and great, stand before God; and the books were opened: and another book was opened, which is the book of life: and *the dead were judged out of those things which were written in the books, according to their works.* And the sea gave up the dead which were in it; and death and hell delivered up the dead which were in them: and *they were judged every man according to their works."*

The Book of Mormon prophet Alma emphasized the importance of righteous works as he gave his final blessing to the people of Gideon. His message is found in *Alma chapter 7, verses 22 through 27:* "I have said these things unto you that I might awaken you to a sense of your duty to God, that ye may *walk blameless before him,* that ye may walk after the holy order of God, after which ye have been received. And now I would that ye should be humble, and be submissive and gentle; easy to be entreated; full of patience and long-suffering; being temperate in all things; being diligent in keeping the commandments of God at all times; asking for whatsoever things ye stand in need, both spiritual and temporal; always return ing thanks unto God for whatsoever things ye do receive. And see that ye have faith, hope, and charity, and then ye will *always abound in good works.* And may the Lord bless you, and *keep your garments spotless,* that ye may at last be brought to sit down with Abraham, Isaac, and Jacob, and the holy prophets who have been ever since the world began, having your garments spotless even as their garments are spotless, in the kingdom of heaven to go no more out. And now my beloved brethren, I have spoken these words unto you according to the Spirit which testifieth in me; and my soul doth exceedingly rejoice, because of the exceeding diligence and head which ye have given unto my word. And now, may the peace of God rest upon you, and upon your houses and lands, and upon your flocks and herds, and all that you possess, your women and your children, *according to your faith and good works, from this time forth and forever."*

Paul taught that there are various levels, or glories in the resurrection. In *1st Corinthians 15, verses 41 and 42,* he explained that "There is one *glory of the sun,* and another *glory of the moon,* and another *glory of the stars:* for one star differeth from another star in glory. *So also is the resurrection of the dead."*

We need to look beyond the concept of escaping the clutches of Satan at the time of death, and realize that mortal life is also the time of probation in which we earn our eventual reward in the kingdom of our Father and our God. I believe this concept is implemented to a far greater extent in The Church of Jesus Christ of Latter-day Saints than it is understood among our Evangelical friends.

Concern #7: Lack of Knowledge of After-Death Events

When I talk with Protestants, I almost always come away feeling that they know almost nothing of future events and experiences which will affect them. Their concept seems limited to death being followed by either heaven or hell—that's about the size of it. I can see why: the typical Protestant book that comments on God's eternal plan doesn't go much farther than that. But there are passages which explain about the spirit world, about the resurrection of the just at the beginning of the millennium, about the resurrection of the unjust at the end of the millennium, and about the final judgment. There are passages that describe in detail the rewards that are promised to the righteous who have been valiant in their testimony of the Christ, and descriptions of life as it will be in the eternal realms.

There's not time in this context to pursue all these passages, but I feel that my observation is valid—many Protestants are woefully ignorant of scriptural teachings concerning God's plan for our eternal future. If they were more knowledgeable they would focus more on what lies ahead, as well as on their concept of being saved.

These, then, are the seven major problem areas I see among the Protestant churches and their teachings concerning salvation:

1. lack of true repentance,

2. rejection of authorized baptism as an essential step toward salvation,

3. assumed guidance of the Holy Ghost without receiving the laying on of hands by one holding authority,

4. assumed invulnerability to falling from grace,

5. assumed immunity on the part of some for ethical and moral responsibilities,

6. failure to seek eternal rewards beyond the time of salvation, and

7. lack of knowledge of after-death events. In my opinion, every one of these problems is a serious challenge to the Protestant doctrine of salvation by belief alone.

Now, before I conclude, I think you need to focus on the question posed by the title of this discussion: Are **you** saved? And let me repeat the personal questions I asked in the beginning. If you think you are saved,

1. What did you do to arrive at that belief?

2. What are you saved from?

3. Can you ever become unsaved?

4. What have you done about true repentance?

5. Have you been baptized by one having authority to baptize you?

6. Have you received the laying on of hands for the gift of the Holy ghost by one who has authority?

7. Have you felt the promptings and guidance of the Holy Ghost?

8. Is He guiding you now, or did he come to you briefly and then not linger with you?

9. Have you entered into the process of sanctification?

10. Have you felt the mighty change in you life that comes with being born again, or is that merely a concept to which you pay lip service?

11. And after all the scriptures we've considered together in this discussion, do you still believe that a one-time expression of belief in Christ is all that is necessary for you to be saved?

Is Your Concept of Salvation a
Something-for-Nothing Insurance Policy?

I've had a lot of life insurance salesmen visit me and present a lot of different kinds of insurance policies. Some seem to be really good values, but I've learned the importance of shopping around before I buy and place my confidence in the product. If had an insurance salesman tell me I wouldn't have to pay for my policy, but just pray a little prayer to the president of the company asking him to forgive my non- payment of the premiums, I'd question whether I really had a valid insurance policy—one that would pay in full when I die. Wouldn't you question that kind of something-for-nothing deal too?

And that's exactly the situation the modern world is in today. There are a lot of people believing that they're "saved," but they haven't met the requirements for salvation the Lord has set down in the scriptures. They don't have a valid insurance policy that guarantees them eternal life in the presence of God after they die. If someone has sold them an invalid bill of goods, or talked them into accepting a something-for-nothing philosophy that won't be counted as valid when they come to the judgment bar of God, then they're going to be left standing outside the pearly gates at the last day.

The Real Question: Not "Do You Accept
Jesus?" but "Does Jesus Accept You?"

The real question will not be "do you accept Jesus," but rather, "does Jesus accept you?" Now is the time to focus on our Savior's warning, found in *Matthew 7:21 to 23.* He has already served notice of the difficulty that will exist at the last day, when he said, *"Not every one that saith unto me, Lord, Lord, shall enter into the kingdom of heaven; but he that doeth the will of my Father* which is in heaven. Many will say to me in that day, Lord, Lord, have we not prophesied in thy name? and in thy name have cast out devils? and in thy name done many wonderful works? And then I will profess unto them, *I never knew you: depart from me, ye that work iniquity."*

Yes, Christ has paid for the sins of all mankind, so that all who choose to come unto him and fulfill his requirements can be saved. But he will save only those who enter in at the strait gate of faith, repentance, baptism by authority, receiving the gift of the Holy Ghost through the laying on of hands, and then enduring to the end in righteousness. Only those who come to him in the way he requires will he accept.

I invite you to ponder these words, and to consider their implications, and then to seek further information and direction from those who hold the authority to speak in the name of Christ—members with priesthood authority in The Church of Jesus Christ of Latter-day Saints.

Let me close, now, with the words of the Book of Mormon prophet Alma. His testimony, in the *7th chapter of Alma, verses 12 through 16,* is one of the greatest expositions of the eternal role of Christ and the doctrine of salvation in all of scripture. Speaking of Jesus Christ, Alma said, "He will take upon him death, that he may loose the bands of death which bind his people; and he will take upon him their infirmities, that his bowels may be filled with mercy, according to the flesh, that he may know according to the flesh how to succor his people according to their infirmities. Now the Spirit knoweth all things; nevertheless the Son of God suffereth according to the flesh that he might take upon him the sins of his people, that he might blot out their transgressions according to the power of his deliverance; and now behold, this is the testimony which is in me. *Now I say unto you that ye must repent, and be born again; for the Spirit saith if ye are not born again ye cannot inherit the kingdom of heaven; therefore come and be baptized unto repentance,* that ye may be washed from your sins, that ye may have faith on the Lamb of God, who taketh away the sins of the world, who is mighty to save and to cleanse from all unrighteousness. Yea, I say unto you come and fear not, and lay aside every sin, which easily doth beset you, which doth bind you down to destruction, yea, come and go forth, and *show unto your God that ye are willing to repent of your sins and enter a covenant with him to keep his commandments, and witness it unto him this day by going into the waters of baptism.* And whosoever doeth this, and keepeth the commandments of God from thenceforth, the same will remember that I say unto him, yea, he will remember that I have said unto him, he shall have eternal life, according to the testimony of the Holy Spirit, which testifieth in me."

That we may all heed and obey his message is my prayer, in the worthy name of our Lord and Savior Jesus Christ. Amen.

RECOGNIZING
TECHNIQUES OF
DECEPTION
IN
ANTI-MORMON
LITERATURE

DUANE S. CROWTHER

C-90 Cassette Tape

In the field of journalism there is great concern about the importance of maintaining a high standard of ethical conduct within the profession. Words are powerful tools—tools which can accomplish much good. But they are also tools which can be easily abused by individuals who might seek to convey misinformation and falsehoods. Journalists have a term for the unethical use of words, the tools of their craft. When someone attempts to twist the truth, or misrepresent the facts by the way they present and phrase their writing, journalists call this unethical conduct "yellow journalism."

"Yellow Journalism" Defined

Let's define the term "yellow journalism" very carefully, because yellow journalism is what this discussion is about. *"Yellow journalism" is the unethical use of words to convey false information, false understanding, or false perception. To use yellow journalism is to intentionally twist the facts, to misrepresent, or to use subtle or blatant writing techniques which*

266

will deceive the reader and distort his perception. Yellow journalism is carefully avoided by reputable authors and journalists who seek to preserve the integrity of their craft.

Professional journalists do their best to protect the integrity of their craft. They can spot yellow journalism "a mile away," as the expression goes. Many journalists are quick to speak up when they see yellow journalism in action. They're anxious to label yellow journalism when they see it, and to clearly identify it as unethical and unacceptable behavior.

The challenging requirements of the editor's art cause one to be very conscious of the way in which words are used. As a writer with more than a quarter of a million of the books I have written in print, and as a professional editor who has prepared well over 200 books for publication, I've read and carefully analyzed the words of many authors. An editor soon becomes extremely sensitive to situations where words are being misused.

That's why I'm speaking out! Today *there's a growing group of authors who are writing religious hate literature based on the wide-scale use of blatant yellow journalism*—books and newspapers and films which are *intended to incite antagonism* against various religious faiths, and to do so to such an intense degree that they stir up persecution, lead to literal abuse, and engender actual hatred against those who are the focus of their attacks.

In their search for targets, some of these authors have become *full-time, professional critics* of The Church of Jesus Christ of Latter-day Saints. But Mormons aren't their only targets. Other groups, including the Adventists, the Jehovah's Witnesses, and the Worldwide Church of God are favorite targets for this group of writers also.

Books and articles and films that make blatant use of yellow journalism as they spread their messages of religious intolerance and hatred are causing a growing problem of ethics among many Christians. Should a Christian bookstore owner, for instance, allow such materials to be stocked on his bookstore shelves? Should a pastor who is honestly trying to serve the Lord Jesus Christ quote from such materials when preaching to his congregation, or recommend that his followers read such books containing serious distortions and contrived untruths? Or should he invite his followers to view films which are blatant distortions of the truth?

National Organizations are Objecting to Anti-Mormon Tactics

Various religious groups are beginning to react to the ethical problem which is growing among them. One such organization, the Arizona chap-

ter of the National Conference of Christians and Jews, recently responded
to one such situation. In March, 1984, after an intense four-month investigation of the anti-Mormon film "The Godmakers," that body issued a statement denouncing the film. Their statement said, in part, *"The film does
not, in our opinion, fairly portray the Mormon Church, Mormon history
or Mormon belief.* It makes extensive use of *half-truths, faulty generaliza-
tions, erroneous interpretations, sensationalism* and is *not reflective of the
genuine spirit of the Mormon faith.* We find particularly offensive the emphasis in the film that Mormonism is some sort of subversive plot—a danger
to the community, a threat to the institution of marriage, and destructive
to the mental health of teenagers. *Our experience with our Mormon neighbors provides eloquent refutation of these charges."*[1]

The Objectives of This Discussion

This brief discussion has been prepared to comment on some of the yellow journalism techniques which the above denunciation of "The Godmakers" makes reference to, along with many others. In a single hour there
is no way I can refute in detail the many derogatory statements made by
anti-Mormon critics. My objectives are

1. to point out often-used yellow journalism techniques,

2. to give those techniques names, and

3. to give each of them a definition or description so the techniques
can be easily discerned by others.

There's not enough time to give indepth examples of all the techniques
I'll mention, but I'll do my best to illustrate many of them with brief
examples.

Your task is to read carefully, fully understand the techniques and definitions I'll discuss, and learn to recognize them when you see and hear
them used.

Before I begin, let me make it clear—I'm not asserting that all anti-
Mormon writers use yellow journalism when they write about The Church
of Jesus Christ of Latter-day Saints. One can write about someone else's
religion rationally, and ethically, and in good taste, even if he disagrees
with the tenets of that church, and there are many non-Mormon writers
who do so as they comment about Mormonism. These comments are

---

1. "Key Religious Group Blasts Anti-LDS Movie," cited in Latter-day Sentinel, Vol. 5, No. 26, March 9, 1984, p. 19.

intended to help you discern whether the writing is fair and unbiased, or whether it embraces the highly unethical practices of yellow journalism. And let me emphatically assert that *yellow journalism truly is intentional deception,* and it is a *wicked* practice—a practice which should be completely foreign to those who have truly undergone the mighty change in their hearts characteristic of Christians who have been born again.

Yellow journalism should be **especially avoided** by Christian writers who place significance in the instruction set forth in the Ten Commandments: "Thou shalt not bear false witness . . . " The use of yellow journalism brands its user as a teller of falsehoods, whose word and personal integrity cannot be trusted, and that kind of conduct should have no place in the field of Christian literature and journalism.

The Unanswerable Falsehood Technique

The *first* of these yellow journalism techniques I'll address is what I have called the Unanswerable Falsehood Technique. In this method of attack upon the Church, *the critic makes sweeping assertations, large or small, which have little or no factual basis nor legitimacy. In short, he tells lies about the Church— its members, or doctrine, or history. And he does so in a book, newspaper or magazine, or some other widely disseminated medium to which Church members are powerless to immediately respond and refute the falsehoods.* Even if a thorough refutation is later made of his charges, his false or overstated assertions take a heavy toll, for they're often accepted at face value by undiscerning readers who know nothing of the facts involved.

Let me give an example. One anti-Mormon book, referring to the Church, asserts that the Mormons "control the lucrative vice industry of Las Vegas." Is this an outlandish claim, or a carefully documented truth? Judge for yourself! The only *proof* (and I use that word with a smile) the author offers is the following statement:

"A count of the Mormon church listings in the Las Vegas telephone directory numbers more than sixty churches and other facilities, which means that probably half of the population is Mormon, and practically all of the population of Las Vegas is directly or indirectly engaged in work related to the vice industry."[2]

---

2. Fraser, Gordon H., *Is Mormonism Christian?* (Chicago, Illinois: Moody Press, 1957, 1964, 1965, 1977), p. 19.

Now that's real research! Just count the number of wards in the Las Vegas area, discover that there are lots of Mormons there, and that then is supposed to indicate that the Mormon Church is involved in the Las Vegas vice industry. There's no validity to the assertation at all, yet the Bible Institute which publishes the book has allowed the allegation to stand through repeated editions of the book.

Presumably, since the book has undergone three revisions and copyright renewals since it was first published, thousands of people have read that false assertion, though who knows how many have been gullible enough to believe it is true? But there is no effective way to reach into the homes of those who have read it and refute the untruth—it's an unanswerable falsehood. Mormons can rebut it in their literature, but there's no way to get that literature into the stores which carry the anti-Mormon books, so it's almost impossible to reach the individuals that falsehood has affected.

The Out-of-Context Technique

A *second* yellow journalism technique is the Out-of-Context Technique. Of course, this is one of the oldest deceptive techniques of all, but it is still among the most widely used by those who engage in yellow journalism. When criticizing the Church, *the critic misrepresents the Church's doctrines or viewpoint by separating phrases or sentences from their original context so the reader will perceive them as having a different meaning or intent from what the author originally wrote or stated.*

Often this is done through the injudicious use of ellipses—those three little dots which are used to indicate that material has been omitted. The use of ellipses is a well-established tool of scholarship, but it may also be utilized for purposes of distortion. For instance, a sentence early in a paragraph may be quoted, then following sentences which greatly qualify the meaning of the original sentence can be omitted, and then a final sentence of the paragraph quoted which would have an entirely different meaning if the omitted words were included. Even if ellipses were used to show material is omitted within the quotation, an *ethical* journalist would not use such an omission to distort the true meaning and intent of what is said.

Let me point out an example of the Out-of-Context Technique as it was used by an anti-Mormon Utah author team. For years this couple has tried to propound a theory that Joseph Smith did not receive his first vision— that he was not visited by God the Father and His Son Jesus Christ. Their theory holds, in part, that Joseph's understanding that the Father and the Son are separate beings gradually evolved over a period of years.

In support of this theory, they assert that the Book of Mormon "taught that there was but one God." In two different chapters of their book they quote from the fifteenth chapter of Mosiah in an attempt to make their point, but both times using the Out-of-Context Technique by selecting only verses 1, 2, and 5.[3] They carefully omitted surrounding verses which refute their theory and clearly show that Jesus and God the Father are separate and distinct beings. They left out the phrases that explain that Jesus was "conceived by the power of God," that the Son became subject to the Father, that the will of the Son was separate and distinct from the will of the Father, and that the Father gave to His Son the power to make intercession for the children of men. Reading all the verses of Mosiah 15 allows the reader to see that these anti-Mormon authors tried unsuccessfully to use the Out-of-Context Technique to support their incorrect theory. Shame on them!

The Inflated Issue Technique

A *third* technique is the Inflated Issue Technique. Critics using this approach *try to make miniscule matters appear to be major reasons for contention and criticism by giving an exaggerated or sensationalized report of insignificant items.* This technique is often *used to sidestep major issues and irrefutable materials* by concentrating attention on less-supported issues.

Two of these non-issue items which are frequently inflated in anti-Mormon literature demonstrate the point. For instance, one recent anti-Mormon book makes the point that "Besides being one of the fastest growing churches in the world, the Mormon Church is one of the richest." Maybe it is, maybe it isn't—I don't know. I'm not aware of *any* church which circulates its financial statements to the world at large, so I'm not going to occupy much of my time trying to find which churches are the richest.

I believe the Lord has prospered the Mormon Church and the saints, and I expect that the prosperity of the Church is a normal result of those blessings. I suspect if other churches could teach as high a percentage of their members to pay a full tithe of their income as the LDS Church has, they would probably prosper more. But the matter really isn't an issue of

---

3. Tanner, Jerald and Sandra, *The Changing World of Mormonism* (Chicago, Illinois: Moody Press, revised edition, 1981), p. 172.

significance. It neither helps nor hinders the truth-seeker in his quest to determine whether the Mormons are truly the Church of Jesus Christ, as they profess to be. The issue is inflated. It's a propaganda ploy, in which antagonists try to somehow infer wrongdoing where no wrongdoing exists.

Another insignificant item often given the inflated issue treatment by anti-Mormon authors is the brief statement, apparently made by Joseph Smith, that he had been shown that there are some inhabitants on the moon. Now I don't know for sure whether there are any inhabitants on the moon or not, nor do any of the anti-Mormon authors who try to make an issue of the matter. Certainly the fact that three of our astronauts took a few faltering steps on one miniscule area of the moon's surface without seeing any inhabitants doesn't provide any evidence of significance. Joseph's comment is not doctrine nor a tenet of the LDS Church, so the matter is just not an issue of any importance.

What's more important to me is that at least Joseph Smith claimed that such a revelation was given to him, while critics of the Church maintain that modern revelation isn't given, and assert that God doesn't speak to man today. Whether revelation is actually granted to man by God is the real issue at stake—poking fun at Joseph's brief allusion to men living on the moon is a diversionary tactic to sidestep that issue.

The Judgmental Opinion Technique

A *fourth* yellow journalism ploy is the Judgmental Opinion Technique. When he uses this technique of deception, *the anti-Mormon critic expresses his personal opinions in such a way that they appear to be statements of fact. Then he makes negative and judgmental comments which assume that his personal opinions have a solid basis, and are legitimate criteria for evaluating the matter at hand.* These judgmental opinions almost always stand without evidence or supporting data.

One anti-Mormon author begins his little micro-book with an attempt to establish himself as an authority on Mormonism by asserting that he subscribes to the Church News, the Ensign, and BYU Studies, and that he's a member of The Society for Early Historic Archaeology at BYU (I'm always impressed by strong, outstanding credentials such as these, aren't you?) Anyway, this individual gives us a classic example of the Judgmental Opinion Technique. He says,

"Your Mormon writers and missionaries cite a number of Scripture passages in their attempt to prove the contention of a total apostasy, but after

studying these I find that not one of them speaks of apostasy as being total, and several of them do not even apply to the Church or Church Age."
And then, because in his judgment the passages he alludes to do not fully
establish the doctrine of the apostasy, he immediately reaches the profound
conclusion that "Without a complete apostasy there was no need for a restoration."[4] He cites five whole passages which he has supposedly examined,
and which form the basis for his opinion, and—sure enough, those passages don't make a very good case that there actually was a complete apostasy
from the Church and gospel of Jesus Christ.

He neglected, however, to examine the *major* Biblical passages on the
subject—the verses that make the reality of the apostasy abundantly clear.
But here he's made his judgment and then, using his opinion as the basis
for his teaching, he announces as a fact that there is no need for a restoration because a complete apostasy never occurred. That's exactly how the
Judgmental Opinion Technique works!

Either-Or Argumentation

The next group of yellow journalism techniques I'll mention are all types
of false or misleading logic. Technique number *five* is called Either-Or Argumentation. In this type of logic, *the critic attempts to eliminate all elements of perspective—all intermediate shades of gray—and pushes the reader
to accept either one extreme or another. And then he loads his premise
so he is comparing apples and oranges, not apples and apples.*

One little anti-Mormon pamphlet, that manages to get love into its title
but not into its contents, does this several times. The author gives a brief,
extremely incomplete description of the Mormon concept of God as *he*
understands it, without a single scriptural reference cited, then presents
seven scriptural passages of his choosing under the title "The Biblical Perspective on God." And then he boldly asserts, "What we truly face is the
fact that either Mormonism is correct or the Bible is correct. One is right,
the other is wrong!"[5] Talk about playing with a stacked deck! That's the
fallacy of either-or argumentation—it's too easy to stack the deck in your
favor. By eliminating other possible conclusions, he "wins" his case by
default.

4. Gruss, Edmond C., *What Every Mormon Should Know* (Denver, Colorado: Accent Books, 1975), p. 28.
5. Decker, J. Edward, *To Moroni with Love* (Seattle, Washington: Life Messengers, no date), p. 10.

The Misuse of Parallels Technique

Technique number *six* is also based on false logic. It's a device called the Misuse of Parallels Technique. *In this type of illogical reasoning, if Item B closely resembles Item C, and C came into existence after B, it is improperly assumed that C was copied or somehow derived from B, or was at least influenced by B.* Other possibilities, like the possibility that there was an Item A which was the common source for B and C, are never even considered.

One biographer of Joseph Smith frequently embraced the Misuse of Parallels Technique. For instance, the Book of Mormon asserts that some of the American Indians have Hebraic origin. Ethan Smith, in a book called *View of the Hebrews,* voiced a similar concept, so this biographer asserted that Joseph must have somehow seen Ethan Smith's book and copied the idea from him.[6] The Book of Mormon tells of a herdsman who fought off rustlers with a sword. She decides this is a parallel that is copied from the Biblical account of David and Goliath. The Book of Mormon tells that the Jaredites brought everything they needed in barges. She sees this as a parallel account borrowed from the Biblical story of Noah's ark.[7]

The Misuse of Parallels Technique has been a favorite yellow journalism technique of anti-Mormon writers. They've tried to use it to explain away things as diverse as the origin of the Book of Mormon and the temple ceremony. They've continually tried to portray Mormonism as having been copied from anything in which they can discover even a remote parallel.

The Argument from Silence Technique

Technique number *seven* is another kind of false logic, the Argument from Silence Technique. Using this technique, one well-known anti-Mormon biographer of Joseph Smith asserts that Joseph was not visited by God in his first vision because "the newspapers took no notice of such a claim."[8]

The same line of reasoning is used to assert that there were no revivals in Palmyra and Manchester, as Joseph Smith asserted in his history, because the newspapers contain no significant report of them. They fail to

---

6. Brodie, Fawn M., *No Man Knows My History: The Life of Joseph Smith, the Mormon Prophet* (New York: Alfred A Knopf, 1957), as reviewed by Dr. Hugh Nibley, *No, Ma'am, That's Not History* (Salt Lake City, Utah: Bookcraft, 1946, 17th printing, 1979), pp. 12-13.

7. *Ibid.*, pp. 13-16.

8. *Ibid.*, pp. 21-22.

point out that the newspapers of the day were usually weeklies, that local reporting was poorly organized, and that they frequently, if not typically let local events go unreported because those events were general knowledge by the time they could get the story into print. The papers saw themselves in a more cosmopolitan light, reporting on political, regional and national issues, even in small communities.

And there are far too many things which go unnoticed by the newspapers even today, in this age of highly professional journalism and reporting, for any rational person to get excited about an argument from silence approach that holds that personal and local religious experiences did not occur just because no reporter wrote up the story.

The Conclusion Contrary to Evidences Technique

Technique number *eight* is yet another kind of false logic, the Conclusion Contrary to Evidence Technique. In this methodology, *the critic refuses to accept the obvious conclusion which an unbiased observer would draw from strong, unimpeachable evidence. He rationalizes, or buries his head in the sand so the evidence can't be presented to him, or does anything else he can to keep from having to accept what clear-cut evidence indicates to be undisputable fact.*

For instance, one critic of the Church wrote, "As for the golden plates, we will simply say that there were not any. No one ever saw them." This author's conclusion stands in direct conflict with a considerable body of well-documented evidence. The testimonies of the Three Witnesses, and of the Eight Witnesses, stand unrefuted, as do the statements of several other associates of Joseph Smith who saw, and in some cases, handled the plates.[9]

The Book of Mormon plates were there—there is too much solid evidence for any *unbiased* observer to deny their existence. Yet this disbelieving anti-Mormon author, rather than carefully report and evaluate that evidence, chose to turn to the yellow journalism Conclusion Contrary to Evidence Technique and misrepresent to his readers, as fact, his false opinion that the Book of Mormon plates did not exist.

---

9. See *The Prophecies of Joseph Smith*, pp.134-154, for a summary of this evidence.

The Specific-to-Generalization Technique

There are other types of false logic which deserve mention in passing, because they show up in anti-Mormon literature. Technique number *nine* is the Specific-To-Generalization Technique. This technique incorrectly *assumes that what happens in one situation is typical of all situations, or that what is experienced by one person is experienced by all persons.*

Critics of the plural marriage which was practiced in the early days of the Church, for instance, have found occasional situations where the union was an unhappy one for the participants. They have reasoned incorrectly, however, that plural marriages were unhappy for *all* concerned. That's just not so, as many a Mormon descendant of a plural marriage can readily testify. We don't practice plural marriage today in the Church, but many of us know that the practice was accepted and lived with honor and marital fidelity by our forefathers, and that strong families, reared in righteousness and love, were the result of those unions.

The Assumed Characteristics Technique

Technique number *ten* is closely related to the Specific-To-Generalization Technique—its the Assumed Characteristic Technique. Terms such as *all, everyone,* and *always* are difficult to use with logical accuracy. When someone uses the Assumed Characteristic Technique while criticizing the Church, *he assumes that all Mormons are alike. Just because one person says something, or does something, that doesn't necessarily mean that* **everybody** *who goes to the same church says, or believes, or does the same things.* Critics like to hang words like untutored, or naive, or fanatical on the Church membership, using the Assumed Characteristic Technique, when no single word can correctly characterize the broad spectrum of LDS Church membership, numbering more than 6,000,000.

The Bandwagon Logic Technique

And then, number *eleven,* there's the Bandwagon Logic Technique, which *reasons that if everyone believes something, that thing must be good, or bad, or true, or whatever point the critic is trying to make.* In the first hundred years of Mormonism, for instance, it became very fashionable to badtalk the Mormons, and many people jumped on the badtalk bandwagon, with all sorts of outlandish assertions and biased statements.

It was often assumed that Mormons were bad just because everybody seemed to be speaking against them. Now, when Mormons are highly respected people in many walks of life, anti-Mormon critics frequently dredge up those wild statements, trying to get people to stay on the anti-Mormon badtalk bandwagon. Thank heaven many people are more discerning now, and willing to think and perceive for themselves.

In summary, *beware of logic that is based on incorrect premises,* or *misdirected logic that leads to erroneous conclusions.* False logic obviously is a powerful technique of deception when used by one skilled in yellow journalism.

The Disregarded Evidence Technique

Technique number *twelve* in this list of yellow journalism practices is the Disregarded Evidence Technique. This technique is often used by anti-Mormon authors against Mormon authors who write carefully documented presentations of basic gospel themes. *If meticulously documented work presents strong, irrefutable evidence of the validity of the Mormon viewpoint, then wily critics will avoid any disputation with that evidence. Instead, they merely refuse to acknowledge that the evidence exists.* They ignore the evidence cited, and separate the author's explanatory and summary statements away from the evidence, then criticize those explanations and summaries as if no supporting evidence exists.

Time after time, when attempting to refute doctrinal teachings expounded by Mormon authors, they will snipe at short excerpts, but they constantly exclude passages where careful doctrinal exposition has been made from the scriptures.

This technique is most visible when an anti-Mormon writer is obviously seeking only negative evidence which supports his own pre-conceived notions. *Those who utilize this technique typically ignore evidence and entire issues which don't support their pre-determined positions.*

A typical area in which anti-Mormon authors use the Disregarded Evidence Technique is in their broad assertions that there is no archaeological nor anthropological evidence that harmonizes with the Book of Mormon. LDS scholars in these areas are very careful not to make extravagant claims concerning external evidences of the validity of the Book of Mormon, but they have amassed an amazing array of evidence—much of it from non-Latter-day Saint scientists—evidence which offers impressive scientific support to the veracity of that record. Much of this evidence has been discovered since World War II, and has found its way into scientific literature only recently.

Anti-Mormon authors are either blissfully unaware of these findings, or else are intentionally disregarding their existence. They quote seriously-outdated sources, raising criticisms which have long since been shown to be wrong. As more and more archaeological and scientific support for historic circumstances in the Book of Mormon come to light, it is clear that this is an area where enemies of the Church will soon be compelled to admit they have circulated much misinformation through the processes of yellow journalism.

Another area where the Disregarded Evidence Technique is often used is in discussions of prophecies uttered by Joseph Smith. One little anti-Mormon pamphlet states, "Joseph Smith gave forth approximately 64 prophecies. Sixty-four times he said, "Thus saith the Lord. Some very comprehensive research has gone into this area. It is easy to do historical research on historical events. Out of 64 prophecies, 58 of them fail the test. Only 6 of them came to pass."[10] I'll comment on the fulfillment of Joseph's prophecies before we're through but let's focus for a moment on the number of Joseph's prophecies, and the so-called comprehensive research which the critic has supposedly done in this area.

It is apparent that the author who supposedly did the research obviously chose to exclude the most comprehensive listing of fulfilled prophecies made by Joseph Smith available in Mormonism, though it has been a standard item in LDS bookstores for over twenty years. The book, entitled *The Prophecies of Joseph Smith,* deals with fulfilled prophecies, showing when and how they were made, and then how they came to pass. The book lists *141 prophecies made by Joseph Smith* which have been fulfilled, plus *184 scriptural prophecies fulfilled by Joseph Smith and the Church* which he restored, and *40 prophecies made by others about Joseph Smith* which he fulfilled. There's another *52 accounts of very choice supernatural experiences* such as healings, instances of divine protection, and other spiritual manifestations which occurred in Joseph Smith's life which would obviously help the truth-seeker learn more about him. The book was written in 1963 and is now in its 15th printing.

10. Decker, *To Moroni with Love, op. cit.,* p. 30.

There is no way the anti-Mormon critic could have missed the book if he truly did what he calls comprehensive research. It's listed and stocked in every major library collection on Mormonism in Utah. One can only assume that he intentionally chose to ignore it. I don't call that seeking truth, by any means.

The Erroneous Time of Fulfillment Technique

Technique *thirteen* is related to the subject of whether prophecy has been fulfilled or not. I call it the Erroneous Time of Fulfillment Technique. The little pamphlet that falsely asserted that most of Joseph's prophecies did not come to pass didn't do the reader the service of listing the prophecies, so I can't comment on his methodology. It did make some superficial comments on Joseph's Prophecy on War, however—a sweeping prophecy which began with the US Civil war but which continues on into the future until the time when God will make a full end of all nations as we know them today.

The Erroneous Time of Fulfillment Technique asserts that the prophecy is false because it has not yet been fulfilled in its entirety. By that same reasoning, many of the prophecies of Isaiah, Jeremiah, Ezekiel, Joel, Micah, Zechariah, John the Revelator, and the Lord Jesus Christ are also false because they're not yet fulfilled. That's nonsense!

The anti-Mormon critic is *attempting to find prophetic fulfillment in the wrong period of time.* And any one who would do that is either scripturally illiterate or has no desire to seek for truth and light.

The Implied Infallibility Technique

Technique *fourteen* is linked to the above situation also. I call it the Implied Infallibility Technique. *Anti-Mormon critics assume that Mormons should believe in the doctrine of infallibility—the teaching that an individual can never make an error.* Bless their imperfect little hearts, it's all right for them to make a mistake, because *they're* only human, and if they make an error that doesn't mean that their work or cause is wrong, or that their church is false. But they insist that Mormons must be *without error,* and interpret any mistake they find as so-called proof that The Church of Jesus Christ of Latter-day Saints is wrong. They especially apply this assumed infallibility standard to Joseph Smith and Brigham Young.

What does the Bible say about prophets who make mistakes? They might do well to recall the events recorded in the book of Jonah, for instance. Jonah, though he was prophet chosen of God, disobeyed the Lord and ran away. God straightened him out with a brief stay in the belly of a fish, and finally got him headed toward Nineveh, with the instruction that he was to prophesy that Nineveh was to be thrown down in forty days.

But the people of Nineveh repented, so God changed the outcome of the prophecy he had revealed to Jonah, and spared the city. And then, do you remember how Jonah sat on the hill and pouted that his prophecy didn't come to pass? The Lord had to teach him a lesson about mercy by letting him sit for days in the hot sun and wind.

What answers does the story of Jonah give us about whether a prophet can be wrong and still be the Lord's prophet? And what does it tell us about prophecies revealed by God which still don't come to pass?

Our anti-Mormon critics, who insist that Mormons must be infallible, would do well to study their scriptures, which show that the Lord does his work through people, and those people are subject to error and all the frailties of humanity. And though those people many occasionally stumble, that does not prove that the Lord's work is false, nor that they are not anxiously engaged in the Lord's work.

The Double Standard of Interpretation Technique

Technique *fifteen* is in the same line of concern. I've called it the Double Standard of Interpretation Technique. Inerrancy is a word often used by fundamentalist Protestants as they talk about the Bible. It symbolizes their belief that the Bible is God's word and is without error. Yet in the Christian world today there are a host of Bible translations which energetically compete for sales leadership in the very competitive Bible market. Some people like the highly literal renderings of the *Revised Version*, the *American Standard Version*, or the *New American Standard Bible*. The *Revised Standard Version*, the *New English Bible*, the *New American Bible*, the *New International Version*, and the *Zondervan's Modern Language Bible* moved into colloquial and modern English. The *Bible in Basic English* is based on a vocabulary of only a thousand words. One of the most popular Bibles on the market today is the *Living Bible,* published by Tyndale House, which is actually a modern English paraphrase of the *King James version.* These titles and terms are well known to most Protestant scholars and many laymen.

Though the wording of each of these various Bible translations and versions is different, and thousands of changes have obviously been made by the groups of scholars who have worked to retranslate or rephrase these

Bible versions, fundamentalist Protestants still hold that the inerrancy of the Bible has been maintained in the various translations. Now I have little quarrel with that, but I do object to the different standard which anti-Mormon critics use when writing about the Book of Mormon. Yes, there have been changes in the exact wording of the Book of Mormon as it has progressed from edition to edition. Language has been updated, grammar corrected, typographical and copying errors have been corrected, phraseology reworked, and so forth. Far, far less of this refining has been necessary on the Book of Mormon than on the Bible. But critics of Mormonism apply the double standard by saying that these changes, from their point of view, prove that the Book of Mormon was not the word of God. Yet the changes in the various Bible versions and translations, which are many hundredfold more, don't change the inerrancy of that volume of scripture, in their opinion.

The same double standard is applied by anti-Mormon critics to Joseph Smith's original translation of the Book of Mormon. They point to a few grammatical errors in the original document, and say that's proof that he wasn't directed by inspiration when he translated, or else the original document would be perfect. But the Bible has similar problems. In the Old Testament, for instance, the writing of Amos, Isaiah, and Joel is considered to be excellent, but Hosea's writing style is so ragged and unpolished that Bible scholars have complained for centuries about his writing. If a few grammatical errors in Joseph Smith's original transcription of the Book of Mormon would indicate that the translation wasn't inspired, wouldn't that also mean that books like Hosea in the Bible are also uninspired? But anti-Mormon critics like to keep their double standard—the standards they insist on for the Book of Mormon certainly shouldn't be applied to the Bible, because it couldn't pass their so-called tests either.

Anti-Mormon critics have the same double standard when they write about occasional additions to Latter-day Saint scriptures in subsequent editions. they somehow believe that additions to LDS revelations prove them wrong. Yet Bible critics point to many passages they assert are additions in the Bible, like chapters 6 and 7 of Micah, 9 through 14 of Zechariah, and chapters 40 through 66 of Isaiah. Does their reasoning prove those chapters are false, or are they applying a double standard of interpretation?

Just one more example. A major precept of Higher Critics, when analyzing Biblical prophecies, is their assumption that a prophet can only prophesy about his own day and time. The Latter-day Saints don't agree with that principle, but that's a topic for another discussion. The point is that anti-Mormon critics use a double standard of interpretation on the Mormons by turning that principle just opposite—they say, for instance, that Joseph Smith's Prophecy on War, recorded in D & C 87, really wasn't an inspired prophecy because lots of people were talking about the danger of a Civil War in the United States about the time he made the prophecy. So prophecying about one's own period **makes** one a prophet in the Bible, according to Bible scholars, but prophecying about events with roots in his own era prove that Joseph Smith **isn't** a prophet, according to anti-Mormon critics who delight in the Double Standard of Interpretation Technique.

The Colored Comment Technique

Technique number *sixteen* is the Colored Comment Technique. When using this deceptive approach, *the critic embellishes statements made by LDS Church leaders or authors with negative adjectives, flippant comments, or other inserted words which in one way or another imply impropriety on the part of the Church leader or the subject he is talking about.* The technique is frequently used when quoting brief phrases or passages verbatim. *Colored adjectives are placed just before the quotation begins,* and few readers are sufficiently astute to note where the quotation marks are placed, and assume the negative adjectives are part of the quotation cited.

Linked with the Colored Comment Technique is *the use of inflamatory words and phrases which distort and exaggerate the reader's perception* of matters being discussed by anti-Mormon writers. Thus one writer uses such flippant comments as "Smith, of course, conjured up a revelation from God . . . ", and "Young was a man of indomitable courage, possessed of a canny nature, but given to fits of ruthlessness now conveniently forgotten by Mormon historians." Those inflammatory comments quickly distort reader perception, and are characteristic of much of the anti-Mormon writing released in recent years.

The Redefined Motive Technique

Technique number *seventeen,* the Redefined Motive Technique, is a real favorite of many anti-Mormon authors. In applying this technique of deception, *the critic expresses his personal, uncomplimentary opinion of what the thoughts or motive of a Church leader or authority or historical figure was, representing his opinion as being fact and beyond question.*

One well-known author of a highly demeaning biography of the prophet Joseph Smith constantly attempted to portray Joseph's emotions and innermost feelings as she envisioned them, using the Redefined Motive Technique. She described Joseph in 1830 as "Still troubled by a sense of inadequacy." At the end of 1832 she had him "Taking himself very seriously as a prophet," yet a year latter he supposedly was "Racked with a sense of impotence and irresolution." Referring to his life several years later, she asserts that "Slowly something of the ruthlessness and cynicism of the frontier began to seep into his own thinking."[11]

Her perceptions of Joseph's thought processes amount to pure fabrication. How did she know what the Church leader's intent really was? And what makes her better qualified than the reader to make such a discernment?

The Misquoted Statement Technique

Technique number *eighteen* is the Misquoted Statement Technique. In this yellow journalism tactic, *the critic quotes or paraphrases statements made by Church leaders, but he alters those statements by inserting words which change either their meaning or their intensity, either completely or partially.* Only readers who actually compare the words of the original statement with the critic's version can detect that this technique has been used.

I experienced a verbal example of this technique at a recent bookseller's convention. A publisher of a forthcoming anti-Mormon book was talking doctrine with me and got on the subject of the Mormon concept of pre-existence, or pre-mortal life. He quoted from memory a supposed statement by an LDS leader, but reduced it down to just one phrase: "Mormons believe Jesus and Satan are brothers."

In this misquoted statement he excluded a host of key understandings: that we believe that all mankind are spirit children of our Heavenly Father, that Lucifer, like Jesus, was one of the oldest, or a son of the morning, that Lucifer rebelled against the Father and was cast out of heaven with a third of our brothers who followed him and thus became Satan, and so forth. And in his misquotation he also omitted the observation that all of the above concepts have Biblical basis. He just reduced the whole doctrine down to the statement that Jesus and Satan are brothers, leaving

---

11. See a summary and critique of these and other statements made by Fawn Brodie in *No Man Knows My History* in Dr. Hugh Nibley's rebuttal, *No Ma'am That's Not History* (Salt Lake City, Utah: Bookcraft, 17th printing, 1979), pp. 21-42.

out the entire understanding that Satan had fallen from a high position of good to become the master of that which is evil.

His statement is like saying, "Martin Luther and Adolph Hitler are brothers." In the sense that both are spirit children of Heavenly Father, and both are descended from Adam, that statement is also true, but it would be very difficult to understand and accept without an adequate explanation of the related concepts. That's the effect of the Misquoted Statement Technique.

The Private Test of Authority Technique

Technique number *nineteen* is the Private Test of Authority Technique. When using this method of attack, *the critic establishes his own private tests of validity. He selects whatever authority he chooses—established procedure, tradition, the views of noted authorities or Bible scholars,* etc. Though the critic may strongly imply that his privately established criterion is based on a firm foundation, *the necessity of fully establishing the validity of this artificial authority remains,* and when the validity is poorly substantiated or lacking, his use of this technique becomes very obvious.

A frequently used example of this ploy arises when Latter-day saints talk with anti-Mormon critics about the nature of God. The Mormons can quote passage after passage from the Bible which speak of God's bodily parts to show that God has a literal body. The typical anti-Mormon reply is that these expressions are metaphors, which they assert are common in the Old Testament. Then, typically, the words of some renowned Bible scholar are quoted, which assert that this kind of metaphor is anthropomorphism— the describing of God in the form of a man. As one author wrote, "The expressions are not meant to be taken literally. Such figurative language is necessary to convey truth which is beyond man's experience."[12]

One wonders how many dozens of passages it takes on this subject before this incorrect assumption is finally identified as exactly what it is—*a personal opinion utilized as a private test of authority, which goes counter to reason and to accepted principles of Bible interpretation and hermeneutics.*

The Misleading Headline Technique

Technique number *twenty,* the Misleading Headline Technique. In this yellow journalism procedure *the critic composes misleading titles, head-*

---

12. Gruss, *What Every Mormon Should Know, op. cit.,* p. 23.

lines or subheadings which negatively influence the reader's perception of what he is commenting upon. The critic counts on the reader's unwillingness to carefully compare the evidence he cites, or fails to cite, with the slanted headline the critic presents, so the reader can evaluate the headline's degree of validity, and he assumes that the reader can easily be mislead.

I glanced at one book, supposedly written to explain why cults prosper, and saw a subtitle which is a classic example of the Misleading Headline Technique. The subtitle read, "The Mormon Secret Police." That peaked my curiosity, because I was unaware that Mormons had a secret police force. I found that the single, half-page quote given as the basis for the section dealt with an event which transpired over a hundred years ago, a battle in southern Utah which anti-Mormon writers have labeled the Mountain Meadows Massacre.

Without treating that episode in this context, let me comment on the technique of conveying misinformation through the subtitle used. Standing without any reference to time or place, it intentionally conveys the contrived untruth that Mormons today have a secret police force. If that author believes there is a Mormon secret police force functioning now, as his misleading headline implies, he should present evidence to that effect, because Mormons certainly don't know of it!

That misleading headline game can work two ways. During the past two decades there have been hundreds of headlines, in newspapers throughout the world, telling about terrorist deeds performed by both Protestants and Catholics in Ireland. Using the misleading headline technique of yellow journalism, an author could easily write headlines such as "Protestant Terrorists Guilty of Murder and Religious Fanaticism," and make it appear that the behavior of warring Irish Protestants is representative of the conduct of all Protestants. But that would be a dirty trick, wouldn't it, to take a reference to another people, in another time and place, and make it appear that it was typical of Protestants in the United States today. But then, that's exactly the same kind of stunt this author has pulled with his Mormon Secret Police headline, isn't it?

The Half Truth Technique

And this allusion to the Mountain Meadows Massacre leads us to yellow journalism technique number *twenty-one,* the Half Truth Technique.

This is a very commonly used ploy in which *pertinent facts which would cast the matter in an entirely different light are intentionally withheld by the critic. He tells only a portion of the truth—only one side of the story—while being fully aware that the other circumstances and aspects, if known by the reader, would obviously cause him to perceive the matter in an entirely different perspective.*

Anti-Mormon accounts of the Mountain Meadows experience, and John D. Lee's involvement in it, are a classic example of the use of the half truth technique. A group of emigrants from Arkansas, together with a rough group of men on horseback from Missouri who termed themselves the Missouri Wildcats, set out for California in 1857, just a decade after the very first Mormons came to the Utah territory. There was a total of 136 individuals in the two parties, which travelled together. The group came from the east to Utah's Salt Lake valley, then traveled south across the desolate southern Utah territory.

About 150 miles south of Salt Lake City, near Fillmore, the Missouri Wildcats became extremely unruly when settlers in the small Mormon outposts refused to sell the supplies they needed to get through the winter to the people in the wagon train. The Missouri Wildcats threatened to destroy the entire community of Fillmore, and also openly boasted that they were participants in the murders and outrages that were inflicted upon the Mormons in Missouri and Illinois.

What were some of those outrageous deeds? In the fall of 1833, for instance, Missouri mobs drove more than a thousand Mormons from their homes in Jackson County, Missouri. In October of 1838, mobocrats burned the Mormon homes at DeWitt, Missouri, stole their livestock, and so menaced the state militia called out to disburse the mob that the militia feared to take action against them. They prevented the Mormons from obtaining food till some actually died from starvation in the area. The same widespread burning of Mormon homes took place at Diahman, Millport, and other Mormon settlements. At Haun's Mill, about 240 mobocrats suddenly rode into the community and opened fire on the inhabitants, brutally massacring men, women, and children alike. Many fled into a building for protection; the mob surrounded it and fired into the building until all inside were dead.

When more than 20,000 Mormons from the surrounding area gathered together for safety at Far West, Missouri, the Missourians surrounded the city. They asked to meet with the Mormon leaders on neutral ground under a flag of truce, but when Joseph Smith and other Church leaders went to meet with them, the Missourians suddenly broke the truce, surrounded them with several hundred men and took them prisoner, with the intention of murdering them early the next morning. Left without their leaders, the Mormon men in Far West were disarmed and marched out of the city, while the mobocrats entered, looted and plundered the entire city, and assaulted and raped hundreds of their women. The entire Mormon community was driven from the state, and most of them made their way to Illinois, penniless, traveling hundreds of miles on foot, many doing so in the dead of winter.

Several years later, when the Mormons had partially recovered from their suffering and had built the largest city of Illinois, at Nauvoo, they again encountered intense persecution, partially because of renewed efforts on the part of the Missourians to harass them. A mob of white men with faces painted as Indians murdered Joseph Smith and his brother, Hyrum, in 1844.

A year-and-a-half later, the Mormons in Illinois were driven out of their homes once again, in weather so bitterly cold they crossed the Mississippi River by walking across the ice. Hundreds died from exposure, and thousands of Mormon graves lie along the trail of their forced flight to the west.

So when these Missourians traveling through Utah boasted that they had been active in the Missouri persecutions of the Mormons, those were the memories their words recalled. But of greater concern were the acts of the Missouri Wildcats as they traveled farther through Utah—they began to destroy the Mormons' crops and tear down the fences and to systematically poison the water springs. Added to this were their repeated threats that they would bring hundreds of men back from California and would then kill every Mormon that was in the mountains.

At Corn Creek, 15 miles south of Fillmore, the Missourians put arsenic in the spring and strychnine in an ox carcass which was fed to local Indians. Ten of the Indians died, along with a Mormon settler. Many of the Mormon cattle drank the water and also died. As the Missouri Wildcats traveled farther south they poisoned wells and springs at numerous places along their route. To poison the water and destroy the meager crops in late summer, in that barren southern Utah outpost area, was literally an act of intended murder—for how could the settlers survive for more than a day or two in the heat of summer without water in that arid desert?

When the ten Indians died, it excited the local Indian tribes, and several hundred Indians gathered at Mountain Meadows and attacked the emigrant train, which repelled the attack, then dug in to endure the Indian siege.

The warriors sent out runners to gather more tribesmen. They also sent runners to John D. Lee, the local Indian agent who was a Mormon, and to several other settlers, demanding that they aid in their attack, and at the same time threatening Lee that if he would not do it they would wage war upon the Mormons and kill everyone in the settlements. Lee and the others sided with the Indians, whose friendship they knew was essential if their tiny frontier colonies were to exist during the months to come.

Apparently the Indians and Lee and the other settlers used the same trick on the emigrants as the Missourians used on the Mormons at Far West—they promised them safe conduct under a flag of truce, then broke that truce when the emigrants had left their position of safety. When the emigrants left their wagon circle the Indians and settlers suddenly ambushed them. All the adults and older children of the emigrants were slain in the battle. Seventeen younger children were spared and later placed in an orphanage in St. Louis.

Now no Latter-day Saint is happy that the Mountain Meadows Massacre took place. But we are weary of the one-sided portrayal it continually receives at the hands of anti-Mormon writers. The way they describe it is a prime example of the Half Truth Technique, and should be clearly identified as such. To hear them tell the story, it was a Mormon attack, not an Indian raid, and it was made on innocent people without provocation, which is a full 180 degrees opposite from the truth—the Missouri Wildcats had murdered and attempted to murder dozens of both the Indians and the Mormon settlers by repeatedly poisoning their water supplies.

The Character Assassination Technique

Yellow journalism technique number *twenty-two* I've called the Character Assassination Technique. The professional hatewriters have used this artifice to the limit, especially in their references to Joseph Smith. *They quote copiously from statements made about Joseph, but never examine whether those statements are truthful, accurate, and unbiased. Their intent is to portray only their predetermined viewpoint* that Joseph was a scamp, rather than to examine evidence which would refute their conclusion.

I listened to the news the other night and heard three Democrat presidential candidates proclaiming their rhetoric which roundly condemned the character, conduct, and policies of the nation's Republican President. If historians chose to quote only the statements of those Democrat candidates, they would surely have a distorted view of the man who guides the nation.

Any controversial figure will draw criticism from his opponents—Joseph Smith certainly did, but some anti-Mormon writers surely stack the deck when they choose statements and sources they cite about him. *It's become a matter of inbreeding, with anti-Mormon authors quoting other anti-Mormon authors, and excluding all other sources, thus perpetuating half-truths, distortions, and contrived misconceptions and falsehoods.* Informed Mormons find their critics' meager attempts at scholarship ludicrous in this area when they examine the prejudiced and unreliable sources which they continually cite, without making any objective effort to show the other side of the controversy.

A favorite method of attack by anti-Mormon writers attempting to portray Joseph Smith in an unfavorable light is to recite so-called evidence that he was accused in courts of law of various charges. They fail to acknowledge that in his period, a very popular way to "harrass thy neighbors" was to bring frivolous charges against them. The legal procedure of the day was for the accused person to be taken into custody by the law and held for one or more days until the judge would get around to trying the case, so these frivolous charges would delay and annoy, as well as serve as a cause of potential embarrassment.

Time after time, anti-Mormons utilized this ploy against Joseph Smith and other Mormon leaders. And time after time, charges brought against Joseph were not sustained by the courts and dismissed because they were untrue, or frivolous, or based on allegations of misconduct when the conduct involved was not against the law. Many times the charges had their roots in religious bias and bigotry, with individuals attempting to make the law fit their religious prejudices.

For instance, in June, 1830, just three months after the Church was restored, Joseph visited Colesville, New York. On Saturday afternoon, he and several others built a small dam across a stream so baptisms could be performed there the following day. During the night a mob collected and tore down the dam. The Mormons rebuilt the dam, but as the baptisms were being performed, a mob again assembled and taunted them.

Later that day, a constable came and arrested Joseph on a warrant. The charge: being a disorderly person because he set the country in an uproar by preaching the Book of Mormon. That's a classic example of attempting to twist the law to achieve religious ends, isn't it?

The constable told Joseph that those who swore out the warrant were lying in ambush for him, but the constable determined to save Joseph from them because he perceived Joseph to be a different kind of person than the mob had represented Joseph to be. When the mob surrounded the constable's wagon, he gave the horse the whip and drove Joseph out of their reach. When Joseph was brought to trial the next day, he was acquitted of the charge because there was no legal basis for it—Joseph had committed no illegal nor improper act in the eyes of the law.

Just as an aside, this trial was of interest because of the way Joseph obtained help from a local man of integrity who was knowledgeable in the law: John Reid. Joseph Knight, a friend of Joseph's, asked Mr. Reid to represent Joseph. Mr. Reid was in the process of declining when he heard a voice from an unseen source tell him, "You must go, and deliver the Lord's Anointed!" Mr. Reid represented Joseph, and reported that he received a witness that Joseph told the truth. He was apparently guided by the Holy Spirit in his defense, and reported that "Whilst I was engaged in the case, these emotions increased, and when I came to speak upon it, I was inspired with an eloquence which was altogether new to me, and which was overpowering and irresistible."

Another trial, which anti-Mormon writers take delight in commenting upon, took place in 1826, when Joseph was just twenty years old, and before he received the Book of Mormon plates. Recently-discovered court records show that the trial actually did take place. Apparently the trial, once again, was in the nature of a harassment, for the charge once more was that Joseph was a "disorderly person." It was also alleged that he was "a vagrant, without visible means of support," but Joseph's employer, Josiah Stowell, quickly made short work of that falsehood.

The trial focused on Joseph's work, for he had been employed to dig. That's hard work, not vagrancy! But the focus was on what he was employed to dig for, and that supposedly was for a treasure which was believed to have been buried in the area. Now, digging for treasure did not violate any New York State law, so there was no grounds for guilt on that count. The trial also focused on the fact that Joseph apparently had power to see unseen things by looking into a stone. Informed Mormons, who know of Joseph's use of a seer stone and also of the Urim and Thummim, feel no concern at this, for they know of several times when he used this ability to good advantage.

Anti-Mormon writers, however, try to greatly inflate the matter, portraying Joseph as what they call a "glass looker," and attempt to link the situation with matters of the occult. The discovered record gives little detail—what historians have is a bill from Constable DeZeng for the usual pre-trial expenses of a process server and constable, for serving a warrant on Joseph, subpoenaing the witnesses, notifying two justices, ten miles of travel, and attendance with the prisoner two days and one night, presumably the day and night before the trial and the day of the trial itself. Judge Albert Neely's bill of costs has also been found, consisting of 20 words, and identifying the charge as a misdemeanor, and showing that the total costs for the case were $2.68.

And was Joseph Smith convicted of the misdemeanor? The historical records differ on the matter. Fraser's magazine, which printed the brief account of the trial in 1873, contains one sentence that says, "And therefore the Court finds the Defendant guilty." But the witness who kept the notes of the trial recorded a different outcome. Judge Neely asked W.D. Purple, who was later a prominent physician in Chenango County, to take notes on the trial. He recorded that "the testimony of Deacon Stowell could not be impeached, the prisoner was discharged." Anti-Mormon authors, however, eager to portray Joseph as a wrongdoer, never mention Mr. Purple's statement of the trial's outcome, though most of the trial details they quote are from his notes.[13]

The technique of dredging up legal records and evidences of religious differences, supposedly as evidence of poor character, leaves anti-Mormon critics vulnerable to the same treatment of their noted theologians and historical figures. A couple of hours spent perusing sources such as the *Wycliff Biographical Dictionary of the Church,* published by Moody Press, and Eerdmans' *Handbook to the History of Christianity,* produce historical observations such as these: *Martin Luther* was excommunicated as a heretic in 1521. He tells in his letters of being troubled by evil spirits. He condemned people as witches and insisted that they be burned. He fiercely persecuted the Anabaptists. He was a staunch anti-Semite, and urged authorities to burn their schools, synagogues, and homes, to confiscate their books and money, and to ship them off to Palestine. He became irritated at the peasants who supported his reformation, and finally exhorted the princes to "Smite, slay, and stab the murderous and thieving hordes."

John Calvin had to flee from Paris in 1533 because of public uproar against his preaching, and was driven out of Geneva by the city council.

---

13. See Hill, Marvin S., "Joseph Smith and the 1826 Trial: New Evidence and New Difficulties," *Brigham Young University Studies,* Winter, 1972, pp. 223-233.

William Tyndale, the Bible translator, was tried and convicted of treason and heresy in Belgium, and was executed there in 1536.

John Wycliff, in 1377, was summoned before the tribunal of the Bishop of London and was prohibited from preaching for much of his later life. After his death his books were ordered destroyed and his body was exhumed and burned.

John Bunyan spent almost 13 years in jail.

John Milton, the English theologian and author of *Paradise Lost,* was fined and set to prison in 1660.

Philip Melanchthon, Luther's fellowworker and the formulating genius of the Reformation, led a schism in Lutheran ranks immediately after Martin Luther's death.

John Knox, the Scottish reformer, was arrested and held as a galley slave for 19 months; he spent 10 years in exile, and was later arrested for treason.

Thomas Cranmer, the English reformer and first archbishop of Cantebury, was arrested and held in the tower of London. He recanted his protestant views and acknowledged papal supremacy, but was still burned at the stake at Oxford.

John Smythe, the founder of the baptist movement, drifted from the Church of England to become pastor of a separatist congregation in England, then left them and went to Amsterdam where he mingled with the Mennonites. He finally baptized himself and 40 others, by pouring, as he founded what is considered to be the first Baptist church.

Ulrich Zwingli, the Swiss reformer, while still a Catholic priest, was secretly married for three years before he broke with Catholicism.

Conrad Grebel, who performed the first rebaptism that began the Anabaptist movement, was imprisoned in the tower of Zurich for months. He finally escaped, rather than complete the sentence pronounced upon him. The list could go on and on.

The point I am making is this: In each of the above instances, I've told the truth, but told only half the story, and phrased my comments in such a way as to portray the characters of these great men in a critical light. And that's exactly what our anti-Mormon critics do concerning Joseph Smith and other Mormon leaders. And their statements are just as distasteful to Mormons as the above historical allusions would be to them.

The Falsified Quotation Technique

Technique number *twenty-three* is the Falsified Quotation Technique. One of the most serious abuses of yellow journalism occurs when *a critic invents quotations, asserting that they are the words of a Church leader, when in reality they're words of the critic himself or someone else. This technique allows the critic to insert damaging material at will, coloring the perception of the unsuspecting reader.* Sometimes he will even insert statements from other books as if they were statements made by the individual that he is criticizing.

The Straw Man Approach

Technique *twenty-four* is the Straw Man Approach. This is often used when anti-Mormon authors grossly misrepresent Latter-day Saint doctrines. *In this technique, the user of the yellow journalism method sets up an easily refutable argument that is supposed to represent the position of his opponent, though it really is not representative of the opponent's belief or position. The critic then attacks and refutes the straw man he has created, leaving his reader with the impression that a real opponent has been defeated.*

This technique is frequently used by anti-Mormon authors to misrepresent doctrines of The Church of Jesus Christ of Latter-day Saints. Let's take the anti-Mormon version of the Latter-day Saint doctrine of the nature of God, as an example. How's this quote as a masterpiece of mixing non-doctrinal items, which are not clearly based on scripture, in with basic Mormon beliefs which are firmly established in the Bible and other scriptures? One anti-Mormon writer falsely portrayed Mormon doctrine in this manner: "Jesus Christ in Mormon theology was a spirit-child of god as are all human beings and was born as the son of Adam-God and Mary. God is the father of the spiritual bodies of all mankind; Jesus is a brother of man. Jesus was supposed to have been a polygamist, having married two Marys and Martha at Cana."[16]

Does that offend you Latter-day Saints as much as it does me to have someone misrepresent our doctrines so grossly? The critics will never

---

16. This treatment combines the Latter-day Saint doctrine found in the scriptures with non-doctrinal private views of church members and non-members alike. This then represents the whole as being representative of the Church's theology; which it is not.

convert Mormons with that kind of misrepresentation and straw man approach. Yes, it is Mormon doctrine that Jesus is a spirit child of God. No, it definitely is not Mormon doctrine, and never has been, that the father of Jesus Christ was Adam. It is Mormon doctrine that Jesus was born in the flesh as the son of God the Father, who is not Adam, and the virgin Mary. Yes, it is Mormon doctrine that God is the father of the spirits of mankind. And yes, it is Mormon doctrine that Jesus is a spirit brother of all men. But no, it is not Mormon doctrine that Jesus was a polygamist, or that he was married to two Marys and Martha.

Our anti-Mormon critics need to recognize one vital key to understanding Mormon theology. Perhaps a few Latter-day Saints need to grasp this principle a little better too. In the Mormon view, *the term Doctrine pertains to religious precepts regarded as statements of eternal, unchanging truths. Doctrine is found in the scriptures, and is limited to subjects so clearly stated in a broad pattern of scripture that they are beyond controversy.* In The Church of Jesus Christ of Latter-day Saints, things are canonized and become scripture by the common consent of the representatives of the Church assembled in General Conference.

Doctrine constitutes the basic belief of the Church, and is the standard of orthodoxy of the membership. Now there are lots of things said by various individuals in the Church which are interesting, and which sometimes add important new viewpoints and understandings. This includes writings of Church authors, discourses given in Church meetings by members and leaders, notations in Church histories, and lots of other material. These things are of value, but *they're not doctrine—they're personal opinions and commentaries.* If they are considered to be of great value to the Church, and an important new contribution to our understanding of the Lord's will for us, we canonize them. Joseph Smith said lots of things, Brigham Young had lots to say, and we hold their words in esteem, but we do not regard all their statements as doctrine. To make them doctrine, we canonize them, and make them part of our scriptures. *Inclusion in scripture is the standard by which doctrine is determined within Mormonism.*

Yes, there are, and have been many deep thinkers in the ranks of Mormonism, who have pondered many lines of thought. We recognize the profundity of their thinking, and acknowledge that they may have been guided by inspiration in their insights. But the mere fact that they have said something, no matter what their position in the Church, does not automatically make it our doctrine—it is the canonization process which defines the doctrine of The Church of Jesus Christ of Latter-day Saints.

Protestantism has its own philosophers and deep thinkers. They study the writings of Karl Barth, Wolfhart Pannenberg, John Macquarrie, Reinhold Niebuhr, Paul Tillich, and others who have stood on the frontiers of Protestant theology. Do they speak for Protestanism? Do they speak for Christianity? Just as their writings are pondered, and considered, but not regarded as official statements of Protestant doctrine, we do not consider discourses by Orson Pratt, or Orson Hyde, or Joseph Smith or Brigham Young, for that matter, to be official statements of the doctrine of the Church. Some of their words have been canonized, others have not.

The canonization process is what designates it to be Mormon doctrine. But anti-Mormon critics constantly attempt to portray non-doctrinal items as being Mormon doctrine, while carefully avoiding many items which are doctrine. *They are snipers, attacking at the fringes, rather than being willing to address the basic issues.*

Now I have presented two dozen different types of yellow journalism techniques I've observed in anti- Mormon writings. There are more, but there's no time to consider them in this discussion. *My intention has been to point out techniques of dishonesty which are frequently used against the Church.* Hopefully I've presented them with sufficient definition and description that you can recognize them when you encounter them. I invite you to go back and review this discussion several times, and to take notes on these techniques and characteristics.

A Review and Quiz on Yellow Journalism Techniques

These techniques are sufficiently complex that some of them are difficult to remember. To help you recall them, and to aid you in better identifying them, I'm going to take a few moments and review all twenty-four of the techniques I've discussed. I'll do it in the form of a quiz. I'll mix up the list, and give you the definitions. See if you can recall the names of the techniques before I give them to you. Are you ready— here we go!

What technique is being used when the critic tells only a portion of the truth, while intentionally withholding other information he knows will cause the reader to perceive the subject in an entirely different perspective? That's number 21, the HALF-TRUTH TECHNIQUE.

Here's the next one. Name the technique used when the critic incorrectly portrays an easily defeated faked issue as representing a major position of his opponent. Then he attacks and defeats this fake issue, giving the reader the impression a real issue has been met and overcome. That's number twenty-four, the STRAW-MAN TECHNIQUE.

What yellow journalism technique is being used when the critic incorrectly reasons that a specific situation is typical of all situations, or that the same thing which one person experiences is experienced by all people? That's number nine, the SPECIFIC-TO-GENERALIZATION TECHNIQUE.

What do we call it when a critic makes false or improper assertions in some widely disseminated publication medium to which Church members are unable to respond because of lack of media or audience access? That's number one, the UNANSWERABLE FALSEHOOD TECHNIQUE.

Give the name of the technique used when the critic refuses to accept the obvious conclusion any unbiased observer would draw from strong, umimpeachable evidence. He accepts other conclusions without evidence, rather than accept indisputable facts which would prove him wrong. That's the CONCLUSION CONTRARY TO EVIDENCE TECHNIQUE, number eight.

What's the name of the technique when a critic requires absolute infallibility, or error-free behavior, from his opponent, while accepting errors among his own ranks? The critic attempts to establish that any error at all on the part of his opponents is absolute proof that his opponent's cause is false, but he applies this all-or-nothing stance only to his opponents, though the same criteria would prove his own cause wrong. That's number fourteen, the IMPLIED INFALLIBILITY TECHNIQUE.

And what is the name of the technique when the critic selects, and cites as unimpeachable authority, a theory or source which lacks factual validity, and then evaluates his opponent using that theory as his standard? That's number nineteen, the PRIVATE TEST OF AUTHORITY TECHNIQUE.

Here's an easy one. Name the technique used when the critic makes up his evidence—he invents statements, or draws them from other sources, and misrepresents them as being the words of his opponent, or of an authoritative source he cites against his opponent. That's number twenty-three, the FALSIFIED QUOTATION TECHNIQUE, isn't it?

And another easy one: the critic assumes that if "everyone" believes something, that widely held belief is true and valid. Which technique is that? Number eleven, the BANDWAGON LOGIC TECHNIQUE.

What is it called when the critic interprets evidence one way when it pertains to his opponent, but a different way when it pertains to his own cause? That's the DOUBLE STANDARD OF INTERPRETATION TECHNIQUE, number fifteen.

Name the literary trick used when the critic assumes that something is true just because he is unaware of evidence which contradicts his assumption of its truthfulness. That's number seven, the ARGUMENT FROM SILENCE TECHNIQUE.

And what do we call it when a critic gives an exaggerated or sensationalized report of an unimportant item, attempting to make it a significant issue and to portray it as a reason for criticism and contention? That's the INFLATED ISSUE TECHNIQUE, number three.

Give me the name of the technique in which the critic erroneously assumes something is stolen, copied or influenced by something else which has slightly similar characteristics, and refuses to consider that they may have no interrelationship, nor that they both might be derived from other sources. That's number six, the MISUSE OF PARALLELS TECHNIQUE.

Name the technique in which a critic uses inflammatory language which distorts or exaggerates the reader's perception of items about which he writes. Or, when quoting from his opponents, he places flippant comments or other negative words next to the quotations so the unsuspecting reader will think they're part of the quotations. That's the COLORED COMMENT TECHNIQUE, number sixteen.

What technique is used when the critic incorrectly assumes that all people of a large group are alike? He assumes that if one person says or does something, everyone in the same group will say, do, or believe the same thing. That's number ten, the ASSUMED CHARACTERISTIC TECHNIQUE.

Here's another easy one. The critic cites inaccurate, biased, and defamatory comments about an individual, disproportionately emphasizes his misdeeds and imperfections, and excludes information about his virtues and accomplishments. That's number twenty-two, the CHARACTER ASSASSINATION TECHNIQUE.

Tell the name of the technique used when the critic eliminates vital elements of perspective, and pushes the reader into accepting one of two extreme viewpoints. He slants the decision in his favor by withholding pertinent information or by choosing alternatives which are not direct opposites. That's number five, the EITHER-OR ARGUMENTATION TECHNIQUE.

And what yellow journalism technique is being used when a critic, faced with strong, irrefutable evidence, intentionally sidesteps it and refuses to even acknowledge that the evidence exists? He criticizes other issues, or the manner of presentation of the evidence itself. That's number twelve, the DISREGARDED EVIDENCE TECHNIQUE.

What is the name of the technique when the critic states his personal, uncomplimentary view of what he supposes to be the thoughts, motives and innermost feelings of his opponents, even though no actual evidence exists to support his supposition? That's number seventeen, the REDEFINED MOTIVE TECHNIQUE.

Name the technique in which the critic expresses his personal opinion in such a way that it appears to be a statement of fact. Then he makes criticisms based on the assumption that his unsupported opinion has validity. That's number four, the JUDGMENTAL OPINION TECHNIQUE.

What yellow journalism technique is involved when the critic quotes or paraphrases statements made by his opponents, but he alters those statements, changing their meaning or intensity so they will be improperly understood by others? That's number eighteen, the MISQUOTED STATEMENT TECHNIQUE.

Here's another easy one. What is it called when the critic composes slanted titles or headlines which negatively influence the reader's perception or understanding of the subject reported? The MISLEADING HEADLINE TECHNIQUE, number twenty.

And the last two are easy ones too. Name the technique in which, when quoting, the critic separates material from its context, and presents it so the reader will perceive it as having a different meaning than that which the author originally intended. That's number two, the OUT-OF-CONTEXT TECHNIQUE.

And the final question in this review—what technique is being used when the critic fails to discover prophetic fulfillment by intentionally searching in the wrong period of time? He looks for completion of prophecies dealing with future events in the past, and vice versa. That's number thirteen, the ERRONEOUS TIME OF FULFILLMENT TECHNIQUE.

Well, there's the list—a whole basketfull of dirty tricks.

How do you use them? If you encounter the writings of anti-Mormon critics, and can bring yourself to read them, let me suggest that you take this list I have given you and use it as a means of analyzing and evaluating the writing. Of course, you are also evaluating the integrity of its author.

If you find repeated use of these techniques of yellow journalism, that will tell you that the author, and what he has written, is lacking in validity and is not to be trusted. Avoid both that individual and his writing.

Questions to Ask When Evaluating Anti-Mormon Materials

Let me suggest ten questions that should be considered as you try to place the critics and their criticism in personal perspective.

1. *Does this person have my personal interest and my eternal wellbeing as his prime motive?* He's apparently wanting me to disassociate myself from the Church. I would do well to evaluate whether he is truly seeking my best interests in the comments he makes.

2. *Does he offer a better doctrine to me than the doctrine of The Church of Jesus Christ of Latter-day Saints?* In other words, is he offering a valid substitute which will enable me to attain my eternal goals, or is he just attacking and tearing down my faith with no appropriate alternative offered?

3. *Do I perceive him to be a person of integrity, whose comments I trust,* and whose views I take to be his best effort to achieve a full understanding of truth?

4. *Is he a seeker after truth? Is he striving to be fair, and is he unwilling to misrepresent my Church's doctrines and history* as he attempts to portray what he believes to be true?

5. *Is he knowledgeable and well informed about the doctrines and history of Mormonism,* or is he merely parroting the critical trivia which has been produced in recent years by opponents of the Church? And likewise, is he well informed about the doctrines and history of his own church?

6. *Is he free from ulterior motives?* Do I find him to be an individual who is unmotivated by jealousy, hate, greed, or other gross motives?

7. *Is he free from a profit motive?* Does this person stand to profit in some way, either financially or in the acclaim of the world, by his criticism of the Church?

8. *Does this individual claim to be an authorized spokesman for the Lord Jesus Christ,* or is he merely a bystander repeating things he has heard from others?

9. *Do I feel the Holy Spirit in him and in me when I'm in his presence?* Do I feel that Spirit bearing witness to me of the truthfulness of his comments, or am I left cold and uninfluenced by the promptings of the Spirit as he talks to me or as I read his writings?

And 10, *What will I be or become if I follow his teachings and example? Will his teachings bring me closer to God and his eternal kingdom,* or will his teachings lead me away from God?

How to Respond to Those Who Write and Circulate Anti-Mormon Material

How should Latter-day Saints respond to those who write anti-Mormon literature and attempt to use it to harm the Church and its members? Several passages of scripture give us insights about such individuals.

First, the Lord Jesus Christ, in his Sermon on the Mount, stated a principle which is directly applicable to the anti-Mormon criticisms of authors who stoop to the use of yellow journalism. The Lord said, in *Matthew 7, verses 1 and 2: "Judge not that ye be not judged, for with what judgement ye judge, ye shall be judged: and with what measure ye mete, it shall be measured to you again."*

When you're handed literature which judges and criticizes the Church, I would suggest that you *first evaluate the literature and its author, to see if he is using the techniques of yellow journalism.* Evaluate the critic himself, and whether he is writing with integrity, before you allow his words to affect your perception of the Church and of the gospel of Jesus Christ. If you find he is using yellow journalism tactics, actually list those instances, so you *have a written basis for judging what he has written.* That will help you discern whether he speaks the truth or not.

Second, determine whether an objective of the critic is to foster dissension within the Church, and whether he is coming to you with an arguing attitude and a spirit of contention. If you believe that his objective is to create dissension and to cause strife and contention, you'd do well to remember the Lord's teaching concerning the source of that spirit in *3rd Nephi, chapter 11, verses 28 through 30.* You'll recall that these words were spoken by the Savior, just after he appeared in the new world following his resurrection. He said, "There shall be no disputations among you, as there have hitherto been; *neither shall there be disputations among you concerning the points of my doctrine,* as there have hitherto been. For verily, verily I say unto you, *he that hath the spirit of contention is not of me, but is of the devil, who is the father of contention, and he stirreth up the hearts of men to contend with anger, one with another.* Behold, this is not my doctrine, to stir up the hearts of men with anger, one against another; but this is my doctrine, that such things should be done away."

Now the leaders of the Church, perhaps with this passage in mind, have wisely counseled the Saints not to seek confrontations and public debates with these individuals. That is good counsel, and should be followed.

But some critics of the Church are growing bolder, attempting to organize and fan anti-Mormon sentiment to cause Latter-day Saints to lose their employment, trying to pressure publishers of periodicals into not carrying advertisements of books written by Mormons or products manufactured by them, and seeking to exclude Mormons from trade associations and business opportunities.

There is nothing in the counsel of the Brethren which holds that Mormons should turn the other cheek to the extent that we abrogate our rights as American citizens, or that we fail to use our proper legal recourse to prevent infringement by these people on our civil rights.

If they transgress the laws of the land in their efforts to retard your personal progress through libel, slander, illegal trade restraints or other unlawful activities, then seek proper legal counsel and, with that professional guidance, utilize the laws of the land which have been written for your protection to halt their infringements upon your liberties.

But what about those humble followers of Christ who are members of various churches of today who are being led astray by the teachings of these anti-Mormon critics? The anti-Mormon books which are being circulated today, though professing to be written for Latter-day Saints, really have little revelance for informed LDS Church members. *The things they write aren't even in the ball park of Mormon life and belief and experience.* Rather, they're written and marketed for non-Mormons. And *the purpose of these books is to spread misinformation, distrust and hate.* We know that those who intentionally spread strife and contention by circulating falsehoods and half-truths are not doing the Lord's work, and are not pleasing in His sight. They are the ones who are fighting against the Lord's work and will be judged by the Lord at the last day.

Third, there is a wise example set forth in the Bible that they would do well to follow. We read about it in the fifth chapter of Acts. You remember that shortly after the resurrection of the Savior, when the apostles were preaching in Jerusalem, the high priest and the Sadducees rose up against them, laid hands on the apostles, and cast them into the common prison. But that night an angel brought them forth out of the prison and told them to go back and preach in the temple. When the apostles were again apprehended and brought before the high priest, Peter voiced the intent which motivated them all, saying, *"We ought to obey God rather than men."* But the high priest and members of the Sanhedrin were offended and took counsel how to slay the apostles.

Then, as we read in *Acts 5, verses 34 through 39,* "Then stood there up one in the council, a Pharisee, named Gamaliel, a doctor of the law, had in reputation among all the people, and commanded to put the apostles forth a little space; and said unto them, Ye men of Israel, *take heed to yourselves what ye intend to do as touching these men. . . .* I say unto you, Refrain from these men, and let them alone: *for if this counsel or this work be of men, it will come to nought: But if it be of God, ye cannot overthrow it;* lest haply ye be found even to fight against God."

That is wise counsel. If there are those of other churches who are uncertain how to interact with members of The Church of Jesus Christ of Latter-day Saints, they would do well to stand back and watch, and not attempt to persecute the Saints or militate against them in any way.

A *fourth* item of scriptural instruction pertinent to the subject comes, once again, from the Lord's Sermon on the Mount. The same counsel which tells Latter-day Saints how to evaluate the activities and intentions of others applies to those who would judge the Mormons in the last days. we read in *Matthew, chapter 7, verses 16 to 20,* where the Lord said, "Ye shall know them by their fruits. Do men gather grapes of thrones, of figs of thistles? Even so every good tree bringeth forth good fruit; but a corrupt tree bringeth forth evil fruit. . . .Wherefore *by their fruits ye shall know them."*

And *fifth,* let's comment on one final principle, found in section ten of the Doctrine and Covenants. Today I'm sure there are opponents of the church who are firmly convinced that Mormonism is wrong, and is leading its members in error. And they believe their role is to help combat that which they perceive to be error, and to lead people to truth as they understand it. Unfortunately, in many instances, critics of the Church have attempted to win souls away from the Gospel by falsifying and circulating half truths, mixing truth with error, and by doing other deceitful acts intended to harm the Church.

Even before the Church was restored, in the summer of 1828, a problem of this kind occurred. You recall that Joseph Smith had translated 116 manuscript pages of the Book of Mormon, which subsequently were lost from the possession of Martin Harris. It appears that these pages fell into the hands of enemies of the Church, who intended to hold them and wait until Joseph had retranslated that portion of the Book of Mormon, then alter the things that he had previously written and produce these pages in a mock effort to depict Joseph as being unable to translate the same things twice.

The Lord spoke to Joseph on the matter and gave a significant statement concerning the motive and methodologies of those who fight against the Saints. Specifically, he established this principle, in *Doctrine and Covenants section 10, verse 28:* "Verily, verily I say unto you, wo be unto him that *lieth to deceive because he supposeth that another lieth to deceive,* for such are not exempt from the justice of God."

As he described what these men were doing, the Lord revealed Satan's approach to combatting the Church, and offered a solemn warning to those who would do so. He said, in *Doctrine and Covenants, section 10, verses 20 through 28:*

"Verily, verily, I say unto you, that Satan has great hold upon their hearts; he stirreth them up to iniquity against that which is good; And their hearts are corrupt, and full of wickedness and abominations; and they love darkness rather than light, because their deeds are evil; therefore they will not ask of me. *Satan stirreth them up, that he may lead their souls to destruction.* And thus he has laid a cunning plan, thinking to destroy the work of God; but I will require this at their hands, and it shall turn to their shame and condemnation in the day of judgment. Yea, *he stirreth up their hearts to anger against this work. Yea, he saith unto them: Deceive and lie in wait to catch, that ye may destroy;* behold, this is no harm. And thus he flattereth them, and *telleth them that it is no sin to lie that they may catch a man in a lie, that they may destroy him.* And thus he flattereth them, and leadeth them along until he draggeth their souls down to hell; and thus *he causeth them to catch themselves in their own snare.* And thus he goeth up and down, to and fro in the earth, seeking to destroy the souls of men. Verily, verily, I say unto you, *woe be unto him that lieth to deceive because he supposeth another lieth to deceive, for such are not exempt from the justice of God."*

It is my solemn prayer that the words I have spoken, and the passages and principles I have cited, will help us all to better discern what is true and uplifting and good and the Lord's will and work. And I ask it in the name of our Lord and Redeemer, Jesus Christ. Amen.

LIST OF QUOTATIONS

INDEX

A

Aaron— 24, 90, 92, 150; priesthood of, given by John the Baptist, 34.

Abimelech— 74.

Abraham—53, 74, 98, 113; Book of, 98.

Adam—98, 113, 143, 145; fall of explained, 273.

Ananias—baptized Paul, 88.

Angels—appeared in Kirtland, 113.

Answers to Tough Questions—250.

Anthon, Charles—visited by Martin Harris, 41, 42, 61, 69.

Anthropomorphism—152.

Anti-Mormon materials—questions for evaluating, 299.

Anti-Mormon writers—how to respond to, 300.

Antichrist—manifested in NT times, 20.

Antinomianism—defined, 260

Apostasy—coming recognized, 29.

Apostle's Creed, The—133.

Apostles—foundation of the church, 81; false, 21.

Apostles, Twelve—foundation of the church, 26; Matthias called, 27.

Ariel—name of Jerusalem, 64.

Arius—doctrine disputed, 129.

Atonement—overcame sin, death, 238; explained, 240.

Augsburg Confession—1530 A.D., 130.

Authority—necessary to baptize, 90; by laying on of hands, 90; Chain of, broken during apostasy, 14.

Azariah, the priest—93.

B

Baptism—252; essential for salvation 86; 3,000 at Pentecost, 87; to put on Christ, 89; Paul rebaptized converts 89; entry to the church, 92; become members through, 194; salvation requires, 199; required for salvation, 213; commanded, 251; purpose defined, 253; rebaptized for invalid baptism, 255; rejected by Protestants as essential, 252.

Baptism for the dead—220.

Barnabas—26, 27.

Barth, Karl—295.

Basic Bible Doctrines—234.

Benjamin, King—165, 247.

Bible—84; various translations, 280.

Blood—redeemed through Christ's, 187.

Body, Spiritual—142.

Book of Mormon—persuades to Christ, 187; confirms Bible witness, 188.

Book, closed Bible not a, 83.

Book, sealed vision of all prophecy, 41; prophecy of, 62.

Born Again—needed to enter kingdom, 86; redemption leads to being, 200; begotten of Christ, 201; cleansed and changed by, 214; defined, 246.

Brodie, Fawn M.—274.

Buena Vista, Battle of—121.

Bunyan, John—unexemplary conduct, 292.

C

Calvin, John—22, 130; unexemplary conduct, 291.

Carthage, 3rd Council of—84.

Carthage, Illinois—120.

Catholicism—lacked authority, 22; Protestant doctines vs. 22.

Catholics—church lacks characteristics, 29, 30.

Celibacy—17, 30.

Y

Yahweh—170.
Yellow Journalism—defined, 266.
Young, Brigham—98, 109, 295; spoke in
     tongues, 110; to preside over church,
     110.
Young, Joseph—110.

Z

Zechariah—chapters added to book of, 281.
Zeezrom—192.
Zion's Camp—100.
Zondervan Pictorial Bible Dictionary
     —245.
Zwingli, Ulrich—130; unexemplary con-
     duct, 292.